WHAT IS MARRIAGE?

MARRIAGE IN THE CATHOLIC CHURCH

WHAT IS MARRIAGE?

by
Theodore Mackin, S.J.

PAULIST PRESS   *New York / Ramsey*

Acknowledgments

In this volume passages are quoted from the following titles with the permission of their publishers: from *Ancient Israel,* by Roland DeVaux, copyright © 1961, used with the permission of McGraw-Hill Company. From *The New American Bible* copyright © 1970 by The Confraternity of Christian Doctrine, Washington, D.C. From *Jerusalem in the Time of Jesus,* by Joachim Jeremias, copyright © 1969, all rights reserved by Fortress Press. From *Dictionary of the Bible,* by John L. McKenzie, copyright © Macmillan Publishing Co., Inc. 1965. From *The Documents of Vatican II,* Walter M. Abbott and Rev. Joseph Gallagher, eds., copyright © by Follett Publishing Co., 1966. From *The New Testament and Rabbinic Judaism,* by David Daube, 1973 edition copyrighted by Arno Press. From *Papal Teachings: Matrimony,* arranged by the Benedictine monks of Solesmes and translated by Michael J. Byrnes, copyright 1963 by the Daughters of St. Paul. From *Studia Canonica,* Vol. 13.1, published by the Faculty of Canon Law, Saint Paul University. From *Alexandrian Christianity,* edited by John Ernest Leonard Oulton, D.D. and Henry Chadwick, B.D.; Volume II: The Library of Christian Classics, Published in the U.S.A. in MCMLIV, and used with the permission of The Westminster Press. From *The Theology of Marriage: The Historical Development of Christian Attitudes Toward Sex and Sanctity in Marriage,* by Joseph E. Kerns, S.J., 1964, and from *The Meaning of Marriage,* by Dr. Herbert Doms, translated by George Sayer, 1939—both with the permission of Andrews and McMeel, Inc., formerly Sheed and Ward, Inc.

Library of Congress
Catalog Card Number: 81-84386

ISBN: 0-8091-2442-4

Published by Paulist Press
545 Island Road, Ramsey, N.J. 07446

Printed and bound in the
United States of America

Contents

Foreword 1

1 Introduction 5

2 The Primitive Christian Understanding of Marriage 38
Palestinian Jewish Marriage Custom, 38. The Religious Reality
of Jewish Marriage, 40. The Theory of Marriage in Palestinian
Judaism, 41. The Genesis Account of the First Couple, 43.
Marriage and the Covenant of Unequals, 50. Marriage According to the Synoptic Gospels, 52. The Instruction on Marriage
in 1 Corinthians, 54. Paul and the Possibility of Divorce and
Remarriage, 57. Marriage in Paul's Exhortation to the Ephesians, 61. Notes to Chapter 2, 66.

3 Christian Marriage in the Roman Empire 69
The Definitions of Marriage in Roman Law, 73. Marriage in
the Christian Communities of the Empire, 76. Notes to Chapter 3, 79.

4 The Fathers of the Church and the Defense of Marriage 80
The Gnostic Christians, 80. Orthodox Attitudes Sympathetic
to Gnosticism, 82. Diverse Gnostic Attitudes Toward Mar-
riage, 83. Valentinus and the *Pléroma,* 86. The Androgynous
God of the Gnostics, 87. The Orthodox Answer to the Gnos-
tics, 88. The Reply to the Antinomian Gnostics, 89. The First
Sin and Sexuality, 90. Marriage's Inferiority to the Celibate
Life, 93. The Traditions of Marriage-for-Procreation, 97. The
Christian Inheritance from Rabbinic Judaism, 100. The Influ-
ence of Philo, 102. The Patristic Use of the Pagan Sources, 104.

Aristotle and the Reasons for Marriage, 107. The Classical Authors and Friendship in Marriage, 111. The Reply to the Antinomian Gnostics, 116. Ambrose and Jerome on the Motives for Intercourse, 119. Notes to Chapter 4, 122.

5 Augustine on the Nature of Marriage 127
The Goods of Marriage That Excuse Its Use, 129. When Intercourse Is Sinful, 130. Augustine's Interpretation of Original Sin, 131. The Nature of Concupiscence, 134. Augustine's Marriage Ethic in Principle, 136. The Meaning of "The Goods of Marriage", 138. Augustine's Secondary Goods of Marriage, 139. Notes to Chapter 5, 142.

6 Marriage in Europe and the Medieval Canonists 145
A Collision of Cultures, 146. The Roman Procedure in Marrying, 148. Prolongation of the Disagreement About the Act That Creates a Marriage, 152. The Dispute and the Medieval Canonists, 154. Hugh of St. Victor, 155. The Theologians of Paris and the Bolognese Canonists, 158. Gratian's Definition of Marriage and the Object of Marital Consent, 161. Peter Lombard, 164. Resolution of the Dispute, 168. Gregory IX, the Decretals and Definitive Resolution, 170. Papal Use of the *Institutes'* Definition, 171. The Situation of Marriage at the Middle of the Thirteenth Century, 172. Notes to Chapter 6, 174.

7 The Theologians and the Nature of Marriage 176
The Albigensians, Cathars and Marriage, 176. Albert the Great, 178. Thomas Aquinas, 179. Aquinas and Marriage as Contract, 180. Aquinas on Marriage as Friendship, 181. Bonaventure on Marriage, 183. Duns Scotus, 185. Marriage Understood as Contract, 186. Disagreement About the Object of Marital Consent, 189. Notes to Chapter 7, 190.

8 The Definition of Marriage and the Code of Canon Law 192
Late Medieval Collections of Decretals, 192. The Problem of Clandestine Marriages, 194. The Council of Trent's Decree, *Tametsi*, 196. The Definition of Marriage at the End of the Medieval Age, 198. Tomás Sanchez, 199. Goals of Marriage and Object of Consent: The Fixing of a Position, 201. Cardinal Gasparri and the Code of Canon Law, 204. Marriage in the Code of Canon Law, 207. The Ends of Marriage, 209. Cardinal Gasparri's Use of the Sources, 212. Pius XI and *Casti connubii*,

215. The Hierarchy of Ends and Controlling Subordination, 218. Notes to Chapter 8, 222.

9 **The Modern Catholic Challenge to the Canonical Definition ...** **225**
The Personalist Philosophers and Theologians, 225. The Critique of the Definition Implicit in the Challenge, 229. The Sexual Nature of Human Beings According to the Personalists, 231. The Meaning of Marriage and the Goals of Intercourse, 233. Reaction of the Church's Magisterium, 235. The Reaction of Pius XII, 237. The Conflict on the Eve of Vatican II, 239. The Effect of the Changed Image of the Church, 241. The Case for the Defense of the Canonical Definition, 243. Notes to Chapter 9, 245.

10 **The Second Vatican Council and the Nature of Marriage** **248**
The Theological Commission's *schema* on Sexuality and Marriage, 249. Challenge to the *schema*, 252. Defense of the *schema*, 255. The Debate and the Compromise in the Council, 257. The Constitution on the Church in the Modern World (*Gaudium et spes*), 259. Final Debate on the Council's Statement on Marriage, 262. Detailed Statement in *Gaudium et spes*, 265. Procreation and Nurture in Marriage, 269. The *Expensio modorum* for *Gaudium et spes*, 271. The Encyclical Letter of Paul VI, *Humanae vitae*, 274. Notes to Chapter 10, 278.

11 **The Defining of Marriage Since Vatican II and *Humanae vitae*** **283**
The Definition in the Revised Marriage Law, 283. The Revision of Canon 1013, 288. The Consent That Creates a Marriage (Canon 1081), 291. Marriage Jurisprudence Since Vatican II, 297. Early Post-Conciliar Jurisprudence, 299. First Juridical Recognition of the *Communitas vitae*, 1969–1972, 300. Early Opposition to the *Communitas vitae*, 303. The Accelerating Jurisprudential Controversy, 1973 to the Present, 305. Denials of the Juridical Relevance of the *Communitas vitae*, 308. A Decision of the Roman Signatura, 313. The Signatura on the Nature and Object of Marital Love, 318. Paul VI's Discourse to the Roman Rota of February 9, 1976, 320. Some Implications of the Discourse, 322. Questions and Doubts That Remain, 322. Notes to Chapter 11, 324.

12 **Critical Reflections** **328**
The Modes of Defining, 329. Questions About Method in De-

fining Marriage, 330. A Definition of Marriage the Matrix of the Sacrament, 332. Why a Juridical Essence in Marriage? 334. The Sacrament as Source and Model for the Definition, 339. Intent in *Gaudium et spes* in the Defining of Marriage, 345. Notes to Chapter 12, 350.

Index of Proper Names 351

Subject Index 356

Index of Published Works 360

Scripture Index 364

to my father

FOREWORD

This volume is not another attempt by a celibate clergyman to instruct the married about marriage. It is an examination of a particular facet of the Roman Catholic Church's reflection on and teaching about marriage—its effort to define the nature of marriage.

The history of this effort shows that it has been mainly the work of lawyers in the Church, of the canonists, some of whom have been bishops, those who by their mission are the teachers and governors in the Church. Consequently much of this examination goes on within the arena of the Church's law. But the designing of the law, and its explanation, have necessarily reached outside the law to other disciplines—to philosophy, to theology, to the interpretation of the Scriptures, and in recent years to psychology and sociology. So the examination is an uneven mixture of all these disciplines, and the alert reader will detect in which of them the writer is more informed, in which of them less so.

The Catholic effort to define marriage has had a long history. Depending on how one interprets this history one can conclude, or not, that the definition has been changed as this history has moved along. The most recent apparent change was made in the Second Vatican Council, in the assembly of Catholic bishops from throughout the world during the years 1962 to 1965. The bishops' statement on marriage in their Pastoral Constitution on the Church in the Modern World (*Gaudium et spes*) is phrased in language so different from the ecclesiastical documents of the centuries preceding it that their intent to change the Catholic understanding of marriage seems undeniable.

But there are Catholic scholars, jurists and churchmen who deny either the intent or the fact of change by the Council. They contend either that the bishops in council proposed the traditional definition but in nonjuridical terms, or that the admittedly different description of marriage is only that—a description, but not an intended juridical change. This denial has become one side of a current debate; the debate in turn forms the current and latest stage in this history of defining.

In tracing and examining a history an author ought ordinarily to maintain neutrality. But where the course of the history has itself been arguable—has the Catholic Church changed her understanding of marriage?—and especially where the argument is the latest part of the history, neutrality has been less easy to maintain. I have chosen not to maintain it; I think the Catholic Church has made this change. Whether the reader will agree with this judgment will depend on his or her own assessment of the evidence. I hope that I have treated this evidence fairly.

As an examination this volume occupies the uneasy borderland between a specialized and even esoteric subject matter and an intended reading audience who are not specialists and who are presumed not to command the esoteric conceptual system and vocabulary in which the specialists communicate. So the anticipated reader—the intelligent, curious, but uninformed non-specialist—may have to be patient with this effort to translate the esoteric into the familiar.

Since the language in which the Catholic Church's teachers speak to one another and to the people is Latin, there was from the beginning the question whether to leave key passages in that language or to take them out of it by translation. I have decided to do both, to leave at least the crucial phrases in Latin but to provide instant translation of them in parentheses or in footnotes.

It will be helpful at this point to provide a mini-glossary of Latin terms that appear again and again in the Catholic marriage law and therefore in this volume.

The following Latin nouns have been and are still used to designate marriage: *matrimonium, coniugium, nuptiae.* Married persons are *coniuges, nupti,* or more abstractly *partes* (the "parties" to a marriage). To marry is *nubere* or *matrimonio inire.* The wife is *uxor,* the husband *maritus* or *vir.*

Two Latin barbarisms distinguish two "moments" in the history of a real-life marriage. *Matrimonium in fieri* (marriage in becoming) designates a couple's act of creating their marriage. More concretely, since about the twelfth century in Western society the term designates exclusively the exchange of wedding vows. *Matrimonium in facto esse* (marriage in its actual existence) designates what the exchange of vows creates: the abiding state of marriage. *Matrimonium in fieri* occupies a few moments starting the history of a marriage; *matrimonium in facto esse* is the marriage throughout the rest of its history.

In recent years the Catholic legal vocabulary has recovered the ancient Roman substantival phrase used in defining marriage, *individua vitae consuetudo.* This is translated "a single (or undivided) sharing of life."

Consortium used as a substantive with the same reference may be misleading because unchanged from its Latin form it has gained currency in contemporary commercial and political vocabularies. Predicated of marriages in antiquity and now in our time, it designates the marital union, the shared life of the husband and wife.

I wish to express my thanks to the following persons for their help in my preparing this volume: to Rev. Thomas J. Green, Dean of the Faculty of Canon Law at the Catholic University of America, and to Rev. James Provost, his colleague there, for sharing their expert knowledge of the Catholic marriage law and for providing me with texts of this law's revision not otherwise available at the time; to Rev. Lawrence Wrenn, *Officialis* (presiding judge) of the tribunal in the Archdiocese of Hartford, for the same kindness; to Monsignor Marion Justin Reinhardt, *Officialis* in the tribunal of the Diocese of Brooklyn, for his advice and for welcoming my attendance at nullity hearings in his court; to Rev. William Schumacher, *Vice-Officialis* in the tribunal of the Archdiocese of Chicago, for his advice and for arranging a helpful meeting with his colleagues in that court; to Rev. Urbano Navarette, S.J., formerly Dean of the Faculty of Canon Law in the Pontifical Gregorian University, Rome, and now rector of the university, for conveying his understanding of the Catholic marriage law at crucial points; to Rev. Josef Fuchs, S.J., of the Faculty of Moral Theology at the same university, for his help in interpreting recent Catholic magisterial documents; to Rev. Peter Huizing, S.J., retired dean of Canon Law at both the Gregorian University and the University of Nijmegen, and *relator* of the subcommission that drafted the revision at certain points; to His Eminence Cardinal Pietro Palazzini, for offering me his interpretation of the sacramentality of Christian marriage; to Monsignor Porter J. White, Canonical and Theological Consultant in the Archdiocese of Baltimore, for his help in interpreting certain points in the revised marriage law; to Rev. William Rewak, S.J., now president of Santa Clara University and formerly rector of its Jesuit community, for generously subsidizing the work of research that has gone into this volume; to Rev. Robert Dailey, S.J., professor in the Jesuit School of Theology in Berkeley, for his critical reading of the first draft of this volume; to Patricia Roca, graduate student at the same school, for reading the same draft and patiently criticizing its prose for intelligibility; and to Theresa Fowler, for proofreading the entire final draft—a maternal gift of no small dimensions.

1. INTRODUCTION

Anyone acquainted with the decisions of the Catholic diocesan marriage courts since about 1971 in such countries as Canada, the United Kingdom, Holland, Germany, Australia and the United States will find the following fictional case familiar in its details. It concerns a Catholic woman's allegation before such a court (whose formal name is the Diocesan Tribunal) that her supposed marriage is null, and her petition to the court to declare it so. In this fiction the court accepts the petition and takes evidence from the principals and from witnesses. It has the former examined by psychologists. It evaluates the evidence and finds in the petitioner's favor. It declares the supposed marriage of four years to be null. That is, it judges that despite her exchange of wedding vows, her cohabitation with her putative husband, and the birth of their child, the woman has never been married. She has always been single. She is now free to marry—not again, but for the first time. (Her child will not as a consequence of this nullity be considered illegitimate. According to Catholic law legitimacy—a legal category to begin with, not a moral judgment nor a biological point of fact—is attained if at the time of either the child's conception or its birth at least one of its parents believes in good faith that he or she is validly married to the other.)

A tribunal officer, an advocate, was appointed by the court to prepare and present her petition. (Different courts now assign different officers to the preparing and presenting of petitions. In the tribunal of Hartford, Connecticut, for example, a judge-instructor does this.) After studying the evidence gathered by another court officer, a diocesan notary, he decided that there was probable cause for finding nullity. And from the evidence he advised her to assert, as the ground for her allegation of the marriage's nullity, essential incompatibility between herself and her supposed spouse, dating from the wedding and before. He assured her first of all that according to the jurisprudence regnant in the court she was petitioning, essential incompatibility of the parties was regularly acknowledged as a cause nullifying attempts at marriage. He added that in his opinion the evidence of her conduct and of her supposed husband before, during and after their life together would probably support her allegation of incompatibility convincingly enough to elicit a judgment of nullity from the judges of the court. In the event it turned out that his opinion on the second point was as accurate as his knowledge on the first.

It is important to note this early in the introduction: Margaret Smith's allegation that her supposed marriage to Ian Jones was flawed fatally by incompatibility, and the court's agreement with her, were judgments by no one that either of them was simply and finally incapable of ever marrying. (Assigning names here to the principals is part of the fiction, but it will help the fluency of the narrative.) That question was not addressed in the court's action. What the judges said expressly was that Margaret and Ian were incapable of marrying one another—or, to hone the judgment to its proper fineness, that they had been incapable of doing so at least at the time they exchanged marital consent in their wedding vows. What the judges said implicitly was that if both could later marry validly, each would have to do so with another partner. Or, to come back to the same fineness, they could marry one another only after demonstrating that they had removed from their relationship the causes of their incompatibility—a wasted implication, since neither of them cherished the relationship enough to try to heal the incompatibility.

I have said that with the help of the notary and the advocate Margaret was able to gather and present evidence sufficient to convince the court that her allegation of essential incompatibility was accurate. What was the nature of this evidence? (Although the case I am outlining is fictional, as I have said, it lies too close to life in a number of tribunals in the countries I named earlier. The evidence of incompatibility shares the fiction, but is just as close to life outside those tribunals.[1])

The History of the Attempted Marriage

Margaret was twenty-three at the time of the wedding, while Ian was twenty-eight. Both were energetic and intelligent. She had earned her master's degree in comparative literature just before the wedding. He had earlier earned a bachelor's degree in economics, and after completing a series of courses but not a degree in business management, he had risen rapidly through the lower levels of a major overseas shipping firm and climbed into its middle management.

While he had a surface interest in Margaret's enthusiasms—classical music, nineteenth-century American painting, poetry of just about any epoch, quiet evenings with a few close friends listening to the music and reading poetry (some of it private composition)—his own deep and committed interests lay elsewhere. He was ambitious to move up. And his rapid rise into middle management by his thirty-second birthday showed that he knew how to do it.

He was aware that this took time and energy away from his marriage, but he insisted that the scrambling and climbing were neither for ego-building nor for money in itself. His father had died when Ian was ten, leaving him and an older sister to be reared by their mother in a frugality he had not forgotten. He intended never again to feel poverty's restriction on his freedom and happiness. His point made to Margaret more than just rhetorically was that while it was nice to listen with friends, in a setting of wine and candlelight, to stereo LP's of von Karajan directing the Vienna Philharmonic, it is much nicer listening to him direct it in the Festspielhaus in Salzburg, some 6,000 miles and $3,000 distant.

So far there had been only disagreement but hardly incompatibility. However, radical personality differences underlay the disagreements. Ian was aggressive, unreflective, had little quiet in him, and could not stand solitude—not even solitude for two. He was voluble in any case, and after three drinks he became a runaway monologist. But he used language mainly for emotional effect, minimally to communicate. Always he had trouble listening. The more he succeeded professionally, the less he tolerated open and equal exchange, even with Margaret. Once deeply into and taken over by his work he found no time for the long, searching conversations she needed. Having found out that resolute decision-making manifested strength among his colleagues, he took up the tactic with Margaret of announcing family decisions unilaterally. During the second and third summers after the wedding he forsook his two-week vacation in exchange for days off at Christmas and during the year, explaining to her that this earned points in the competition for promotion. He urged her to visit her parents in place of the fortnight with him in a seaside cottage she had talked about and planned for.

His lovemaking was perfunctory in style, about six times in ten unsatisfying because of partial impotence brought on by fatigue, preoccupation and simple lack of enthusiasm. He refused to discuss his lame and halting sexuality. His covering explanation and intended consolation were that on some future day or night he would have the desire and the energy for the tactile poetry that Margaret wanted.

He agreed to have a baby, at first reluctantly but then less enthusiastically in the hope that her preoccupation with the child would deflect her emotional need from him to it.

Margaret's personality was point for point misfitted to his. She needed quiet time, although not necessarily alone; she wanted Ian with her there. She was keenly sensitive to nuances of mood. Even before the wedding, but when it was too late to back out, she had begun to suspect that his unawareness of her feelings was conscious but veiled impatience. She needed constant assuring that she was understood and cared about, all the more since none of Ian's hurried verbal assurances ever came near touching her need. She resented his spending hours developing and maintaining a numerous assortment of business acquaintances. Early in the marriage she had been his consort in the unceasing round of receptions and parties that took up his evening hours. But soon, out of boredom and out of resentment at her ornamentary role in it all, she left him to go alone and stayed home—also alone, sometimes angry and sometimes depressed. He returned the anger, aiming it at her selfish failure to be supportive during what he considered a short but trying period of struggling upward mobility that was as much for her good as for his.

The rest of their history together was the familiar one: longer absences on Ian's part; more reclusion on hers, varying between total preoccupation with the baby, and neglect of the baby and everything else to make room for interminable escapist television-watching; increasingly frequent arguments, brief and blistering, in which she was badly overmatched and almost always driven to tears.

At the urging of a friend who cared and at Margaret's pleading with him to do it to save the marriage he twice went with her to a professional marriage and family counselor. In the two sessions he got, he insisted, as much of an understanding of their trouble as he needed. He refused to participate beyond the two sessions because at minimal profit to him they either took up the heart of his business day or interfered with his evening schedule. What angered Margaret most, and to her mind worked as the fatal flaw, was his refusal and probably his inability to face the mangled reality of their relationship, to acknowledge it and talk about it honestly. He excused himself from the pain of this by insisting that there was nothing wrong that couldn't be healed by her growing up and acting like an adult.

The tribunal had no difficulty in getting Ian as well as Margaret to undergo examination by its court-appointed psychologist. As the latter found out, the possibility of an annulment appealed to Ian. He would be unburdened of a wife already dragging heavily on his upward momentum, while she was still young enough to marry again soon and free him from having to support her. The new husband might also adopt the child and reduce even that responsibility to nil.

The judges also interviewed Ian's sister. She was two years his senior, an intelligent and discerning woman. She told them the dreary story of the death of his affectivity during childhood and adolescence. First a remote and despotic father, then a demoralized and compulsively drinking mother, had been its assassins.

The Point of Law in the Decision

The tribunal's judgment was that Ian's and Margaret's attempt at marriage four years earlier had been null. It named as cause of the nullity that they had been unable to form with one another the *intima communitas vitae,* the intimate community or sharing of life that belongs to the nature itself of marriage according to contemporary Catholic teaching. From before their first meeting they had been blocked by a fundamental incapacity for forming this union with one another, for carrying on the intimate sharing in all of life.[2]

An essential point in the court's reasoning to this decision was that because the relational incapacity had its causes in Ian's and Margaret's separate emotional characters, and because development of these characters had been substantially completed by the time of the wedding (hence by that time the incapacity had already been established), they had become incapable of the consent needed to create the marriage. There was a moral principle at the core of the judges' reasoning: no one can make a valid act of consent, whether contractual or covenantal, to form and sustain a relationship he or she is incapable of forming and sustaining. This is true even if the incapacity is verified solely in the relationship that one has tried to form and sustain.

Just under the surface of this logic is the fact that Margaret's securing the judgment of nullity depended on the court's interpretation of the nature of marriage. Notice of this takes us into the theme of this entire volume—the Roman Catholic Church's understanding of marriage in the last third of the twentieth century. It is a changed conception, some say so changed as to be substantially different from what it was during the first two-thirds of this century and for about seven centuries earlier. With the earlier conception as ruling criterion of judgment, the court would have rejected Margaret's allegation that her supposed marriage was null for the reason she adduced—essential incompatibility. Indeed her petition entered on this ground would not even have been accepted by the court. The records of the Church's tribunals show no annulments granted before 1969 on the ground of two persons' inability to form with one another a life of intimate sharing. And annulment on this ground would have been unacceptable in principle before December 1965. For it was only in that month of that year that the bishops of the Second Vatican Council promulgated their Pastoral Constitution on the Church in the Modern World, *Gaudium et spes*. It was only in this document that the Church recovered the ancient understanding of marriage as *intima communitas vitae et amoris coniugalis*—an intimate community (or sharing) of marital life and love.[3]

What was the Catholic Church's conception of marriage before the Second Vatican Council? In its most exact form, the form that had served until *Gaudium et spes* as the functional definition in the Catholic marriage courts, is contained in its several parts in the Church's Code of Canon Law promulgated in 1917. Before we state it and study it briefly it is appropriate to note that although one may now justifiably speak of this definition in the past tense, as a conception it is nevertheless part of the Church's Code of law that is still in effect. The entire Code is at present writing (in the autumn of 1980) under revision, including its Title VII, *De Matrimonio*. The revision of Title VII has been completed since the spring of 1978, but awaits promulgation along with the entire code when the revision of its other parts will have been completed. Meanwhile the Code's interpretation of marriage has been supplanted unevenly in its parts by the interpretation taken from *Gaudium et spes*. Both the supplanting and the unevenness have been evident in the marriage courts.

The Definition of Marriage in the Code of Canon Law

Using the term literally, there is no "definition" of marriage in either the 1917 Code of Canon Law or in *Gaudium et spes*—no formal, taxative definition of it.[4] That is, in neither is there an assigning of marriage to a generic category of existence and then a determining of its specific category. What the Code has done is to include within itself three schemata within which marriage has been conceived of in the history of the Church's dealing with it. Therefore to understand the Code's conception of marriage one must piece together the discrete elements of each schema. There is the schema of the ends of marriage, primary and secondary (this is the schema incorporated most explicitly in the Code). A second schema of the *bona,* the goods or blessings of marriage, coming down from the age of the Fathers and consecrated by St. Augustine, is itself contained as a sub-set among the ends of marriage. The third schema, Scholastic-juridical in origin, names the essential properties of a marriage.

None of these appear in the Code's first words about marriage, in its Canon 1012. For particular reasons of history that we shall review later this canon says, in its paragraph 1, that "Christ our Lord has raised the very contract of marriage between baptized persons to the dignity of a sacrament." Thus the canon contains an assumption of fact, that the essence of any marriage is a contract. It asserts an historical event, that Christ raised the marriages of his baptized followers to a sacrament. And in its paragraph 2 it asserts a religious fact: "It is impossible for a valid contract of marriage to exist between baptized persons without its being a sacrament." But being a statement in a code of law, the canon does not explain when the event took place in history, nor how it is that any marriage of two baptized persons is a Christian sacrament.

The kind of contract a marriage is the Code explains implicitly as the canons immediately following go on to specify the components and the characteristics of this contract. They borrow from the above-named schemata in doing so. Canon 1013.1 says that the primary end of any marriage is the procreation and nurture of children. ("Nurture" translates the canon's Latin noun *educatio* better than does its English transliteration because the canon intends the full physical, emotional and intellectual upbringing of the child. The redundancy "procreation and nurture of children" appears throughout the Code and in most Church documents with which I am acquainted.) The same canon, still in its paragraph 1, says that a marriage's secondary end is mutual help and the remedying of concupiscence. (Some modern authors—Bouscaren and Ellis among them—seek to dull the cutting edge of the Latin *remedium concupiscentiae* by translating it "the allaying of concupiscence." But a careful reading of St. Augustine's theory of marriage, whence the concept got its long-lasting impetus, shows that he meant exactly what the Latin says, a *remedium,* a healing of a kind of psychological illness. I hope to show this in a later chapter incorporating the key pertinent texts from Augustine's essays, *De Nuptiis et Concu-*

piscentia, De Peccato Originali, De Adulterinis Coniugiis and *De Genesi ad Litteram.* "Legitimate relief" may be included in Augustine's conception, but it does not express all he meant.)

Since the ends of any relationship are found in the goods it can realize for the parties to it, to name its primary end is to name the most valuable of these goods. And if the relationship is said to be in nature a contract, this most valuable good is the principal object of the contract. It is what the parties entering it must contract for; it is the advantageous thing or situation or experience which, before all other things, situations or experiences, they must commit themselves to realize for one another.

(Since in the attempt to define marriage we are already in the domain of exactly used words, it is worthwhile pouncing here on an exactness. The Latin noun for "end" in Canon 1013.1 is *finis.* This noun is also commonly translated in English as "purpose." But synonymizing these two translating English nouns can cause confusion, since in real life the end of a certain kind of conduct is not always identical with a person's purpose in engaging in it. His purpose is his motive. And his motive is the future good he hopes to gain from the conduct. Marriage as defined in the canon according to its primary end is an example here of the potential confusion. I doubt if the primary *purpose,* the dominant motive, of many men and women in marrying is to procreate and nurture. Moralists and canonists using the Latin language avoid the ambiguity here by distinguishing the *finis operis* [the end] from the *finis operantis* [the purpose].)

Canon 1013.2 states the essential properties, or characteristics, of a marriage. It says that these are two, unity and indissolubility. The first of these, *unitas* in the Latin of the Code, is better translated as "exclusivity," since what the Latin noun designates in context is monogamy.

To say more exactly what *indissolubilitas* designates we must first take note of one adjective in this paragraph. The two properties just named are said to be *essential* to a marriage. Taken at ontological face value the adjective indicates that for a relationship to be a marriage, it must have these two characteristics, monogamy and indissolubility.[5] Or to say the same thing in negative form, if a relationship, even though intended by the partners to produce and nurture children, is however intended by them to be either not exclusive or not indissoluble, or neither, it is not a marriage.

But what *indissolubilitas* designates is not an intent in the minds of the parties; it designates a property of the contract itself. It does not say that the parties must intend to honor their contract unfailingly; it says that the contract once entered cannot be voided as long as both parties live, because such is simply the nature of the contract. Only the death of one or both can dissolve it. Therefore the consent that creates the contract is irreversible—not in the sense that trying to do so is forbidden, but because to do so is impossible. And intending against the indissolubility of one's potential marriage while making the act of consent nullifies the attempt at contracting.

More elements of the Code's conception of marriage are found in a later part of its Title VII. This is first of all in Canon 1081, which specifies the act that alone can bring a marriage into existence. Paragraph 1 of this canon encapsulates an authoritative decision which ended a long and painful debate among canonists during the eleventh and twelfth centuries. The debate pitted the Roman against the central European tradition about the kind of act or acts needed to create a marriage. (In a later chapter this debate will get the explanation it merits.) But Canon 1081.1 says: "A marriage is created by the consent of the parties lawfully expressed by persons capable according to the law; and for this consent no human power can substitute."

That is—to spell out briefly the implications of the paragraph's first clause—a marriage is brought into existence not by betrothal plus intercourse bypassing expressed consent, nor by the husband's leading his bride across the threshold into their new home after the consent, nor by her father's or her guardian's handing over the bride into her husband's authority, nor by a combination of mutual consent followed by intercourse. As variant interpretations these all had their moment in the debate mentioned above. The canon asserts that a marriage is created by the parties' expressed consent and by only this. Such consent is indispensably necessary in order to create a marriage. And by itself it is sufficient to do so.

Our concern lies now with paragraph 2 of this Canon 1081, which specifies the object of the consent that creates a marriage. It says to what the parties consent in creating a marriage: "Marital consent is an act of the will whereby each party grants and accepts a permanent and exclusive right over the body regarding its acts which are of themselves apt for the generation of offspring." The earlier canons made clear that the consent creating a marriage is contractual. Here in its own way Canon 1081.2 reiterates Canon 1013.1 in the latter's naming procreation and nurture as the primary end of marriage. And putting these two canons together we get this: that the object of the contractual consent and the primary end of the contract, the most valuable good it can secure, are almost identical—almost but not quite.

For note that Canon 1081.2 does not say that the object of marital consent is procreation itself. It does not even say that this object is the right to procreate, a right whose exercise the spouses could freely relinquish while retaining the right itself—as happened among those husbands and wives of saintly report who lived virginal marriages. We can penetrate to the meaning of this clause by going through an inch of legal psychology. Contractual consent is, at base, a decision of the will—or more accurately the decisions of two wills, each decision conditioning the other's effect—by which the parties give over to the other something of value that is his or her own.

In this light, what Canon 1081.2 names as the thing of value given over by marital consent is each party's right over his and her body's genital function oriented to conception. Said another way, the thing of value exchanged contractually is not the parties' sexual acts themselves, but each one's personal and private *right* to his and her own sexual acts.

This careful identifying of the act of marital consent and of its object has historical reasons energizing it. I shall name but one for now. No canonist in the twelfth or thirteenth century, when the identifying was done, wished to deny the Catholic tradition that Mary and Joseph were truly married. Neither did any wish to challenge the tradition of Mary's deliberately chosen and perpetual virginity, nor the codicil to this tradition saying that before her marriage Mary had taken a vow not only of celibacy but of perpetual virginity. (St. Augustine suggested that she had made a conditional vow that she would remain unmarried and a virgin unless God willed otherwise.) But the canonists' problem was to explain how she could maintain her physical virginity but nevertheless marry if the objects of marital consent were understood as the conceiving of children and sexual intercourse themselves. However, they agreed that if they were to define the object of this consent as a person's *right* to sexual acts, it could be concluded that Mary had exchanged this right with Joseph (and had thus really married him), but with the understanding that the right would never be claimed in act. Thus the historical phenomenon of virginal marriage, not unheard of during the centuries preceding and surrounding the canonical debate about the object of marital consent, helped produce the solution to the dilemma about Mary's virginal marriage. The solution, in turn, explained the canonical possibility of the phenomenon.

This specification of the object of marital consent also keeps the way humanely open for the marrying of men and women who cannot conceive and bear children because of sterility for whatever reason. Though either or both be sterile, they can nevertheless exchange the right to their sexual acts. Hence the precise wording of the final clause of Canon 1081.2: ". . . acts which are *of themselves* apt for the generation of offspring" [italics added]. That is, though a woman be post-menopausal in age and condition or have had a hysterectomy, or though a man have had a vasectomy or his sperm count be so low as to make conception impossible, they can nevertheless exchange the right to the sexual acts including intercourse because they can presumably perform the latter, the act of itself apt for conceiving.

This exchanged right to sexual acts is said also to be an exclusive right, or a right given over in exclusivity. The correlate to this, already identified in Canon 1013.2, is marriage's essential property of monogamy. While the exclusivity of the exchange of rights according to Canon 1081 clearly implies a prohibiting *norm* concerning adultery, it does not imply about it what Canon 1013 implies about polygamy, namely that it is impossible. What it implies, or rather what it does, is to define and in a sense to establish adultery. That is, it establishes for the married that sexual acts had with any person other than the one with whom oneself has exchanged the exclusive right to such acts are in fact adulterous. Canon 1013 implies not that adultery, like polygamy, is impossible, but that it is evil; and what is evil about it is that it is a violation of the right once one's own but now given over to one's spouse in perpetuity.

Canon 1081 and its wording also help account for a piece of vocabulary common and, until the Second Vatican Council, useful in the Church's marriage law. Since according to the law sexual intercourse in a marriage is the substance of an exchanged right, and since rights exist and are exercised in the land of debts justly owed and justly claimed, it is appropriate from this point of view to refer to intercourse in marriage as "rendering the debt." This conceptual setting, combined with the centuries-old custom of marriages entered not for love but by parental arranging, produced a repertory of legal-moral questions about the motives for which and the conditions under which spouses may justly "demand the debt" from one another, or might "refuse the debt."[6]

That much of an excursus through the two canons of the 1917 Code which contributed most to the Catholic Church's pre-Vatican II understanding of the nature of marriage readies the way for a return to Ian and Margaret. It is clear why their allegation of nullity on the grounds she cited would have earned slight consideration at best in a jurisprudence drawn from that understanding. Compatibility as a man's and a woman's ability to enter and sustain together an intimate sharing in marital life and love is entirely separable from their ability to engage in sexual acts with one another, and thus to exchange the right to them. The ability to share in the sense intended by the bishops of the Council is not needed as a condition of their ability to exchange the right. Turning this disjunction about and restating it in an admittedly tendentious and brutal way, they could otherwise detest one another and expect to live a lifetime at an icy emotional distance from one another. But provided they were nevertheless willing to exchange, and were capable of exchanging, the perpetual and exclusive right to all their sexual acts apt of themselves for conceiving, they could, according to the 1917 Code, become husband and wife.

As I understand the history of Catholic theological and juridical thinking about marriage over the last thirty years, they were just such anomalies as this that helped drive the 1917 conception out of its normative place in the jurisprudence of the marriage courts. Under this norm the ability to marry—or the capacity to do so, to use the noun preferred in the marriage courts—was the capacity to constitute a contract. In a most general way this capacity was verified at two points. First was the capacity to carry through the kind of act that contracting is. (A four-year-old child cannot do this. Neither can a feeble-minded person, nor one under the influence of a heavily amnesiac anodyne such as demerol, nor can a person emotionally paralyzed by fear.) Secondly, even for a person with his perfectly clear wits about him this capacity to constitute a contract or not was verified in his ability or not to exchange the contractual good after he had constituted the contract. (Sexual impotence is the prime example of an incapacitating disability here, since according to the Code one's right to sexual acts including intercourse is precisely the good exchanged in the marital contract. But no one can give over to another the right to an act he cannot perform.)

Not that sexual impotence was the only annulling disability under the jurisprudence derived from the Code. The essential properties it ascribes to marriage—exclusivity and indissolubility—were territories in which such disability could be found. A man or woman incapable of fidelity, incapable of confining his or her sexual acts exclusively to the spouse, could be found incapable of marrying. (In 1957 a precedent-setting decision was handed down by the Church courts which ruled that a woman suffering apparently incurable nymphomania had been for this reason incapable of marrying, and her supposed marriage was declared null.[7]) A man or woman suffering from a mental illness allowing intervals of lucidity during which he or she could make an act of contractual consent, but which made impossible the permanent stable cohabitation and sexual exchange substantial to the marriage contract, could also be found incapable of marrying.

It is important in the Catholic jurisprudence ruling nullity cases to distinguish between the incapacity of a person to form a marriage with anyone, and the relative incapacity of two persons to form a marriage with one another. The latter is the annulling incapacity I have already reviewed in this chapter's extended paradigm under the title "essential incompatibility." And I have already said that this relative incapacity was not acknowledged as a ground of nullity before 1969, because the conception of marriage from which a jurisprudence acknowledging such an incapacity came to life in the Church courts only after the publishing, in December 1965, of the Second Vatican Council's Pastoral Constitution on the Church in the Modern World. But before this date and this document even a person's private incapacity to marry at all was interpreted narrowly—as narrowly as the two essential properties of marriage stated in the Code of Canon Law. It was *Gaudium et spes* that expanded the meaning of capacity and incapacity beyond boundaries that pre-conciliar jurists had imagined possible.

The Conception of Marriage in *Gaudium et spes*

What did the Catholic bishops intend in writing their chapter on marriage at the beginning of Part II of *Gaudium et spes?* Did they, as the Church's appointed teachers, mean to offer to her people—and indeed to all the world—a conception of marriage different from the one that was fixed in the Code of Canon Law as the product of centuries of philosophy, legislation and jurisprudence? The history of the document's composition shows beyond a doubt that persons functioning at the heart of the Council were convinced they meant to. This history would not contain the severe disagreement, the prolonged debate between two clearly defined alliances of bishops, if this conviction had not been both clear and attended with alarm.

Even so, *Gaudium et spes,* like Title VII of the Code, contains no formal definition of marriage and attempts none. What the bishops plainly sought to do was to present a fresh description of marriage. The description contains a partial phenomenology of marriage. It is found mainly in paragraph 48 of the document, although in the chapter's introductory paragraph 47 it refers to marriage in passing as a partnership of love (*communitas amoris*).

The first thing the bishops say about marriage (in paragraph 48) is that it is an intimate partnership, or sharing, of marital life and love (*intima communitas vitae et amoris coniugalis*). In the same sentence they add that marriage, precisely as such a sharing, has been founded by the Creator and is governed by his laws. And still in the same sentence they make the crucial point that a marriage is formed by the marital covenant (*foedere coniugii . . . instauratur*), a covenant whose nature is one of irrevocable personal consent.

Continuing with their specification of the kind of act that creates a marriage, the bishops say that the partners do this by a human act in which they mutually give and accept one another (. . . *actu humano quo coniuges sese mutuo tradunt atque accipiunt*). They then link their descriptive definition with ancient tradition by saying that marriage is endowed with various goods and ends (*variis bonis ac finibus*), and these, when realized, serve for the continuation of the human race, for the personal growth and eternal salvation of the individual family members, and for the dignity, peace and prosperity of the families themselves, and indeed of the entire human race.

As the compromise resolution of a long and painful disagreement in the Council's last session over the place of procreation in marriage's nature, the bishops say that marriage as an institution and married love itself have as a natural characteristic of themselves (*indole naturali*) an orientation to procreation and nurture. Marital love and marriage reach their completion, come to their full flowering, in children (*suo fastigio coronantur*).

The dynamics of a marriage, what makes up the substance of married life, they designate as the spouses' living of a covenant (*foedus*), an intimate conjoining of their persons and actions (*intima personarum atque operum coniunctio*), a giving of mutual help and service (*mutuum sibi adiutorium et servitium praestant*), a constant growing in a sense of unity. The bishops end this descriptive defining in paragraph 48 by returning to their own introductory epithet: marriage is an intimate union, a mutual self-donation of the persons (*intima unio . . . mutua duarum personarum donatio*). (The rest of the paragraph turns to a descriptive analysis of the sacramental nature of the marriages of Christians, while paragraph 49 is the same kind of analysis of marital love.)

Consequences of the Changed Conception

If I were the tribunal judge writing the decision on Margaret Smith's petition, I would make these paragraphs of *Gaudium et spes* the major premise of my conclusion in favor of the nullity of her supposed marriage.

And since the conclusion would be a judgment interpreting a point of fact according to Church law, I would also use as a premise a religious claim made by that law for centuries, namely that the only valid marriage two Christians can have is a sacramental marriage. Consequently I would judge it sufficiently evident that Margaret and Ian, both Roman Catholics, had in their relationship with one another shown the antecedent incapacity to consent to the following:

(a) to the giving of themselves to one another for one another—and particularly as Christians to make the kind of mutual self-bestowal found in Christ's sacrificial love for the Church;

(b) therefore to the forming of a covenant of love and fidelity (far from faithful in this religious covenantal sense, they had from the beginning moved apart in alienation, even though there was no evidence of sexual conduct with third parties);

(c) therefore to the forming and maintaining of a communion of their persons.

Since they had been, at the time they exchanged their wedding vows, incapable of doing any of these, they were incapable of making the consent that creates a marriage. Especially were they incapable of making the self-giving consent that creates a sacramental marriage, the only kind of marriage that they as Christians, according to Catholic marriage law, could have possibly created.

Questions That Remain—and Disagreements

Obviously the conception of marriage given the Church in *Gaudium et spes* has inspired a jurisprudence that has broadened the grounds for nullity, and has thus opened a way out of destructive relationships for such victims of their own indiscretion as Ian and Margaret. But this conception has not bred unity, clarity and peace about marriage among Catholics generally. In the rest of this introductory chapter I will outline some of the as yet unanswered questions, some of the unresolved disagreements, that have followed in the wake of *Gaudium et spes*. And this outline may serve as a preview of fuller treatment in later chapters.

The first question here is one I have yet to see asked in all the critical examination brought to bear on *Gaudium et spes*. This question asks about the process of describing marriage, about even the methodology of defining it descriptively that the bishops employed. A method of defining is either prescriptive or descriptive. To use the former is to design, to invent something that has not yet existed. The definer in this case knows the nature of what he defines because he designs this nature. He cannot err about this nature in definition; he can only later realize it imperfectly if he tries to fashion a concrete example of it and does so less than flawlessly.

Nowhere is there evidence that the bishops of Vatican II thought that they were defining marriage prescriptively. On the contrary, they were explicit (in paragraph 48 of *Gaudium et spes*) about God's authorship of marriage. They professed to be describing what he had given to the human race—a relationship, an institution that was already there, apparently in its established nature—aeons before the Catholic Church and her bishops came into existence. Consequently, if they adverted to their method at all, they were convinced that they were defining descriptively.

But whoever sets about defining a thing or a relationship does this accurately in the degree he describes accurately the reality he seeks to define. His effort at accuracy is complicated if two further conditions obtain: first, if he finds plural models of the reality he seeks to describe in his definition, and, second, if he wishes to use his definition to instruct the members of a society in right conduct. Given these complicating conditions, now he has not only the task of describing accurately, but the prior task of choosing that one among the plural models whose description (become his definition) will best serve the society he wishes to instruct.

Immediately it occurs to one to ask whether, given the diversity of societies in the human race and their diverse needs, it is possible to *describe* a single conception of marriage that can be *prescribed* helpfully for these diverse societies. Because the bishops insisted that the single conception of marriage they acknowledged is God's design, presumably they found this conception in the Sacred Scriptures. But there are plural conceptions of marriage there. And the earliest that is historically verifiable, the polygamous marriage of the Hebrew patriarchs, hardly fits the one design that the bishops acknowledge. Moreover, there are societies today, in Asia and Africa, whose culture does not produce marriages that fit this design. Insofar as the bishops' definition in *Gaudium et spes* is descriptive, it is more nearly a description of marriage in European and American societies. What they may indeed have done is to draw a descriptive definition of marriage from its model in one culture and prescribed it as a definition for marriage everywhere and (such being the universal reference of definitions) in all ages.

This temporal reference of the definition raises a second question. Let us suppose that in *Gaudium et spes* the bishops did offer a new conception of marriage, or offered anew an ancient one that had been forgotten. In either case they set aside a definition of marriage that had reigned in the Church for seven centuries, one whose clearest formulation is in the 1917 Code of Canon Law. It was an amalgam of Roman law and Germanic tradition. At its core was the concept of marriage as consensual contract. And the bishops removed and replaced it presumably because they found that it served the Catholic people poorly in the second half of the twentieth century.

What is the nature and what is the value of definitions that are relinquished when they cease to serve a society well? Are they really descriptions of the given nature of a certain kind of natural relationship—a nature so given of a relationship so natural that one feels justified in saying that it is the Creator's design? Or are they really variant formulations for the well-being of men and women who seek to live in society in variants of this relationship at different times and in different places? If so, has the Catholic Church in Vatican II designed the last of these formulations in her history or only the latest in a series? If only the latest in a series, what holding power does it have as a norm for measuring the validity and invalidity of presumed marriages?

Marital Love

Since *Gaudium et spes* calls a marriage a man's and a woman's intimate community or sharing of marital life and love, did the bishops who drafted this formulation mean to say that a kind of love is essential to marriage? They said too that a man and woman form their marriage by an act of covenanting. The conception is clearly drawn from the biblical model of God's love for his people. So in this did they imply that a covenantal love is needed essentially for the forming of a marriage? They added that by this covenanting a man and woman give themselves to and accept one another, and in living their married life they are joined in an intimate union of their persons, and help and serve one another. Did they in these clauses too imply the essentiality of love in a marriage?

To some readers this composite question may seem a pseudo-question. What other could the answer be than affirmative? But since about two years after the close of Vatican II this apparently tranquil territory of interpretation has been the arena of one of the most serious canonical, philosophical and theological debates among Catholic teachers. An emphatically negative answer has come from a Pope (Paul VI), from the subcommission that drafted the revision of the Catholic marriage law, from a majority of the forty cardinals of the *plenarium* who supervised this revision, approved its final draft and sent it on to the Pope, from some judges of the Church's appellate court for marriage cases (the Rota), and from many canonists around the world. Not even the consideration (by those who thought of it) that at least the sacramental marriages of Christians are sacraments precisely in that they image on earth the love of Christ and his Church—not even this could convince them of the essentiality of love in a marriage. The issue is a stark one: if a kind of love is essential to marriage, only those men and women capable of this love are capable of marrying. And which among all the kinds of love in human experience may this essentially needed love be?

All the persons named just above, Pope Paul and the others, admit that a specific love lies close to the essence of marriage, that it is ordinarily the cause bringing a man and a woman into their marriage, that it is indispensable for the fulfillment and happiness available in marriage, but not that it is an element of marriage's essence—on this they have insisted. This is to imply that the consent needed absolutely for the creating of a marriage need not be an act of love, though it may be motivated and accompanied by love. Implicit too in the negative insistence is the denial that the conduct most specific to the self-giving and accepting in marriage, which is sexual intercourse, need be an act of love even to make it *marital* sexual intercourse.

A later chapter in this volume will review the history of this disagreement and denial. In studying this history one finds, again, no difficulty in identifying the principal reason for the denial. Who can say exactly what marital love is? Or, even if this were possible, who can verify that it is present or absent in a real-life heterosexual relationship? Love is an elusive reality. The boundaries of its different kinds are vague and the several kinds overlap. The kinds of love that have led men and women into marriage have varied from epoch to epoch and from culture to culture. On the record men and women have destroyed marriages in the name of love. So, despite the bishops' saying so much about love in *Gaudium et spes* (the document's paragraph 49 is virtually an apostrophe to marital love), and despite Pope Paul's saying quite exactly what the characteristics of marital love are when writing his encyclical letter *Humanae vitae* in 1968 (he named its full humanness, its totality, its faithful exclusivity and its fecundity), the major officers of the Church's *magisterium* have insisted that what a man and woman create when they give themselves to one another in their wedding vows is not a relationship having love as one of its essential components. Whether these teachers in the Church have thought themselves compelled logically to deny also that the act of self-giving in the wedding vows is in essence an act of love has never been made clear.

A Changed Conception of Marriage and the Sacrament

It would be consistent with everything said thus far to add that the Church's changed understanding of marriage has brought also a change in her theology of marriage as a sacrament. But the converse is closer to the truth. The ancient Catholic anthropology saying that every marriage is a contract could live peacefully with the theology saying that every marriage of two Christians is a sacrament as long as "sacrament" in marriage was accepted to mean what it meant to St. Augustine—a *sacramentum,* a sacred seal of commitment. His understanding of this *sacramentum* of marriage was that the commitment in marriage is not primarily of the spouses to one another, but a joint commitment of both to God. And the prior fact that by their baptism both were already "sealed" with the indelible *sacramentum* of baptism had the effect of making their commitment to God in marriage indelible in the sense of indissoluble. So this was for Augustine the *sacramentum* of marriage, an unbreakable seal of commitment in marriage to God. More than once, in answer to the question asking how their marriage continues to exist and what in it still exists if one spouse abandons the other and attempts a second marriage, he answered that this is the *sacramentum.* It is the perdurance of this in the souls of both spouses that forbids either's attempting remarriage while the other still lives. This *sacramentum* he likened to the sacerdotal character, also a *sacramentum,* that remains indelibly in the soul of a priest even if he be removed permanently from all priestly function.[8]

As I suggested above, this fifth-century interpretation of the sacramentality of Christian marriage is congenial to the thirteenth-century interpretation of marriage as a contract. What the sacrament is here understood to do is to make a marriage a sacred contract. This in turn makes possible a convincing analogy. Just as baptism, in the sense of a character abiding in the soul, serves functionally as a cause of grace in the sense of divine help given to lead a Christian life, so the contract-become-sacrament serves functionally as a cause of sacramentally healing grace. This healing grace is understood in turn as a gratuitously given divine help for fulfilling the duties of marriage. And again in turn these duties are understood as the obligation to secure either the three goods of marriage for which the spouses have contracted, namely offspring, fidelity and permanence, or these duties are identified in an overlapping way with the ends of marriage, namely procreation and nurture, mutual help and the remedying of concupiscence. The grace of the sacrament is then understood to be a divine help for the spouses in attaining these ends, which are those of the marriage contract. In short, the sacrament is understood to make possible, or even to facilitate, the keeping of the contract.

Interpreting history with the help of hindsight it is easy to understand which point of view, contract or sacrament, was to become the controlling one and which the controlled as the contingencies of history from the thirteenth century onward forced the development of Catholic thought on marriage. The nature of the act consummating marriage offers a sample of this predictability. If the question about this act had been "What is needed in order to fulfill a sacred commitment to permanent fidelity?" the answer could not have omitted the survival of both spouses in fidelity in the same marriage until the death of one of them. But in fact the question about the consummating act was asked not about the sacrament but about the contract. To this question the answer inevitably contained the conclusion that since the contract is consummated by the first complete exchange of the contractual good—by the first act of complete intercourse after the marital consent—so too is the sacrament. And since, according to Augustine's explanation, the indissolubility of the marriage of two Christians comes of its being a *sacramentum,* consummation fitted to the contract brings on the indissolubility caused by the sacrament. (This inconsistency was thought to be repaired by the canonists of the twelfth century who relocated the indissolubility in the contract itself by redefining it as non-voidable even by the parties who had originally made it. Their warrant for inventing this unique contract was their supposition that in saying "What God has joined no man must separate" Jesus referred to the contract they had in mind.)

But once Catholic minds became increasingly aware of the implications in the central image of marriage as sacrament—it is a living sign of God's covenantal love with his people, and, more exactly, according to the

New Testament model, it is a living sign of Christ's love relationship with his Church—the contract's domination of the sacrament was bound to be challenged. Now at last the question, or at least one of the earnest questions, in the reshaped Catholic curiosity asks: "What must go on in the marriage of two Christians if it is to be a sign of such a love relationship as that?" The sacral and theological term "to be a living sign" is translated accurately into our usual language as "to manifest a reality, to tell accurately about it, by acting it out—by re-enacting it," as for example an embrace may manifest love by acting it. But if we are to ask what must go on in the marriage of two Christians if it is to be such a sign, we must back up and first ask what must be in their souls if they are to come to the wedding capable of acting out such a love relationship. Whatever the ability or inability of Margaret and Ian to create a merely secular marital relationship, a contract, and sustain it, it is clear from the evidence that they were incapable of joining in the unafraid, undefensive self-giving love that would re-enact sacramentally the love relationship of Christ and his Church.

The Indissolubility of Marriage

From the instruction of Jesus as this is remembered in the Synoptic Gospels and in St. Paul's First Letter to the Corinthians, Christians know that a man's getting rid of his wife is contrary to God's will, and that his seeking to marry another woman after getting rid of his wife is a contradiction to God's will that is adultery. But the simplicity of this instruction is only apparent, as the Catholic Church has found out through experience. For one thing, in virtually every culture in every society a marriage comes into existence in plural stages. This being so, one must ask if the unfailing fidelity that Jesus demanded in marriage is expected from the onset of the first of the plural stages in marrying, or not until one of the ensuing stages. Among his own people a couple created a marriage in two stages. The first was the *kiddushin,* deceptively translated into English as "betrothal"—deceptively because it was far more unlike our own engagement than like it. If a Jewish girl in Jesus' society were marrying for the first time, her *kiddushin* lasted a year. If she were a woman remarrying, it lasted a month. If the couple broke off the *kiddushin,* they did so by divorce. According to the tradition of at least southern Israel, the betrothed were permitted sexual intercourse during the *kiddushin* in order to test their fertility.

The first generation of Christians was almost entirely Jewish in ethnic and cultural makeup, and there is no evidence that their manner of marrying was different from what their families had been doing for generations. Consequently Jesus' demand could not avoid being applied to their marriages in some version of the questions, "Do we disobey his word if we end our relationship during the *kiddushin?* Or is it not until that year has ended and the second and ordinarily lasting phase, the *nissuin,* has begun that a husband's dismissing his wife is the sundering he has forbidden?"

As Christianity moved out of Palestine and Syria, during its second generation, and out of the diaspora synagogue communities of the empire and into the mainstream of Hellenistic-Roman society, the question had to change its trajectory. By the year 55 or 60 A.D. the older forms of Roman marriage which kept the wife in virtual childhood all her married life had fallen into disuse. Almost all the women whom the law allowed to marry entered a *matrimonium liberum,* a free marriage. They chose their own husbands, and engagement was reduced to much the same status it has in our own Western tradition. The marriage itself was created simply by the mutually expressed consent of the parties. Consequently there arose the new and different shape of the question: "Does the Lord's demand for unfailing fidelity, now that there is no longer the trial period of *kiddushin,* bind from the moment of consent?"

Four hundred years later Christian marriage found itself again moving into societies and cultures whose processes of marrying were multiphased. Lombards, Franks and Germans all had variations on some form of handing over the bride and of marriage sealed by the first act of intercourse. In some parts of central Europe the consent of the young spouses, particularly of the bride, counted for little. Two sets of parents did the substantial consenting. So again the question had to be reasked and again redirected: At which step in the process of marrying does Jesus' demand for unfailing fidelity take its binding effect? The history of Catholic disagreement about the answer to this question shows that over seven hundred years would go by, and the Church would pass its one thousandth anniversary, before the apparently final answer came from papal authority: not until the marriage is consummated by the first act of intercourse does it come under this demand. This is a qualification that is not in Jesus' remembered words. And by this time the unfailingness he had demanded was on its way to being understood as the indissolubility invented by the canonists of the twelfth century.

I am convinced that the understanding of marriage in *Gaudium et spes* (as also in Paul VI's *Humanae vitae*) compels yet another reasking of the question, and in a more challenging way than ever. From the time of the great canonists of the twelfth and thirteenth centuries until the Second Vatican Council the question had become, in its inclusive form, "Granted that Jesus' demand of all spouses that they stay unfailingly with one another means that they pass a certain point in the creating of their marriages at which these become indissoluble, what is this point?" And there also is a question of minor interest generally, but important to the curious canonist and theologian, "What is there in the marriage after that point that makes it indissoluble, incapable of being ended except by the death of one of the spouses? For example, what does the first act of intercourse after consent do to a marriage to finally make it, as the Church's *magisterium* insists, radically indissoluble?"

But the conception of marriage coming from *Gaudium et spes* and *Humanae vitae* makes different questions unavoidable. From this conception one cannot readily infer that what a Christian man and woman do when they marry is to enter a contract rendered a sacrament by their baptismal character, and therefore rendered also an essentially unretractable commitment to God that they will stay married—a contract-sacrament from which they are powerless to withdraw even by mutual agreement. On its own terms the changed conception implies that by their covenantal commitment the spouses *will* to be unfailing in their marital commitment and love, that they *will* to begin and never desist from a self-giving that builds gradually into an intimate communion of persons. In light of this is it still accurate to identify the object of Jesus' demand for unfailingness as indissolubility, which is a characteristic of a contract? Do the question and the discussion now turn instead on the unfailingness of the intention, of the will and of the effort in each of the partners?

The bishops of Vatican II appear to have been alert to this difference. It is true that in paragraph 50 of *Gaudium et spes* ("The Fruitfulness of Marriage") they refer in passing to "the indissoluble covenant between persons" as one of a marriage's characteristics (*indoles foederis inter personas indissolubilis*), thereby moving the canonical indissolubility of the contract invented in the twelfth century backward in history to fit the biblical covenant. But at the beginning of paragraph 48 they state that the act creating a marriage is a man's and a woman's "irrevocable personal consent." Thus they seem to imply that the irrevocability of the consent creating the covenant shares equally with the indissolubility natural to the covenant itself as the ground for any marriage's unbreakable permanence.

Curiously, when the bishops said these things of marriages—that they are indissoluble covenants created by irrevocable consent—they were referring not only to the consummated sacramental marriages of Christians. One would expect that they had limited their reference to these marriages, since according to Catholic doctrine these are the only kinds of marriage having radical indissolubility. All other marriages, though deemed indissoluble since the twelfth century, have in fact been held dissoluble. There is one power on earth that can dissolve them; this is "the power of the keys" given by Christ to Peter and his successors, the bishops of Rome. These marriages are said by the irreverent to have dissoluble indissolubility.

This raises the question broached much earlier in this chapter about descriptive and prescriptive defining. Since the bishops defined all marriages according to a covenantal model, a covenant that is naturally indissoluble, where did they find this model? Has there ever been in the Judeo-Christian tradition an indissoluble covenant? It is not to be found in the Old Testament, since it is clear in both Torah and the prophetic books that God's covenant with Israel was conditional and voidable. From his side God promised unfailing fidelity *provided* that Israel kept faith. It is equally clear that Israel's infidelity could destroy the covenant. God's promise to bless and protect Israel held on condition that Israel from her side remained faithful to her covenantal commitment. If she did not, the blessing and protection would turn into a curse and destruction.[9]

Let us say then that the model for this imperishable covenant of marriage is found in the New Testament, in Christ's love relationship with his Church. And let us set aside for now the question whether the Church can, like Israel, prove unfaithful to her side of the covenant. This can account for the bishops' defining the marriages of Christians, who presumably live according to the new covenant, as indissoluble covenants. But can it account for what the bishops really did, which was to define the marriages of all human beings, of non-Christians, of non-believers, of atheists, as indissoluble covenants?

Let us admit also for the moment that such a model can be prescribed reasonably for all marriages, even the most secular, since even the latter are called to be irrevocable commitments to indissoluble fidelity. But if such marriages are made what they are *in nature* by the same model that makes consummated Christian marriages *in fact* indissoluble, why are not the former also made in fact indissoluble? The Catholic discipline of divorce since the sixteenth century does not treat them as such. Since that time this discipline has said that the papal power of the keys "to bind and to loose" can dissolve a marriage provided that it is not a sacrament.

Since nothing in *Gaudium et spes* hints that this discipline has been either ended or changed, it appears that from the same set of causes the bishops concluded to two kinds of indissolubility, one of them dissoluble. The impression that a varying history of prescription has gone on is strengthened by a move that I have already noted and one that I have not. The first is the bishops' relocating, in *Gaudium et spes,* the ground of marriage's indissolubility from the pre-Vatican II non-voidable-contract-marriage to the newly recovered irrevocable-covenant-marriage. The second seems a counter-move to the first and calls for detailed explanation.

Pope Paul VI made this move, if I understand his words correctly, in a discourse, on February 9, 1976, to the judges of the Roman Rota, the Church's highest appellate court in marriage matters. What occasioned the discourse were the decisions of the Dutch marriage courts in the ecclesiastical province of Utrecht declaring that they had found marriages to have simply ended by disintegration, by dying out. The judges ruled this way by reasoning from *Gaudium et spes'* defining marriage as a man's and a woman's intimate sharing in marital life and love, and concluding that when the sharing had ended irrevocably, the marriage had disappeared— because that is what a marriage is, an intimate, covenantal sharing. Pope Paul overruled these judges, saying that even though the love and the sharing disappear permanently from the relationship, the marriage remains nonetheless. It does so because the cessation of the sharing does not touch the essence of a marriage. This is a juridical entity, the marital bond. (Curiously Paul did not mention this essential heart of marriage when offering his own descriptive definition of marriage in his encyclical letter of 1968, *Humanae vitae.*)

Thus, although Paul did not, in this 1976 discourse, make the juridical bond synonymous with the marital contract of the 1917 Code that *Gaudium et spes* ignores, it seems nevertheless that he moved the ground of marriage's indissolubility from the irrevocable covenant back to where it had been before the Council—into the contract's non-voidability. For there is no other bond in marriage conceived as contract than the contract itself. Or did Paul mean to keep marriage the covenant but redefine it as the juridical bond he thought necessary in order to keep marriage's indissolubility? If he did, his biblically modeled covenant become juridical bond is as striking an innovation in our time as marriage the non-voidable contract was in the twelfth century.

Marriage and Procreation

There is a statement in paragraph 48 of *Gaudium et spes* that marks a crucial turn in the Catholic theology of marriage, in the moral theology of married conduct, and in the theology of the Church itself. This statement reads, "The marital institution itself and marital love have as a natural characteristic an orientation to procreation and nurture. Indeed they come to their natural completion in procreation and nurture."[10]

My reason for making this seemingly exaggerated claim for a statement sounding so conventional in the history of Catholic pronouncements on marriage may emerge against the background of some fresh history comprehending the Catholic theology, moral theology and canon law of marriage.

For at least fifteen centuries, from St. Augustine to the middle of this century, the claim that marriage has two inherent ends—procreation and nurture the primary end, mutual help and the remedying of the concupiscence the secondary end—had stood consecrated at the center of the Catholic teaching on marriage.[11] But in the late 1920's and in the 1930's this centuries-old teaching came under challenge by some Catholic European philosophers and theologians thinking and writing not in the Scholastic tradition but from phenomenological and personalist principles. Heribert Doms' book-length essay of 1935, *Vom Sinn und Zweck der Ehe* (On the Meaning and End of Marriage) was the best-known and most influential of these challenges (it had gone through two editions in French translation by 1937, and was translated into English in 1939 as *The Meaning of Marriage*). As Doms' title indicates, he urged thinking not in terms of the ends of marriage, but in terms of its meaning.

The officers of the Church's *magisterium* replied to the challenge in two especially memorable statements. On April 1, 1944 the Congregation of the Holy Office condemned the opinion denying the traditional hierarchy of subordinated ends of marriage. Seven years later Pope Pius XII, in a discourse to representatives of the Union of Italian Catholic Obstetricians (on October 29, 1951), condemned the same opinion at far greater length, with a far more detailed counter-reasoning, and in far more severe tones. (I shall review these condemnations, and the controversy that evoked them, in a later chapter and at greater length.)

Once the bishops of Vatican II decided to issue a statement on marriage and family—in fact an apostolic constitution including them as one of its major elements—they refused to skirt this once-controverted but now apparently settled issue that lay at the center of Catholic thinking. This was a surprising and controverted decision itself on the part of the bishops, since in face of the condemnations already on record from the Holy Office and Pius XII, they seemed to have very good reason to treat the issue as closed. Instead they treated it as still open, and used language which, in the footnote judgment of the American editors of the documents of the Council, was intended to keep it open.[12]

The place in marriage of procreation is stated again in *Gaudium et spes* at the beginning of paragraph 50 ("The Fruitfulness of Marriage"):

> Marriage and marital love have, as a natural characteristic of themselves, an orientation to procreation and nurture. Children are really the most valuable gift of marriage; they contribute richly to the good of their parents. . . . Hence, while not making the other ends of marriage of less value, the authentic conduct of marital love and the entire meaning of family life coming from this conduct have this aim, that the spouses be ready with courage to co-work with the love of the Creator and Savior in the continual increase and enrichment of his family.[13]

Anyone who has read the history of the debate and the maneuvering within the Mixed Commission of cardinals and bishops governing the debate on this part of *Gaudium et spes,* and in the subcommission that drafted its chapter on marriage and the family, knows what an angry interlude that debate became. (This too I shall review in the later chapter promised above.) But one must acknowledge the seriousness of the reasons in the minds of those bishops who wanted no changing of the traditional teaching on the subordinated ends of marriage. For, to return to a point hinted at earlier, the theology of the Church's *magisterium,* of her duty of teaching, was at issue. What must be the consequences for this theology if an ecumenical council ignores a Pope within fourteen years of his clear reiteration that the distinction and subordination of the ends of marriage belong to the perennial and common doctrine of the Church? And from a pastoral point of view, what could the bishops expect to be the effect in the mind of the married population of the Church once the moral consequences of this change began surfacing?

To name the first and most evident consequence in the ethics of contraception, it is common experience for the married that sustaining the primary end of marriage (procreation and nurture) can not only create a conflict with that part of the secondary end that is mutual help, but it can also threaten the marriage itself as a relationship of love. Having no other choices than to either accept another child, perhaps a sixth or seventh, or to end all lovemaking with intercourse, can bring the spouses to a destructive dilemma.

As long as the primary end was said resolutely to be primary, there was at least a principle by which consciences could be bound to make the primary end prevail in conduct over the secondary. And the spouses could struggle within their dilemma as best they might. But what follows for consciences if the erstwhile primary end, as happened in *Gaudium et spes,* loses its primacy and is demoted to equality with marriage's other end? Presuming that one continues to think in terms of the ends of marriage, the claims of the secondary end are no longer secondary and become at least equal in moral valence. And if serious necessity bolsters these claims in an irreconcilable conflict with procreation and nurture—a necessity as serious as saving the marriage—there is no principle, no compelling reason why procreation could not be suppressed while intercourse continues in order to save the marriage.

What eventually happened is commonly known. Three years after the Council the Catholic *magisterium* in the person of Pope Paul VI gave up speaking of the ends of marriage at all. In his encyclical of July 25, 1968, *Humanae vitae,* he replaced them as an ethical principle with two essential meanings of sexual intercourse, the unitive and the procreative.[14] He wanted to make these meanings serve as a premise for the condemnation of contraceptive intercourse in the same way that the now displaced primary end had served earlier. To do this he stated that the two meanings are equal in value and inseparable in conduct. This became a double addition to the history of the Church's defining of marriage—that a marriage has not ends but meanings, and that these meanings are equal and inseparable.

Critical curiosity may give in to the temptation to ask, again, whether this is descriptive defining or prescriptive. If it is the former, where in human experience did Paul find that marriage's unitive component—the need, the desire and the effort to form the communion specific to marriage—is inseparable from procreation? For centuries the Church has honored as saints a number of spouses who chose to live celibate marriages. Deliberately they separated the unitive meaning of their marriages from the procreative. Does Paul's defining of marriage according to these two inseparable meanings imply a revised retrospective judgment on their marriages?

But closer to our own time and experience, Paul's defining marriage according to these two meanings has its most obvious effect in the verification of men's and women's ability to marry. They must be able to bring to reality the unitive meaning of their marriage as well as the procreative. But what are the details of this meaning? What is the complex reality a couple must be able to bring into and sustain in existence if they are to be able to marry? Let us suppose that Paul provided these details in paragraphs 8 and 9 of the encyclical:

> . . . By means of the reciprocal personal gift of self, proper and exclusive to them, husband and wife tend toward the communion of their beings in view of mutual personal perfection, to collaborate with God in the generation and education of new lives. . . .
>
> [Marital love] is first of all fully *human,* that is to say, of the senses and of the spirit at the same time. It is not, then, a simple transport of instinct and sentiment, but also, and principally, an act of the free will, intended to endure and to grow by means of the joys and sorrows of daily life, in such a way that husband and wife become one only heart and one only soul, and together attain their human perfection.
>
> Then this love is *total,* that is to say, it is a very special form of personal friendship, in which husband and wife generously share everything, without undue reservations or selfish calculations. Whoever truly loves his marriage partner loves not only for what he receives, but for the partner's self, rejoicing that he can enrich his partner with the gift of himself.
>
> Again, this love is *faithful* and *exclusive* until death. . . .

We have now no way of knowing if Paul intended that this descriptive definition of marital love define also what he called the unitive meaning of marriage. In this regard it is curious that the judges of the Roman Rota, the Church's highest appellate court in marriage matters, seldom quote from *Humanae vitae* when explaining the principles of the law whence they draw their decisions. This may be because they think Paul did not, in the passage quoted above, detail what he understood by the unitive meaning of marriage. Or it may be because they fear that he did do so.

The Consummation of Marriage

Under the contractual model the only conduct truly essential to a marriage is sexual intercourse. Completed after the consent, what the intercourse is said to accomplish even by its first episode alone is the consummation of the marriage. For to consummate a marriage, as long as one thinks of it as a contract, is to complete the contract—as the exchange of wedding vows is no more than the constituting of the contract as yet incompletely because it is only the promise to exchange the contractual good (which is the right to sexual intercourse).

But under the covenantal model—which presents marriage as a man's and a woman's giving and accepting of their selves into an intimate sharing

of marital life and love—the conduct essential to marriage is far more inclusive and varied. Since this is so, can any one kind of marital conduct be
the completion of the covenant? Can any one episode of any one kind of
conduct be its completion? Indeed does the concept of completing the marital covenant at some one point within the history of the marriage have any
real referent at all?[15]

Or to come at the same questions obliquely, how does the specifically
marital conduct which follows the first creating of the covenant in the
wedding vows relate to that first creating? The judges in the Dutch marriage courts mentioned earlier said that the subsequent conduct is a prolongation of the first creating of the covenant, that the creating of a
marriage is not a once-for-always event in an indivisible unit of time, but is
a continuing process. (It hardly need be said that Pope Paul disagreed with
them in his discourse of February 1976, since it was obvious that according to the judges' interpretation a marriage would simply cease to exist if
and when the process of self-giving and accepting should cease irrevers-
ibly.)

If, notwithstanding, the Church keeps the notions of consummated
and non-consummated marriages (and she has), if so much more essentially marital conduct than a single complete act of intercourse is now needed
to consummate the covenant, and if the Church holds to the rule that a
non-consummated marriage can be dissolved by papal authority, does it
not follow that an unidentifiably greater number of marriages may be di-
vorcible than is commonly acknowledged, or even suspected?

On the other hand what is the quality of justice in Catholic judicial
proceedings ruling on marriage when marriages are called covenants but
their consummation is defined as the completing of a contract, and the territory of dissolution is therefore restricted to non-consummated contracts?

Finally, once marriage is understood according to the biblical covenantal model, does not completion, or consummation, consist of keeping the
covenant and bringing it to its fullness? But since the completion in question is that of a person-to-person relationship, how is one to judge when
such a relationship is complete? Doesn't completion vary enough from
couple to couple and their unique needs and capacities—and isn't happiness in marriage (surely an ingredient and measure of its completeness)
different enough from culture to culture—to make futile any attempt to
define consummation univocally? Some Catholic bishops of Africa
brought an example of this difference to the papal subcommission revising
the marriage law. Among their people a marriage is traditionally not
deemed complete until the wife has borne her first child. In an agricultural
society in which the continuation and continuity of the extended family is
essential for survival, fertility in the wives is indispensable. In this society
marriage is traditionally understood as primarily a children provider. By
what justification could a different culture's definition of consummated
marriage be forced on the African farming people?

Marriage the Matrix of the Sacrament

Here at the end of this introductory chapter I wish to return to the consideration of the sacramentality of Christian marriages.

Every one of the Christian sacraments (Catholic doctrine says there are seven) has among its essential elements one that can accurately be called its matrix. This is the human ritual, the visible-tangible-audible action, the drama in miniature, which is the sacramental rite. In the Eucharist this is the consecrating, the sharing and the consuming of the one bread and the one cup. Bathing, or at least washing, with water is the matrix of baptism. In confirmation it is the laying on of hands and the anointing with oil.

In every instance the human matrix is made for the participants an effort at saving, a coming to them of Jesus' rescuing death and resurrection, by the action of God's Spirit in and through this matrix. He uses it as his instrument of saving and sanctifying. It becomes a successful effort, an effective saving and sanctifying, when the Spirit's action is met by the faith of the participants.

To understand how the effective signing action of the sacrament takes place, one must first understand that these two essential components of the sacrament condition one another, each in its own way. The action of the Spirit is conditioned by the specific dramatic content of the matrix of the sacrament in question. Thus baptism is a cleansing rather than a nourishing because it is a washing rather than an eating or drinking. The converse is true in the Eucharist. But it is the one Spirit who acts in and through the different dramatic actions in each.

In every sacrament too the matrix is conditioned reciprocally by the action of the Spirit. Baptism is more than a mere physical washing (and in its earliest form, which was immersion, it was more than merely a bath) because the bathing and now the washing are enlivened and used by the Spirit to give them a different meaning and therefore to produce a different effect.

Marriage was not finally and universally accepted by the Roman Catholic Church as a saving sacrament in the Christian community—as not only a sacred sign but a personally sanctifying sacred sign—until the twelfth century. It is significant in the history of the theological interpretation of marriage that just at that time the dominant interpretation of the matrix of the sacrament of marriage—the natural relationship—was that it is a contract. This set the conditions for a contest I have already pointed out in that arena of the Church where law and theology occasionally meet. Was the contract to be interpreted in terms of the sacrament? Or on the contrary was the sacrament to be interpreted in terms of the contract?

It was no contest, really. A moral anxiety among canonists and theologians, among the officers of the *magisterium,* overbalanced everything in favor of the contract. The sacramentality of Christian marriages was never allowed its full value. For while in the middle of the twelfth century hardly anyone doubted that the marriage of two Christians is a sacred sign, most doubted that it could be a sacred sign through which sanctifying grace, substantial holiness, could be brought to the spouses. The reason for this doubt was a commonly shared one. Everyone knew what goes on in marriage: erotic love, bodily passion running out of control, sin-infected flesh satisfying itself sexually. There is grace given in the sacrament, so the explanation went, but it is not sanctifying; it is medicinal. It is a divine help for keeping passion not only inside one's marriage, but even within it confined to the one innocent and therefore permissible motive for having intercourse, which is to conceive a child. It is grace fitted perfectly to enable spouses to deliver the good of their contract, and to keep their passion within the terms of the contract.

What is more, with the contract ruling speculation about the sacrament, it could keep attention centered on that element within the latter that Augustine had called the *sacramentum,* the seal of faithful commitment. This in turn could ennoble the contract and strengthen its binding force. No one thought it a real contract, in the sense of a commitment to exchange consumable property. Most understood it as the consensual personal contract familiar in Roman law, but now illumined by the ancient model that is the biblical covenant of God and his people. The banal way to name the contract was to say that it is a service. But it is a service motivated by high values: to conceive, bear and nurture children for the family, for the nation, for the Church, ultimately for God; to help one's spouse avoid sins of sexual passion. The contract has also among its goods that it offers the most favorable setting for the best of all human loves, agape, the love substantial to friendship, the disinterested concern for the loved one's happiness.

But here again the changed conception of marriage coming from the Second Vatican Council forces questions. What must happen to the interpretation of the sacrament now that its human matrix is said no longer to be a contract but a covenant—a mutual giving over and accepting of the selves, an intimate sharing, a union of persons (as *Humanae vitae* says) meant to lead to personal fulfillment, and all these meant in turn to climax in parenthood? For one thing, a psychology of erotic love is now both welcome and necessary for searching out the meaning of the sacrament. And this brings a unique difficulty to the understanding of a marriage as a saving and sanctifying sacrament. The twelfth-century canonists and theologians reluctant to concede that a sexual relationship could be the subject of Christian holiness were not being Manichean or merely fastidious. There is a difficult paradox here, one that comes near to being a contradiction. Christ's love, one of the loves meant to be mirrored in a marriage that is a sacrament, is not self-seeking, but self-giving. It does not long for its fulfillment as a thing of this life; it gives up that fulfillment for the space of this life, consciously and freely. It did not take possession of the beloved—of the missing other half of oneself, according to Plato's myth of the androgyne—in order to finally fill up personal emptiness. It "emptied itself" for the sake of the beloved's happiness. And it did this not for the sake of one chosen beloved, but, in a way that ordinarily thins and disperses passion, for the happiness of many, including those who would never return or even acknowledge this love. How could erotic passion, a passion seeking its own life and fulfillment, and doing it preferably in the most pleasurable experience available to men and women, mirror Christ's love that expressed itself and came to climax as a victim of the capital punishment reserved by the Romans for barbarians and slaves?

In another quarter, how are Catholics now to understand the indissolubility said to be caused by a marriage's being a sacrament if the matrix of the sacrament is no longer understood to be a non-voidable contract but a community, a sharing that human experience shows can come to an end, and if the community and sharing are said to be caused by a marital love that as both attitude and action can die? But if the matrix of the sacrament can die, how can the sacrament survive? And since in Catholic tradition it is the sacrament that is finally the cause of the marriage's indissolubility—not the covenant and not even the contract to which Paul VI returned when faced with this question—if the sacrament dies what else can cause this indissolubility?

Margaret's and Ian's relationship never got to the point of being able to concern itself with these questions. But if it had lasted and had matured into a marriage, they might have found them waiting to be asked and answered. This diagnosis of their invalid attempt at marrying, and the questions the diagnosis has bred, are not much more than a beginning glance at the situation of marriage in the Catholic Church in the last decades of this century. A patient inspection of it would show that marriage in the Church has arrived at this situation only after a continuous journey lasting almost nineteen centuries. Trying for an accurate understanding of the situation calls for tracing this history in at least its more significant features.

NOTES

1. The real-life case on which I have modeled this fiction was adjudicated in the tribunal of Paterson, N.J., on March 19, 1975. It is reported in the Canadian canon law review, *Studia Canonica,* Vol. 9:1 (1975) pp. 178–184. An essay helpful in understanding the ground for nullity in this case is "Essential Incompatibility as Grounds for Nullity of Marriage," in *The Catholic Lawyer,* Vol. 16 (1970) pp. 173–187. Its authors are Marion Justin Reinhardt, Presiding Judge of the Brooklyn tribunal, and Gerard J. Arella, Defender of the Bond in that court.

2. From the 1975 decision by the Paterson tribunal I quote here the clauses of its report that seem to me to touch the heart of an attempt at marriage nullified by the incompatibility of the parties. "The Plaintiff . . . is alleging what appears to be essential incompatibility on the grounds that neither party to the marriage was able, or at least willing, to fulfill the intimate personal needs of the other to such an extent that it rendered the establishment of a *consortium vitae conjugalis* impossi-

ble. . . . What is absolutely crucial here is that the needs of both parties have not been and cannot be fulfilled. These fundamental needs are inherent to the personality of each individual, and when consent in marriage is given, it is because each party to the consent believes that the other is willing and able to supply his or her psychological and emotional needs. . . . We have chosen to judge this case of A.B. and C.D. under the heading "essential incompatibility." We believe that this heading most properly fits their marital situation and most adequately describes the reason for the inevitable rupture of their marriage. . . . The couple is said to be essentially incompatible when their personalities clash, relative to one another, to such an extent that they are unable to carry through the covenantal consent articulated in the wedding ceremony. . . . The question is not whether the parties are able to assume the obligations and responsibilities with respect to *any* partner, but rather that this particular couple could not, or did not, complement one another in their mutual married state. . . ." (*op. cit.*, pp. 180–181)

3. This phrase from *Gaudium et spes* is the first in its paragraph 48. The entire document in its authorized edition is in *Sacrosanctum Oecumenicum Concilium Vaticanum II, Constitutiones, Decreta, Declarationes*. Cura et Studio Secretariae Generalis Concilii Oecumenici Vaticani II, Romae, 1966. The best-known English translation of *Gaudium et spes* is in *The Documents of Vatican II*, Walter M. Abbott, S.J., General Editor, N.Y., 1966, pp. 183–308. The chapter on marriage, "Fostering the Nobility of Marriage and the Family," which is Chapter 1 of Part II, "Some Problems of Special Urgency," is in pp. 249–258 of this edition.

4. The English-language analysis of the Catholic law on marriage that is both most manageable and accessible is in T. Lincoln Bouscaren and Adam C. Ellis, *Canon Law: A Text and Commentary*, Third Revised Edition, Milwaukee, 1957; Part Five: Marriage, pp. 445–630.

5. There is a sense in which a marriage's primary end is also one of its essential properties. For if procreation and nurture were not marriage's primary end, it would be some other kind of relationship—sexually realized, perhaps, but not marriage in exactly the same sense as that intended by the canon. And since there is no known way in which two men or two women can together conceive a child, this definition voids even the possibility of a homosexual marriage.

6. For example, as early as St. Augustine's time custom had set a two-month grace period after the wedding vows during which the bride could in justice refuse the debt to her new husband, and he in turn could not demand it with justice warranting his demand. The reasons legitimizing the custom were three: to allow the bride, and the groom too if he wished, time to decide against the still unconsummated marriage in favor of entrance into monastic life and the dissolving of the marriage by monastic vows; to allow time to prepare the festive celebration of a marriage as yet no more than contracted by the consent exchanged through procurators; and to impress on the new husband, by delaying his gratification, that in gaining the right to sexual intercourse he had made no easy gain of a trivial thing.

By the sixteenth century the period of grace had been shortened at least in Spain to two weeks. Toward the end of that century the Spanish Jesuit moralist, Tomás Sanchez, posed the question whether a new husband sins in claiming the exercise of his right with violence if his bride continues to deny it to him beyond the two weeks. He replied that after the grace period the husband claiming the exercise of his right with violence sins at least not against the virtue of justice, since he only claims a right his bride has already granted him. But whether he sins against the virtue of charity depends on the kind and degree of violence he uses. (In

De Sancto Matrimonii Sacramento Disputationum, Tomus Primus. Posterior et Accuratior Editio, Venetiis, 1726. Liber Secundus, *De Essentia et Consensu Matrimonii,* Disputatio XXII, Quaestio 4a).

7. This was an appellate decision handed down by the Roman Rota on June 21 of that year, and written by the Rotal judge Sabattani. The decision is examined and explained by John R. Keating in his volume. *The Bearing of Mental Impairment on the Validity of Marriage: An Analysis of Rotal Jurisprudence,* Rome, 1973, pp. 158–161.

8. Where Augustine says this in Chapter 24 of his *De Bono Coniugali* he does not say that the perdurance of the *sacramentum* makes divorce, and remarriage following it, both impossible. Although he says that the marriage bond, apparently because of the *sacramentum,* is not ended except by the death of the spouse, what he says follows from this perdurance is that ". . . because of this sanctity *it is wrong* for a woman, leaving with a divorce, to marry another man while her husband lives. . . ."

He wrote that in 401. Seventeen years later, when writing the first book of his *De Nuptiis et Concupiscentia,* Augustine offered a different reason in explaining why it is that even though one spouse commits adultery, the other may not divorce him or her and remarry: "So much do the vows once pronounced perdure among spouses still living that those who have separated remain spouses to one another rather than to the [new] partner to whom they have cleaved. For with the latter they would not be adulterers unless they remained spouses to the former. . . . Thus there remains, as long as they live, a certain marital something [*quiddam coniugale*] that neither separation nor intercourse can remove" (Cap. 10).

9. This theme of the conditioned covenant runs especially through the Book of Deuteronomy. The choice set before Israel and the contradictory consequences of choosing either fidelity or infidelity are especially explicit in these passages: "Thus, then, shall it be: if you continue to heed the voice of the Lord, your God, and are careful to observe all his commandments which I enjoin on you today, the Lord, your God, will raise you high above all the nations of the earth. . . . But if you do not hearken to the voice of the Lord, your God, and are not careful to observe all his commandments which I enjoin on you today, all these curses shall come upon you and overwhelm you. . . . The Lord will put a curse on you, defeat and frustration in every enterprise you undertake, until you are speedily destroyed and perish for the evil you have done in forsaking me" (Chapter 28, verses 1–2 and 15–20). "Here, then, I have today set before you life and prosperity, death and doom. If you obey the commandments of the Lord, your God . . . you will live and grow numerous, and the Lord, your God, will bless you in the land you are entering to occupy. If, however, you turn away your hearts and will not listen, but are led astray . . . I tell you now that you will certainly perish" (Chapter 30, verses 15–18). The condition was stated most clearly and succinctly in the Book of Exodus: "Therefore, if you hearken to my voice and keep my covenant, you shall be my special possession, dearer to me than all other people, though all the earth is mine" (Chapter 19, verse 5).

10. The Latin text reads "Indole autem sua naturali, ipsum institutum matrimonii amorque coniugalis ad procreationem et educationem prolis ordinantur iisque veluti suo fastigio coronantur" (*Sacrosanctum Oecumenicum Concilium Vaticanum II, Constitutiones, Decreta, Declarationes,* p. 755).

11. It is not true, as some theologians have maintained, that Augustine said of *fides* (fidelity), *proles* (offspring) and *sacramentum* (permanence) only that they are

goods of marriage, and that later canonists turned *proles* into its primary end. If
one accepts that in the following statement *causa* signifies "end," Augustine made
the point clearly enough, when cautioning against the practice in his day of prolonged sexual abstinence within marriage, that procreation is *also* the primary end
of marriage: "For the propagation of children is the first and natural and legitimate
end [*causa*] of marriage. Hence those who marry because of their inability to contain themselves ought not so temper this evil that they exterminate the good of
marriage ... which is the procreation of children" (*De Adulterinis Coniugiis,*
Liber II, Cap. 12)

12. This note 168 reads as follows: "The Commission charged with drafting
this text made every effort to avoid any appearance of wishing to settle questions
concerning a hierarchy of the 'ends' of marriage. Thus, the passage includes a
beautiful reference to children as 'the supreme gift of marriage,' but this sentence
makes it clear that the present text cannot be read as a judgment on the relative
importance or primacy of ends" (*The Documents of Vatican II,* p. 254). An earlier
and kindred footnote, no. 155, is the following: "Here, as elsewhere when the question arises, the Council sedulously avoids the terminology of primary and secondary ends of marriage. It insists on the natural ordering of marriage and conjugal
love to procreation but without recourse to such formulations. The same teaching
is repeated in Art. 50, and the Council's care to avoid distinguishing 'primary' and
'secondary' is again evident" (p. 250).

13. *Sacrosanctum Oecumenicum Concilium,* etc., p. 760. This is my own
translation of the passage.

14. This implicit defining, indeed redefining, of marriage is in paragraphs 12
and 13 of the encyclical. The authorized text is in *Acta Apostolicae Sedis,* Vol. 50
(1968) no. 9, pp. 481–503.

15. The sensitivity of the Church's teachers for the need of changed thinking
on the subject of consummation has been made evident in more than one place.
The following instance is surely not typical of the earlier and traditional jurisprudence on consummation, but the official ruling in the case was both logically possible and logically consistent given the accepted understanding of marriage as a
contract and of consummation as the completing of the contract. On August 2,
1958 the Sacred Congregation for the Sacraments handed down a decision answering the question whether a marriage is consummated if, in order to have intercourse at all, the wife must so drug herself that she becomes semi-conscious and at
times even unconscious. The congregation's reply was affirmative.

A more generic question was asked of the latter congregation at the same
time: whether in order to consummate the marriage both partners need have the
capacity, both before and during the intercourse, to place a truly human act. This
was to ask if both must be aware of their conduct and carry it on by free consent.
The congregation's reply contained a distinction. In order that the intercourse be
an exercise of the virtue of justice whereby each party discharges a debt owed in
justice, both must be able to place a human act—intercourse had knowingly and by
choice. But in order to consummate the contract, to place the act which of its nature is apt for realizing the marriage's primary end, neither awareness nor consent
is needed. (Where both parties are Christian this unconscious penetration and semination were presumably thought also to consummate the sacrament.)

The sensitivity for the need of changed thinking about consummation that I
mentioned at the beginning of this note has shown up most clearly in the following
way. Since 1966 a papal commission has been at work revising all of the Catholic

Code of Canon Law, with a special subcommission at work on the marriage sector of the law. Canon 1015 in the Code being supplanted by the revision defines the act that consummates a marriage. Canon 1015 said that a marriage is consummated if that act takes place between the spouses to which the marital contract is oriented by its nature. The new canon (245.1) says of consummation that it is accomplished if the spouses place that act *in a human way (humano modo)* which is apt of itself for procreation and to which marriage is of its nature oriented. The subcommission's own explanation for adding the modifier is that it is found in a paragraph in *Gaudium et spes* describing conjugal love: "This love is uniquely expressed and perfected through the marital act. The actions within marriage by which the couple are united intimately and chastely are noble and worthy ones. Expressed in a manner truly human *(modo vere humano)* these acts signify and promote that mutual self-giving by which the spouses enrich each other with a joyful and thankful will." This explanation is given in the official journal reporting the work of the papal commission revising the Code, *Communicationes,* Vol. 5 (1973) 79.

2. THE PRIMITIVE CHRISTIAN UNDERSTANDING OF MARRIAGE

Since it is accurate enough to date the establishing of the community of Jesus' followers as a church within the decade 27–37 A.D., we may put the end of the second Christian generation at the turn of the first century. By that time two major traditions, the Jewish and the Hellenistic-Roman, had formed the character of early Christian life in community. By the end of these sixty years the confluence of these two traditions in Christianity was complete. Each had had time to make its contribution to Christian life in full strength. Each had conditioned the other. And even though the first communities of Jesus' followers in Palestine had been destroyed, or at least dispersed, during the devastation of Judea and the siege of Jerusalem by the Roman army under Vespasian and then Titus in 68–70, the Jewish influence continued past that date because the first Christian communities outside Palestine had been formed mainly from the synagogue communities scattered around the eastern half of the empire. Consequently, though the Hellenistic-Roman character eventually overwhelmed at least Jewish custom as the Jewish portion of the Christian population dwindled, the Jewish vision of marriage left its effect in the early Christian consciousness. It is this vision that we must seek to understand first.

Palestinian Jewish Marriage Custom

Among Jesus' people marriage was regarded as obligatory. The male who had reached eighteen years but had not yet married could be compelled by a court to do so. While girls, as also boys, could not be married before puberty, the former were ordinarily married as soon as they reached it, which was set at twelve years and six months. Thirteen was the earliest age at which a boy might marry. These early ages for marrying hint clearly at the meaning of Jewish marriage in Palestine at that time. It was for family decisively and in multiple ways. The principal motive for marrying was to provide children so as to preserve the husband's family, to keep his and

38

his father's name from dying out, to keep the tribe, the nation itself as the people of God in existence—withal to honor the ancient covenant commitment with Yahweh to be a light to the nations. Since infant mortality was high and life-expectancy low even for those who survived until adulthood, it was important that the childbearer marry at the onset of puberty so as to bear as many children as possible.

Hesitant belief in personal survival beyond death reinforced this tradition. If a man had no heirs, even if he had daughters but no sons, he risked having his name die out; the memory of him might vanish and be lost to his people forever and in every way. Hence marriage was before all else what Christian tradition would later call an *officium,* a dutiful vocation, a vocation motivated by *pietas,* loyal loving concern for one's parents and one's people. The Jewish people itself had already been given and had accepted the *officium* mentioned earlier, to be a light to the nations. Obviously it could be faithful to this vocation only if its sons and daughters bore and nurtured children.

The Jewish people of Jesus' time were not a defining people in the Western sense of assigning an entity to generic and specific categories of existence. But if one were to ask in terms of these categories about the essence of marriage among this people, no more exact answer could be given than that it was an abiding relationship between a man and a woman intended mainly although not exclusively for children.

Although the negotiations between the two families to settle the dowry and the *mohar* (the bride-price given by the husband-to-be to the girl's father) were contractual in form, the marriage itself was not thought of as a contract.[1] For one thing an element essential to a contract was missing. The mutual consent by the contracting parties themselves to the exchange of a contractual good was deemed functionally unnecessary. Jewish fathers in consultation with their wives negotiated their children's marriages; the wills of the fathers held good for those of their children. The latters' marital consent was more an obedient acceptance of the partners chosen for them, although loving parents took their children's desires into consideration, especially if the desire were against the tentatively chosen partner. Thus the marriage was a covenant between two families. It was made orally by the parents, but by Jesus' time the covenant was confirmed legally in writing.

The preferred source wherein to search for spouses for one's children was one's own relatives, within those forms and degrees of kindred permitted marriage by Torah and the traditions of the fathers. Marriage between uncle and niece was not uncommon; the girl's father found a husband for her among his own brothers. Marriage of cousins was common. This marrying within the family gained two understandable advantages. One could be less uncertain about the quality of a spouse in the uncertain human enterprise of marrying. And there was less likelihood of divorce if a dissatisfied husband had to answer to his brother for dismissing the latter's daughter from his house. And if she did fall victim to divorce, there was considerable comfort for her in having to fall back only to a family she had never really left.

When the girl married she became a member of her husband's family. Since he owed obedience to his father as long as the latter lived, so too did his wife. She became in effect her father-in-law's newest daughter. Often enough the newly married pair, especially if they were quite young, lived in the paternal household. When they did, the young wife took her place as an added daughter in the household managed by her mother-in-law under her father-in-law's authority.

The Religious Reality of Jewish Marriage

Was this marriage a religious reality or was it secular? The question would have been meaningless for a Jew of Jesus' time, for he simply recognized no division in life between these two realms. All of life for him was religious because all the world came from the hand of God. Getting married was one form of faithful response to God's covenant invitation to his people Israel. Marriage in turn was God's gift to men and women as part of his creation. According to the creation poem of Genesis his work of creating came to its climax in the sexually differentiated pair who were given the *officium* of using their sexuality in order to populate the earth and rule it. According to the Genesis parable of the garden the sexually different and therefore desirable creature, the woman, was given to the man as God's gift to him to relieve his loneliness. He made them two and sexually different expressly so that they could become one—even "one flesh," one person before God and the people. The sexual uniting was holy because it was God's creation and given as his gift. Yet it was of this world and worldly, not sacred in the sense of the ancient fertility cults' sexuality interpreted as participation in genital activity of the gods. It was not sacred precisely because it was created and therefore creaturely in substance. It was created by a supra-sexual deity, therefore by one who could not be imitated sexually and in this way bribed by sexually magic ritual.

Because in the parable of the garden God "brought the woman to him" (the man) as a gift to relieve his loneliness, marriage at least in this ancient tradition could only with difficulty be construed as a contract. An added difficulty against this was the fact that the most excellent religious model for the husband-wife relationship proposed by the prophetic tradition could hardly be contractual. This was the husband-bride relationship of God to Israel pictured by the prophets Hosea (1:1—3:35), Jeremiah (2:1–2) and Ezekiel (16). Common acceptance of this religious metaphor as a normative model, where it was done, overweighted the husband's authority in the marriage severely. The model presumed the wife's infidelity and need to be disciplined; it gave the husband a divine warrant to discipline her. But for this reason alone the model blocked the possibility of seeing Jewish marriages as contracts. As the bride Israel could not negotiate with God, could not in justice hold him to contractual conditions, neither could the Jewish wife with her husband. She could expect and demand that he care for her, protect her, forgive her, but none of these as obligations in justice. As God had promised these to Israel only out of love and in sovereign freedom, so, according to this model, the wife could expect these from her husband only as a gift of his love freely given.

I have said that the marriage itself was not understood as a contract, and that where this prophetic model was in the forefront of awareness, any temptation to understand a marriage contractually was suppressed. But given the contractual nature of the marriage arrangements, especially as these were detailed in the *ketuba,* the inclination to think of the relationship as contractual must have been strong. But since the pre-marital agreement had been struck not between the spouses but between the families, the inclination was to think of these as the contractors.

The solemnization of the Jewish marriage was, in the senses I have explained above, both religious and non-sacral. The *kiddushin,* the year-long trial period (literally "the sanctification"), was sealed and begun with the handing over of the *mohar* to the bride's father. The boy and girl were dedicated to one another and held to sexual fidelity. The bride's intercourse with a third person during that year, but only hers, was considered adultery. In northern Israel the two were forbidden intercourse with one another until after the wedding feast. In the south, in Judea, betrothal and marriage were in effect the same in permitting intercourse.

The wedding feast lasted a week. All of it was deemed religious, as I have said, but the core of the "liturgical" part of the celebration was a series of seven benedictions read by the father of the groom. No part of the feast took place in either temple or synagogue. No priest, levite or rabbi had a part in it as an exercise of his office. It was a family affair, supervised and conducted by parents. It was private in that sense but thoroughly public in the sense that the entire village might join in the celebration. Since the groom's father presided over the celebration, it ordinarily took place in his home. The bride's father gave her away, and the groom's father took her for his son. The ceremony ended and climaxed with the groom's leading his bride in procession to his home. If he was quite young, this would be his parents' home.

The Theory of Marriage in Palestinian Judaism

To search for a theory of marriage in the society of Jesus' people is to risk forcing the analytic habits of the Western mind on a people who were not concerned with defining. We may in fact find the ingredients of a theory. But they are scattered in forms of discourse none of which was intended to be a formal definition. These are religious parables, wisdom sayings, legal prescriptions, folk-legends, prophetic declarations and interpretations. But they do not say abstractly what a marriage is, marriage conceived of in the detached way peculiar to the Greek mind and its heirs. They say how the first marriage was created and why it was, how the Lord

wants men and women to relate to one another, what is the deeper meaning of a husband's and wife's fidelity and infidelity to one another, and so
forth.

We may presume safely that Jesus and his hearers knew intimately
the passages from the Jewish Scriptures I shall review here briefly—knew
them with an intimacy and a connaturality we must despair of attaining.
Whether they would agree that the meaning modern inquirers find in them
is really there, we can only conjecture. In trying to ferret out the meanings
of these passages, I shall stay with those that are accessible and unforced. I
shall try especially not to read later Christian interpretations back into
them.

But I shall in a few places try to find meaning that demands inspect-
ing passages in first one focus then another. This chapter's interest bears
upon the Jewish understanding of marriage in Jesus' time. But at certain
points the understanding is itself an interpretation in his time of passages
in Jewish Scripture dating from centuries earlier. One example of this
comes quickly to mind.

The Book of Deuteronomy, chapter 24:1, contains a prescription
against a husband's remarrying a woman he had once divorced. In English
translation it reads, "When a man, after marrying a woman and having
relations with her, is later displeased with her because he finds in her
something indecent, and therefore he gives her a writ of dismissal and
hands it to her, thus dismissing her from his house. . . ." The author or authors of this passage taught and wrote in the seventh century before
Christ. They presumed that it was both possible and permissible for a Jewish husband to dissolve his marriage by dismissing his wife. They presumed too that the cause—and perhaps one among multiple causes—·
justifying this dismissal was named in this verse, with the substance of the
cause or causes encapsuled in its terms "something indecent in her" (*erwath dabar* in the Hebrew of Deuteronomy).

In Jesus' time the rabbis, the people's teachers, debated the meaning
of the verse. Those who were heirs and disciples of the Rabbi Shammai of
a generation earlier followed their master in saying that it named but one
cause, the "something indecent," that this term specified what it may be in
a wife that so evokes displeasure in her husband as to justify his dismissing
her, and that this indecency is her adultery or some conduct equivalently
delinquent.

The disciple-heirs of Rabbi Hillel, a contemporary of Shammai, argued that there is a disjunction in the second clause of the verse, and that
therefore it names distinct causes for a husband's dismissing his wife. One
is the "uncleanness" designated by *erwath dabar*. The other is whatever
causes the husband's displeasure, including the uncleanness.

In the twentieth century we can try (probably futilely) to determine
what the Deuteronomic teachers had in mind when writing this clause.
But, and this is a second focus for inquiry, we can try to determine exactly

the references Jesus' people found in it, and then, from the distance of nineteen centuries, go on to yet a third focus and, by studying Jesus' argument with a group of Pharisee rabbis reported in Mark 10 and Matthew 19, try to understand how he himself interpreted Deuteronomy 24:1, what he thought of the debate in his own day, and whether he thought a marriage to be the kind of relationship that allows a husband to end it, and end it by dismissing his wife. (And by trying to answer this last question we can join the unending Christian debate turning on whether Matthew's version of Jesus' argument with the Pharisees records accurately his allowing one ground for a husband's doing this.)

Obviously the second and the third of these foci hold the principal interest for us. For this is an examination of the history of the Christian understanding of marriage; and this understanding began with Jesus and those of his people who became his followers, whom he formed into a community, and who have passed down to us his understanding within the setting of their own interpretation of it.

The Genesis Accounts of the First Couple

In Jesus' argument with the Pharisees mentioned above, the latter appeal to Torah against him, specifically to Moses as the giver of the law. They reach back to Deuteronomy 24:1, but not, as in the Hillel-Shammai debate, to argue whether one or multiple causes of dismissal are legislated in the passage. They cite it to prove against Jesus that their long-accepted practice of dismissing wives, which they saw him challenging, was introduced by Moses himself.

Jesus too appeals to Torah. However, he goes not to Moses and Deuteronomy, but "to the beginning," to the accounts of the first couple in Genesis 1 and in Genesis 2. He ignores what modern scholarship has rediscovered, that these are separate and even discordant accounts—the Garden parable in Genesis 2 dating from the Yahwist scholars of the ninth century, the creation poem in Genesis 1 from the priestly scholars of the Babylonian captivity in the fifth century. He ignores too the fact that neither is a factual record of the first generation of the human race, but the one an etiological parable accounting for the origin of sin and suffering in the human race, the other a poem professing in faith the Lord's relationship to the universe as its designer and creator. He treats them as his people apparently understood them, religious statements of how it was in the beginning of the race, and especially of how the Lord willed things to be in the beginning—especially of how he willed that husbands treat their wives.

The facet of marriage's meaning in these passages that Jesus saw to be crucial, and contextually crucial for his argument with the Pharisees, is evident in those verses that he quoted from the passages against them. Into a single assertion about the husband-wife relationship he conflated Genesis 1:27b, "male and female he created them" (Mark 10:7; Matthew 19:4), and

Genesis 2:24, "That is why a man leaves his father and mother and clings to his wife, and the two of them become one body" (Mark 10:8; Matthew 19:5).

I say Jesus' quoting these words from Torah was crucial in context because he prefaces his quotation with "But from the beginning of creation . . ." (Mark 10:7a). He makes clear to the Pharisees that their interpretation of the husband-wife relationship, which allowed the husband to unilaterally dismiss his wife, is not the relationship that the Lord intended and still intends. This implies that their interpretation is an innovation, and an innovation that contravenes the Lord's intention. Moses allowed the dismissal (according to Matthew's version) or commanded it (according to Mark's) for a reason that is not a compliment to the husbands of many centuries: because they have been hardhearted, stubborn against the will of the Lord revealed in the verses Jesus quotes.

Once Jesus took the argument back to the Genesis passages, his hearers may well have scanned in memory all that these verses had to say about this first man-woman relationship as the Lord had designed it. The motive for his bringing the woman into existence was made clear: "The Lord God said, 'It is not good for the man to be alone' " (2:18a). This hints at a need, even a weakness in the man. He had been put to live in a garden of delights, to keep it and rule over its denizens. But still his life was incomplete. Therefore the Lord God's decision: "I will make a suitable partner for him" (2:18b). (The "helpmate for him," found in so many English translations, conveys the meaning poorly, for the Hebrew noun means literally "someone alongside him," "someone suited to him." The being that the Lord God will provide for his loneliness will be the correlate to his need, not so much a helper as a partner.)

When, according to the parable, the forming of all the other animals had failed to produce the suitable partner, the Lord God "cast a deep sleep on the man, and while he was asleep he took out one of his ribs and closed up its place with flesh. The Lord God then built up into a woman the rib he had taken from the man" (2:21–22). So it is a being of his own kind who is given to him because it is not good for him to be alone, a being so close to him as to be formed of his own flesh and bone. But this being is also strikingly different from him, and the difference is sexual. His partner is a woman.

The man's welcome to her, his verdict on his partner, is rich in meaning: "This one at last is bone of my bones and flesh of my flesh." To understand these words as no more than the man's acknowledgment that the woman is of the same material stuff as himself, or even that she is derived from his own flesh and bone, is to catch the words' least meaning. "Flesh and bone" make up a word-pair appearing more than once in the Old Testament. "Flesh" by itself not only can mean one component of the body, but in a certain context it means bodily and even human frailty. It means "flesh-weakness." Bone can have the meaning of strength and power—"bone-strength." But when combined the two terms signify more than just the two realities in juxtaposition. Together they create a new meaning, and a meaning that goes beyond physical power and weakness. Flesh-weakness and bone-strength are antitheses in combination, and the antithesis includes not only the two extremes but all degrees between them. They include the full range of a person's character traits, from his weakest to his strongest.

Thus when the man says of the woman that she is "bone of my bones and flesh of my flesh," he means that she shares his strength and his weakness and all that lies between them. She is his partner in every contingency of his life. Theirs is a companionship that is not sundered by changing circumstances. It is one of constancy, of abiding loyalty.[2]

Just before the parable moves on to tell (in Chapter 3) of the man's and woman's tragic disobedience, the author pauses for his own comment (in 2:24), and it is this comment that Jesus quotes from the parable in his argument with the Pharisees. In the comment the author apparently tries to make even clearer the intimacy and the totality of this first sexual relationship. He does so by pointing out one of their first consequences: "That is why a man leaves his father and mother and clings to his wife, and the two become one."

The two verbs in the comment belong to the language of covenant. They say that a man "abandons" his father and mother (the Hebrew is *asav*). He does so to enter a new covenant, this one with his wife. He joins or clings to her (the verb is *davaq*, also a covenantal term).

This formulary reinforces a second layer of meaning in the "flesh-bone" word-pair I have examined just above. While thus paired they designate the full range of a person's life, from his thinnest frailty to his most effective power; but where in the Jewish Scriptures outside this Genesis parable two persons are said to be "flesh and bone" to one another, this tells of their forming a covenant, or strengthening it, or restoring it.[3]

If Jesus had this meaning in mind when quoting to the Pharisees this comment of the Yahwist author, he was pointing out to them what they had apparently forgotten. To be husband and wife a man and woman enter and live a covenant commitment to one another. And it is a most precious commitment, more precious than even a man's commitment to his father and his mother. Jesus included the last verse of the comment: ". . . and the two of them become one body." The reference here is not primarily to sexual union, although this is implied and included. "Body" here carries some of the meaning indicated above, a person's nature in its mortality and fallibility. By extension it designates beyond that a person's human identity. Therefore, in repeating this, the Yahwist's last comment on the man-woman union, Jesus points out that they become as one person. (Since this is so, he seems to imply, how could a husband dismiss his wife? He would have to dismiss his own person.)

And this intimate union is God's design, as Jesus had hinted in the first words he quoted from Genesis—from the creation poem: "God made them male and female" (1:27b). Since God it was who designed this union and brought it about, Jesus has the reason for his own verdict on the custom of husbands among his people dismissing their wives: "So then what God has joined, man must not separate."

Disobedience and Betrayal

That much was the ideal. That is marriage as God designed it and means it to be lived. And Jesus appealed to the divine will behind this design as to the compelling force behind his own demand that the husbands among his people no longer dismiss their wives. But was the design the reality with which the spouses among his people lived? And had not the Lord changed and qualified his original intent, so that in quoting Moses against Jesus the Pharisees were not going apart from the divine will but instead were only citing the great lawgiver's clarification of that will's change in regard to marriage?

For the parable makes clear that it was the woman who led the man into disobedience to the Lord. It was indispensable for the purpose of the parable that the man have sinned; that the woman have sinned was of only secondary consequence. It is an etiological parable. It intends to say how sin and misery got into the human race, into all of it down through its history. Unlike the myths of Israel's neighbors that for the most part blamed the caprice of the gods for human misery, the Jews insisted that human foolishness and disobedience had brought it. Sin is the source of our misery. But for a patrilineal society it was necessary that the sin's effect be explained as coming down from the father if it was to affect his children, his children's children, and all generations for the rest of history. Therefore the man had to have sinned.

But the tempter in the parable went not to the man; he went to the woman. It was her curiosity that he worked on, her hunger for independence, her Promothean desire to be "like the gods who know good and evil." No doubt he was confident that the surest way to bring down the man was to first bring down his woman. Once he had done that, the man would be easy. The woman would bring him down.

The strategy worked to perfection: "The woman saw that the tree was good for food, pleasing to the eyes, and desirable for gaining wisdom. So she took some of the fruit and ate it. And she also gave some to her husband who was with her, and he ate it" (3:6).

For nine centuries, from the first telling of this parable by the Yahwist teacher until Jesus' time, the reading of this part of Torah reminded Jewish husbands that it was the first wife who had perpetrated the most tragic disobedience imaginable, that she had exploited her husband's weakness, his need for her, to lure him into disobeying the Lord. Given to him by the Lord as his companion in covenant, she had betrayed him. And the consequences of the betrayal had been all the misery and evil in history, beginning with their oldest son's murdering his brother. In a spineless attempt to exonerate himself the man had explained to the angered Lord God how he had come to disobey him: "The woman whom you put here with me—she gave me the fruit from the tree, and so I ate it" (3:13). Apparently the Lord God agreed that this weakness for his wife was exactly the reason for the man's disobedience, for he said later in telling him his punishment: "Because you listened to your wife and ate from the tree of which I had forbidden you to eat, cursed be the ground because of you . . ." (3:17).

And his punishment for the woman was fitted perfectly. First, "I will intensify the pain of your childbearing" (3:16a). And then because she had lured her husband into sinning by exercising her mastery over his need for her, she will be punished in turn in her sexual need for him: "Yet your urge shall be for your husband" (3:16b). And finally the most condign punishment of all for her: "And he shall be your master" (3:16b).

It was not difficult for every Jewish husband down to the time of Jesus to hear in this sentencing of the first wife the warrant to carry it out on his own wife. In a society that believed almost doctrinally in guilt by genetic association it was forever tempting for husbands to see whatever in their wives' conduct that displeased them both the repetition of the first wife's disobedience and the guilt for it that still deserved punishing. As for the first marriage's being a covenant, if anything still remained of it after the betrayal of its covenantal trust, at best it was a covenant of unequals, a covenant of suzerainty, with the husband as gracious lord covenanting with his vassal-child wife to support and protect her, while she covenanted to obey and to serve him in return for the protection.

Roland DeVaux tells of some of the lived-out consequences of this lordship of husbands among Jesus' people:

> It has already been said that the wife called her husband "ba'al," or "master"; she also addressed him as "adon" or lord; . . . she addressed him in fact as a slave addressed a master, or a subject his king. The Decalogue includes a man's wife among his possessions, along with his house, his land, his male and female slaves, his ox and his ass. . . . Her husband can repudiate her, but she cannot claim a divorce; all her life she remains a minor. The wife does not inherit from her husband nor daughters from their father, except where there is no male heir. . . .[4]

Joachim Jeremias supplies more detail when describing the condition of women and wives in Jesus' time:

> The wife's first *duties* were household duties. She had to grind meal, bake, wash, cook, suckle the children, prepare her husband's bed and, as repayment for her keep . . . to work the wool by spinning and weaving. . . . Other duties were that of preparing her husband's cup, and of washing his face, hands and feet. . . . These duties express her servile relationship with her husband; but his rights over her went even further. He laid claim to any-

thing his wife found . . . as well as any earnings from her manual work, and he had the right . . . to annul her vows. . . . The wife was obliged to obey her husband as she would a master—the husband was called *rab*—indeed this obedience was a religious duty. . . . This duty of obedience went so far that the husband could force a vow upon his wife, but any vows which put the wife in a discreditable position gave her the right to demand divorce before the court. . . . Relationships between children and parents were also determined by the woman's duty of obedience to her husband; the children had to put respect for their father before respect for their mother, for she was obliged to give a similar respect to the father of her children. . . .

Two facts are particularly significant of the degree of the wife's dependence on her husband:

(a) Polygamy was permissible; the wife had therefore to tolerate concubines living with her. Of course, we must add that for economic reasons the possession of several wives was not very frequent. Mostly we hear of a husband taking a second wife if there was dissension with the first, but because of the high price fixed in the marriage contract, he could not afford to divorce her. . . .

(b) The right to divorce was exclusively the husband's. . . . In Jesus' time (Matt. 19:3) the Shammaites and Hillelites were in dispute over the exegesis of Deut. 24:1, which gives, as a reason for a man divorcing his wife, a case where he finds in her "some unseemly thing," *'erwat dabar*. The Shammaites' exegesis was in accord with the meaning of the phrase, but the Hillelites explained it as, first, the wife's unchastity (*'erwat*) and, secondly, something (*dabar*) displeasing to the husband; either gave him the right to put away his wife. . . . In this way the Hillelite view made the unilateral right of divorce entirely dependent on the husband's caprice. From Philo (*De spec. leg.* III, 30) and from Josephus (*Ant.* 4.253), both of whom knew only the Hillelite point of view and championed it, it appears that this must already have been the prevailing view in the first half of the first century A.D. However, reunion of the separated parties could take place; also by reason of divorce there was a public stigma on the husband as well as on the wife and daughters . . . ; then too when he divorced his wife, the husband had to give her the sum of money prescribed in the marriage contract; so in practice these last two facts must often have been obstacles to any hasty divorce of his wife. As for his wife, she could occasionally take things into her own hands and go back to her father's house, e.g., in the case of injury received. . . . But in spite of all this, the Hillelite view represented a considerable degradation of women.

... to have children, particularly sons, was extremely important for a woman. The absence of children was considered a great misfortune, even a divine punishment. ... As the mother of a son the wife was respected; she had given her husband the most precious gift of all.

As a widow too a woman was still bound to her husband, that is, if he died without leaving a son. ... In this case she had to wait, unable to make any move on her side, until the brother or brothers of her dead husband should contract a levirate marriage with her or publish a refusal to do so; without this refusal she could not remarry.

The conditions we have just described were also reflected in the prescriptions of religious legislation of the period. So from a *religious* point of view too, especially with regard to the Torah, a woman was inferior to a man. She was subject to all the *prohibitions* of the Torah (except for the three concerning only men ...), and to the whole force of civil and penal legislation, including the penalty of death. ... However as to the *commandments* of the Torah, here is what was said: "The observance of all the positive ordinances that depend on the time of the year is incumbent on men but not on women."

As a woman's religious *duties* were limited, so were her religious *rights.* According to Josephus, women could go no further in the Temple than into the Courts of the Gentiles and of the Women. ... During the time of their monthly purification, and also for forty days after the birth of a son ... and eighty days after the birth of a daughter ... they were not allowed even into the Court of Gentiles. ... By virtue of Deut. 31:12 women, like men and children, could participate in the synagogue service ... but barriers of lattice separated the women's section. ... In the liturgical service, women were there simply to listen. ... Women were forbidden to teach. ... In the house, the wife was not reckoned among the number of persons summoned to pronounce a benediction after a meal. ... Finally we must record that a woman had no right to bear witness, because it was concluded from Gen. 18:15 that she was a liar. Her witness was acceptable only in a few very exceptional cases, and that of a Gentile slave was also acceptable in the same cases ... e.g., on the remarriage of a widow, the witness of a woman as to the death of the husband was accepted.

On the whole, the position of women in religious legislation is best expressed in the constantly repeated formula: "Women, (Gentile) slaves and children (minors)." ... like a non-Jewish slave and a child under age, a woman has over her a man who is her master . . . and this likewise limits her participation in divine service, which is why from a religious point of view she is inferior to a man.[5]

From a distance of nineteen and a half centuries it is impossible to know with certainty how much this subservient condition of wives in Jesus' time among his people was due simply to the customs of a patriarchal culture, and how much was the consequence of husbands' asserting the lordship they had found granted them in Genesis 3:16b. No doubt the two causes converged and reinforced one another; custom and inclination were justified by what was taken to be a divine decree. And insofar as the decree was understood to be a warrant to punish, the punishment was thought in turn to be for the violation of a covenant. That the violation was also thought to have the first husband's manipulable need as one of its contributing causes could not have diminished the inclination to punish.

Marriage and the Covenant of Unequals

Four among Israel's great prophets chose, at one point or another in their utterances, to interpret Israel's history as that of a wife struggling with the relentless temptation to infidelity, and succumbing to it frequently. The husband to whom Israel was said to again and again prove faithless was the Lord, Yahweh. The prophets who chose this explanatory metaphor were, in the sequence of their teaching, Hosea in the middle of the eighth century, Jeremiah at the end of the seventh century, the anonymous poet who prophesied toward the end of the Babylonian captivity in the middle of the sixth century, and whose oracles are in chapters 40 to 55 of the Book of Isaiah (he is sometimes called Deutero-Isaiah), and Ezekiel, a contemporary of the poet just named, perhaps his companion during Judah's exile in Babylon.[6]

The reason for these prophets' using the metaphor of Yahweh-husband and Israel-wife was to hold up to the people of Israel a mirror in which to see their religious apostasy when it took place, its nature and its seriousness. About its nature they meant, by using the metaphor, to make clear that the apostasy was the violation of a covenant; its seriousness they conveyed in their prophecies of terrible punishment for the people and the land.

A scenario runs through the metaphor. In each case—and most especially in Hosea and Ezekiel—the scenario makes the metaphor a miniature dramatic allegory. The stages in the drama are these: a gracious king (Yahweh) takes for wife a girl (Israel) poor, abandoned, scorned, even (in Hosea) a prostitute. He makes her his queen and wife, promising her unfailing love and asking the same from her. She promises, forming with him a covenant of love. But soon she succumbs to the temptations of false lovers who know of her weakness. She prostitutes herself to them in exchange for their passing favors. Her lord-husband, to punish her, strips her, disgraces her before her lovers, and reduces her to her original destitution. But this punishment is not vindictive, and it is not forever. Her lord-husband does not abandon her; he does not go back on his promised love in the face of her faithlessness. The punishment is love-motivated. It is intended only to bring her to her senses. And when it will have done this, her lord will take her back to himself.

The genesis of the allegory in the different prophets is not easily tracked down. The latter three of them may have borrowed it from their predecessor, Hosea, although the theme of the gracious prince who takes the peasant girl for his wife is virtually universal in the literatures of mankind. If Hosea did in reality take a prostitute for his wife, if he did promise unfailing love to her, experienced her infidelity, punished her, but took her back because of his covenant of love, he found in his own marriage an image with which to tell his people how Yahweh loved them and would treat them because of their faithlessness, and eventually despite their faithlessness.

One obvious consequence of the prophets' using this metaphor was to set before their people a unique interpretation of the latter's relationship to God. Whether the people understood it or not, and whether understanding they welcomed it, they were told that as a people they were Yahweh's wife. Therefore the fidelity to him expected of them was that of a devoted wife.

That was the use of the metaphor to illumine a fact about the Israelites as a nation. But the metaphor once established, and the first illumination once accomplished, a second and reciprocal illumination became possible. Now Jewish husbands and wives had their marriages illumined; the Yahweh-Israel union became the model on which they could fashion their own marriages. And as such a model it could easily move on to become a norm mandating the kind of marriage Jewish spouses *must* have. (As we shall see presently, St. Paul, in his Letter to the Ephesians, most explicitly set this model before the spouses of that Asia Minor community. And because of the inclusion of this letter in the New Testament writings, the model has become the main source of the Catholic theology of Christian marriage as a sacrament.)

I think the following things ought to be noted about the content of the metaphor and about its use for interpreting the early Christians' understanding of marriage. First, nothing of the nature of a contract was to be found in it. Parties to a contract negotiate its terms; each leads from a position of relative strength, even if the quantities of the two strengths be unequal. When each sets his terms for the contract, he is establishing what he can later claim in commutative justice from the other. But in the Yahweh-Israel covenant there was no negotiating, no setting of terms by Israel, no claiming in justice by either. The relationship began with an act of self-giving, rescuing love on the part of Yahweh. He took an entirely gracious initiative and did so in complete freedom. He invited Israel into a love-relationship. This invitation she was free to accept or reject. And even after both had entered the covenant, both remained free. In the historical scenario of the metaphor Israel was free to prove faithless, and she had the power to void the covenant. The only effect she could not work was to destroy Yahweh's love. He chose freely to pursue her despite her faithlessness. The permanence of their relationship came from his unfailing will to have her as his spouse.

The metaphor-model proposed the most exquisite of all the kinds of love. Some of its characteristics I have named just above. It contains a care for the beloved's happiness, a care that cannot be defeated. Its beginning and wellspring is a desire for this happiness, not a lover's private need nor his desire to gain for himself. It contains patience, the will to forgive in the sense of willingness to start over again after infidelity. Above all else it contains commitment, the will to give oneself unreservedly for the well-being of the beloved.

But when the metaphor is turned to use as a normative model for husbands and wives in Israel at least two dangers of misuse appear. The potential for this misuse is rooted in the inapplicability, at crucial points, of the *personae* of the metaphor—Yahweh and Israel—to real-life husbands and wives. And the misuse could surface vividly where the metaphor was applied in rigid, person-for-person allegorical fashion to such husbands and wives. This application would fairly invite the husband to play the role of the sovereign lord, with all the graciousness, the freedom, the taken-for-granted fidelity, and the pursuit in unrelenting forgiveness on his side. Correlatively the wife would be expected to be weak, capricious, in need of protection, control, forgiveness—and of course punishment.

Such an acting out of such an asymmetric covenant relationship the prophets themselves never urged. In fact it is not clear that any of them even proposed the metaphor of Yahweh-husband and Israel-wife as a normative model for the spouses among their own people. But as I have already intimated, St. Paul did just this in Ephesians 5 after transposing the *personae* of the metaphor to Christ-husband and Church-bride. He borrowed the image obviously from his own Jewish prophetic tradition. What the prophets had done was to fix the image in the Jewish consciousness centuries earlier, available there for use as soon as a man as visionary and poetic as themselves should come ready to use it.

But I will put off the examination of Paul's use of the metaphor for the moment, in order to first examine what Jesus said of the nature of marriage, at least by implication, in his instruction reported in the Synoptic Gospels.

Marriage According to the Synoptic Gospels

First, Jesus accepted and validated the covenantal concept of marriage proposed by the Yahwist teacher in Genesis 2. This we have already seen in Jesus' quoting against the Pharisees, in both the Markan and the Matthean versions of his dispute with them, the words, "This is why a man leaves his father and his mother and clings to his wife."

He insisted that marriage has become a relationship fixed in the human race not as an invention of men and women themselves, but as invented by God. This is evident in his first quotation from Torah in both Mark and Matthew, taken from the creation poem of Genesis 1: ["But from the beginning] God made them male and female." And this is not merely a statement of how marriage began.It is a statement made with contentious motive. That is, Jesus meant by this to claim against the Pharisees and the husbands among his people that they had no competence to dissolve marriages—or at the very least no competence to dissolve them in the traditional way, by dismissing their wives. He reinforced this meaning with his own clinching assertion, "So then what God has joined, man must not separate" (Mark 10:9 and Matthew 19:6).

Just before this declaration of God's unassailable act of uniting the spouses, he asserted about the marriage relationship itself that in the husband's separating from his father and mother and clinging to his wife, the two of them become "one flesh." Both Matthew and Mark have Jesus say this a second time after first quoting the phrase from Genesis 2, and in his repetition reformulating it just slightly, apparently in order to get the clarity and emphasis he wanted. Mark has him say, "Thus they are no longer two, but one flesh." Matthew, following the Septuagint version of Genesis 2, has a small but interesting rhetorical variant of the same repetition. Where Mark has Jesus say, "they are . . . one flesh (*eisin . . . mia sarx*), Matthew following the Septuagint puts the numeral adjective at the end of the phrase, in the place of greatest emphasis (*eisin . . . sarx mia*) as if to insist that the two, the husband and the wife, are indeed *one* flesh.

In the Hebrew clause that Jesus quoted from the Yahwist teacher—*veh haiyoo l'vasahr echad*—the substantive, *l'vasahr,* signifies literally "body." Obviously neither the Yahwist nor Jesus could have meant that in becoming husband and wife a man and a woman metamorphose into a single body. Hence the implied simile, "They become like a single body," signifies the closest union imaginable. If of two distinct persons it is said that in some sense they become equivalently one body, in some sense they become equivalently one person. This sense is found in the domain in which they are husband and wife, namely in the domain of social interaction. Thus the conclusion: before the people, and in the law of the people, they are equivalently but one person.

A thousand years later the author of the New Testament Letter to the Ephesians (perhaps Paul himself) drew from the Yahwist's effort to express the oneness of a husband and wife. What he drew must have seemed to him the most obvious conclusion: "Husbands should love their wives as they do their own bodies. He who loves his wife loves himself. Observe that no man ever hates his own flesh; no, he nourishes it and takes care of it as Christ cares for the Church. . . . " Then to make his reference and his application transparently clear he takes verbatim from Genesis this verse that ends ". . . and the two shall become one flesh."

The Instruction on Marriage in 1 Corinthians

Sometime during the year 56 or 57, while in Ephesus on his third missionary journey, St. Paul wrote a letter to the Christian community in Corinth that he had founded six or seven years earlier on his second missionary journey. His main purpose in writing this letter was to instruct this community about a series of doubts and problems they had conveyed in a letter to him. Chapter 7 of the letter contains Paul's answers to their questions about sexuality and marriage. I quote here the most pertinent of these answers.

> 1. Now for the matters you wrote about: "Is it better for a man to have no relations with a woman?" 2. But because of sexual immorality it is better for each man to have his own wife, and for each woman to have her own husband. 3. Let the husband fulfill his obligation to his wife, and likewise the wife her obligation to her husband. 4. A wife has no authority over her own body, rather her husband has it; just as a husband has no authority over his own body, but his wife has it. 5. Do not deny one another, except perhaps by mutual agreement for a time, so as to devote yourselves to prayer. Then return to one another so that Satan may not put you to the test through your lack of self-control. 6. I say this to you by way of counsel, not of command. 7. I would that all were as I myself am, but each has his or her own gift from God, one person one gift, another person another.
>
> 8. To the unmarried and to the widows I say that it is good for them if they remain as I am. 9. But if they cannot contain themselves, let them marry. For it is better to marry than to burn. 10. To the married I proclaim—not I, but the Lord does— that a wife must not depart from her husband. 11. But if she departs, she is either to remain unmarried or is to be reconciled with her husband. And a husband is not to dismiss his wife.
>
> 12. To the rest I say, not the Lord, if a brother has a wife who is an unbeliever, but she is willing to live with him, he is not to dismiss her. 13. And if a wife has a husband who is an unbeliever, but he is willing to live with her, she is not to dismiss him. 14. For an unbelieving husband is sanctified by his wife, and an unbelieving wife is sanctified by her husband. If it were not so, your children would be unclean. But in fact they are holy. 15. But if the unbeliever wishes to depart, let him or her depart. The brother or sister is not to play the slave in such cases. For God has called you to live in peace.[7]

From the evidence available here in Paul's answers it seems likely that a Gnostic attitude had penetrated the minds of some of the Corinthian community, an attitude suspicious of the moral rightness of marriage and of sexuality within marriage. It seems evident too that some of this community had returned to the practice of going to the temple prostitutes in the city. The latter is evident from the passage (6:13–20) immediately preceding this instruction on marriage. In it Paul exhorts the Corinthians to think of themselves, of their bodies, as temples of the *living* God.

We could understand Paul's answers to the questions about sex and marriage if we knew exactly what these were. But we have only Paul's answers, and thus must infer the questions from them. The importance of not having the questions emerges in the first verse of this chapter 7. In it does Paul (as I suppose he does in my translation) repeat back to the Corinthians their own question as a preparation for answering it? Or in it does he begin immediately with an answer to their question? If he does the latter, the verse must read, "Now for the matters you wrote about, it is better for a man to have no relations with a woman." Nothing in the syntax of the verse tells the reader which is the correct interpretation, and the written Greek of Paul's time had no punctuation. In either case, the answer and the implicit question hint clearly at the Gnostic influence mentioned above, its distrust of sexual activity, its belief that the Christian life is holier in those who rise above the needs of the flesh. It is not likely that Paul would concede so important a point to adversaries with whom he was otherwise so uncompromising. Furthermore, if he were stating flatly that it is good that a man have no sexual contact with a woman, and this not even in marriage, what he says later in his instruction would be a poorly fitted and contradictory continuation of this original thought.

For Paul would here be advocating not only, as he does later in the letter, that it is *better* for both men and women who are as yet unmarried to remain so. He would be proposing an ascetic best way for all Christians. The predicate adjective in his instruction is *kalón.* This would mean that it is "good," "excellent," that a Christian man have no sexual relationship with a woman. (In the New Testament the word is sometimes an understatement for "the right thing" or "the necessary thing to do." Thus in Mark 7:27 Jesus tells the Syrophoenician woman who has asked him to cure her daughter, "It is not *kalón* to take the children's food and throw it to the dogs." And in Mark 9:43 Jesus tells his hearers, "And if your hand should cause you to sin, cut it off; it is *kalón* for you to enter into life crippled, etc.") And the predicate, *me háptesthai,* which is translated so frequently ". . . that he not touch," had, in the usage of Paul's time, a general sexual reference. The Septuagint Old Testament, that version read by the Corinthian Christians, uses the verb to refer to physical intercourse with or without marriage.

Taking this verse then as Paul's restatement of the Corinthians' own question, we have his answer to it in verse 2: "But because of sexual immorality (*pornéia*) it is better for each man to have his own wife, and for each

woman to have her own husband." Paul's careful use of the possessive re-
flexive pronoun *heautoû,* and of the adjective *ídion,* points to monogamous
marriage. But more than this, the reply names what is, in Paul's mind, a
principal office or function of marriage. It is to serve as a safeguard against
sexual sins—sins of whatever kind, as the generically referenced *pornéia*
indicates. (This thought was to be seized on by Christian teachers in succeeding centuries and used in their defining of marriage. It is included in
the Catholic Code of Canon Law, in Canon 1013.1, where it appears as an
element of the secondary end of marriage, which is to be a remedy for concupiscence.) Paul returns to the same thought of marriage as safeguard later in this letter (verses 8 and 9) in his instruction to those not yet married
and to widows: ". . . it is good for them if they remain as I am. But if they
cannot contain themselves, let them marry. For it is better to marry than
to burn."

As Paul develops this instruction in verses 3 and 4 he advances a
thought that must seem to the modern Christian to juridicize marriage
and even the expression of love in marriage. Whatever the truth of this,
Paul says something about marriage that was singular in his time—singular unless he is reiterating an interpretation of marriage begun by Jesus
himself and taught to Paul during the years of his own learning the Gospel. He says: "Let the husband fulfill his obligation to his wife, and likewise the wife her obligation to her husband. A wife has no authority over
her own body, rather her husband has it; just as a husband has no authority over his own body, but his wife has it." A modern Christian may wince
at finding the apostle writing of sexual intercourse as an obligation, or even
a debt, owed by spouses to one another, and writing of husbands' and
wives' marital relationship as containing authority over one another's bodies. But Paul's contemporaries—at least those bred in the tradition of Torah and of its rabbinic interpreters—would have winced for another
reason. This was Paul's assertion of equality between husbands and wives,
and equality exactly on the juridical ground of authority and obligations
owed. He insists that husbands owe the debt of sexual intercourse to their
wives just as much as the latter do to them, that wives have just as much
authority over their husbands' bodies as the husbands have over theirs.

And none of this comes from Paul as mere suggestion and counsel.
He asserts it all and commands it; his verbs in this part of the letter are in
the imperative. (Nor is this the first letter in which Paul innovated this
idea of equality of the rights and obligations of spouses. In 1 Thessalon-
ians, written seven or eight years earlier, when instructing the Christians of
this Thracian community about sexual conduct, he had said, "He [God]
wants you to keep away from fornication, and each one of you to know
how to use the body that belongs to him." Even if this last clause refers to
a man's or woman's own body, it bespeaks an exercise of authority, and an
equal exercise of it.)

When the Catholic canonists of the twelfth and thirteenth centuries
bent to the work of defining marriage formally, and sought reasons to in-

terpret it as a contract, they found reasons with a clear scriptural warrant here in 1 Corinthians. For two persons to be under obligation to pay a debt to one another is for them to be in a contractual relationship, all the more so where the obligations are equal. And where in addition the persons in such a relationship hold an authority over the other that had originally been the other's, this points to a conveyance, to an exchange between the parties of just this authority. This seems clearly a contractual exchange. It also appears to identify the contractual good that is exchanged, namely each party's right to his or her own body, specifically in the domain of the sexual conduct appropriate to marriage. With the benefit of hindsight on the centuries we can see Paul here supplying the entire medieval and modern Christian community with major portions of the definition of marriage it would make its own.

Paul's appreciation of marriage as a safeguard against sexual sins appears again in verses 5–7. Here he advises (but does not command) the Corinthian spouses that they not deny one another the "marriage debt" except for a limited period, only if the brief abstention is agreed on by both, and only for the motive of devotion to prayer. After the brief interruption they are to resume normal marital relations, but not so much in order to overcome temptation as in order to finesse the tempter, as it were, ". . . in order that Satan not put you to the test through your lack of self-control." (The verb here is *peirázein,* the same that is used in the Synoptic tradition to explain why the Pharisees came to Jesus to begin the dispute with him over divorce—not to tempt him, but to put him to the test. Mark uses it in his version of the testing in 10:2, as does Matthew in his, in 19:3.)

And again Paul expresses the wish that all the Corinthians be as he is at the time, living a life of celibacy. But he grants that to be able to live either form of life—sexually active in marriage, or celibate (whether in fact married or not)—is a gift of God: ". . . but each has his or her own gift (*chárisma*) from God, one person one gift, another person another." Here is another point of origin in Paul that would be remembered later in the history of Christian thinking on marriage, namely that life in marriage, being a gift from God, is one of the acknowledged "vocations" in the Church. In contemporary parlance we may even call it one of the formally established roles that make up the collectivity that is the Christian community.

Paul and the Possibility of Divorce and Remarriage

From the evidence in Paul's replies in verses 10 to 16 the Corinthian Christians had put to him two questions about spouses' separating and divorcing—or more accurately said, two different questions about two kinds of marriages whose spouses might separate and seek to dissolve. And from the fact of their putting both kinds of questions it is evident that both kinds of marriages were to be found in their community. In one of them both spouses are Christians; in the other one spouse is Christian, the other an unbeliever. Apparently the question about the first of these asked if either spouse might dissolve it. Paul's reply to this he insists is not his own, but a command that he has from the Lord. He divides the question in order to cover the cases of both husband and wife. The wife is not to "separate." But if she does, she has two options: either to be reconciled with her husband or to remain unmarried.

The Greek verb Paul uses here, which I translate "separate," causes some difficulty for the interpretation. This is *chorízein;* it is a verb that was used commonly under Roman law to designate one way of dissolving a marriage (the other way consisted of dismissing a spouse).[8] Ordinarily it was used in the active voice to designate what a spouse did in dissolving the marriage in this way: he or she "separated" the marriage. But here in verse 10 Paul uses the verb in the aorist of the passive infinitive with the negative particle, and uses it about the wife only: *me choristhénai*—she is not to be separated. With the hope that one is not being finer in the exegesis than Paul was in the writing, one may yet ask whether this command (really the Lord's) was aimed in fact at the husband, although indirectly through the wife. For it commands what must not be done to the wife, and it is something which only a husband could do. If the command is aimed rather at the husbands, it is more nearly like Jesus' command as this is recorded in the Synoptic tradition, which forbade Jewish husbands to dismiss (*apolúein*) their wives. And Paul is correct in saying that this command he has from the Lord, although his own version of it is slightly disguised.

But this leaves Paul with no command about dissolving marriages fitted to Christian wives married to Christian husbands. The omission would have been inconsequential in an instruction to Christians living under Jewish law, which allowed wives no divorce action of any kind. But it is a significant omission for wives living under Roman law, which allowed them the same divorce actions it allowed husbands. Yet here again Paul's honesty emerges in conveying Jesus' command of a generation earlier. For neither had he had a command for the Jewish wives of Palestine—for the obvious reason, again, that a command to not do what the law forbade them in any case would have been pointless. The upshot of this is that Paul's command to the Corinthian Christian wives married to Christian husbands touches only their conduct after having been dismissed by such a husband. What this is we shall see in a moment.

The Lord's command which Paul directs to the husbands in this kind of marriage cites almost exactly Jesus' command to Jewish Palestinian husbands recorded by the Synoptics: they are not to dismiss their wives. (Paul uses the verb *aphiénai* to designate this unilateral dismissing where the Synoptics had used *apolúein*. But their meaning is synonymous.) Here again Paul hews faithfully to Jesus' instruction. But in doing so he leaves untouched the legitimate question the Corinthian spouses could have asked in reply to his reply, namely whether, apart from dissolving their marriages by the obviously forbidden dismissal of the wife by the husband, they could yet do so by the other action permitted by Roman law—the "separating" of the marriage. We can only conjecture what Paul's answer might have been. About it we can be sure only that it would have had to be his own counsel, since he apparently knew of no instruction on the point from Jesus. This is not to say there was none, since the same Synoptic tradition carried Jesus' trenchant command, "What God has joined, man must not separate." And the second verb here is exactly the *chorízein* that the vocabulary of Roman law used to designate the divorce action that attacked the marriage rather than dismissing the spouse. That Paul does not quote this dominical command where it would have been so useful for his instruction to the Corinthians is an omission I have never found explained.

However one interprets this family of verbs as Paul uses them in this context, it is clear that in conveying the mind and will of Jesus about Christian spouses' dissolving their marriages by the dismissal of the other spouse, where both are Christian this is forbidden—absolutely and unexceptionably forbidden. Paul offers no explanation for why it is forbidden. It is enough for him that it is the Lord's command.

But Paul's choice of words in another sector of his reply leaves a second uncertainty in its wake. In verse 10 he said that a wife must not be separated from (and by) her husband. But where, in verse 11, he states the options available to a wife who has in fact been thus dismissed by her Christian husband, he begins "But if she is separated. . . ." Does Paul here mean to say that what is absolutely forbidden by the Lord's command is nevertheless possible? To use later Catholic terminology in asking the same question, does Paul here admit implicitly the dissolubility of even the marriage of two Christians while stating unequivocally the impermissibility of its dissolution by dismissal?

That this is the case is supported by Paul's choice of adjective to designate one of the options available to a dismissed Christian wife: she is to remain unmarried—*ágamos*. This adjective Paul had used as a substantive in verse 8 to designate two other social categories in the Christian community, the unmarried and the widows (*hoi ágamoi kai hai chérai*). He uses the same adjective again in verses 32 and 34 to designate the unmarried who are better able than the married to attend to the things of the Lord. Thus, as far as Paul's choice of words reveals his meaning, he says that the effect of a wife's being separated (or dismissed) from her marriage is that she becomes unmarried—she is once again single. (But consistently with the uncertainty of meaning in the passage, verse 39 later seems to gainsay this, for here Paul says ". . . a wife is bound to her husband for as long as he lives.")

In the second kind of marriage about which the Corinthian Christians had asked, one spouse was a believer but one was not. From his replies we can tell that Paul had been asked two questions about such a marriage. And in replying Paul took care to explain that the instruction in his answer was not from the Lord but from himself.

However the first of the questions was formulated, it manifested the anxiety of some of the Corinthians lest their marriages to non-believing spouses harm them in their effort to live as Christians. Paul replies that just the reverse is what happens: the non-believing spouses are sanctified by their marriages with Christians. The evidence for this Paul supplies by dint of some rabbinic logic: if the the Christian spouses were harmed by their marriages with non-believers, the children of their marriages would not be holy. But the contrary is the truth about these children. They are holy. Therefore in the marriages whence they are born the non-believing parent must have been sanctified by the Christian. Therefore too if the non-believing spouses are willing to live in peace with the Christian, the latter are not to dismiss them. And Paul directs this counsel as expressly at Christian wives as at Christian husbands, thus conceding to the wives an equality with their husbands in the question of dismissing a non-believing spouse.

The motive Paul offers the Christian spouses for not dismissing their non-believing partners is not that Jesus had forbidden such an act, but that the reason suggested by the Corinthians for doing so was a false assumption of fact.

The second question Paul must have been asked about such religiously mixed marriages had in mind relationships in which the non-believing spouse was unwilling to live with the Christian, but chose to separate. The verb Paul uses to designate this separation is again *chorízein,* whose common reference in Roman law was to one of the kinds of divorce action available to either spouse. But this time the verb is in the middle voice (*chorízetai*), which indicates an action completed within the person carrying it on, not something done either by that person to another, or to him by another. Here it is appropriate to translate the clause (verse 15), "If the non-believer wishes to depart, let him or her depart."

From the one counsel to the other Paul's shift in choice of verb is not without significance. Where he first addressed Christian spouses who had non-believing spouses willing to live with them in peace, he said that the former were not to dismiss the latter (the verb there is *aphiénai*). This was an action available to the Christian spouses that Paul counsels them not to take. But then when he advises Christian spouses who have non-believing partners unwilling to live with them and wanting to depart, he directs the verb *chorízein* to the latter. He leaves the initiative to them; the Christian spouses are to do nothing other than to let the departure-dissolution take place.

This examination of Paul's instructions to the Corinthian Christians—his relayed command of the Lord to those married to another Christian, and his own counsel to those married to a non-believer—searches into a most important sector of the early Christian understanding of the nature of marriage. Presumably Paul tells the Corinthians things acceptable throughout all the Christian communities of the time. Nothing he said conflicted with what these had learned of Jesus' teaching coming from a generation earlier. What then do we conclude from his telling Christian

wives that if they are separated from their Christian husbands (and in doing so he uses a conventional verb of the time indicating the dissolving of a
marriage), they must either be reconciled to their husbands or must remain
unmarried (and here he uses the same adjective with which elsewhere in
the passage he expressly designates both those who are not married and
those who have never been married)? And what conclusion do we draw
from Paul's counseling Christian spouses that if their non-believing
spouses depart from the marriage, they are not to stop them from doing so
(and in advising this he uses a conventional verb of his time referring to
the dissolving of a marriage)? From his choice of words it appears that
Paul did not think a marriage to be a relationship impervious to dissolution. The kind of separation-departure of spouses that would leave them
still husband and wife, the "separation from bed and board" familiar in
Catholic tradition, was unknown to either the Roman or the Jewish law of
the time. Presumably had Paul counseled this literally novel kind of separation, he would have had to explain both its nature and his reason for insisting it was the only kind of separation possible, or at least the only kind
permitted them.

And in the case of the Christian spouse whose non-believing spouse
has departed, Paul did not repeat to the former his earlier command to the
two believing spouses who are separated by the husband's action that the
wife must either be reconciled or remain unmarried. Paul would have been
bound in conscience to repeat this command if he had thought that in this
second case to remarry was either impossible or forbidden or both. We
may say, at the end of this brief review of Paul's instruction in 1 Corinthians, that if Paul had ever heard of Jesus' own command, "What God has
joined, man must not separate," he did not understand it as either a declaration that such a separation is fundamentally impossible (and hence that
what is forbidden is an attempt at the impossible), or that such a separation is forbidden beyond all exception. Apparently at least, he understood
a marriage to be a relationship that is not impervious to dissolution even
this side of the death of one of the spouses.

Marriage in Paul's Exhortation to the Ephesians

I suggested above that the most evident Christian borrowing of the
prophets' vision of Israel as the spouse of Yahweh has occurred in the Letter to the Ephesians. There, in chapter 5, it is transposed into a relationship in which Christ is the husband and the Church his spouse.[9] The
passage, with verses numbered for the sake of explanation, is the following:

18. And do not besot yourselves with wine (this is only dissipa-
tion), but be filled with the Spirit, 19. singing to one another in
psalms and hymns and spiritual canticles, singing and chanting
to the Lord in your hearts, 20. giving thanks always and everywhere to our God and Father in the name of Our Lord Jesus

Christ, 21. deferring to one another in the fear of Christ, 22.
wives to their own husbands as to the Lord, 23. for the husband
is the head of the wife just as Christ is the head of the Church, he
who is savior of the body. 24. And as the Church defers to Christ
so also should wives to their husbands in everything. 25. You
husbands should love your wives

Just as Christ loved the Church
and gave himself up for her,
26. so that he might sanctify her,
purifying her in the bath of water
and the Word,
27. so that he might take to himself
a glorious Church,
having no spot or wrinkle
or any other such thing,
but one that is holy and faultless.

28. In the same way husbands ought to love their wives as
they do their own bodies; a man who loves his wife is loving himself. 29. For no one has ever hated his own flesh, but he nourishes it and cares for it, just as Christ does the Church, 30. for we
are the living parts of his body.

31. "For this reason a man will leave his father
"and his mother and will cling to his wife.
and the two of them will become one flesh."

32. This mystery is a profound one; and I mean this about
Christ and the Church. 33. Therefore you too, each one of you,
ought to love his own wife as he loves himself, so that the wife
may respect her husband.[10]

This exhortation has been misunderstood persistently enough at certain points to merit a brief but exact explanation of what Paul says in it
about the character of a marriage where both spouses are Christian.

First of all the passage has two main contextual features that help to
determine its meaning. This instruction to the spouse is located, according
to a standard format of Paul's letters, in the latter part of the letter, in its
disciplinary and hortatory part following the earlier doctrinal part. But
here in Ephesians there is an obvious conceptual bridge joining the first
part to the second. In the former Paul explained that Christ has brought a
new life to those who accept and believe in him, a life energized by his
Spirit. In the latter part he draws the conclusions from this fact by describing (and exhorting) how this new life is to be lived in specific points of conduct and in specific relationships within the Ephesian Christian
community. Thus from Chapter 4:25 and following he instructs in detail:

25. See to it, then, that you put an end to lying. . . . 26. If you are
angry, let it be without sin. The sun must not go down on your

wrath; 27. do not give the devil a chance to work on you. 28. The man who has been stealing must steal no longer. . . . 29. Never let evil talk pass your lips. . . . 31. Get rid of all bitterness, all passion and anger, harsh words, slander, and malice of every kind. 32. In place of these, be kind to one another, compassionate, and mutually forgiving, just as God has forgiven you in Christ.

This exhorting to specific kinds of right conduct continues on into the first twenty verses of chapter 5. At this point Paul moves on to single out three relationships within the community for special attention: parents and children (6:1–4), masters and slaves (6:5–9), and the relationship with which we are now concerned, husbands and wives (5:21–33).[11] Each of these he deems a love relationship because of the Spirit-filled Christians comprising it. The conduct he explains and urges in each is demanded by, and will be the product of, the Spirit-energized love shared by these Christians. This conduct is not what Paul would expect of parents, children, masters, slaves or spouses living merely conventionally decent lives.

The second contextual feature is Paul's intent in the passage. It is not to explain how God in Christ relates to human beings in several ways. Such doctrine there is in the passage, but it is there in the service of his instruction and exhortation about conduct. Consequently if we look here for the results of Paul's "defining" Christian marriage, we find him doing so only as a secondary intent. He implies the nature of this marriage only in order to make clear to the Christian spouses why they should regard and treat one another in a special way.

Here an old and disputed point of exegesis can be taken care of succinctly. The Vulgate Latin translation of verse 32, *Sacramentum hoc magnum est* (rendered in the seventeenth-century Catholic Douay version as "This is a great sacrament"), does not have marriage as its referent. Therefore it does not say of the marriage of two Christian spouses that it is a sacrament. In Paul's Greek—*tò mystérion toûto méga estín*—*mystérion* does not denote exactly what the modern theological term "sacrament" denotes, a religious re-enacting wherein persons manifest the action of God in Christ in the world, and thereby grow in their relationship to both. The primary sense of *mystérion,* as Paul uses it here, is that of a sensate manifestation of God's invisible plan for the human race. He says in the same verse 32 that he means the term to describe and evaluate the relationship of Christ and the Church.

A not so commonly known point of exegesis, and one not now so unanimously agreed on, calls for an explanation that cannot be so brief. It has to do with verses 5:21 and 5:22. To begin with, verse 21 is both a coda to those that precede it and a bridge to those that follow. What precedes is pure exhortation, Paul urging what the Ephesians' conduct should not contain and urging what it should contain. The latter runs a list, with the recommended kinds of conduct named from verse 19 onward in the participial form of the verbs continuing the thematic exhortation in verse 18:

"singing . . . chanting . . . giving thanks." Then without a break in thought
or rhythm Paul adds the bridging phrase in verse 21, ". . . deferring to one
another in the fear of Christ."

It is at this point that the Vulgate New Testament, and every English
translation I know of that imitates it, breaks the rhetorical flow and even
the continuity of thought in a way that is arbitrary.[12] All go so far as to
make the next verse (22) the introduction of a new paragraph, and in addition translate the Greek verb in a way that perverts Paul's meaning:
"Wives, be subject to your husbands as to the Lord." But the phrase that
the Vulgate and its imitators render ". . . be subject to . . ." has in some of
the most ancient Greek manuscripts no verb at all, not even a last participle in the series of participles begun in verse 10 with "singing." And in
those manuscripts that do show the clause to contain a verb, this is the
participial form, *hypotassómenoi,* which indicates that this is the last in a
series of conduct forms that Paul urges on his Ephesian readers, since, as I
have pointed out, all the forms preceding it in this series are also indicated
by participles. If in this phrase as Paul himself wrote it the verb is absent,
or is at best present in its participial form, the process of his thought is
this: the Christians of Ephesus ought to defer to one another; and of the
forms of deference to be named in sequence, one is that of wives to their
husbands.

Central to Paul's thought here is the exact signification of the Greek
verb that is translated in the Vulgate as a predicate adjective: "Mulieres
viris suis *subditae* sint," and in the English as "Let wives be subject to their
husbands." The Greek verb in its middle voice, *hypotássesthai,* signifies "to
defer to," "to give way to." It is the kind of thing friends do habitually in
order to maintain their friendship. Scholars do it when they carry on discussion in order to learn rather than to conquer. Even commanders of
combat units within the same army do this in order that all may conquer
together. The verb by itself carries a generic signification; it is for the user
of it to bring his meaning to more exact focus. This is what Paul does here:
he goes on to explain in what way the Ephesian wives are to defer to their
husbands, as he then explains how the husbands are to defer to their wives.
His words as we have them here are not a command, nor even an exhortation, to Christian wives of all succeeding generations to obey their husbands.

Yet, though Paul sees the deference needed in a marriage to be mutual, he shares the cultural assumption of his age that wives are in fact under
obedience to their husbands. He does not challenge other substantial
points in the social structure of the civilization he lived in, not even the
master-slave relationship he discusses in chapter 6, verses 5–9. There is no
ground for assuming that he would challenge the accepted arrangement of
the husband-wife relationship.

But while accepting the arrangement he urges a profound change in
the motives that animate it. If Paul understood the Genesis story of the
first man and woman and their disobedience as a factual historical ac-

count, he believed that God's original intent had been that women *not* be subject to their husbands. He read in the early part of the story that the first woman had been created as the man's helping partner, as the sharer in his vocation to tend the garden that God had meant to be the permanent home of themselves and their children. But he read also at the story's end that it was a consequence of her sin and as a punishment for it that she had had her husband set over as her lord. Thus as long as sin reigned in the world, women's inferiority was a punishment, and punishing treatment was appropriate to this inferiority.

But Paul believed that Christ's death and resurrection had broken the reign of sin. The victory had not been complete, but at least one of the worst consequences of the long victory of sin—helplessness in slavery to the basest human inclinations—was at an end. Those who believed and who accepted the Father's and the Son's gift of the Spirit could live compassionately and with trust within life's accepted social structures.[13] I think this is what Paul believed had been made available to Christian spouses: the Spirit's gift of being able to *not* continue in their marriages the ancient punishment for their ancestors' disobedience. Instead they could now love and trust one another, but asymmetrically, with the husband caring and protecting, and the wife depending and obeying. Whether Paul might have moved on to think that, with the passing of time and the growth of faith, hope and charity in the Church, another structure for marriage would be better—as with the passing of time the Church saw to the abolition of slavery—we can only conjecture.

An analogous change of heart within an unchanged social relationship appears in Paul's Letter to Philemon. From Rome Paul wrote to the Colossian Christian of that name, urging him to take back his runaway slave boy, Onesimus, who had escaped as far as Rome. Law and custom in the Empire called for Philemon to punish the boy severely, even to the point of killing him if he chose, all the more so because the boy had apparently stolen from the household when taking flight. All the householders of Colossae who knew of Onesimus' theft and flight, and all the slaves as well, would wait to see if Philemon applied the conventional punishment. If he did not, master-slave discipline in the city would be challenged and a serious undermining of it would have begun. But even knowing all this, and knowing how he was forcing Philemon into a most painful dilemma, Paul nevertheless wrote:

> Therefore, although I feel that I have every right to command you to do what ought to be done, I prefer to appeal in the name of love. Yes, I, Paul, ambassador of Christ and now a prisoner for him, appeal to you for my child, whom I have begotten during my imprisonment. He has become in truth Onesimus [Useful], for he who was formerly useless to you is now useful indeed both to you and to me. It is he I am sending to you—and that means I am sending back my heart. . . . Perhaps he was separated

from you for a while for this reason: that you might possess him forever, no longer as a slave but as more than a slave, a beloved brother, especially dear to me; and how much more to you, since now you will know him both as a man and in the Lord.

It is not unlikely that Paul meant about husbands and wives, now that they were married in the Lord, that they no longer regard one another as master with the right to punish, and faithless child-wife needing to be punished. In place of this he hoped and urged that their love for one another might imitate the love of Christ and his bride, the Church. The husbands especially had to sense a fundamental change of things aborning when Paul pointed out that because of this love Christ gave himself up, sacrificing his life for his bride. If husbands were to continue being lords to their wives in some sense, this new sense included the assumption that their wives are more precious to them than their own lives.

NOTES

1. These negotiations were summed up and their results specified in the *ketuba,* "the writ of marriage." It stated the financial obligations I have mentioned, mainly that of the husband to the wife (the *mohar,* given to her through her father). But it specified agreement on other matters as well, such as the place and date of the wedding feast. The usual formula of the *ketuba* also obligated the husband to work for his bride, to honor her, support her, and maintain her in accordance with the custom of Jewish husbands. One of the purposes, and one of the effects, of the *ketuba* was to limit the freedom of the husband to divorce his wife capriciously.

2. I have taken this interpretation from Walter Brueggemann's essay, "Of the Same Flesh and Bone," in *The Catholic Biblical Quarterly* 32.4 (1970) pp. 532–542.

3. *Op. cit.,* pp. 539–540.

4. *Ancient Israel,* New York-Toronto-London, 1961, p. 39.

5. *Jerusalem in the Time of Jesus,* London, 1969, pp. 359–376.

But always, of course, human nature challenges and triumphs in some degree over tradition, doctrine and law. The Jewish Scriptures themselves, both canonical and deutero-canonical, contain verses, chapters and entire books in praise of women, of Jewish women faithful in marriage, and of Jewish women who used their sexuality to save their people. Of the beautiful widow Judith it is told that she ended a siege of Bethulia and saved her people from slaughter and slavery by seducing (and beheading) a Babylonian general. Esther was chosen by the Persian king Xerxes as his favorite wife, and by her pleading she saved her people from pogrom in his empire. The Book of Tobit tells of the tender, most caring love between a young Jewish husband and wife, one that began with the blessing and gift by the girl's father as he gave Sarah to Tobiah: "She is yours according to the decree of the Book of Moses. Your marriage to her has been decided in heaven! Take your kinswoman; from now on you are her love, and she is your beloved. And tonight, son, may the Lord of heaven prosper you both. May he grant you mercy and peace" (7:11).

That these stories are thoroughly legendized takes nothing from the value of their witness to another side of the popular Jewish mind regarding women. And it is to be noted that the writing down of these folk documents and finally their inclusion (Tobit excepted) among Israel's sacred writings were all the work of Jewish male teachers and authorities.

Certainly the most explicit praise of women in Jewish sacred writings is the portrait, in the final chapter of the Book of Proverbs, of the ideal wife. That she was regarded as anything but a child is evident in such verses as the following:

> When one finds a worthy wife,
> her value is far beyond pearls.
> Her husband, entrusting his heart to her,
> has an unfailing prize. . . .
> She picks out a field to purchase;
> out of her earnings she plants a vineyard.
> She reaches out her hands to the poor,
> and extends her arms to the needy. . . .
> She makes garments and sells them,
> and stocks the merchants with belts. . . .
> She opens her mouth in wisdom,
> and on her tongue is kindly counsel.
> She watches the conduct of her household,
> and eats not her food in idleness.
> Her children rise up and praise her;
> her husband too extols her.

6. The pertinent passages are Hosea 1—3:35; Jeremiah 3:1–10; Isaiah 54:5–10 and 62:1–5; Ezekiel 16.

7. The translation of this passage is my own.

8. For the meaning of *chórizein* in the early Christian context see W. F. Arndt and F. W. Gingrich, *A Greek-English Lexicon of the New Testament and Other Early Christian Literature,* Second Edition . . . Chicago and London, 1979, p. 890.

9. The question whether Paul is the primary author, or author at all, of Ephesians is not pertinent to this essay. Ephesians is accepted in the canon of the Christian Scriptures, and the exhortation in this chapter to the Ephesian spouses has contributed substantially to Christian thinking on marriage from the second century onward.

10. The translation of this passage is my own.

11. Paul repeats this exhortation in condensed form in Colossians 3:18—4:1: "You who are wives, be submissive [i.e. defer] to your husbands. This is your duty in the Lord. Husbands, love your wives. Avoid any bitterness toward them. You children, obey your patents in everything as the acceptable way in the Lord. And fathers, do not nag your children lest they lose heart. To slaves I say, obey your human master perfectly, not with the purpose of attracting attention and pleasing men but in all sincerity and out of reverence for the Lord. . . . You slaveowners, deal justly and fairly with your slaves, realizing that you too have a master in heaven."

12. St. Jerome's arbitrariness in rendering the passage as he did in his Vulgate New Testament is threefold. First, he insisted that verse 22 have a verb, in face of the fact that the oldest New Testament codices disagree on this point, with Sinaiti-

cus and Alexandrinus including *hypotássesthai* in the imperative, but Vaticanus (the oldest of the codices), Ephraem Rescriptus and Codex Bezae Cantabrigiensis excluding one. Second, he made verse 22 into an independent statement, breaking it off from its obvious place at the end of the preceding series of clauses. Finally, he translated the verb *hypotássein* according to a meaning not common to it in biblical terms, viz., "to be subject to."

13. On this signification see Markus Barth's explanation in *The Anchor Bible,* Vol. 34A, *Ephesians, Translation and Commentary on Chapters 4–6,* Garden City, 1974, pp. 608ff.

3. CHRISTIAN MARRIAGE IN THE ROMAN EMPIRE

It is to be expected that as long as the demographic center of the early Christian communities was Palestine, the marriages of Christians would be Jewish in social structure, and the Christians' motives for marrying would be fundamentally Jewish, as would their experience of married life itself. The same is true about the Christian communities that sprang up around the then known world, generally in the major cities of the empire, such as Alexandria, Antioch, Ephesus, Corinth, Thessalonika and Rome. There the Christians were for the most part erstwhile members of these cities' synagogue communities who, on hearing the Christian evangelists, accepted Jesus as their long-awaited messiah and joined the ranks of his followers.

But gradually, as the proportion of Jewish converts in these first- and second-generation Christian communities diminished against the growing proportion of Gentiles, the structure and experience of marriage, as well as the motives for marrying, inevitably became those of the Hellenistic-Roman civilization of the time. And this demographic transformation brought with it significant cultural and legal changes.

In this civilization marriage had lost all its ancient religious meaning except among the few patrician families that supplied the priests to conduct sacrifice in the imperial temples. The old liturgical wedding ceremony of *confarreatio,* with its elaborate ritual including sacrifice to Jupiter, had disappeared except among these families. Among them it lingered until as late as 394, thirteen years after Christianity had become the established religion of the empire. In that year the emperor Theodosius I finally abolished the traditional priesthood and sacrifice.

For everyone else marriage had become simply a secular association of a man and a woman. And in a society otherwise addicted to regulating life by statutory law, marriages in the empire bore a surprisingly slight weight of juridical control.[1] The meaning of marriage, the process of marrying and the experience of being married in the empire until about Justinian's reform of imperial law in 536 showed the following elements.

There was first of all the legal matter of *connubium*. This was a determination of the law verifying persons' capacity to marry at all. The law denied *connubium* to slaves altogether, and consequently the possibility of marriage between citizens and slaves and between freedmen and slaves. To the latter was allowed only *contubernium* with one another, a kind of legitimized concubinage. It differed from citizens' marriage within *connubium* in that the slave owner could block the exercise of *contubernium* and could end it at will. The children born of slaves' *contubernium* were illegitimate, with the consequence that they became slaves at birth. They also became the added property of their mother's owner, who could keep and rear them, sell them, or simply kill them if he or she deemed them a burden. Since their parents could own no property, the children of slaves could inherit none. If the citizen wife permitted, and often even if she did not, female slaves were kept in the household to help serve the sexual needs of the male head of the house and of his sons. For the female slaves this was a duty to which they were expected to put up no resistance.

Roman citizens were forbidden *connubium* with foreigners. Sexual liaison with them was permitted, but children born of such unions were illegitimate and could therefore not inherit. *Connubium* was also forbidden within certain degrees of consanguinity. These differed according to different legal reforms, but at one time extended to include even the seventh degree of kindred in the collateral line. *Connubium* was also forbidden between freed slaves and their erstwhile owners, and between citizens of patrician rank and freedmen.

Girls were legally capable of marriage at the age of twelve. Boys were capable when puberty in them was verified by inspection and by experience, usually in about their fourteenth year. Betrothal was a mutual promise to marry. It could take place as much as five to seven years earlier than the age of marriage, that is, when the boy and girl were, in the language of the law, no longer *infantes* or *infantiae proximi,* but "could speak with understanding of what they said." In Justinian's code of 536 this legal capacity was presumed in children of seven years. Obviously the betrothal in such cases was arranged by whoever held the *patria potestas* over the children, the legal responsibility accorded a father. This could be the natural male parent or it could be a tutor, a man holding power of attorney, so to speak, not so much over the child's person as over whatever personal fortune had come to it or might come to it in the future. In fact betrothal was largely a financial arrangement, a contract without any form of law. Obviously when children were betrothed at a tender age, this was an arrangement completed by two sets of parents, or possibly by tutors on one or both sides.

Boys were allowed a clear right of dissent against the partners chosen for them in betrothal. The girl's right to do so was less clear in the law. Her *paterfamilias* could betroth her against her will. Against this she had the right of dissent, but one not always effective in its exercise. Sons and daughters were in practice often allowed to choose their mates, but this freedom was conditioned in turn by the approval of whoever held *patria potestas* over them. He had the authority to veto any choice they made. During the Roman republic, beginning as early as the fifth century B.C., marriage by *coemptio* was a common arrangement. Legally this was a conveyance, a fictitious purchase of the bride by the groom. She was transferred from the *potestas* of her father or tutor into that of her husband. She was in both relationships legally a child. This arrangement was also called a marriage *in manu,* a passing of the girl from the hand of the *paterfamilias* to that of her husband. *Coemptio* disappeared gradually during the years of the empire until by the time of the classic Roman jurists in the second and third centuries it was a thing of the past. Its place had been taken by the *matrimonium liberum,* the free marriage.

As early as the Law of the Twelve Tables, dating from 450 B.C., free marriage was acknowledged as an option for women. That is, once she had reached the legally marriageable age of twelve years a girl could declare herself *sui iuris,* a legally free woman. From that time on no one had *patria potestas* over her. She could, and usually did, take a guardian, a *curator,* who administered her estate until she was twenty-five. She could betroth herself to and marry whom she chose. And in marrying she remained a free person; she did not pass into the *potestas* of her husband. Her estate remained her own; her husband could not touch it.

Indeed the woman so fortunate as to be a Roman citizen and married as such enjoyed a status singular among wives of the ancient world. Although she ordinarily took her husband's name, she was regarded as his equal. If he had social status, she shared it. Their home was as much hers as his, and in this home she had "first place" status according to law and tradition. This equality extended to her right to dissolve the marriage. And since Roman marriage was by tradition monogamous, no wife had to share her husband with another wife. But custom tarnished this equality severely by demanding fidelity of the wife but permitting the husband concubines and easy access to prostitutes and to female slaves.

About the procedure for marrying in Roman society, after the disappearance of the ancient ceremony of *confarreatio,* and with the diminishing to rarity of the marriage by *coemptio,* any fixed and traditional ceremony dwindled and disappeared. In the free marriage, which was the usual form as the imperial epoch began, there was virtually a formless transaction. There was no exchange of gifts. The conjunction of three causes was required to create a marriage and sufficed for doing so. The first was *connubium* possessed by both parties, the citizen's right to marry. Then there was *maritalis affectio,* the desire and the will of the parties to be married to one another. It was this *affectio* that differentiated marriage from any other kind of relationship. Finally this *affectio* had to be manifested in some mutual consent that could be verified. If the bride had not declared herself *sui iuris* but still lived under the authority of a *paterfamilias* or of a *curator,* his consent too was required.

Roman law before its classical period beginning in the second century recognized a quasi-expression of consent as sufficient to create a marriage. This was called *usus.* If a woman lived in sexual intimacy with the same man for one uninterrupted year, he acquired *manus,* or authority, over her provided their intent in living together was eventual marriage—although the laws specifying this effect of intent joined with duration may have been simply a way for the man to acquire *manus* over a woman already his wife by cohabitation alone. She could avoid coming under his *manus* by taking advantage of the *trinoctium,* a verifiable absence from him within that year of three successive nights.

As the free marriage, the *matrimonium liberum,* became from early in the empire the common arrangement of marriage, inevitably free divorce grew with it in availability. In theory at least marriage under Roman law was understood to be a stable, lasting relationship. And before the imperial epoch, during the republic and before, divorce had been kept in check by the custom that all serious decisions regarding marriage had to be submitted to a family council. But in practice marriage was divorced easily and frequently under Roman law by the time Christianity came to birth. Such dissolution required no judicial act by the state. The spouses needed to allege and prove no grounds in order to dissolve their marriage. They needed only to withdraw their *maritalis affectio* in a verifiable way—to "separate the marriage"—as we saw in the preceding chapter.

Because of the predominance of the free marriage and the reluctance of Roman law to prescribe any specific form of marital consent, traits of contract in this marriage were virtually non-existent. Because of the acceptability of the marriage by *usus* there was ultimately nothing to distinguish marriage from concubinage except the *maritalis affectio.* It was not until after the collapse of the empire in the West that elements of contractuality began to infiltrate marriage law and custom. The presence or absence of the *affectio* was naturally difficult to prove. This posed for authorities a minimal problem regarding the poor, the residual slave population and non-Christians. But among illustrious families the problem was taken as severe, since with the verification of a marriage there could go a transfer of considerable wealth and identification with a powerful family. So it became common even in the late Western empire to draw up in advance of the marriage a settlement of the size and nature of the dowry and of the nuptial gifts. Since this led to the popular error that the settlement touched the substance of marriage, the emperor Theodosius II in 428 enacted a law declaring the incidental character of the *dotis instrumenta,* the settlement of the dowry (*Constitutio Theodosii* 3, 7, 3).

One hundred years later, in 529–530, Justinian decreed that when a man and a woman living in concubinage, and having or being about to have an illegitimate child or children, began to regard one another with *maritalis affectio,* they could, by drawing up a dotal instrument, legitimize their children already born or conceived (*Constitutio Iustiniani* 5, 27, 10–11). In 542 he decreed that in order to be valid the marriages of *illustri* and higher dignitaries "must be marked by the conclusion of a marriage contract" (*Iustiniani Novella* 117, cap. 4). But Theodosius had already in his *Codex* decreed that every marriage concluded by mutual consent of the partners in the presence of several friends was valid (*Codex Theodosianus*—438 A.D.). Any secular or religious ceremony surrounding the consent was expressly placed outside the law's requirements for validity. And in his own reform Justinian had already decreed that the mutual consent of both parties sufficed for a valid marriage without further formalities (*Iustiniani Digesta* 35, 1, 15). What this also said, in the spirit of the third-century jurist Ulpianus' axiom, *Consensus non concubitus facit matrimonium,* was that a marriage is created not by intercourse nor by *usus,* but by the parties' consent.

One should not read later Catholic canon law back into this imperial legislation, even though the latter came from Christian emperors. Mutual consent according to this law did not bind spouses inseparably for life. It simply created a relationship and a socio-economic situation which lasted as long as the spouses chose to have it last. The *maritalis affectio* was the essence of the marriage. As long as it lasted, that is, as long as the man and woman willed to be husband and wife and regarded one another as spouses, the marriage lasted. When the *affectio* ended, the marriage ended—at least as far as imperial law was concerned.

The Definitions of Marriage in Roman Law

Distinct from these legislated characteristics and conditions of marriage were two definitions of it contained in Roman law of the imperial epoch.[2]

The first of these definitions is found in the *Digesta* (23, 2, 1) of the sixth-century Christian emperor, Justinian. It is attributed to the jurist, Herennius Modestinus, whose death three centuries earlier, c. 244, had marked the close of the period of classical jurisprudence in Roman law.

> Marriage is a union of a man and a woman, and a community [or sharing] of the whole of life, a participation in divine and human law. (*Nuptiae sunt coniunctio maris et feminae et consortium omnis vitae, divini et humani iuris communicatio.*)

The second definition is found in Justinian's *Instituta* (1, 9, 1), and although he is not there identified as its author, Domitius Ulpianus, a contemporary of Modestinus (d. 228), is said traditionally to be its author.

> Marriage, or matrimony, is a union of a man and a woman, a union involving a single [or undivided] sharing of life (*Nuptiae autem sive matrimonium est viri et mulieris coniunctio, individuam consuetudinem vitae continens.*)

Some scholars have challenged the authenticity, in whole or in part, of the definition attributed to Modestinus, saying that at least the last clause about divine and human law is a later Christian interpolation. Those who deny its classic jurisprudential authenticity altogether urge that the concept of marriage as a community of the whole of life is a later insertion of the Christian idea of permanence. That the fundamental permanence of marriage is not a Christian invention, and that Roman marriage had its origin in ancient religious consciousness, diminishes the force of the criticism.

Both definitions are descriptive, generic and therefore minimal. They intend to say what a relationship long in existence, indigenous to the definer's culture, is in itself. The key generic term in each is "union" (*coniunctio*): whatever else a marriage is, it is first of all a union. And both definitions agree that it is a union of one man and one woman (the possibility of polygamous or homosexual marriage is thus ignored by both definitions if not excluded). It is in the added, specifying clauses that the differences of one definition from the other emerge. But first it is important that the meaning of the shared generic term *coniunctio* be understood.

Consistently with its minimal, generic reference the term designates only the "living together" of the man and woman. It is a term that could be predicated of the *contubernium* to which Roman law limited slaves; it could even refer to the merely physical association of animals in their mating and shared nurture of their young as long as this lasted. By itself *coniunctio* designates nothing specifically human—not a union of minds and wills, and not any inherent end of marriage other than the implication that the union is a valuable relationship and should be preserved and perfected. The term brings into the definition of marriage a legal imprecision, since a couple can be married without in fact living together, without forming a stable community.

From this point the two definitions diverge. Modestinus' first differentiating phrase specifies that the *coniunctio* is a community, a sharing, of the whole of life. The etymology of *consortium* helps to understand this. Of the word's two components, *con-sors,* the second designates a person's lot in life, the first a sharing. Persons joined in a *consortium* are thus sharers in life's experience.

The *omnis vitae,* the "whole of life" of which a marriage is said to be a sharing, can have two meanings which are not mutually exclusive. The *omnis* can refer to the duration of life, and according to this reference the terms would say that a marriage is a permanent union. Or the *omnis* can refer to the quantitative inclusiveness, so to speak, of what the spouses share. Nothing—at least nothing of significance—in either spouse's life is left unshared. The effect of combining both meanings is to say that everything of significance in both lives is shared as long as both live. While this is not identical with the indissolubility of marriage as this trait was understood by St. Augustine and Catholic thinkers after him, it is clearly an excellent human matrix for it.

In his definition taken into the *Instituta* Ulpianus has "involving a single [or undivided] sharing of life" where Modestinus has "sharing of the whole of life." Both clauses seek to convey the notions of community, of sharing—to convey moreover the inclusiveness and the stability of the sharing. But Ulpianus' definition at this point lacks the exactness of Modestinus'. Fellhauer notes that "J. Gaudemet, in his essay 'La definition romano-canonique du mariage,' claims that while *consortium* evokes the old Roman familial community (extremely close-knit, united in private worship as well as by *patria potestas*), *consuetudo* designates etymologically 'common customs,' whence life in common. *Individua vitae consuetudo* is, however, a less expressive, less happy term."[3]

The final element of Modestinus' definition—"[A marriage is] . . . a participation in divine and human law"—has no equivalent in that of Ulpianus. If this clause is a later Christian interpolation, it may be an attempt to write more effectively into the law a claim for the wife, in the Christian understanding of marriage, which began with Jesus' denial to Jewish husbands of their right to dismiss their wives, and which was strengthened by St. Paul's insistence that husbands and wives share equal obligations and equal rights. An assertion that the wife shares in human and divine law, or rights, along with her husband, would strengthen her case considerably. But it is not necessary to say that the clause is such an interpolation. Roman tradition at least ideally accorded the wife a dignity of station equal to her husband's. And the *matrimonium liberum* that had become the usual structure of marriage since early in the empire gave at least informal legal status to her equality in such significant quarters of the marriage as her right to choose her own spouse. In either case the clause states that the husband and wife carry on a sharing (*communicatio*) of rights both human and divine. This seems to specify and strengthen even further the assertion of the definition's preceding phrase: "A marriage is a sharing in the whole of life." Within this inclusive sharing a husband and wife enjoy (equally?) rights that are both divine and human in their source and in their value.

It is obvious that in their defining—or redefining—of marriage the bishops of the Second Vatican Council went back to these articles from classical Roman law on marriage and borrowed almost verbatim from them. But even centuries before the Council these ancient definitions had had their effect on Catholic marriage law. Fellhauer evaluates this effect:

> It was in some ways fortunate for the early Church to find itself situated in a society where the law of marriage was the Roman law. There was much about Roman marriage which the Church could readily accept. It was monogamous, in principle permanent, in design procreative. Roman marriage was ideally a complete community of man and wife, a *corporum-coniunctio totius vitae,* which implied the duty of conjugal love. The Roman wife, unlike the woman in many other cultures, was accorded dignity

and respect. The Church added, of course, to this understanding
of marriage its own notion of indissolubility.[4]

Marriage in the Christian Communities of the Empire

A student of marriage expecting to find in the history of the first
Christian generations any striking difference between pagan marriages and
Christian marriages is bound to be disappointed. Differences there were,
but they were not the kind that met the eye. To begin with, since almost all
married Christians were adult converts, they had been married before becoming Christian. If both spouses had converted, or even if only one had,
they were made "holy" not by their marriage (whether thought of as a sacred sign or not), but by their baptism and their conduct in the Christian
community. Those who did marry after becoming Christian thought of
marriage in its essence just about what their pagan parents and siblings
thought of it. It was an association of a man and a woman distinguished in
nature from all other associations by a mutual *maritalis affectio* that could
be motivated in various ways: to provide children for the family, to have a
partner for help, for comfort, for pleasure, or—a reason rare because few
early Christians belonged to illustrious families—in order to join two great
family fortunes.

But there were significant differences of attitude. Within the first and
second Christian generations the intensity of eschatological expectation
had two inter-related effects. Where communities were convinced that history was nearing its end and that Jesus would soon return to judge the nations and to consummate his kingdom as he had promised, marriage was
understood to lack any significant purpose. Insofar as it might be for children, for the historical survival of the family, why marry for this purpose if
history was soon to end? There is no evidence of any conviction at this
time that men and women might wait for the end in more steadfast faith
and hope because they waited in the intimate company of a believing and
trusting spouse. One reason and one only argued for marriage in such a
setting of expectation: if one had not the gift of continence, it was better, as
Paul had said to the Corinthians, to marry than to burn—to burn while
waiting for the judgment and perhaps to burn after it as well.

Secondly, since the things of this world were passing away, since all
the great baggage of the world's business-as-usual was losing its meaning—
and marriage, family and family life were taken for granted to be this
world's business—an alert Christian freed himself or herself from all that.
A new life was available, a Spirit-filled life in the risen Christ, a life whose
epicenter was the taking of the good news of this new life as far and widely
as possible. Marriage and family life were at best irrelevant to this work, at
worst a crippling burden and a tie to the now unimportant past. To see and
to feel this freedom and to want it was a charism, the gift of celibacy. It
was what everyone ought to pray for even if not everyone received it. It
was the reason why Paul, a most charismatic man, advised all in the com-

munity that though they did well to marry, they did better not to (see 1 Corinthians 7:25–38).

One of the most significant differences about marriage among the early Christians was that they ignored the imperial law denying *connubium* to slaves and foreigners, the right to *matrimonium iustum* (the kind of marriage that could have legitimate children with the right to inherit), and limiting their sexual relationship to *contubernium*. From the beginning the Christians, in contravention of the law, opened to their slave members marriage with citizens. Pope Callistus I (217–222) was criticized by the Christian writer Hippolytus in his *Philosophoumena*[5] for violating civil law by allowing Christian women citizens to marry freedmen and even slaves. This was the first appearance in Christian history of "the marriage of conscience," a marriage kept secret from civil authority in violation of the law. And this conduct of Pope Callistus is the oldest solid evidence we have of effective episcopal intervention in the marriages of Christians. (Bishop Ignatius of Antioch's urging a century earlier, in his letter to St. Polycarp, that Christians marry under the authority of their pastor-bishops was effective only in the manner of exhortation.)

A second difference from ordinary Roman attitude and custom was the Christian rejection of divorce and the infidelity that led to it. Whatever the conduct of individual spouses, the words of Jesus were fixed in the Christian consciousness as normative: "But I say to you, he who even looks at a woman to lust after her has already committed adultery with her in his heart" (Matthew 5:28). A man who became Christian knew of this, and presumably accepted it and converted because he wanted to live in such a moral climate. He knew the Christian demand that wives be cherished and that the same moral obligations bind husbands and wives equally. The modern Christian may be hard put to appreciate the stark contrast of this with the normal genital whimsy of the Roman husband, for whom wife-stealing and wife-trading were common enterprises, and for whom the call at the neighborhood brothel was almost as usual as the business lunch of today.

What may be the most surprising lack of difference between early Christian marriages and those of their pagan neighbors was the manner of marrying, the ceremony or lack of it. We have already seen that no specific form for manifesting marital consent was imposed by Roman law except toward the end of the empire in the West on illustrious families high in imperial government. The Christians saw equally no reason to impose a specific ceremonial manifestation of consent. Marriage for them too was an affair of the family. Neither bishop nor priest was required to be present, and ordinarily none was. The fathers of the two families did the arranging in most cases. And at the wedding, if there was such a ceremony, the father of the groom presided. He and those whom he had invited witnessed the manifestation of consent—manifested simply or manifested multiply in some combination of handing over the dowry, of giving the pledges (the *arrhae*) including the wedding ring, of handing over the bride

by her father or the wedding page, of the *domum ductio* (the groom's leading his bride to their new home).

How thoroughly accepted was this non-religious and familial formation of marriage is evident in Canon 54 of the Synod of Elvira in Spain in
306. Its bishops accepted that the marriages of Christians were to be celebrated in the same way as those of pagans. The synod also accepted in
principle the authority of Roman legislation over Christian marriages, and
condoned Christians' taking marriage cases before the Roman courts.
There was in fact no distinct Christian wedding ceremony obligatory on all
members of the Church for the first nine centuries of Christian history.

Christian pastors entered the wedding ceremony only gradually and
at first informally. This occurred where they were invited to the wedding
feast and were asked to bless the bride and the groom. As pastors of Christian communities bishops often took over the care of orphan girls and
functioned as *paterfamilias* for them in helping them to find husbands. Although this practice was at first forbidden in the West, need and custom
gradually overcame the stricture and bishops came more and more to arrange the marriages of orphans and, as participants in the ceremony at
which the father of the groom, not the bishop himself, presided, to give the
bride in marriage. The actual presence of a bishop or priest at the ceremony, and his approval and blessing, were required by papal decree in the
fourth century only for the marriages of the lower ranks of clergy and of
catechumens. In the latter case the marriage was of an unbaptized person
with a baptized.

The oldest evidence of Christian marriage solemnized with a priest or
bishop officiating dates from the fourth century. From that time until the
eleventh century the liturgical setting of Christian marriages was enriched
progressively. But again, until the eleventh century, solemnization of marriage *in facie Ecclesiae* (in the presence of the Church) was never obligatory except for members of the lower clergy. It was forbidden for second
marriages and for those whose lives before marriage had been less than exemplary. As late as 866, according to evidence in the *Responsum ad Bulgaros* of Pope Nicholas I, marriages by mutual consent were accepted as
valid despite the lack of any ceremony at all, whether of a family, civil or
ecclesiastical nature.

Gradually from the fourth until the twelfth centuries the Church took
over full control of the marriages of her people. And gradually her law
came to consider marriage to be in essence a contract. (How it did so we
shall consider in a later chapter.) But it was not so in the beginning. Marriage understood as a contract is a product not of Jewish nor of Hellenistic-Roman law and custom. By the time of the classic Roman jurists in the
third century it was clearly enough established that the manifestation of
mutual consent was sufficient to create a marriage. But this was not considered consent in and to a contract. It did not have as its immediate object
to create obligations, but to bring the *consortium omnis vitae* into exis-

tence. Roman marriage was not a consensual contract but a state of life realized by the partners and ruled minimally by law.

Nor did the idea that the procreation and nurture of children are the primary end of marriage come from Roman law and tradition of either the classic or Byzantine periods. They were held implicitly during the Roman kingdom before 500 B.C. to be the primary end; so too during the early republic when the purpose of marriage was manifestly to preserve the cult of the family deities. But in the classical period the end and the *forma* of marriage were identical. These were the *consortium omnis vitae*, the joining and the sharing of the entirety of two lives in one.

NOTES

1. The source material on marriage in the Roman empire most available to an English-reading public is to be found in P. E. C. Corbett, *The Roman Law of Marriage*, Oxford, 1930. More general treatises are W. Buckland, *A Text-Book of Roman Law from Augustine to Justinian*, H. Jolowicz and B. Nicholas, *Historical Introduction to the Study of Roman Law*, F. Schulz, *Principles of Roman Law*. A widely-used treatise in French is by Gabriel LeBras in *Dictionnaire de Théologie Catholique*, "Mariage," Vol. 9.2. Recently David E. Fellhauer, a judge in the diocesan tribunal of Dallas, has published an excellent concise review of the history of the development of the Catholic understanding of marriage. It is titled "The *Consortium omnis vitae* as a Juridical Element," and occupies the entire volume 13.1 (1979) of *Studia Canonica*, the review of The Canon Law Society of Canada.

2. For this analysis of the two definitions I have borrowed heavily from the essay by David Fellhauer indicated in the preceding note, as also from Corbett's *The Roman Law of Marriage*.

3. *Art. cit.*, p. 16.

4. *Loc. cit.*, p.17. Fellhauer concludes this part of his essay: "The Roman-law definitions of marriage were themselves significant. The two celebrated formulations indicated explicitly the permanency of married life and evidenced an understanding of marriage as a unique conjugal community, an *individua consuetudo vitae*—or, in the more expressive phrase of Modestinus, a *consortium omnis vitae*. The two definitions evidently describe more than the legal aspects of marriage, but rather marriage as an ethical and social reality. Perhaps it is partly for this reason that the Roman-law definitions were destined to have a life of far greater duration than the culture from which they sprang." (*Ibid.*)

5. Liber IX, cap. 12 (PG 16:3386).

4. THE FATHERS OF THE CHURCH AND THE DEFENSE OF MARRIAGE

Unlike the Roman jurists Modestinus and Ulpianus, none of the teachers of the Church during the three and a half centuries before Augustine inquired about the nature of marriage as a social institution taken in abstraction from marriages in their real-life situation. Nor is it certain that Augustine himself ever did exactly that. The compelling reason for this absence of detached speculation was that these Church Fathers' teaching about marriage was in great part a counter-attack against assaults on marriage that cut at its very heart. This was first the Gnostic teaching that marriage is evil, and the paradoxical teaching of some Gnostics that sexual intercourse is of such high value that it must be freed from the burden of procreation. And once the Gnostic threat was subdued, the Manichees repeated the same condemnation of marriage.

The case that the Fathers had to make against the first of these challenges was simple and fundamental. It was to verify that marriage is not evil but good, and that sexual intercourse in marriage that intends procreation is good. The second challenge was more subtle: how to show that though sexual intercourse is good, it is not excessively good; that it is God's gift but is not an avenue to happiness—and is certainly not, as a few Gnostics insisted, *the* avenue to it.

Gnosticism as a religious interpretation of life and as a sectarian movement antedated the birth of Christianity.[1] It infiltrated the Church shortly after the latter's birth, as soon as it had left the womb of the first community in Jerusalem. It fastened itself like a parasite in a number of the nascent communities in the eastern Mediterranean basin and then moved westward. Its intent, and its threat, was to mutate the very nature of the way of life that had come from Jesus. It was in itself a mixture of Iranian myths, Jewish mysticism and Jewish magic. It fed on Greek and Chaldean philosophy and mysticism. It proposed itself, in its Christian form, as a champion of the freedom from the law brought by Jesus, and after him by Paul. The Gnostics considered themselves the superior Chris-

80

tians, in fact the only accurate and faithful interpreters of the Gospel. This was as much their statement of simple fact as an elitest boast, for they contended that the true Gospel consists of a secret knowledge, a *gnosis,* meant for an excellent few because only a few are capable of gaining this knowledge. And one of the indispensable conditions for gaining it was also the ground for the Gnostic contempt for marriage: a person must be sufficiently spiritual to do so. For the Gnostic this meant sufficiently free from the enemy of the spirit, which is corporeality in all its needs, desires and conduct.

The Gnostics held to two major points of doctrine that more than all others disagreed with orthodox Christian doctrine.[2] One was a predeterminism, a denial of the part played by free will in either a person's salvation or damnation. The most glaring by-product of this was the religious-anthropological categorization and distribution of the human race worked out by the Roman Gnostic, Valentinus. He saw all mankind divided into a tiny and elite group of "the spiritual," a somewhat larger group of "the psychic," and a huge majority of "the earthly," or "the animal." "The spiritual" Valentinus held to be predetermined to salvation, and nothing in their conduct could alter this fate. "The earthly" were just as immutably predetermined to damnation. As for the "the psychic," their fate alone depended on their free decisions in belief and conduct. Predictably the cadre of "the spiritual" was made up exclusively of the true Gnostics.

The second major point of Gnostic heterodoxy was their pessimistic view of the world and of the human race. This was no mere moral discouragement or psychological morosity. It was a cosmic pessimism. It saw evil not in the deprivation or perversion of goodness, but as a component of the universe equally as real as goodness. This pessimism was an ontological dualism; it fused moral evil with ontic evil, as it fused moral goodness with ontic goodness. Conveniently for the Gnostic system, the spiritual component of the universe is good, the material is evil. And this dualism-pessimism dictated a fundamental Gnostic attitude toward marriage and sexuality. These are obviously material, bodily enterprises. So radically, at their source and in their nature, they are evil. And since they are ontically evil, indulgence in them by a man or woman is morally evil.

Because the material sector of the universe was taken as evil, the Gnostics had to revise the traditional Jewish-Christian interpretation of the Creator and creation. The creator of this sector cannot be the good God whom Jesus revealed to be his Father and the father of the saved. Its creator is rather an inferior deity, a demiurge, who is evil. The God Yahweh-Elohim whom the Old Testament presents is this evil deity. Indeed the entire Old Testament is an earthly document produced by earthly men who have gone to their predetermined damnation.[3] Therefore what it says about marriage and sexuality—whether in commendation of marriage or in condemnation of certain kinds of sexual conduct—is at best worthless and at worst misleading and corrupting. The entire law set forth in the Old

Testament is fit to govern only the earthly, those men and women of animal souls. "The spiritual" have risen above this law; their perfect knowledge (their *gnosis*) has gained for them the freedom of the true sons of God that St. Paul claimed and preached.

Certain Gnostics offered variant explanations of this dualistic creation, bizarre borrowings from Eastern spiritualism. I shall review them presently and suggest how they affected the Gnostic attitude toward marriage and sexuality.

But to come at this attitude from a less crude source, one must note how orthodox Christianity itself fed the Gnostic inclination to spiritualism and thence to dualism. The Gnostics claimed to find clear support in the New Testament, in certain passages whose meaning they twisted to their own purposes.

Beginning with the assumption that Christians now live in a new age, the age of the Kingdom, they interpreted Jesus' words, "But woe to those who are with child or have infants at the breast in those days" (Matthew 24:19 and Luke 21:23) to mean that in the Kingdom there is, by Jesus' will, to be no childbearing. They found the same meaning in his words, "The children of this world take wives and husbands, but those who are judged worthy of a place in the other world and in the resurrection from the dead do not marry . . . for they are the same as the angels" (Luke 20:35–36). And they easily turned Jesus' disapproval of the man invited to the banquet who excused himself with "I have married a wife and so cannot come" (Luke 14:20) into the conclusion that those who marry are excluded from the eschatalogical banquet at the end of time. They pointed out too that Jesus himself had never married, and neither had John his precursor; they noted that Paul had married but had left his wife, and had told the Corinthians (as they understood his counsel): "It is good for a man not to touch a woman" (1 Corinthians 7:1).

Orthodox Attitudes Sympathetic to Gnosticism

Much as the orthodox Christian teachers might condemn the Gnostics' contempt for marriage and procreation as a threat to the human race itself, they could hardly have denied, had it been pointed out to them, that attitudes of their own unwittingly supported the Gnostics they condemned. Any Christian who took seriously Jesus' exhortation, "You must therefore be perfect as your heavenly Father is perfect" (Matthew 5:48), had to translate this into conduct as well as into attitude. Where in the multiple repertory of human conduct might he realize this perfection? Moreover, religious-moral perfection is a comparative state. The context itself of Jesus' exhortation had been his comparison of his new law with the law his followers had heard "said of old," and a comparison made to the consistent disadvantage of the old. Consequently it was easy for the Christian teachers to pick out the highly visible sexual irresponsibility of their pagan neighbors and locate the Christian effort at perfection, and concentrate it, in sexual conduct.

Not by way of forbidding marriage and the sexuality proper to it did they do this, since these were allowed and were even the object of the Lord's command in Genesis, but by extolling the life of virginity—with the obvious help from the preferential counsel Paul had given in 1 Corinthians 7: "I should like everyone to be like me" (verse 7); "Those who have wives should live as though they had none" (verse 29); ". . . an unmarried woman, like a young girl, can devote herself to the Lord's affairs; all she need worry about is being holy in body and spirit. The married woman, on the other hand . . ." (verse 34).

Diverse Gnostic Attitudes Toward Marriage

In Book 3, Chapter 5 of his *Stromata*[4] Clement of Alexandria explains that the Gnostics' dualist view of creation led to two disagreeing attitudes toward marriage and sexuality. These were the extremes of a rigorous and negative asceticism on the one hand, and a licentious, all-is-innocent antinomianism on the other. (Some modern scholars have identified a compromise position lying between these two extremes.) Whether and in what degree Clement's, and also Irenaeus', descriptions of the several sub-species of Gnosticism are accurate we have no way of knowing. But their accuracy is not at issue here, nor to the point. The point is their perception of the Gnostic threat whether accurate or inaccurate. For it was from this perception that the orthodox patristic defense of marriage came. It was their understanding of the Gnostic abuse of marriage and sexuality that produced their reasoned claim for the value of both.

The best-known of the ascetic Gnostics were the three, Marcion (in Rome, with his complete community having its own hierarchy and liturgy), Tatian (an Assyrian, converted probably in Rome, and a disciple there of Justin, the apologist and martyr), and Julius Cassianus (a dissenter from Valentinian Gnosticism, who taught in either Antioch or Alexandria ca. 170; he is identified with yet another Gnostic sub-group, the Encratites or "Self-Controlled").

It was Marcion especially who insisted that the Old Testament is the work of earthly, sensuous men, who in it tell of the inferior God, the evil creator of the material universe. According to Marcion it was this God who, as the Book of Genesis records, gave the command: "Increase and multiply." This was of a piece with his design to fill the earth with brutish men and women. No true Christian, no spiritual or even psychic believer in the Gospel, would listen to this command; none would engage in sexual intercourse and thereby increase the number of the brutish who are in any case predetermined to damnation. Therefore Marcion simply forbade his followers to marry or to engage in sexual conduct in any circumstance.

About Julius Cassianus we know only from Clement's reference to him in Book 3, Chapter 13 of the *Stromata*. Clement quotes there from his treatise, *Concerning Continence and Celibacy*, his condemnation of sexual intercourse, and in it gives a fair sample of the Gnostics' hermeneutic in defense of their position.

> At any rate in his book *Concerning Continence and Celibacy* he says these words: "And let no one say that because we have these parts, that the female body is shaped this way and the male that way, the one to receive, the other to give the seed, sexual intercourse is allowed by God. For if this arrangement had been made by God, to whom we seek to attain, he would not have pronounced eunuchs blessed; nor would the prophet have said that they are "not an unfruitful tree" [Isaiah 56:3], using the tree as an illustration of the man who chooses to emasculate himself of any such notion."[5]

The Gnostics whose teachings seem known in greatest detail were a group established in Alexandria, by the middle of the second century the intellectual capital of the Roman-Hellenistic world. These were the Carpocratians, a group of disciples gathered during that time and instructed by and taking their name from their master, Carpocrates. Clement lays the heaviest weight of blame upon the Carpocratians for bringing general suspicion of sexually dissolute conduct upon all Christians, even though Tacitus (in his *Annals* 15:44) and Pliny (in his *Epistles* 10:96) had reported this reputation in the first century. Celsus, the bitter pagan critic of Christianity (in his *On True Doctrine*, ca. 177–180), may have been in part the cause of Clement's judgment of the group. Celsus considered their religious ritual as licentious as the orgies of the devotees of Antinoous, the homosexual child favorite of Hadrian, who after drowning in the Nile in 130 was made by that emperor the object of a hero cult at Antinoopolis in Egypt.

In his *Against the Heresies*, Book 1, Chapter 25,[6] Irenaeus attempts a summary of Carpocrates' teaching. According to it the material universe has been created by the inferior angels. But Jesus, the son of Joseph of Nazareth, used in an extraordinary way his power of *anámnesis*, the Platonic recalling of what his spirit had gazed on in the divine sphere before being incarnated in birth. By dint of this he gained power from the Father, the highest and good God, by which he escaped from the control of the world-creators. Jesus gained this power by his purity and steadfastness. But those souls after Jesus who can gain the same power, now by true knowledge and by magic, can make the same escape from the world-creators. Since they have this power and have freed themselves from evil control, they can engage in any kind of conduct without danger. The moral right and wrong detailed by human law are no more than human conventions about what harms souls still vulnerable to harm. But they, the Carpocratians, are free and above this harm. They have already been saved by their faith and love, and of course by their secret knowledge. Finally, in order to avoid reincarnation after one's spirit has once departed the earthly sphere, the Gnostic must, before his departure, have every kind of experience—especially in the domain of sexuality. In this sense the Carpocratians interpreted Jesus' admonition (in Luke 12:59), "I tell you, you will not get out [of the debtors' prison] until you have paid the last farthing." Hence Irenaeus' indictment of the male Carpocratians (in *Against the Heresies,* Book 1, Chapter 25), that in their arrogance the teachers and spiritual leaders among them seduce their women followers, live with them, and—ironically—get them pregnant. It was entirely consistent with such ethical premises that the Carpocratians should make a religious ritual of sexual intercourse a means for entering the Kingdom of God. In any case Clement accuses Carpocrates and his associates (in *Stromata,* Book 3, Chapter 2) of even turning the last moments of the Eucharistic agape into a ritual of "holy" copulation.

The morality of the antinomian Gnostics was grounded in part in their singular cosmogony, their theory of the origin of the universe. This was explained in multiple ways by the many Gnostic sub-groups, and Irenaeus has an elaborate rehearsal of it in the first five chapters of Book 1 of *Against the Heresies.* But in general the cosmogony involved a monadic self-multiplication, a kind of caricature of the generation of the divine Word explained by orthodox theologians in the developing doctrine of the trinity of persons in God. Thus, at the beginning of all and the source of all was the entity called the Monad. It—or he or she, because the entity proved indeed fertile—was alone at first. But it seemed good to its unity not to be alone. It generated the Idea, then had intercourse with it, and from this came the invisible spirits, the "powers" of the universe.[7] These, when generated in the pre-ordained full number, will make up the *pléroma,* the fullness, of the universe.

To a fuller explanation of this notion of the *pléroma* I shall return in a moment. But two other representatives of the antinomian Gnostics deserve mention. One of these were the Nicolaitans, a group surfacing early in Christian Gnosticism. Their *Book of Apocalypse* was composed in the last few years of the first century, and in his letter to the Church in Ephesus the author mentions this group: "But you have this much in your favor: you detest the practices of the Nicolaitans, just as I do" (2:16). The others were the followers of Prodicus in Rome. They too defended their attitude and their conduct by twisting to their purpose New Testament passages on the theme of liberation. They called themselves "lords of the Sabbath" and "royal sons," and deemed themselves bound by no law. Clement accused them (in *Stromata,* Book 3, Chapter 4) of committing adultery in secret, considering themselves already predestinately saved, so that nothing they did could change this blessed fate.

Valentinus and the *Pléroma*

The notion of the *pléroma* makes its most developed appearance among the Gnostics in the teaching of Valentinus. He was an Egyptian who claimed to have studied under a certain Theodas, a personal disciple of Paul. He first taught in Alexandria, then came to Rome, and stayed and taught there until Hyginus became bishop of the city and Pope, from 135 to 160. Valentinus' followers became the best known of all the Gnostics.

Valentinus approved of marriage, but his reason for doing so was most unusual. The remote source of this reason was the Platonic-Hellenistic notion that earthly structures imitate heavenly structures, and that accordingly earthly conduct ought to imitate its heavenly models. According to Valentinus the godhead, which is the *pléroma,* consists of thirty spiritual beings, the aeons. The *pléroma* began its cosmogonic history with the aeon *Bythos* (Depth or Abyss) and his consort *Sige* (Silence). Their marriage produced *Nous* (Mind) and *Aletheia* (Truth). This pair in turn produced *Anthropos* (Man) and *Ecclesia* (Church). These eight form the cosmic Ogdoad, and from it the rest of the *pléroma* evolves gradually until the full thirty aeons are attained. In this Gnostic sect the sacred marriages of the aeons served as the model for the Gnostic bride and groom on earth. The latters' experience of marriage and sexuality were a counterpart and an imitation of the very life of the godhead; the experience was a foretaste of the final happiness of the Valentinian spouses after death.

(The concept of the *pléroma* was taken into the christology of the early Church, a christology that antedated Valentinus' teaching. We find it expressed clearly in the Christus-hymn of Paul's Letter to the Colossians, 1:15–20. The poet, whether Paul himself or some anonymous Christian, says first (in verse 16) that the totality of all things, *ta panta,* in heaven and on earth, was created in Christ. The poet gives a sampling of the hierarchy he has in mind: Thrones, Dominations, Sovereignties, Powers. All these were created through Christ and for Christ. In verse 19 he seals his thought by using the word itself: the divine plan from the beginning has been that the *pléroma,* the fullness and the fulfillment of the universe, be found in Christ. And (in verse 20) this is to be done by Christ's bringing all creatures together in peace by his death on the cross. That this faith-assertion about Christ is a reply to the Gnostic belief is hardly to be doubted.)

The Gnostic linking of the *pléroma* of aeons to their sexual conduct lay in this, that some of them thought this fullness would come only through the emission of their seed by spiritual men on earth. Apparently with each emission another of the aeons took its place in the hierarchy of celestial beings. If the orthodox teachers of the time searched for some purpose for sexual intercourse—some purpose beyond the act itself, nobler than it, one that would take it beyond mere pleasure-seeking—these Gnostics offered them a noble find. What nobler purpose could a man's and a woman's intercourse on earth have than to generate a spiritual being and thereby bring the divine history nearer its goal? This was to do the work of the godhead itself. And it was perfect without any reference to human reproduction.

The other group of Gnostics of this middle way between asceticism and sexual license were Basilides, his son Isidore and their followers. Basilides himself taught in Alexandria between 120 and 140; he claimed to have received his doctrine from a certain Glaukias, the interpreter of St. Peter. He taught that to marry is not a sin, that it is better, as St. Paul said, to marry than to burn. But, he insisted, marriage and its sexual involvement are obstacles to Christian perfection. Irenaeus had different information about Basilides. He reported in Book 1, Chapter 24 of *Against the Heresies,* Basilides' saying that marriage and the bearing of children are from Satan, but that the practice of lusts is at the same time a morally indifferent matter.

The Androgynous God of the Gnostics

Running through much of this Gnosticism, and apparently coming from rabbinic teaching of the time, was a belief in the androgynous character of the divine.[8] An androgynous divine being was said to have played an essential role in creating the universe. (We have seen a hint of this in the Carpocratian cosmogony of the Monad, which was said to have begun creation by generating out of itself Idea.) Thus in implicit contradiction of the premise in the creation poem of Genesis 1 that the Creator transcends sexuality, this cosmogony proposed a creator who is inclusively sexual. And since nature is created in imitation of the divine, divine androgyny is the model and the ideal for human sexuality.

Logically this may lead to two main consequences in human attitude and conduct: sexual intercourse is not for procreation but for the partners' experiencing in themselves the divine ideal—that is, the blending of the sexes instead of their fruitful interaction is the ideal; and the Gnostic, who has the true knowledge of the divine, is to locate the experience of androgynous sexuality, the full repertory of sexual experiences, at the center of his or her life. (According to Irenaeus, Carpocrates believed the latter and advocated it.) One consequence of this attitude for sexuality was to void it of any reason for situating it within marriage, and therefore of any reason for confining it to marriage. For if sexuality finds its reason in richness of experience, marriage would only constrict it and procreation would worsen the constriction.

Whether derived from these quasi-doctrinal elements or only concomitant with them, some Gnostics held that in the communities of true believers the women should be available for marriage, or at least for intercourse, with any man. Presumably this was to be both a sign and an enacting of the full freedom of those who are already saved for having attained the true knowledge.

Clement reports this in Chapter 2 of Book 3 of the *Stromata:* "But the followers of Carpocrates and Epiphanes think that wives should be com-

mon property." He explains how these Gnostics come to this as a conclusion of their theology: the universal righteousness of God intended that in
creation there be no difference and separation; that as all differences are
included in himself and there reconciled in non-difference (here is the androgynous trait of divine sexuality), so in creation there ought to be no difference and separation: "The righteousness of God is a kind of universal
fairness and equality. There is equality in the heaven which is stretched out
in all directions and contains the entire earth in its circle. . . . There is no
distinction between rich and poor, people and governor, stupid and clever,
female and male, free men and slaves. . . . And for birth there is no written
law (for otherwise it would have been transcribed). All beings beget and
give birth alike, having received by God's righteousness an innate equality.
The Creator and Father of all with his own righteousness appointed
this. . . . He did not make a distinction between female and male, rational
and irrational, nor between anything and anything else at all. . . . God
made all things for man to be common property. He brought female to be
with male and in the same way united all animals. He thus showed righteousness to be a universal fairness and equality."[9]

The Orthodox Answer to the Gnostics

Such, in review, was the double and disparate Gnostic attack on marriage as the orthodox Christian teachers perceived it (Clement's and Irenaeus' perception of it was typical). From the rigorist right, so to speak,
came the condemnation of marriage and sexuality as evil, the invention of
an evil deity; from the antinomian left came the claim that all and any kind
of sexual conduct is at least permitted to those who are already freed from
the world-creating powers and their obsolete law, and even demanded of
those who would imitate on earth the divine ideal and thus begin divine
beatitude here. In either case marriage was the victim—a fatality—either
condemned as evil or ignored as meaningless.

It was comparatively easy for the Fathers to counter the fundamental
claim of the ascetics that marriage, sexuality and procreation are evil.
(Clement undertakes this in Chapter 5 of Book 3 of the *Stromata*. Irenaeus
distributes his refutation of all the Gnostics through Books 2 and 3 of his
Against the Heresies.) To counter this claim it was necessary only to verify
two points of fact against the ascetics. The first was that marriage is the
invention of the one and true God, the creator of all the universe, and is
therefore good a priori, from its cause. The second was the a posteriori fact
that Christian marriages have produced martyrs and virgins, and therefore
cannot be fundamentally and in every case evil.

About the first of these points of fact the Fathers meant more than
that men and women have a natural need and desire for marriage designed
into them by God. They read as factual history both the creation poem in
Genesis 1 and the Garden of Eden parable in Genesis 2 and 3. Consequently they understood these divinely inspired "histories" to say that the initial

form in which God created the human race was that of a heterosexual couple made man and wife from the moment of the woman's formation from
the rib taken from the man's side (in the Garden parable) or from the simultaneous beginning of their existence (in the creation poem). This point
of interpretation of the history of marriage became a principle of almost all
else they taught about it. For example they reasoned from it to the falsity
of the Gnostic (and later the Manichean) charge that marriage is a sinful
state. At least in its primitive and pure state before the first couple's sin it
must have been innocent because God invented it. Clement pointed to this
in Chapter 12 of Book 3: "If marriage . . . is a sin, I do not see how a person can say he knows God when he says that the law of God is a sin. But if
'the law is holy,' marriage is holy." Irenaeus' form of refutation is in Book
1, Chapter 28: "Saturninus and Marcion, who are called the Continent,
preached abstinence from marriage, frustrating that age-old creation of
God and implicitly finding fault with Him who made human beings male
and female so that they could reproduce themselves. They introduced abstinence from what they described as 'animal-like,' ungrateful as they are
to Him who made everything, God".

But these ripostes grounded in what the Fathers regarded as historical
fact did not identify the interior goodness of marriage. For them to argue
that marriage is good because it has a good source and produces good fruit
was not yet to explain wherein lies its inherent goodness. It was the challenge coming from the antinomians on the left that drove the Fathers to
search for this goodness in marriage.

The Reply to the Antinomian Gnostics

The issue that the sexual permissiveness of the antinomians forced on
the Fathers was at first level one of conduct, of adultery in face of God's
command, "Thou shalt not commit adultery," and of fornication in face of
its condemnation in the New Testament by Jesus (Mark 7:22) and by Paul
(1 Corinthians 6:12–20; 10:6–10). The issue also had its public counte-
nance that I have already mentioned, the scandal taken by high-minded
and disciplined pagans like Tacitus, Pliny, Celsus and Porphyry. Their
harsh judgment of the Christians, just because it drew on enough fact to
make it plausible, demanded a reply from the Christian authorities. These
gave it readily. But the reply had to be more than just a restatement of the
facts, a correction made by pointing at examples of Christian continence
that were extraordinary.

For beyond the merely moral problem thrown up by the antinomian
Gnostics' teaching and conduct was the deeper and subtler question that
surfaced at the point where the two Gnostic attacks on marriage converged. Against the ascetics' condemnation of marriage and sexuality it
seemed sufficient to insist on marriage's origin in the creative will of the
one and true God. But from the antinomians came the apparently absurd
suggestion that sexuality is good because valuable in itself—valuable as an

experience that asserts and demonstrates freedom, or that cooperates in completing the *pléroma* of the universe, or that enables men and women to imitate on earth the conduct of the spirits, or that gives them a foretaste of the bliss that awaits them in the next life. These values were proposed as transcending the ordinary morality of man-made law. None of them needed marriage as locus and instrument of their realization. And none of them had any necessary link with procreation. The grave challenge then to the Fathers was not so much to verify the goodness of marriage and sexuality, but to verify a meaning for sexuality that could justify the Jewish and Christian tradition that insisted it be kept within marriage.

The First Sin and Sexuality

Before examining the Fathers' search for this meaning and purpose we must take note of an assumption that rules their thinking on the subject inside and out, from top to bottom. It was an assumption about a moment in history, an assumption about it that had become all but doctrine. This was that the narrative early in the Book of Genesis of the sin of the first man and woman is an account of what actually happened at the dawn of history. The first husband and wife disobeyed God's command; they ate the fruit of a tree which he had forbidden them to eat. All of human life since that moment—all of human life collectively and every human life singly—has been affected disastrously by that first sin, and will be so affected until the end of time.

Sexuality and marriage have been caught up in the disaster, caught up in an especial way because the Genesis narrative shows that the dynamic of the temptation leading to the sin began with a fatal curiosity and pride in the first man's sexual partner. The centrality in the sin of the couple's sexuality is evident in the punishment laid upon the woman. Childbirth, the fruit of her sexual activity, was henceforth to be an agony for her. Despite this she would crave her husband sexually. Because of this, and because she had led him into sin, he would until the end of time be her lord.

Seeing the first disaster-bringing sin as occurring in a moment of time in a married couple's history suggests that before that moment their marriage had been different. And supposing too that their marriage and its conduct before the sin was God's design, the suspicion is inescapable that the sin has done something disastrous to this design. This complicates our earlier questions about marriage's meaning and purpose. What was God's original intent for it? What had he meant marriage to be for a race of men and women he had intended to remain obedient and sinless? What has the first couple's sin done to his intent, his plan for marriage? Destroyed it utterly? Damaged it, but reparably? Changed it in some important way? Left it untouched?

It hardly needs to be said that none of the Fathers proposed the last of these as an answer. The most detailed consideration of the effects of the first sin on God's plan for marriage is, of course, Augustine's. It will be examined later as part of the inclusive outline of the Fathers' answer to the question about the meaning of marriage forced on them by the Gnostics and then the Manichees. But for the moment it is interesting to glance at some samples of the most radical speculation on the consequences for marriage of the first sin. This includes the thesis that in some way sexuality, and derivatively marriage, are effects of the sin, and that had the sin not been committed, there would be no need for sexuality and hence for marriage.

The most resolute advocate of this thesis was Origen, a pupil of Clement at Alexandria and his successor, at the beginning of the third century, in the headmastership of the catechetical school in that city. He put the case with little qualification: one of the effects of the first couple's sin was that marriage came into existence. This was really of a piece with his theory of the source of evil in human experience. He thought that human beings themselves come into existence as angelic spirits that fall from preexistent beatitude into the condition of souls trapped in human bodies. In short, the genesis itself of the human race has been a kind of cosmic misfortune, and sexuality is an unfortunate if necessary instrument for providing bodies for the fallen spirits. St. Jerome's criticism of Origen's theory tells us what this was: "How can the Apostle Paul write, 'I wish the young widows to marry and beget children'? Is he commanding marriage so that the bodies born of women may furnish prisons for angels who have fallen from heaven and are turned, according to you, into souls?"[10]

A century later two other of the Greek Fathers suggested what was in effect a mitigated version of Origen's interpretation. They did not, like him, see the sinfulness of the human race to be the fallen condition of angels. Rather it is a state of moral guilt and of consequent interior disorder brought on by the disobedience of the first man and woman, the parents of the race. Gregory, bishop of Nyssa in Cappadocia in the second half of the fourth century, suggested a conclusion that he was convinced must be drawn from Jesus' reply to the Sadducees' attempt to trap him in their dilemma about the woman who had had seven consecutive husbands: "You are badly misled because you fail to understand the Scriptures and the power of God. When people rise from the dead, they neither marry nor are given in marriage, but live like the angels in heaven" (Matthew 22:29–30).

Gregory reasoned that since the life of those restored to original innocence after the resurrection at the end of time will be like that of the angels, then the innocent life of the first parents before their sin must also have been like that of the angels. He pointed out the obvious, that there was no need for sexual intercourse in this once-regnant angelic condition:

> For although there is no propagation among the angels, as we have noted, their host is still in some sense infinite in number. . . .
> Therefore if we had not fallen because of sin from the condi-

tion and rank in which we were equal to the angels, not even for us would there have been any need of marriage to increase our kind.[11]

Gregory's implication is clear enough: God had had in mind another way for effecting the increase of the human race, a way identical with or at least similar to the way he had created the myriad angels. That human beings are instead produced by sexual intercourse is a change of plan, and it is a change brought on by the sin of the first parents, which Gregory thought (echoing Origen's thought from a distance) had as its effect a fall from an angelic state. He does not here say that a sexuality that would have been kept innocently dormant was awakened and set loose by the first parents' sin. He apparently means that sexuality had been kept in reserve as a kind of backup system for propagating the human race. If this is what he means, he also implies clearly that what the correlated heterosexual capacity in fallen mankind is for is procreation, and for nothing else.

John Chrysostom, bishop of Constantinople and a contemporary of Gregory, agreed that marriage has come into existence as a consequence of the first couple's sin. But he thought it intended to serve one more purpose than Gregory cited. This is to provide men and women, indeed the whole of mankind, with a refuge for lustful passion.

> That age [the generations following immediately on the first sin] demanded it [marriage] with human nature raging and neither standing firm against the attack of sensuality nor having any port to flee to for safety in the storm.
>
> What was commanded? That they live in continence and virginity? Why that would have caused a greater fall and a more vehement flame. . . . That is why virginity was not given in the beginning; or rather, that is why, though virginity did exist in the beginning—even before marriage—marriage thrust itself on the scene and seemed necessary; whereas if Adam had remained obedient, there would have been no need of it.
>
> "But who," he says, "would have begotten so many thousands of men?"
>
> Since this anxious fear haunts you, I ask in turn where Adam came from and Eve came from when there was no marriage.
>
> "What then? Is that the way all men were to have been born?"
>
> Whether in this way or some other way is not for me to say. The point is that God did not need marriage to fill the earth with men.[12]

Chrysostom's logic is simple and his interpretation cruel, both in what they offer explicitly and in what they only imply. God has at his disposition plural ways of producing human beings. His way of forming Adam and Eve shows this. Presumably he could have continued to produce the entire race in the same way even after the first sin. But the sin brought a compelling reason for setting human sexuality to this task. The reason? To keep this sexuality within control. The form of the control? First of all by giving sexuality something reasonable to do and, one may hope, thereby luring it away from lustful vagrancy.

Soon after Chrysostom wrote this in Constantinople Augustine was to begin nearly a quarter-century's development of the thought that marriage is a *remedium*—a refuge and a medicine—for lust. But I think that there is this difference in their thinking: Augustine, as we shall see, insisted that among the reasons for marriage procreation is primary. But for Chrysostom, at least in this essay, marriage's primary reason is precisely to serve as a refuge for sexuality turned wanton by the sin of the first parents. Its service for procreation is a divine afterthought and fundamentally unnecessary.

Marriage's Inferiority to the Celibate Life

These judgments on marriage by Origen, Gregory and Chrysostom were not speculative assessments of its nature taken in abstraction. They were evaluations of marriage's place in history, of its function in human conduct that has been perverted seriously by the sin of the first couple. They took for granted that the perversion is hereditary and that it is universal in sexual relationships in all ages and places until the end of time.

This was the taken-for-granted, real-life situation of marriage with which any of the Fathers who set out to answer the Gnostics had to reckon. However urgently they sought to demonstrate against the ascetics that marriage is good, they had to begin with the sad acknowledgement that its goodness carries in it somewhere the infection of sin. (Against the antinomians the acknowledgement was used as the premise in the argument demonstrating that sexual intercourse is not the beginning on earth of eternal happiness nor cooperation with the spirits in completing the *pléroma*.)

It was this mood of marriage as somehow wounded and drained of its original value that the Fathers met when they looked in the New Testament for divinely inspired evidence to use against the Gnostics. What they found there were not assertions of the sin-infection that had got at marriage. The Gospels especially were too Jewish to forget that marriage as a man-woman relationship established in history is one of the Lord God's most precious gifts. What they found was rather a kind of obverse correlate of marriage as sin-infected.

Running as an all-embracing theme through the New Testament is the assumption that with Jesus' death and resurrection an old and tired age had come to an end, the age of sinfulness and the law, and that the new age has begun, the age of the Kingdom, of hope, of loving care, of eager waiting for the climax of history. (Many modern Christians fail to notice this theme, probably because nineteen centuries after the Gospel's first proclamation they sense themselves standing at the end of an old and tired age.) The simplest version of this attitude in primitive Christianity was that history is divided into the old and obsolete on the one hand, and on the other the new creation brought by Christ. Marriage's unfortunate place in this vision of things was that good though it may have been in God's original intent, it now belongs to the old and the obsolete. It is tolerable in the new age and has uses (about which most Christians were vague in face of their belief that history was soon to end). But it is passé.

Another facet of this vision and this mood was the conviction that since Christ's resurrection has brought the new age, anything of life carried across into it from the old age must experience redemption. It must be cleansed of its old sinfulness. In an earlier chapter we saw a quite concrete example of this redemption and purification of the old. The moral-religious principle underlying Jesus' reply to the Pharisees who came to test him on the issue of divorce was that the question in which they formulated their test had lost its meaning. The husband-wife relationship was now simply different from what they assumed it to be. The wife is not the husband's property to be disposed of at his pleasure. Their relationship is two-in-one flesh, as God had intended in the beginning that it be.

This theme of sexuality and marriage cleansed and redeemed surfaces again and again in multiple guises throughout the New Testament. What I propose to do for the next few pages is to review the main variations on this theme. The reader will probably notice quickly that one variant is the conviction that marriage as a condition or state of life has a preferred rival, the state of dedicated celibacy. One should also not forget that in every New Testament passage an orthodox teacher found expressing sexuality and marriage's redemption or need of redemption, a Gnostic teacher could find a divinely inspired vote of no confidence.

Paul's instruction on marriage sent to the Corinthian Christians in his first letter to them (scholars say really his second letter to them, since an earlier one has been lost) stuck vividly in the early Christian mind just because it touched the kinds of concerns about marriage shared by many of the young churches. Paul is careful to set the unshakable premise that the married state is not sinful (verse 28), that it is a gift from God (verse 7), that those who are already married should remain so (verse 24) because a time of crisis and coming judgment is not the time for a substantive change of life ("I tell you, brothers, the time is short. . . . For the world as we know it is passing away . . ." (verses 29 and 31), and that it is better to lead a normal married life than to be tormented by unrelieved sexual urgency (verse 9b).

These points established, Paul then registers his doubts and worries. Although it is good as a safeguard against sin that spouses keep up sexual relations, he prefers that they be like himself—married (probably) but living a celibate life removed (probably) from his wife (verse 7). It is good that a man have no sexual relations at all (almost certainly the Fathers understood verse 1—"A man is better off having no relations with a woman"—as Paul's own mind, not as his rhetorical repetition to the Corinthians of their own letter's first question to him). While the married state is surely not sinful, it is full of trials (verse 28) and of its nature it distracts spouses from attention to the Lord and takes them away from his work (verses 32–35). A man who has an unmarried virgin in his care does well if he gives her in marriage, but he does better if he persuades her to continue unmarried (verses 36–38). (Some prefer to interpret the instruction as saying that such a man does well if he himself marries the girl. But the verb that Paul uses—*gamízein*—does not support this. It signifies "to give in marriage.") Because the time is short, it is better for the married to live as though they were not; celibacy is the better survival condition for the Christian about to enter the crisis of judgment or of persecution (verse 29). A far more urgent formulation of this advantage is Jesus' own in his eschatalogical discourse: "It will go badly with pregnant and nursing women in those days" (Matthew 24:19; Mark 13:17).

The advice (that may well be Paul's) to two young heads of Christian communities about marriage for men of their station tells more of the attitude accepted in the earlier churches. To Timothy he insists that a bishop must be a man of one wife (1 Timothy 3:2); to Titus that a presbyter must be the same (Titus 1:6). This does not mean that otherwise accepted polygamy is forbidden the heads of the Christian communities. It means either that these must not remarry if their marriages end in dissolution (less likely) or more likely that they must not remarry even though their marriages end with the death of the wife. Why Paul gives this advice he does not explain. But his implication is clear that for the heads of the communities he prefers celibacy.

Certain words of his advice in 1 Corinthians take on special impact when combined with two other lapidary Pauline statements about sexual desire. If the reader of 1 Corinthians 7:5 and 7:9 draws from these verses that Paul saw only one justifying reason for marriage in a time of crisis—that it offers protection from sins of the flesh—what conclusion is he to draw when he reads Paul writing to the Romans (13:14), "Rather put on the Lord Jesus Christ and make no provision for the desires of the flesh"; and to the Galatians (6:7–8) "A man will reap only what he sows. If he sows in the field of the flesh, he will reap a harvest of corruption; but if his seed-ground is the spirit, he will reap everlasting life"? The reader could succumb easily to the temptation to run the logic of the two statements in reverse and conclude that only those who make no provision for the desires of the flesh put on the Lord Jesus Christ, and that only those who sow in the seed-ground of the spirit rather than in that of the flesh will reap everlasting life.

What the anti-Gnostic Fathers could find about marriage in the Gospels favored the celibate life over marriage less explicitly. But what was there implicitly was no less powerful a preferential judgment. To begin with, according to the Infancy Narrative in Matthew and Luke Jesus was conceived not by sexual intercourse but by miraculous divine intervention. His mother was a virgin at his birth, and according to an added element in the early tradition she kept her virginity throughout her married life. John, the man who prepared the way for Jesus' ministry, his precursor in announcing the imminent kingdom, was remembered as a desert-dwelling celibate.

Becoming a committed follower of Jesus during his ministry seemed to call for a life torn free from home and family and by implication from marriage. True, Jesus' first disciples, and the select twelve among them, were married. But his call to them was away from their married lives: "With that they brought their boats to land, left everything and followed him" (Luke 5:11). Jesus was uncompromising in the need to set his work ahead of even the dearest ties of love: "Whoever prefers father or mother, son or daughter to me is not worthy of me" (Matthew 10:37b); "If anyone comes to me without turning his back on his father and mother, his wife and children, his brothers and sisters, indeed his very self, he cannot be my follower" (Luke 14:26).

In a statement akin to these Jesus put off the members of his own blood family to make clear who are his true kin: "He said in reply, 'Who are my mother and my brothers?' And gazing around him at those seated in the circle he continued, 'These are my mother and my brothers. Whoever does the will of God is brother and sister and mother to me' " (Mark 3:33–35; Luke 8:19–21). This necessary willingness to leave all things and all loved ones for the following of Jesus will be rewarded in the next life with beatitude that is beyond measure: "Moreover, anyone who has given up home, brothers or sisters, father or mother, wife or children or property for my sake will receive many times as much and inherit everlasting life" (Matthew 19:29; Luke 18:28–30). Again, as above, it was easy to revise the logical consequence here and to interpret the giving up of everything and everyone as a condition for gaining everlasting life.

The likelihood that gaining eternal life itself may be conditioned by a person's willingness to forego marriage is suggested by an easily optional interpretation of three other Gospel passages. One of them, Jesus' reply (in Matthew 22:29–30, Mark 12:18–27 and Luke 20:27–38) to the Sadducees who tried to trap him in a *reductio ad absurdum* about life after death, we have already seen. He shattered the Sadducees' argument by pointing out that among those risen from the dead there is neither marrying nor giving in marriage, but only an angelic life. When, in one of his parables on the eschatalogical banquet, he contemned those who offer insufficient excuses for refusing to come to it, he included one man who said "I am newly married and so I cannot come" (Luke 14:20).

Such an inventory of New Testament passages disfavoring marriage is of course selective and tears them from their contexts, some of which point to other meanings than the serious disadvantage of married life for the followers of Jesus. But the passages were there to be used by the Christians of the middle second century—by the Gnostic ascetics for building their case, by the orthodox Fathers for challenging that case as best they could. The latter were not helped, as I have said, by the fact that Jesus' words most clearly in praise of marriage, on his side of the debate with the Pharisees, were almost exclusively taken from the Old Testament that the Gnostics rejected. These words were therefore a dulled polemical weapon for use against them. Paul's exhortation to holiness in family life in Ephesians 5:22—6:4, and in Colossians 3:18–21, could be taken as words of counsel to men and women who had already made the unfortunate choice of marrying and forming a family. How strapped for scriptural ammunition against the Gnostics the orthodox Fathers could find themselves is exemplified in Clement's feeble attempt (in *Stromata,* Book 3, Chapter 10) to make Jesus' words, "Where two or three are gathered together in my name, there I am in the midst (Matthew 18:20), to refer to a family of Christians. As for procreation itself, the only New Testament passage favoring it explicitly as an instrument in the economy of salvation was the word of instruction to women in 1 Timothy 2:15: "She [women in general] will be saved through childbearing, provided she continues in faith and love and holiness—her chastity being taken for granted." But even this careful encomium of motherhood is the literal bottom line of a gentle scolding of Christian women for stepping out of their submissive place by attempting to teach in the community, to exercise some kind of unspecified authority. Motherhood is part of the life-pattern defined also by the slightly earlier admonition in the same letter, "A woman must learn in silence and be completely submissive . . . she must be quiet" (verses 10–11). The reason volunteered for this womanly silence and submissiveness played perfectly into the hands of the Gnostic ascetics: "I do not permit a woman to act as a teacher, or in any way to have authority over a man; she must be quiet. For Adam was created first, Eve afterward; moreover it was not Adam who was deceived but the woman. It was she who was led astray and fell into sin" (verses 12–13).

The Traditions of Marriage-for-Procreation

Such were the passages in their Scriptures available to those Fathers who searched in them for the comparative values of marriage and celibacy. As they interpreted them they saw themselves with no choice but to institute their defense with the acknowledgement that marriage is the religiously and morally inferior state, the default vocation for those Christians lacking in courage. The God who had said it is not good for the man to be alone, and had given him the woman as his partner, had done this in an age that had passed away, within a covenant that had failed in sinfulness. Now in the new age and covenant the same God seemed to have called both men and women to a higher life, up out of the sinfulness to purity and perfection. Since this was just the point that the ascetic Gnostics made the heart of their doctrine and discipline, what was left that the Fathers could say in defense of marriage, that could justify Christians' continuing in it even though it is admittedly inferior and perhaps at its best a safeguard for the weak?

They could go back to the same Scriptures in which they had found the case for the superiority of celibacy. There they could find—and many did find—the Hebrew version of an ancient, multi-source tradition that marriage is an *officium,* a societal duty; it is an institution whose value is pragmatic in that by nature it is meant to serve a purpose beyond itself. This purpose is to provide members for society, for continuing civilization's multiple societies—the family, including its clan and tribal dimension; the state and the sub-groups or classes within the state such as the nobility or the hereditary priesthood; and, if it is distinct from all the aforementioned, the religious society, the *ecclesia.*

In the tradition of Israel it was taken for granted that whatever the motives impelling this or that man to marry, the relationship itself had been invented by God, and invented for fertility, for offspring and family. The very words in which he was thought to have invented marriage were God's command to the first couple to procreate and use this procreation socially: "Be fertile and multiply; fill the world and subdue it" (Genesis 1:28).

How close to the core of marriage's meaning in this tradition was fertility is evident in the ancient commendation of polygamy and concubinage. In the sagas of Israel's patriarchs the chosen wife, Sarai, was at first unable to bear children to Abram. Because of this she gave her maidservant, Hagar, to him as his concubine, urging him to have intercourse with her so as to come by a son (Genesis 16:1–4). Two generations later Rachel did the same thing for Jacob, her husband and Abram's grandson. Roland deVaux writes of the importance of children to the Israelites:

> In ancient Israel, to have many children was a coveted honor, and the wedding guests often expressed the wish that the couple would be blessed with a large family. As Rebecca leaves her family, she is blessed with the words: "O sister of ours, become the mother of thousands of ten thousands" (Genesis 24:60). When Boaz marries Ruth, the wish is expressed that his young wife may be "like Rachel and Leah, the two who built up the house of Israel" (Ruth 4:11–12). First Abraham and then Isaac received the promise that their posterity would be countless as the stars in the sky (Genesis 15:5; 22:17; 26:4). God promised Hagar, too, that her posterity would be past counting (Genesis 16:10). Children are "the crown of a man" (Proverbs 17:6), and sons are "olive plants around the table" (Psalm 128:3), "a reward, like arrows in the hand of a hero; happy the man who has his quiver full of them" (Psalm 127:3–5).
>
> Sterility, on the other hand, was considered a trial (Genesis 16:2; 30:2; 1 Samuel 1:5), or a chastisement from God (Genesis 20:18), or a disgrace, from which Sarah, Rachel and Leah all

tried to clear themselves by adopting the child which their maids bore to their husbands (Genesis 16:2; 30:3, 9).

All these texts show that the Israelites wanted mainly sons, to perpetuate the family line and fortune, and to preserve the ancestral inheritance. . . .[13]

When it was in the New Testament that the orthodox Fathers searched for the meaning and value of marriage, they could find only one passage suggesting that these may be found in procreation. This is Paul's instruction to Christian women, in 1 Timothy, that we have already seen. Its peculiar value lies in its being a correction of what Paul regarded as certain women's good-willed but mistaken notion of how they could best serve the Christian community. Not by teaching nor by exercising any kind of authority, he insisted, but by their maternity. And in this way they could not only serve the Church but could reach salvation: "She will be saved through childbearing." Since for Paul it was unthinkable that this maternity be found anywhere but within marriage, he was saying equivalently that at least one meaning of marriage for a Christian woman is that as the context of her motherhood it can be also the matrix of her salvation.

In his diatribe, in Romans 1:18–32, against the pagan savants Paul argues obliquely and implicitly for fertility as the meaning of sexuality. The logic of his attack is fairly transparent: the educated but evil men who are his target have refused to acknowledge God the creator's existence and presence in the universe despite the clear evidence of these in the nature he has created. Therefore he has punished them—not by taking punitive action against them, but "by delivering them up in their lusts to unclean practices" (verse 24). These practices he identifies: homosexual intercourse by both men and women. And these practices are unclean because they are unnatural: "Their women exchanged natural intercourse for unnatural, and their men gave up natural intercourse with women and burned with lust for one another" (verses 26b–27).

That much demands the question, "Why is homosexual intercourse not natural while heterosexual is?" The answer can be given only in terms of the one substantive difference that Paul would recognize between the two: heterosexual intercourse can be fertile, homosexual cannot. A conclusion to the reason is then readily available: since the specific and significant difference of heterosexual intercourse from homosexual is fertility, this must be the former's inherent meaning and value. This must be what it is for.

Because the New Testament is a message that presumes men and women are in need of rescue from a sin-wounded condition, what it has otherwise to say about the meaning of marriage amplifies what Paul said so tersely to the women in 1 Timothy. Marriage can be made a means of this rescue into salvation. So here we have marriage defined not as it was designed in its nature by the hand of God, but marriage, wounded like everything else human, put to work in a massive salvage operation. The amplification of this theme in 1 Corinthians 7 touches the rescue from sinfulness in its somber side. Marriage contributes to this meaning by providing a safeguard from sexual sin: "But to avoid immorality every man should have his own wife and every woman her own husband" (verse 2). "... but if they [the widows in the community] cannot exercise self-control, they should marry. It is better to marry than to burn" (verse 8). How far, in Paul's mind, on the nether side of holiness is sexual intimacy is evident in his assumption that it makes prayer impossible, or at least difficult, or is at best inappropriately linked in time with prayer: "Do not deprive one another, unless perhaps by mutual consent for a time, to devote yourselves to prayer. Then return to one another, that Satan may not test you through your lack of self-control" (verse 5).

The positive side of this instrumental service of marriage in the work of rescue from sin is urged clearly in four New Testament sources. Jesus' reassertion, in Matthew 19 and Mark 10, that a marriage is a covenant of equals we have seen earlier; it is no more than a hint of the rich meaning that will be inferred from this covenantal unity in later centuries. Paul is more explicit in his letter to the Corinthians. To the Christian spouses there who are worried that their marriages to pagans may defile them, he insists that the contrary is readily possible and has happened among them: "The unbelieving husband is consecrated by his believing wife; the unbelieving wife is consecrated by her believing husband."

The First Letter of Peter repeats the same possibility for such a religiously mixed marriage. But here a particular facet of the wife's married life is said to serve the Christian work of rescue: "You married women must obey your husbands, so that any of them who do not believe in the word of the Gospel may be won over, apart from preaching, through their wives' conduct" (3:1–2).

The possibility, urged in Ephesians 5, that a husband may do for his wife what Christ does for the Church—heal her, purify her, grace her with holiness—we have seen in an earlier chapter and will review again briefly at the end of this one.

The Christian Inheritance from Rabbinic Judaism

What the Fathers of the first three Christian centuries inherited from Judaism was more than what they read in the Jewish Scriptures. At least those of them who were Jewish or who came from a Jewish milieu (Paul, Matthew and the Matthean editor, the author of the Letters of Peter, the author of Apocalypse; such Alexandrians as Clement and Origen because of the presence in that city of Jewish intellectuals, including Philo's disciples; Justin because he was born in Palestine)—all these must have been influenced by that developing body of Jewish teaching that was eventually gathered into the two Talmuds, the Babylonian and the Palestinian.[14] For example, the condemnation of solitary sexuality, that is nowhere fixed and explicit in the Old Testament, gets into Jewish ethical thought from these rabbinic sources. In Torah a man's loss of seed calls for no punishment; it no more than makes him unclean ritually. He must bathe himself before being allowed to participate in religious ceremony—the same stricture put on a woman in her menstruation and on a married couple after having intercourse, according to Leviticus 15:16–24. But the commentary *Niddah* (13a) in the Babylonian Talmud condemns masturbation severely: "Whoever emits semen in vain deserves death" (a delinquent act's deserving death, according to the rabbinic vocabulary, was a common hyperbole meaning that it is seriously evil). One feature at least of the malice of masturbation seems to be implied in *Niddah* 13b: given the belief among some rabbis that the Messiah will not come until all the souls of the unborn have been born, seed lost in masturbation could have been used to provide a body for one of these souls.[15] As it is, the failure to do so delays the Messiah's coming and derivatively prolongs Israel's unfreedom. The idea that at least the male's sexual capacity is meant to serve a purpose beyond itself—and so to be reserved for this purpose—is clearly present here.

The arch-example in Jewish tradition of the wasting of seed is, of course, the conduct of Onan described in the legendized narrative in Genesis 38. The evil conduct for which the Lord killed Onan must have been, in the minds of the first narrators of the story, his refusal to obey the Law of the Levirate, to conceive a son by the wife of his dead and childless older brother, Er, so that in family annals that child might be reckoned as Er's and keep the latter's name from dying out. But in the Babylonian Talmud the commentary *Yebamoth* (34b) cites rabbis who taught that the evil of Onan's conduct lay in its being unnatural. By implication Onan's *coitus interruptus* could have been unnatural because it was a refusal to use semen according to its natural purpose.

This fixing as a moral criterion of sexual conduct that which is natural in bodily function appears in another quarter of rabbinic teaching. Some rabbis who otherwise condemned *coitus interruptus* as a means of contraception permitted it when a wife was nursing a child Thus Rabbi Eleazar in commentary *Yebamoth* (34b). In commentary *Nid*-ah (45a) Rabbi Bibi in Babylon in the fourth century permitted contraceptive measures to a nursing mother, to a pregnant woman, and to an eleven-year-old girl. The reason for the exception allowed the nursing mother was so that an early subsequent pregnancy would not affect the nursing and weaning of the child already born. It was allowed the pregnant woman lest she suffer miscarriage. It was allowed the eleven-year-old girl, presumably fertile but a year younger than the minimum age for marriage, lest her health be damaged. In each case there was an implied appeal to what is "natural" for a woman and for her child, whether unborn or born and nursing.[16] But here the demand of nature for the persons overrode the demand of nature—the demand of their inherent purpose—of semen and of sexual intercourse.

The Influence of Philo

Among the Jewish teachers who had a lasting effect on the Christian Fathers' attitude toward sexuality and marriage none was more influential than Philo, a contemporary of Jesus and of Paul. A decisive reason for the depth of his influence is that he lived and taught in Alexandria, successor city to Athens as the intellectual capital of the world. It was there that the most active catechetical center of early Christianity was started up by the middle of the second century. What Philo taught was all the more congenial to the Christian teachers there because he was a monotheistic Jew, a man deeply committed to a pure life and to holiness—and fundamentally approving of marriage, in ironic contrast to such Gnostic Alexandrian Christians as Basilides, Valentinus and Carpocrates. Moreover his lifelong work of fusing Old Testament revelation with Greek philosophy, an effort at using the latter to ground the former intellectually and thus make it acceptable to serious-minded pagans, helped provide the Alexandrian Christian teachers with what they needed. This was a philosophically reasoned case against the Gnostics of both persuasions, the ascetics and the antinomians. Philo's ability to supply this case to the generations of Alexandrian Christians succeeding his own was born in his anthropology.

Deeply influenced by Platonism, Philo maintained a sharp dualism of soul and body, of the rational and the sensate elements in human beings. He insisted on the moral necessity of person' freeing themselves from the power of the sensate in them. The Stoic ideal showed itself in his moral teaching, in his urging that the only true good for men is virtue and that the only virtuous relationship of men to their passions is apathy.[17]

Consistently with this anthropology and the moral teaching it produced, the Christians could take the following from Philo about sexuality and marriage. Philo set down a judgment that for later Christians was to take on the status of a first principle. Writing in Book IV, Chapter 15 of his *Special Laws,* he describes the ruinous effect of desire in those foolish enough to let themselves be bound by it. He warns especially against the ruin brought by desire fixed on four objects: money, reputation, office and bodily beauty. Of the last-named he says, "If the object of their desire is bodily beauty, they become seducers, adulterers, pederasts, devotees of lust and promiscuity. And they regard these vile evils as the highest blessings."[18]

Earlier, in Book III, chapter 2, he had undertaken to explain Moses' meaning in each of the commandments of the Decalogue. When explaining the first commandment of the Second Table, "Thou shalt not commit adultery," he had found opportunity to point at the ruinous effect of the desire for pleasure:

In the Second Table the first command is "Thou shalt not commit adultery"—first, I think, because physical pleasure breathes everywhere in the civilized world so powerfully that no part of it escapes its tyranny.[19]

He then uses this near-axiom to explain how desire for pleasure can produce evil within a man's marriage.

> For even that pleasure which is according to nature earns a frequent and serious reproach, when one is ruled by an immoderate and insatiable desire for it. It may, for example, take the form of insatiable gluttony, even though one should eat none of the foods that are forbidden. Or we may see it in woman-lovers, men who hunger constantly for sexual intercourse, who behave shamefully with women—not necessarily with other men's wives but even with their own.[20]

What Philo considers wrong about sexual intercourse otherwise kept faithfully within one's own marriage is that it is "immoderate and insatiable." He does not in these passages specify the exact point that will become crucial for Augustine's sexual ethic, namely the point at which the satisfaction of sexual desire crosses over from moderation to immoderation. We shall see that Augustine drew this line quite exactly.

A hint at where this line is to be found Philo gives in an entirely different treatise, *On Joseph,* chapter 9.[21] By way of explaining to the reader why Joseph, a devoutly moral Jew, resisted the attempt of Pharaoh's wife to seduce him, he has him deliver to her an extraordinarily prolix rebuke even as she tries to drag him to her bed. Joseph explains that not only do men of his race and religion not lie with other men's wives, but that even "before the lawful marriage we have no intercourse with other women, but as men untouched we come in marriage to untouched virgins. And the goal we seek with them is not pleasure but the begetting of lawful children."

In his treatise *On Abraham,*[22] in explaining how God punished the Sodomites and Gomorrhites for their homosexual lust by burning their cities with fire from heaven, Philo contrasted with this the reward given to Abraham for his chastity. He implies clearly enough that this chastity lay, in contrast with the conduct of the Sodomites and Gomorrhites, in the naturalness of the patriarch's intercourse.

> But God took pity on men and women who marry according to the demand of nature, in order to bring children into the world, and gave them offspring in extraordinary abundance. But he abominated and destroyed that unnatural and unlawful intercourse. . . .

Philo's thesis that the only morally permissible intercourse is intercourse within marriage motivated exclusively by the desire to conceive appears in slightly different guise in Book 3, chapter 6 of his *Special Laws*.[23] Here he is explaining those heterosexual relationships listed in Leviticus 18 within which intercourse is forbidden, and explaining the reasons for the prohibitions. In every case the reason is some form of the demand of the law of nature. Thus a man may not have intercourse with a woman during her menstrual period, and the reason he may not is that his seed would be wasted; that is, its release could not be intended for its natural purpose, which is conception.

> Whenever a woman is having her menstrual flow, a man is not to touch her. During this time he must observe the law of nature and refrain from intercourse. He must at the same time learn not to spend his seed in an untimely and purposeless way, for the sake of mere gross pleasure. For it would be as if a farmer, while drunk or in a fit of insanity, were to sow wheat and barley in ponds and streams instead of in his fields. . . .

The same reason, the evil of using his seed unnaturally by releasing it when conception is impossible, forbids a man's having intercourse with a woman he knows to be sterile.

> Those men too must be blamed severely who plow the hard and stony land. And who are these men if not those who have intercourse with sterile wives? Driven solely by the uncontrollable desire for pleasure they deliberately waste and destroy their seed like the most lecherous of men. For what other goal can they have in approaching such women? They cannot do so in hope of children, a hope which they know is doomed to failure. Their only motive must be an incurable incontinence, a lust that they find unbearable.[24]

It is a most significant facet of his sexual psychology, which surely underlies and forces his morality, that the only other motive than conception that Philo could imagine for a man's having intercourse with even his own wife is lechery. It is an assumption that will be taken over unexamined by most of the Christian Fathers and will have one of its more lasting effects on the Christian understanding of marriage.

The Patristic Use of the Pagan Sources

It is easy for the twentieth-century Christian student to not notice, or at least to forget, the interlocking ironies of the Gnostic-orthodox challenge and reply in the second and third centuries. The majority party among the Gnostics, the ascetics, were not anti-Christian. They were men and women passionately concerned to be perfect Christians, who in their search for perfection sought to live above and free of a most elemental and compelling human need. As a prior philosophical warrant for their heroism they called the root of this need evil, and evil the societal institution in which the need had been fulfilled since the beginning of the race. They supported this condemnation by quoting words of Christ and of his apostles and evangelists. In their minds they escaped quoting them against God the creator of marriage and sexuality by denying that the God who on record had created them is the God of goodness, the true knowledge of whom (as against the Old Testament's false knowledge of him) Christ had come to reveal.

The orthodox Fathers, in order to defend sexuality and marriage, which they knew instinctively (but could not prove systematically) to be in some way good, found themselves defending an institution whose specific conduct they thought to be virtually always carried on sinfully. In defending it they could not use confidently the words of Christ and the apostles, because in most instances this use only strengthened the Gnostic case they were trying to destroy. The sharpest irony of all lay in the Fathers' finding the most effective argument against the Gnostics supplied by the pagan philosophers, the very men against whom Paul had railed so bitterly at the beginning of his Letter to the Romans, some of whom were almost doctrinal champions of the proposition that the noblest expression of love is homosexual.

Justin and Athanagoras in the second century, and Clement, Irenaeus, Origin, Tertullian, and Minucius Felix in the third, were students of their own cultural and philosophic traditions. That they knew the main elements of the Platonic, Peripatetic, Stoic and Neo-Platonic teaching on sexuality and marriage is evident in their writings. Therefore they knew that as early as the Academy at Athens the thesis had become axiomatic that human beings seek by nature to live in community. In Book II of Plato's *Republic* the discussants develop this thesis at length, drawing their judgment from the self-evident fact that human beings can survive only if they provide for one another those goods they need absolutely for survival, such as food and shelter, but which are too numerous for everyone to supply for himself.

In Book I, Chapter 2 of his *Politics,* Aristotle repeats the thought in his aphorism, "Hence it is evident that the state is a creation of nature and that man is by nature a political animal."[25] He adds a particular point of evidence to sustain his thesis: all the other animals can make no more than sounds to one another indicating pleasure or pain, but human beings have the power of speech with which they can "set forth the expedient and inexpedient, and therefore likewise the just and the unjust."[26]

The Stoics agreed. Diogenes Laërtius, in Book 7:123 of his *Lives and Opinions* said: "The excellent man will not live in solitude; he is by nature a being of community and inclined to human transaction."[27] In his *Discourses,* Book 1, Chapter 23, Epictetus offers his own even more succinct aphorism in reply to his favorite opponents: "Epicurus understands as well as we do that we are by nature social beings. . . ."[28] Cicero had said the same thing in his more copious style: "From the fact that no one would choose to live in solitude even though it contained an endless abundance of pleasure we easily understand that we have been born for the coming together and joining of mankind, and for sharing that is natural."[29]

Subsumed under that thesis whose truth these ancients regarded as evident in the most fundamental human experience was another that many of them regarded as equally beyond question. It is that marriage, and sexuality within it, are meant by nature to serve the larger, inclusive society, the state. Plato's version of this function for marriage and sexuality emerges in Book 5 of his *Republic* where, of course, it is presented as Socrates'.[30] The discussion here is about the kind of education the guardians of the ideal state should receive as youths and young adults. Between them Socrates and Glaucon raise the question whether girls and young women among the future guardians should receive the same education as boys and young men. Socrates allows that perhaps they should not because the former's "nature" is different. But he asks immediately if the admitted difference of nature is such as to make women's roles in the state different in a way that calls for different education for them. The one significant difference of role does not seem to him to justify a different education.

> . . . but if the difference consists only in women bearing and men begetting children, this does not amount to a proof that a woman differs from a man in respect of the sort of education she should receive; and we shall therefore continue to maintain that our guardians and their wives ought to learn the same pursuits.[31]

Socrates suggests that in regard to the qualities of soul needed for governing, women in general have them all, although just as generally to a lesser degree than do men. As some men are good governors in the state and some poor, so would some women be good, some poor.

So his point is simple enough: what the sexual difference of men and women means, why it exists, is for procreation. That he intends to say this much, and to move beyond it and say that procreation is for the good of the state, becomes clear in his singular (we would say bizarre) plan for the marrying of the young, the conceiving of children and the state's nurture of the latter.

The legislators are to select the young men and women whom they find most suited to become guardians and to produce children apt to become guardians in the succeeding generation. These young men and women will study together. They will exercise together naked in the gymnasium so that they will be impelled by nature toward having intercourse with one another. But this coupling is to be controlled severely by the legislators. No young man may mate monogamously and permanently with any one young woman. All the young people of one sex in the group are to be mated commonly with all those of the other. Socrates' reason for this community of mates is naively humane. It is the good of the state, that it may have peace and right order. For if all the guardian citizens feel toward all the others as husbands or wives, as brothers or sisters, they will share equally in the same joys and pains. All will regard all as members of their one family; there will be no selfishness, privacy, or animosity.

The legislators will see to it that only the best young men mate with the best young women so as to produce the best possible offspring for the state. There will be no intercourse of the weak with the weak. The bravest of the young men may have multiple sexual partners. The babies born of these unions, the best of them, will be taken from their mothers at birth and placed in a nursery (inferior offspring will be done away with). No mother is ever to be able to identify her child or vice versa. She will go to the nursery only to help nurse the babies, with anonymity guarded on both sides.

The thesis could not be more brutally clear: sexuality in men and women is for producing the next generation. This is confirmed by Socrates' judgment that any man having intercourse earlier or later than the ideal years between twenty-five and fifty (and any woman before eighteen or after forty) is suspect of acting out of lust. The same judgment bears upon even a man or woman within these years if he or she has intercourse in a union not approved by the legislators.

Aristotle and the Reasons for Marriage

A modern student informed about the influence of Aristotle on Catholic teaching for the last seven hundred years through his influence on the Scholastics must take care not to indulge anachronism by exaggerating his influence on the Christian Fathers. The fact is that Aristotle's thought had, in the forming of early Christian social morality, an influence that was minor in comparison with that of Plato, of the Neo-Platonics and of the Later Stoics. There is no need to explain here why this was so. It is enough for our purpose to keep in mind that what Aristotle said in his *Nicomachean Ethics* and in his *Politics* about men, women and marriage was to become most influential in the twelfth and thirteenth centuries, once these and his other works had become available in the West in Latin.

It will be helpful to examine Aristotle's thinking on marriage in answer to two questions whose intentions eventually converge. The first asks about the place of marriage in civil society, what its function is there in helping to secure the goods of this society. The second asks what marriage gains for the partners to it, in what ways men and women are helped to their personal good by taking one another as mates. And be it noted that in the passages we shall examine briefly Aristotle writes descriptively rather than prescriptively; that is, he reports the evidence he has turned up as the fruit of his inquiry rather than declaring the way he thinks things ought to be.

It is mainly in his *Politics* that he addresses the first of these questions. In Book 7, chapter 16 he asks who in the state are fit to marry and which are the best ages for men and women respectively to marry.

> Since the legislator should begin by considering how the frames of children whom he is rearing may be as good as possible, his first care will be about marriage—at what age should his citizens marry and who are fit to marry?[32]

Aristotle's answer to his own question is that citizen couples should conceive and bear children only if they are in sound health and only if they are neither too young nor too old. The optimum age for women to marry and begin bearing therefore is about eighteen years, for men about thirty-seven: ". . . then they are in the prime of life, and the decline in the powers of both will coincide." The age at which men should cease begetting children is that at which they reach the prime of their intelligence, which is at about fifty years.

Is this readiness for physically healthy parenting the only criterion by which Aristotle judges the suitability of a man and a woman to be spouses? He no more than hints at another norm, one which is subsequent to the fact of their already having used their sexuality to produce healthy children: ". . . at four or five years later [than the husband's fiftieth year] they should cease from having families; and from that time forward only cohabit with one another for the sake of health, or for some similar reason."[33]

What he thinks this "some similar reason" may be he explains with reasonable completeness in his *Nicomachean Ethics,* at which we shall look presently.

For Aristotle to specify the optimum years of life within which men and women may bear and nurture children is hardly to state that this bearing and nurturing are the principal reason for marrying, the primary goal of marriage as a social institution. But that he thought marriage in its capacity for producing children and nurturing them is at the service of the state he confirms implicitly in answering another of his own questions, about what to do with deformed children or children numerically in excess of what is good for the state.

> As to the exposure and rearing of children, let there be a law that no *deformed* child shall live, but that on the ground of an excess in the number of children, if the established custom of the state forbid this (for in our state population has a limit), no child is to be exposed, but when couples have children in excess, let abortion be procured before sense and life have begun.[34]

Aristotle's judgment that marriage is itself in some way for children appears when we begin to ask and answer the second of our questions, about his opinion of marriage as a form of friendship. In Book 8, Chapter 12 of his *Nicomachean Ethics* he discusses the causes of the friendship that is found between husband and wife. He declares that this friendship is natural; and evidence of the naturalness of it he finds in the undeniable inclination of men and women to pair off—to pair off because they need one another, and with a need that is prior to their need for the state with a priority that is both temporal and natural. Among these needs is that one which is inevitable in the rearing of children. Hence the implied interpretation of this marital pairing: it is by nature for the rearing of children.

> . . . man is naturally inclined to form couples—even more than to form cities, inasmuch as the household is earlier and more necessary than the city, and reproduction is more common to man with the animals. With the other animals the union extends only to this point, but human beings live together not only for the sake of reproduction but also for the various purposes of life; for from the start the functions are divided, and those of men and women are different; so they help each other by throwing their peculiar gifts into the common stock.[35]

This simple interpretation of marriage was one that Aristotle shared with other thinkers of his time. They agreed that it is a vocation of service to the state. When they asked in what ways it serves, they offered two discrete answers, with different thinkers among them specifying one or the other kind of service or some combination of the two.

They could say that marriage serves the state by providing children and thus its perpetuation, or by providing companionship for men and women, or by providing both. (I have found none who chose the second purpose by itself; all opted for either the first or the third.)

Xenophon in his *Oeconomicus* (7:11) said that marriage has in it both goals; it is a sharing of the home and of children.[36] A succinct judgment is quoted from Aristotle himself in Stobaeus' *Eclogues* (II, 7, 26): "Marriage is for the procreation of children and the sharing of life."[37]

Among the earlier Stoics, Pseudo-Aristotle, Phintys, and Hierocles all said the same: marriage has the conjoined goals, to procreate and to provide a sharing of life. The only one among the ancients who is reported to have named only procreation as its goal was Socrates. Xenophon says this of him in his *Memorabilia* (II, 2, 4).[38] One must come down to the later Stoics and to Philo, however, to find the resolute proposition, "The end of marriage is to beget legitimate children."[39]

An exception among these later Stoics, and the fullest elaborator of the double goals of marriage, was Musonius Rufus, born before 30 A.D., the teacher in Rome of Epictetus and of Pliny the Younger. His beginning formula about marriage is that it is a companionship or community of life (a *koinonía*) and of the procreating of children. The spouses are to consider all things as shared and nothing private, not even their own bodies. Every-thing is shared, their souls, their bodies, their goods—everything except their distinct identities as husband and wife. To express fully this sense of shared lives he used the terms *symbíosis, kedemonía,* and *homónoia.* By these he meant that the partners take full care of one another in true devo-tion and have everything in common.[40]

In Musonius' judgment the Creator intends for human beings to mar-ry; it is according to their nature. And he offered four points of evidence for this: the correlated anatomies of men and women; men and women have a natural desire for one another; the intimacy of marriage is the most inclusive and intense of all intimacies, for only spouses share everything; the gods intend for men and women to marry, since Hera, Eros and Aph-rodite attend and supervise marriage and procreation.

Musonius' version of the anatomical-teleological argument for the natural place of procreation among the goals of marriage was typical. His vivid elaboration of it was surely borrowed in its details from the myth of the Androgyne: ". . . the demiurge who created men first cut our species in two, then made for it matched genitals . . . then built into each half an in-tense desire for the other's intercourse and its sharing, and mixed into both a powerful yearning for one another."[41]

Aristotle and the others aside for the moment, it is clear that the argu-ment the orthodox Christian Fathers most needed for their reply to the Gnostic antinomians they found in a sufficiently representative number of the pagan philosophers. That the preservation of the species is the primary goal of marriage and indeed of sexuality itself was asserted as early as Pla-to. In his *Laws* he wrote about legislation that would regulate all sexual problems in an ideal manner and that would have to contain among other features a measure forbidding all intercourse which does not intend pro-creation. In the dialogue it is the Athenian stranger who discourses:

> . . . but was I not just now saying that I had a way to make men use natural love and abstain from unnatural, not intentionally de-stroying the seeds of human increase, or sowing them in stony places, in which they will take no root; and that I would com-mand them to abstain too from any female field of increase in which that which is sown is not likely to grow? . . . Such a law, extending to other sensual desires, and conquering them, would be the source of ten thousand blessings. For, in the the first place, moderation is the appointment of nature, and deters men from all frenzy and madness of love, and from all adulteries and im-moderate use of meats and drink, and makes them good friends to their own wives.[42]

Both of the Athenian's notions—that a man's sexual capacity should be used only when conception is possible, and that (perhaps by this means) men will be kept from lust and even from excessive passion with their wives—became dear to the later Stoics. Ocellus Lucanus formulated the ideal in his *Universal Nature* (4): "Not for the sake of pleasure do we approach one another, but in order to conceive children. . . . The sexual organs are given to man not for pleasure but for preserving the species."[43] Musonius Rufus insisted that ". . . sexual activity is right only within marriage and only when directed to the procreation of children." All other instances are "indecent relationships ruled by lust."[44]

Seneca's renowned assessment of a man's options among motives for intercourse we have thanks to St. Jerome's quoting it in his diatribe *Against Jovinian* (1:49):

> All love of another's wife is shameful; so, too, too much love of one's own wife. A wise man ought to love his wife with judgment, not affection. Let him control his impulses and not be borne headlong into copulating. Nothing is fouler than to love a wife like an adulteress. Certainly those who say that they unite themselves to wives to produce children for the sake of the state and the human race ought, at any rate, to imitate the beasts, and, when their wife's belly swells, not destroy the offspring. Let them show themselves to their wives not as lovers but as husbands.[45]

The Classical Authors and Friendship in Marriage

Helped so little by the ambiguity in their Scriptures about marriage as a friendship, could the Fathers find any more decisive judgments among the pagan philosophers? They could, but even these were divided among those thinkers who saw the possibility of friendship in marriage and those who doubted it.

The marriage that Plato proposed for the guardians in his ideal city-state was taken for granted to be friendship, and its design was motivated by the desire for friendship. All the young men and women were to be husbands and wives respectively to all expressly in order to make their experience of pleasure and pain an equally shared one. The motive in turn for this was that all might have a care for all, instead of being selfishly concerned each for himself or herself or for a private monogamous relationship. Even the anonymous paternity and maternity and the holding of all babies and children in common among the guardians had this care of all for all as its motive.

It goes without saying that married friendship in this form was unacceptable to the Fathers. What then of friendship in marriage according to Aristotle and the Peripatetics? Aristotle himself favored it. But he saw difficulties in it that led him to recommend it in only carefully qualified form. His first difficulty was expressed in his judgment on the nature of women; he had serious doubts that this nature allowed them to be adequate friends to men. This he expresses in his *The History of Animals* (Book 9, Chapter 1):

> The fact is, the nature of man is the most rounded off and complete, and consequently in man the qualities or capacities above referred to are found in their perfection. Hence woman is more compassionate than man, more easily moved to tears, at the same time is more jealous, more querulous, more apt to scold and to strike. She is, furthermore, more prone to despondency and less hopeful than the man, more void of shame or self-respect, more false of speech, more deceptive, and of more retentive memory. She is also more wakeful, more shrinking, more difficult to arouse to action, and requires a smaller quantity of nutriment.[46]

Elsewhere (in his *Politics*, Book 3, Chapter 4) Aristotle judges that a woman's courage is *by nature* less than that of a man: "For a man would be thought a coward if he had no more courage than a courageous woman." And he says in the same place that *phrónesis*, the practical wisdom needed to govern, is found only in the man. The excellence, the *areté*, that he expects to find in woman's nature he appraises in his *Rhetoric* (Book 1, Chapter 5): "Both male and female are here included: the excellences of the latter are, in body, beauty and stature; in soul, self-command and industry that is not sordid."[47]

Out of this evidence gathered, one may suppose, empirically (but with Aristotle never suspecting that the "nature" he perceived in women may have been a product of Athenian men's treatment of them), he drew his conclusion about the nature of the friendship one may expect to find in marriage. This is found in his *Nicomachean Ethics*, Book 8, where first he sets a quasi-principle: "Perfect friendship is the friendship of men who are good, and alike in virtue. . . ."[48]

Returning to the passage already quoted above from Chapter 12 of this book of the *Ethics*, wherein he discusses the friendship of husband and wife on its simplest and most natural ground, we find him saying not that men and women marry naturally when and because in particular instances they have become friends. He says rather that men and women have a natural need of one another. They marry in order to provide for this need in all its facets; and the will to do so is the will to friendship specific to men and women who join in marriage. These needs are the need to provide for the nurture of their children, and to provide too for those services which men and women respectively provide more adeptly. (It is clear how easily this natural joining in marriage to provide for these needs may later be interpreted as a seeking to attain certain natural ends in marriage.)

> Between other kinsmen friendly relations are found in due proportion. Between man and wife friendship seems to exist more by nature; for man is naturally inclined to form couples—even more

than to form cities, inasmuch as the household is earlier and more necessary than the city, and reproduction is more common to man with the animals. With the other animals the union extends only to this point, but human beings live together not only for the sake of reproduction but also for the various purposes of life; for from the start the functions are divided, and those of man and woman are different; so they help each other by throwing their peculiar gifts into the common stock. It is for these reasons that both utility and pleasure seem to be found in this kind of friendship. But this friendship may also be based on virtue, if the parties are good; for each has its own virtue and they will delight in the fact. And children seem to be a bond of union (which is the reason why childless people part more easily); for children are a good common to both, and what is common holds them together.[49]

That marriages may contain friendship growing out of some other part of life than the need to nurture children and provide respective services Aristotle suggests above in acknowledging that ". . . this friendship may also be based on virtue, if the parties are good, for each has its own virtue and they will delight in the fact." Does he here imply that the developing of, and the reciprocal enjoyment of, this virtue is a reason or goal for marrying? Or does he leave the matter at this, that these are by-products found now and then in marriages formed to meet the needs of nurture and service—but formed by men and women having the virtue that he mentions but does not specify? To try to answer these questions would, I think, be to risk drawing inferences from implications that Aristotle himself did not intend.

But it is necessary, if one is to read him accurately as he discusses friendship in marriage, to point out that always and everywhere he considered this a friendship of unequals. This is hinted clearly in the passages already quoted in which he points out the inferiority of women in the realm of social virtues. There is the implication there that between unequals in virtue there can be a friendship only of unequals. And when we examine how Aristotle described (and perhaps prescribed) the living out of this inequality, we find a clear picture of the marital syntax as he knew it and approved of it in his own society.

But there is another kind of friendship, viz., that which involves an inequality between the parties, e.g., that of father to son and in general of elder to younger, that of man to wife and in general that of ruler to subject. And these friendships differ also from each other; for it is not the same that exists between parents and children and between rulers and subjects, nor is even that of father to son the same as that of wife to husband. For the virtue and the function of each of these is different, and so are the rea-

sons for which they are loved; the love and the friendship are
therefore different also. . . . In all friendships implying inequality
the love also should be proportional, i.e., the better should be
loved more than he loves . . ."[50]

The consequence of this inequality that Aristotle designates as the dis-
proportionately greater love with which the wife should love her husband
is repeated in Chapter 11 of this same Book 8 of the *Ethics.* But there he
volunteers a clarification: "The friendship of man and wife, again, is the
same that is found in an aristocracy; for it is in accordance with virtue—
the better gets more of what is good, and each gets what befits him; and so,
too, with the justice in these relationships."[51]

But in Chapter 10 he had made a distinction and set a limit. There are
matters in a marriage that a woman supervises more competently. Over
these a husband exercises a mediated rule by handing them over to the
wife.

One may find resemblances to the constitutions and, as it were,
patterns of them even in households. . . . The association of man
and wife seems to be aristocratic; for the man rules in accordance
with his worth, and in those matters in which a man should rule,
but, the matters that befit a woman, he hands over to her. If the
man rules in everything the relation passes over into oligarchy;
for in doing so he is not acting in accordance with their respective worth, and not ruling in virtue of his superiority.[52]

In his *Politics* Aristotle adds a further precision that makes clear he
does not intend that a husband's rule over his wife be royal or despotic—
the kind of rule appropriate to a master over his slaves. He calls this marital rule constitutional, a rule that he had defined in Book 1, Chapter 7 as
". . . a government of free men and equals."[53] But in Chapter 12 of this
same book he explains why, despite the wife's freedom as a citizen and her
constitutional equality, she is nevertheless to be the one ruled: the man is
fitter than she to command in the familial society.

A husband and father, we saw, rules over his wife and children,
both free, but the rule differs, the rule over his children being
royal, over his wife a constitutional rule. For although there may
be exceptions to the order of nature, the male is by nature fitter
for command than the female, just as the elder and full-grown is
superior to the younger and more immature.[54]

In the following chapter (13) he explains even more specifically the
superiority of the husband that makes him the natural ruler of the marriage: his deliberative power is greater than that of both his wife and his
children.

But the kind of rule differs;—the freeman rules over the slave after another manner from that in which the male rules over the female, or the man over the child; although the parts of the soul are present in all of them, they are present in different degrees. For the slave has no deliberative faculty at all; the woman has, but it is without authority, and the child has, but it is immature. . . . Clearly, then, moral virtue belongs to all of them; but the temperance of a man and of a woman, or the courage and justice of a man and of a woman, are not, as Socrates maintained, the same; the courage of a man is shown in commanding, of a woman in obeying. . . . All classes must be deemed to have their special attributes; as the poet says of women, "Silence is a woman's glory."[55]

In summary and by way of recapitulation, what could the Christian Fathers have found in Aristotle and his contemporaries? First—and what they wanted most to find—was that the bearing and rearing of children is one of the principal reasons for and goals of marrying. But within this goal, which marriages have in common with the mating of animals, there is a clear difference from that mating. For animals do not have to maintain a household. And the different offices in this maintenance and the differing capacities for ruling in the household are the grounds for both the friendship in marriage and the inequality of ruler and ruled within this friendship.

But what is so typically Aristotelian is that marriage and the friendship within it are meant by nature to serve the civil society. This is not to say that there would be no marriage if there were no state. But Aristotle is very clear that the state is the most valuable of all the communities that men form. And this is because its aim is to attain the highest good for human beings, and it does so in greater degree than any other society.

Every state is a community of some kind—and every community is established with a view to some good; for mankind always acts in order to obtain that which they think good. But, if all communities aim at some good, the state or political community, which is the highest of all, and which embraces all the rest, aims at good in a greater degree than any other, and at the highest good.[56]

Thus marriages are by nature for the political community, the state, in that they provide it an indispensable service: they enable it to stay in existence. Thus when, in Chapter 2, Aristotle lists the sub-groups making up the state, he says the following about marriage:

In the first place there must be a union of those who cannot exist without each other, namely of male and female, that the race may continue (and this is a union which is formed, not of deliberate purpose, but because, in common with other animals and plants, mankind have a natural desire to leave behind them an image of themselves), and of natural ruler and subject, that both may be preserved.[57]

(One must take care not to misunderstand Aristotle when he says that the union of a man and a woman is a union of those who cannot exist without each other. Obviously a man can survive a normal lifetime without the intimate companionship of a woman, as a woman can without that of a man. Nor does he mean that they need one another in the sense that Jungian psychology understands, that without a heterosexual intimacy their psychic integration risks incompletion. What he means is that without the sexual union of man and woman the race would vanish.)

This orientation of marriage to the service of the state he returns to in Chapter 13 of the same Book 1. Discussing the virtues appropriate to the various members of the sub-societies within the state, he says that the virtues to be developed in women and children are to be developed in consideration of the good of the state.

> For, inasmuch as every family is a part of the state, and these relationships are the parts of the family, and the virtue of the part must have regard for the virtue of the whole, women and children must be trained by education with an eye to the constitution, if the virtues of either of them are supposed to make any difference to the virtues of the state. And they must make a difference; for the children grow up to be citizens, and half the free persons in a state are women.[58]

Here, available for the Fathers' use, is a goal for marriage outside itself—a good and justifying goal, to serve the larger and more valuable society by keeping it in existence. Where, for Aristotle, this larger society was the state alone, for the Fathers it was the Kingdom of God, both on earth in the visible Church and in heaven in the invisible society of the saints. Pagan philosophy here (should they want to use this Aristotelian version of it) clearly reinforces their argument against the ascetic Gnostics' condemnation of marriage as evil.

The Reply to the Antinomian Gnostics

Irenaeus, Clement *et al.* replied to what they regarded as the new hedonism of the antinomian Gnostics by appealing to the nature of sexuality. The understanding of its nature to which they appealed was the one we have reviewed thus far, that especially of the later Stoics, and most especially that of Philo, the Hellenic-Jewish scholar of Alexandria. The element of this understanding that the Fathers used as the first premise of their argument was that the human sexual anatomy (or at least that of the male, since it was almost exclusively about this that they reasoned) is designed by nature exclusively for impregnating. This is what nature intends the release of semen for, and she intends it for this alone. Two preliminary conclusions, distinct though conjoined, follow from this: first, any deliberate releasing of semen when conception is impossible is a violation of nature; second, any releasing of semen for a motive other than to conceive is a kindred violation. Given the validity of this *argumentum,* the Gnostics who were sexually active in order to have all experiences, or to complete the *pléroma,* or to anticipate in this life the rapture of heaven, stood condemned as violators of nature.

The earliest protestation that the Christians live by this morality is that of Justin Martyr, in his *First Apology,* written in Rome to the emperor in defense of the Christians between 155 and 165. Responding to the popular accusations against the Christians of sexual immorality he insisted (Chapter 1:29) about his community, "Either we marry with only one thought, to have children; or if we forego marriage, we keep ourselves continent at all times."

Athanagoras, like Justin a Christian apologist and his contemporary, addressed his *Supplication for the Christians* to the emperor and the Roman people in 177. Like Justin he insisted that the Christians marry only in order to have children. To illustrate and to undergird this protestation rationally he adopted the agricultural metaphor we have seen used by Philo and the later Stoics. He used the metaphor by explaining that in sexual conduct Christians imitate and obey nature; they do not have intercourse during pregnancy: ". . . as the farmer, throwing the seed into the ground, awaits the harvest, not sowing more upon it, so the procreation of children is the measure of our indulgence in appetite."[59]

Almost the same thought was set forth at the end of the second century by another Christian apologist, Minucius Felix, in his *Octavius* (31, 5). He explained to his pagan contemporaries, "With a good heart we cling to the bond of one marriage; in our desire for children we have only one wife or none at all."[60]

But nowhere in this singleness of motive both so claimed for the Christians and demanded of them as in the writings of the Alexandrians. Clement comes back to the principle repeatedly that a man must have intercourse only in order to beget a child. He adds the negative side of this, that a man must in his soul exclude any other motive. And among the other motives Clement takes dead aim at pleasure, the satisfying of bodily desires. He also suggests a rule that divides moderate sexual activity from immoderate: the intending and the seeking in this activity nothing else than to conceive a child. A resounding hint at his understanding of marital love is in his supposition that if a husband goes to his wife impelled only by desire, he does not love her. He loves her only if he seeks to beget a child by her.

He says in his *On Virginity,* Chapter 17, "The man who has taken a wife in order to have children should also practice continence, not even seeking pleasure from his own wife, whom he ought to love, but with honorable and moderate desire, which is to beget children."[61]

He repeats virtually the same instruction in his *Stromata,* Book 3, Chapter 7: "A man who marries for the sake of begetting children must practice continence, so that it is not desire he feels for his wife, whom he ought to love, and that he may beget children with a chaste and controlled will."[62]

How thoroughly Clement had borrowed this marital morality from the Stoics and from Philo is evident in his reflections, in Book 3, Chapter 7 of the *Stromata,* on the nature of sexual desire and its proper place in a man's or woman's life. He accepts the Stoic ideal and goes beyond it, but admits that surpassing it is beyond unaided human strength.

> The human ideal of continence, I mean that which is set forth by the Greek philosophers, teaches that one should fight desire and not be subservient to it so as to bring it to practical effect. But *our ideal* [emphasis mine] is not to experience desire at all. Our aim is not that while a man feels desire he should get the better of it, but that he should be continent even respecting desire itself. This chastity cannot be attained in any other way except by God's grace.[63]

The insistence that marital chastity and love demand that a husband confine his intercourse exclusively to the begetting of children is Origen's as well. In his *Third Homily on Genesis* (6) he urges that the truly circumcised Christian does not commit adultery; but more than that, he has intercourse with his wife only in order to conceive offspring.[64] In his *Fifth Homily on Genesis* (4) he uses Seneca's argument from the conduct of animals, pointing out that there are some women who, like animals, "serve lust without any restraint; indeed I would not compare them to dumb beasts. For beasts, when they conceive, know not to indulge their mates further with their plenty."[65] Once a woman is pregnant, in other words, the one motive justifying intercourse is *in suspenso* until she has delivered that child and can conceive again.

The African Christian rhetorician Lactantius repeated this by now settled and hardening marital rule for marital intercourse in his *Divine Institutes,* Book 6, Chapter 23. He uses the Stoics' teleological argument to undergird the rule reasonably—that the structure and function of anatomy tell us its natural purpose:

> God gave us eyes not to see and desire pleasure, but to see acts to be performed for the needs of life; so, too, the genital part of the body, as the name itself teaches, has been received by us for no other purpose than the generating of offspring.[66]

And again, God has implanted a sexual instinct in all animals so that impelled by "this most burning desire they can propagate and multiply the species."

Toward the middle of the third century a collection of disciplinary canons was circulated in the communities of Syria. Thanks to the common Christian inclination of the time to gain authority for such documents by attributing them to early and authoritative authorship, the collection was given the title, *Didascalia Apostolorum* (*The Teaching of the Apostles*). The canons condemn specific kinds of sexual conduct as immoral: sodomy, bestiality, fornication, adultery. They include with these intercourse during pregnancy (6:28) and name as the reason for the latter's immorality that the intercourse is against nature—that is, it is not used to beget a child but in order to have pleasure.[67]

Before finally coming to Augustine, who developed and in a sense sealed this synthesis of marital anthropology and morality, unequal glances at two of his contemporaries are in order. Ambrose was bishop of Milan when Augustine came to that city to teach rhetoric in 384. As pastor of the Christian community there he taught constantly, and most of his teaching was elucidation of the Scriptures. In his *Exposition of the Gospel According to Luke* (Chapter 1, verses 43–45) he explained why Elizabeth was embarrassed at conceiving a child in her old age. She understood, Ambrose explained, what every good Christian must know, that intercourse is to be reserved for conception, so that the elderly who cannot conceive are suspect of sinful desire if they exercise their marital right. She was vindicated, of course, by the miraculous conception of John the precursor, and thereby provided evidence that her intercourse with Zechariah took place under divine impulse.[68]

Jerome expressed his mind on the subject with none of Ambrose's gentleness. In Book 3, Chapter 5 of his *Commentary on the Epistle to the Galatians* he stated succinctly that the activities of marriage itself, if they are not modest and do not take place under the eyes of God, so that the spouses' only intention is to conceive, are filth and lust.[69] But his reflection on intercourse in marriage that was to be repeated in Christian communities uncriticized for the following fifteen centuries is found in his choice of translation of verses 16–22 of the Book of Tobit, Chapter 6. Joseph Kerns in his *Theology of Marriage* explains the historical context of Jerome's translating this Jewish legend that he was reluctant to admit belongs to the Scriptures:

> Aware that the Jews were not including the Book of Tobit in their official Old Testament collection, he told the bishops Cromatius and Heliodorus, who had urged him to translate it, "I've satisfied your desire, not my own taste. I've done my best with it." This last remark touches on a fact that is also important. The text he had worked from was in Aramaic. Mistrusting his knowl-

edge of that language, he had a Jew translate it aloud into Hebrew, which he would recast into Latin and dictate to a scribe.
Even with so complicated a procedure he finished the book in a
day.[70]

There are other versions of the passage in question, the most common
of them available in Greek in three different recensions. (It is from them
that *The New American Bible* translation of the Book of Tobit is made.)
And in 1955 fragments of the book in Aramaic and Hebrew were recovered from Cave IV at Qumran. These fragments agree substantially with
the Greek recensions, so it is possible to compare Jerome's version with
them.

What is striking is that none of the Greek recensions, nor the Qumran
fragments, even contain the verses 16 through 22 that Jerome has in his
Vulgate. In fact his translation is the only one in the history of the Jewish
and Christian sacred writings that contains it. Where Jerome got it, whether from the Aramaic text whose translation his Jewish friend dictated to
him in Hebrew, or from his own mind so impatient with women and sex
generally, we shall probably never know.

The verses contain the advice of the young Tobiah's companion and
guide, the angel Raphael, about how to avoid the fate of the seven preceding husbands of his bride-to-be, Sara. All had died violently in the wedding
chamber on their wedding night, struck down by a demon before they
could consummate their marriage. In instructing Tobiah Raphael points
out why his predecessors had perished:

> Listen, I am going to show you those whom the demon can con-
> quer. Those who at the time of their marriage banish God from
> their thoughts and give themselves over so completely to their in-
> stincts that they have no more intelligence than a horse or a
> mule, the demon is stronger than they. But you, when you marry
> her, spend three days in continence, having no concern but pray-
> ing with her. . . . After the third night, in the fear of the Lord
> take the maiden, prompted not so much by instinct as by the love
> of children. . . .

That Jerome, even if this passage is his own invention, was not of a
mind discordant with the Jewish folk-author who first produced the story
in the second century B.C. is evident in some words of prayer Tobiah ut-
tered on his wedding night after having vanquished the demon not by intended continence, as Jerome would have had the reader believe, but by
the magical use of a fish's liver and heart. The prayer and Tobiah's con-

duct immediately following it suggest that Jerome may indeed have tapped a vein of Jewish folk morality. For Tobiah addresses the Lord thus:

> You made Adam and you gave him his wife Eve
>   to be his help and support;
>   and from these two the human race descended.
> You said "It is not good for the man to be alone;
>   let us make him a partner like himself."
> Now, Lord, you know that I take this wife of mine
>   not because of lust
>   but for a noble purpose.
> Call down your mercy on me and on her,
>   and allow us to live together to a happy old age.

They said together, "Amen, amen," and went to bed for the night (8:5–9).

The noble purpose to which Tobiah referred in his prayer is identifiable in the theme of the entire story: he took Sara to wife in order to preserve the name and the home of his father, Tobit.

To say that the Fathers' response to the Gnostic challenge gave birth to the Catholic Church's definition of marriage would be to stretch a cause-effect relationship perhaps too far. But the relationship in some degree is undeniable, and it is a transparent example of the way in which a particular response to a challenge in a particular epoch can grow eventually into an accepted teaching of the Church. In the simplest estimation of it what the Fathers' response had to be was this: a verifiable statement of the moral character of sexuality and marriage that could prove them good against the ascetics' condemnation of them, but a statement that could at the same time restrain sexuality's use severely against the antinomians' turning it to the completing of the cosmos and to the anticipation of heavenly beatitude.

To get this moral statement the Fathers went to the pagan thinkers and borrowed their philosophy of sexuality's nature. This philosophy says that whatever the goods coming from heterosexual union, and they are many, the most fundamental of these is the preservation of the race by the service of the state. This is the naturally given goal of both the sexual anatomies and of their function (that the other animals use them only for preserving their species reinforces this evidence). Consequently for human beings to use their sexuality according to nature they must confine it within marriage and use it there for procreation. And a codicil to this moral conclusion seems obvious: since what it is for according to its nature is procreation, to allow any other motivation in using it is to act against nature. This is especially true if the other motive is to have pleasure.

This is not yet to fix the principle that procreation is the primary end of marriage. But it is to assemble all the elements of it and to name the evidence supporting the principle. Only another epoch of challenge and response was needed to arouse the minds that could formulate it. But the kind of challenge needed to evoke just that response was not the one that followed immediately on the Gnostic conflict. The Manichees were the ones who provided the next challenge, but it was not substantially different from that of the Gnostics. They were the next in the long series of marriage's despisers and condemners.

Augustine was the Christian teacher who answered the Manichees most thoroughly and forcefully. In doing so he explained the goodness of marriage in a detailed formulation that became a kind of first principle of Christian thinking on marriage for centuries afterward. He was also to supply a detailed answer to another question, one that lurked unavoidably around the philosophers' and the Fathers' condemnation of sexual pleasure. This pleasure seems just as natural to sexuality as procreation. It has accompanied sexual experience from the beginning; it is more usually the product of the experience than is procreation. Why then is it against nature to seek this pleasure, especially if it does not hinder procreation? And the kin of that question, drawn from human experience: Why do men and women seek this pleasure so relentlessly? And yet another question forced by that one: Since this pleasure is so powerful as to overwhelm even the will of the earnest Christian to suppress it—and there is no evidence that it will ever diminish or that it will ever go away and leave men and women in peace—has the economy of redemption done anything for the Christian living under this pleasure's assault?

NOTES

1. A standard and readily available study of the primitive Church's encounter with Gnosticism is Robert A. Grant's *Gnosticism and Early Christianity,* N.Y., 1959. John T. Noonan has a brief but inclusive explanation of the Christian Gnostics' teaching and practice regarding marriage and sexuality in his volume, *Contraception,* N.Y., 1965, Chapter 3.

2. For centuries the teachings of the Gnostic masters were known mainly through the works of the orthodox Christians who wrote to refute them. Principal among these were Irenaeus of Lyons' *Against the Heresies (Adversus Haereses),* whose proper title is *The Detection and Overthrow of the Pretended False Gnosis* (its five books were composed probably during the decade 180–190), and Clement of Alexandria's *Miscellanies (Stromata),* Book 3, whose first four chapters are a kind of character profile of the Gnostic attack on marriage and exaltation of sexuality. But archeological findings in the twentieth century have turned up a treasure of original Gnostic writings. Probably the most informative of these are two documents discovered in 1945/56 in a library of Gnostic documents at Nag-Hamâdi (Upper Egypt). One is *The Gospel of Thomas,* a Sahidic-Coptic version (dating from the later fourth or early fifth centuries) of an earlier Greek original. The other

is *The Sacred Book of the Great Invisible Spirit,* otherwise known as *The Gospel of the Egyptians.*

3. Paul's own ambiguity about the exact binding authority of a law which he himself believed and taught had been superseded shows up in his First Letter to Timothy. After reading the passage (1:5–10) one could not be sure from it whether Paul intends that the Law—which for him and his fellow Christians meant the Law of Moses—really binds any but sinners: "What we are aiming at in this warning is the love that springs from a pure heart, a good conscience, and sincere faith. Some people have neglected these and instead have turned to meaningless talk, wanting to be teachers of the law but actually not understanding the words they are using, much less the matters they discuss with such assurance. We know that the law is good, provided one uses it in the way law is supposed to be used—that is, with the understanding that it is aimed, not at good men, but at the lawless and unruly, the irreligious and the sinful, the wicked and the godless. . . ."

4. An available and most readable English version of this work is in the series, *The Library of Christian Classics,* Vol. 2, *Alexandrian Christianity: Selected Translations of Clement and Origen* . . . by J. E. L. Oulton and Henry Chadwick, Philadelphia, 1954.

5. *Op. cit.,* p. 83.

6. Irenaeus' treatise is available in *The Ante-Nicene Christian Library: Translations of the Writings of the Fathers Down to A.D. 325,* edited by A. Roberts and J. Donaldson, Vol. 5, Irenaeus, Vol. 1, Edinburgh, 1867.

7. Paul took worried notice of this cosmogony involving the emanation from the highest deity of a hierarchy of spirits. He is very explicit about this in Colossians 2: "See to it that no one deceives you through any empty, seductive philosophy that follows mere human traditions, a philosophy based on cosmic powers rather than on Christ" (verse 8). . . . "Thus did God disarm the principalities and powers" (verse 15). . . . "Let no one rob you of your prize by insisting on servility in the worship of angels" (verse 18).

8. David Daube tells of this rabbinic tradition in his *The New Testament and Rabbinic Judaism,* Part II, *Legislative and Narrative Forms,* Chapter 3, "Precept and Example," N.Y., 1973.

"The question arises . . . What is the precise force of this argument, 'male and female he created them'? At first sight it looks quite irrelevant, speaking neither in favour nor against divorce; or perhaps in favour, seeing that God created two independent beings. Modern commentaries incline to slur over the difficulty. The true explanation lies in the fact that, for the Rabbis, this verse contains the doctrine—familiar to the readers of Plato—of the ideal, androgynous man, the doctrine that when God created the first man, he created him as both man and woman in one.

"The reasons why the Rabbis connected the doctrine with just this verse are two. For one thing, they had to harmonize this verse, 'male and female he created them', with the narrative according to which Adam came first and Eve was only subsequently formed from one of his ribs. A plausible solution was to maintain that the original Adam was a composite being, and that this was the meaning of the verse in question. For another thing, the Hebrew text wavers between singular and plural. It starts by using the singular 'man'—'God created man in his image'—and then goes on to put the plural 'them'—'male and female he created them'. What sort of being might it be, the Rabbis asked themselves, of whom one could equally well speak in the singular or plural? Again the answer was that the verse must refer to the androgynous man.

"That this interpretation of the verse goes back to the New Testament times is certain. Philo has it. It occurs in many different Rabbinic sources. Moreover, the Rabbis inform us that the authors of the LXX, for the enlightenment of their gentile public, slightly altered the verse 'male and female he created them': they translated 'a male with his female parts he created them', or 'male and female he created him'—'him' in the singular . . ." (p. 72).

9. In *Alexandrian Christianity,* pp. 42–44.

10. *Epistola* 100, 12 (PL 22:823) (In Joseph Kerns, *The Theology of Marriage,* N.Y., 1964, Ch. 3, p. 31).

11. *On the Fashioning of Man* (*De Opificio Hominis*), ch. 17 (PG 44:87,190) (in Kerns, *op. cit.,* p. 32).

12. *On Virginity,* ch. 17 (PG 48:546) (in Kerns, *op. cit.,* pp. 32, 33).

13. *Ancient Israel,* p. 41. About polygamy in Israel DeVaux writes, "It is hard to say whether bigamy of this kind, referred to in Deuteronomy 21:15–17, was very common, but it was probably no more frequent than with the Bedouin and fellahs of modern Palestine, who, for all the liberty allowed them by Moslem law, are rarely polygamous. Sometimes self-interest leads a man to take a second wife, for he thus acquires another servant; more often it is the desire for many children, especially when the first wife is barren or has borne only daughters. There is also the fact that the Eastern woman, being married young, ages very quickly. The same motives played their part, no doubt, in ancient Israel" (*op. cit.,* p. 25).

14. "*Talmud* (Aramaic *talmûd,* 'teaching'), the name of a collection of Jewish rabbinical literature. The name Talmud properly belongs to only a part of the collection, but it is popularly used to designate the entire collection. . . .

"The core of the Talmudic literature is a collection of rabbinical opinions called the *Mishna;* this collection was made by Rabbi Judah ha-Nasi in A.D. 200. The rabbis whose opinions are collected in the Mishna are called *Tannaim,* 'teachers.' . . .

"The Mishna itself became after its publication the subject of rabbinical study, and two commentaries upon the Mishna, composed by compiling the opinions of rabbis who lived after the Mishna, were prepared. Each of these is called the *Gemara* or the *Talmud* indifferently; they are distinguished by their place of origin as the Palestinian Talmud, prepared in the rabbinical schools of Palestine, and the Babylonian Talmud, prepared in the schools of Babylonia. . . .

"There are other bodies of rabbinical literature similar in form and content. The *Tosefta* (additions) is a collection of opinions of the Tannaim found outside the Mishna. . . .

"The Mishna-Talmud can be described generally as an interpretation of the law, i.e., of the Pnt as a divinely revealed guide of morals and conduct. Almost any description, however, fails to describe the form and contents of the collections. The object of the interpretation is chiefly to settle problems of casuistry: to determine the obligations of the law as precisely as possible. . . . The traditions of the elders are treated as of equal value with the law and are submitted to the same discussion and interpretation" (McKenzie, *Dictionary of the Bible,* Milwaukee, 1965, p. 866).

15. For this information on rabbinic opinions I have drawn from Noonan's volume, *Contraception,* pp. 70ff.

16. See Noonan, *op. cit.,* p. 71.

17. This anthropology and the morality it bred are especially evident in Philo's treatise, *On the Fashioning of the World* (De Opificio Mundi, 50:144).

18. I have translated the Greek of these passages from the *Loeb Classical Li-*

brary edition of Philo's works, in ten volumes, Cambridge and London, 1939. Book 4 of the *Special Laws* is in Volume 8 of this edition.

19. *Op. cit.,* Vol. 7, p. 478, par. 8.

20. *Ibid.* par. 9–10.

21. *Op. cit.,* Vol. 6, par. 40–45, pp. 162–164.

22. *Op. cit.,* Vol. 6, par. 136–137, p. 70.

23. *Op. cit.,* Vol. 7, par. 32, p. 494.

24. *Ibid.,* par. 34–35, p. 496.

25. *The Basics Works of Aristotle,* edited by Richard McKeon, N.Y., 1941. 1253a, p.1129.

26. *Ibid.*

27. Quoted in A.C. van Gaytenbeek, *Musonius Rufus and the Greek Diatribe,* Assen, 1962, p. 68.

28. In *The Stoic and Epicurean Philosophers,* edited by W. J. Oates, N.Y., 1940, p. 263.

29. *De Finibus,* III, 20, 65ff. Quoted in van Gaytenbeek, *op. cit.,* p. 69.

30. *The Dialogues of Plato,* translated by B. Jowett, in two volumes, N.Y., 1937, Vol. 1, pp. 714ff.

31. *Loc. cit.,* p. 716.

32. *Basic Works,* 1334b, p. 1301.

33. *Loc. cit.,* 1336a, p. 1303.

34. *Loc. cit.,* 1335b, p. 1302. He no more than glances at the moral issue in abortion by adding ". . . what may or may not be lawfully done in these cases depends on the question of life and sensation."

35. *Op. cit.,* 1162a, p. 1073.

36. Quoted in van Gaytenbeek, *op. cit,* p. 64.

37. *Ibid.*

38. In van Gaytenbeek, *op. cit.,* p. 64.

39. *On Joseph* (43), *op. cit.,* Vol. 6, p. 165.

40. In Van Gaytenbeek, *op. cit.,* p. 62.

41. *Op. cit.,* p. 68. Of the same teleological evidence Musonius' pupil, Epictetus, wrote in his *Discourses* (I, 6, 9) ". . . the male and the female and their desire for coitus and their ability to use those parts devised for this purpose, do not these point to a craftsman?"

42. *Dialogues,* Vol. 2, 839, p. 588.

43. *The Nature of the Universe,* sec. 44 (in Noonan, *op. cit.,* p. 67).

44. In van Gaytenbeek, *op. cit.,* p. 71.

45. In Noonan, *op. cit.,* p. 67.

46. *Basic Works,* 608b, p. 637.

47. *Op. cit.,* 1277b, p. 1182.

48. *Op. cit.,* 1156b, p. 1061.

49. *Op. cit.,* 1162a, p. 1073.

50. *Op. cit.,* 1158b, pp. 1065–1066.

51. *Op. cit.,* 1161a, p. 1071.

52. *Op. cit.,* 1160b, p. 1070. And to be honest, as he believes, to all the evidence, he acknowledges the exceptional instances in which women rule in a marriage because of their inherited wealth: "Sometimes, however, women rule because they are heiresses; so their rule is not in virtue of excellence but due to wealth and power, as in oligarchies" (*ibid.*).

53. *Op. cit.,* 1255b, p. 1135.

54. *Op. cit.,* 1259a, p. 1143.

55. *Op. cit.,* 1260a, pp. 1144–1145. Aristotle's evaluation of friendship in mar-riage—the natural inequality of husband and wife—is by no means exclusively his. A generation earlier Xenophon in his study of married and domestic life, *The Oe-conomicus* (Book 4), emphasized a husband's honor rather than his devotion to his wife. That which is to join them in mutual care is rather their concern for material things than anything else. Those among the ancients who thought that husband and wife ought in marriage to form a friendship of equals were few and not famous. Hierocles, an Alexandrian Neo-Platonist, thought that a marriage in which the partners share everything gives the greatest satisfaction. Antipater of Tarsus, a fourth-generation member of the early Stoa, in his *On Marriage* insisted that mar-riage should be a perfect mixture, as of water and wine; the partners should share everything equally. Both these authors are cited in Stobaeus IV, 22–25 (in Van Gaytenbeek, *op. cit.,* p. 65).

56. *Politics,* Book 1, chapter 1, *op. cit.,* 1252a, p. 1127.

57. *Op. cit.,* 1252a, pp. 1127–1128.

58. *Op. cit.,* 1260b, p. 1145.

59. N. 33, in *Ancient Christian Writers,* J. Quasten and J. C. Plumpe, editors, Vol. 23, Westminster and London, 1956, p. 74.

60. In *The Fathers of the Church,* Roy J. Deferrari *et al.,* editors, Vol. 10, N.Y., 1950, p. 388.

61. CSEL, 2:45.

62. *Alexandrian Christianity,* p. 67.

63. *Op. cit.,* p. 66.

64. In Noonan, *op. cit.,* p. 102.

65. *Ibid.*

66. *Ibid.,* pp. 103–104.

67. *Ibid.,* pp. 102–103.

68. CSEL, 14:28.

69. In Kerns, *op. cit.,* p. 42.

70. *Ibid.*

5. AUGUSTINE ON THE NATURE OF MARRIAGE

The historical setting of Augustine's thinking and writing on marriage was in great part his reaction to challenges to marriage coming from two sources that were almost polar opposites.[1] On the one side there was the Manichee condemnation of marriage, or at least of procreation, as essentially evil; on the other there was a charge against him personally coming from certain Pelagian Christians who insisted that his refutation of the Manichees was so qualified as to leave him in fundamental agreement with them.

The Manichee Christians with whom Augustine dealt were members of a worldwide religious movement that had infiltrated the Christian churches. The Manichees took their name from their prophet and founder, Mani, a Parthian born in Babylon in 216, who claimed to be as a youth the recipient of a divine revelation that disclosed to him the truth of the cosmos and of history, and that set him in a vocation to carry this disclosure to all the human race. At heart Manicheeism was Gnosticism reborn, since it proposed salvation through a perfect knowledge, or *gnosis,* and through the living out of the consequences of this knowledge.

Manichee doctrine proposed a dualistic structure of the universe. The dual and opposed elements are Good-Evil, or Light-Darkness. Behind these names it is spirit that is Light and goodness, matter in all its manifestations that is Darkness and evil. The doctrine divided the history of the universe into three epochs: the *initium,* when spirit and matter were separate, having been created by the respective good and evil deities, before the cosmic (and *cosmogonic*) conflict that introduced the second period, the *medium,* and formed the universe as it now exists; the *medium* is the epoch that witnessed the creation of Adam and the human race. During it spirit and matter are intermingled and are in constant conflict. But also during it the third and final epoch, the *finis,* is being prepared through the work of the Ambassadors of Light, who have succeeded one another since Adam. The *finis* will be the eschatological age, wherein the original separation of spirit and matter, of Good and Evil, will be repaired.

Meanwhile during the *medium* the entire cosmos is in struggle, and the struggle goes on in microcosm within every human being. Those who would emerge victorious from it into the Kingdom of Light must live a severely ascetic life. They are the demands of this asceticism that divide the human race into three classes of persons.

There is the tiny and elite group of the *electi,* who can live and must live the Manichee ascetic ideal in the highest degree. In its negative features this asceticism is abstention, withdrawal, separation from all that is evil in essence or leads to evil. Thus the *electi* must have nothing to do with wine, with meat, agriculture, hunting, business, sexuality, marriage. They must keep a triple guard over the person: by the *signaculum oris* (the seal over the mouth) they must avoid blasphemy and evil foods; by the *signaculum manus* (the seal on the hands) they must avoid work and the destruction of plants or animals; by the *signaculum sinus* (the seal on the duct) they must avoid any sexual activity.

The *auditores* make up the far more numerous sector of the Manichee church. Their asceticism, though obligatory, is less strict. They need fast only once a week, on Sunday. Marriage is tolerated for them, as is concubinage. But they must not procreate.

Outside the Manichee church all others are the damned, whose souls are fated to return by metempsychosis to this life after death in the bodies of animals, until eventually they end in hell for all eternity. These are the human beings who, among other kinds of evil conduct, procreate in their marriages.

The attack against Augustine from the opposite quarter came mainly from Pelagius' disciple, Julian. Again, it was that Augustine's defense of marriage against the Manichees was a half-hearted one. In truth Augustine was caught in a kind of cross-fire of twisted meanings. He insisted against the Manichees that marriages since the fall of the first parents (therefore since the dawn of creation) are not fundamentally evil. He based this insistence on evidence available to all. For even if the great majority of marriages are lived sinfully even by Christian spouses, the cause of this cannot be the state of marriage itself. Marriage can yield verifiable goods, and in fact does so among many Christian spouses.

But the Pelagians charged him with conceding too much to and even siding with the Manichees in acknowledging this fact of the sinfulness in almost all marriages. They acknowledged no real historical fall of mankind from original grace, and could thus see no fundamental difference between the human condition vis-à-vis sinfulness after the first sin and before it. Consequently by conceding the general sinfulness of marital conduct since the fall, Augustine had, they thought, acknowledged the fundamental sinfulness of marriage.

What Augustine did then, in order to counter both attacks, was to defend the fundamental goodness of marriage against the Manichees, and this on two levels, or at two moments in marriage's history. The first was marriage as God originally intended it, before its being damaged by the first sin. This was marriage as a kind of ideal institution, almost but not quite detached from its incarnation in real-life men and women. The second moment or level was marriage since the first sin, as it has been lived and will be lived in real life until the end of time. He claimed goodness for marriage in this "moment" too, but from different evidence than that supporting its pristine, ideal goodness.

The Goods of Marriage That Excuse Its Use

Augustine's claim for marriage against the Manichees was that it is good a priori because it is God's creation, and a posteriori because three observable goods are found in it. In the latter he seems to have had two meanings that are linked in marriage's history. As designed by God it is to contain these goods and can do so; and even after its being damaged by the first sin and by sinfulness ever since, many marriages (especially those of devout Christians) still contain them.

The goods he had in mind are three: fidelity (*fides*), offspring (*proles*) and the sacrament (*sacramentum*), which in his thought-system has many meanings, but seems in this case to designate persevering commitment. His first and briefest formulation of these is in The Good of Marriage (Chapter 24, n. 30): "These are all the goods on account of which marriage [itself] is good: offspring, fidelity and the sacrament."[2]

He offered two other fuller formulations of these goods. In the *Commentary on the Literal Meaning of Genesis* (Book 9, Chapter 7, n. 12) he explains:

> This [good] is threefold: fidelity, offspring, sacrament. Fidelity means that one avoids all sexual activity apart from one's marriage. Offspring means that a child is accepted in love, is nurtured in affection, is brought up in religion. Sacrament means that the marriage is not severed nor the spouse abandoned, not even so that the abandoner or the abandoned may remarry for the sake of children. This is a kind of rule set for marriage, by which nature's fruitfulness is honored and vicious sexual vagrancy is restrained.[3]

Yet a third formulation is in his treatise *On Original Sin* (Book 2, Chapter 39):

> Marriage is therefore a good in all those elements that belong to marriage. And these are three: the orientation to procreation, the fidelity in chastity, and the sacrament of marriage. Because of the orientation to procreation it is written, "I want that the young widows should marry, bear children, become mothers of families." Because of the fidelity in chastity a wife has not authority over her body but her husband has it; as likewise a husband has not authority over his body but his wife has it. Because

of the sacrament of marriage, what God has joined no man must separate.[4]

Augustine's logic in citing these goods that have been found in many marriages is that they cannot come from an essentially evil cause. But since he was pointing at evidence in real life, his claim of these three goods took on an inescapable apologetic stance. For he had elsewhere already admitted that because of the first parents' sin passed down to all succeeding generations, sexual intercourse even within marriage has been almost without exception an exercise in sinfulness. Thus these goods produced in marriage, that would otherwise have verified its goodness simply, now in Augustine's mind become excuses for marriage. Indeed if his supposition about the almost inevitable sinfulness of sexual intercourse even within Christian marriages is accurate, even these marriages need a justifying excuse. Such is his argument: even in sin-infected marriages the intent and the hope of realizing these goods provide the excuse for risking the sinfulness and even perpetrating it.

When Intercourse Is Sinful

The reasons for Augustine's thinking that sexual intercourse even within marriage is sin-infected since the fall of the first parents deserves a detailed explanation even at the cost of delaying the explanation of his understanding of the three goods. Let me borrow from Chapter 6 of *The Good of Marriage* to set out schematically his moral judgments on intercourse in different circumstances and for different motives.

1. Intercourse can be without sin only within marriage. It is in fact sinless even there if it is motivated only by the desire of conceiving a child, and provided that consent is given to no other pleasure than to that coming from anticipation of a possible conception. (It was the rare instances in which motivation is so confined and pleasure so carefully focused that produced Augustine's judgment that intercourse is almost never without sin.)

2. Intercourse is had with venial sin within marriage when a spouse engages in it impelled by concupiscent passion and/or if there is accompanying subsequent consent to the carnal pleasure attending the act. (Later, in Chapter 10, Augustine says that if one of the spouses no more than renders the marriage debt to the other passion-driven and therefore sinfully motivated spouse, he or she thereby saves the other from fornication and does not sin provided that there is no subsequent consent to the carnal pleasure in the act.)

3. Intercourse is had with mortal sin if it is with any person other than one's spouse; and it is mortally sinful also with one's spouse if it is done in any way that avoids the possibility of conception. (In Chapter 11 Augustine says that for the wife to do the latter is worse than her countenancing her husband's adultery.)

In effect, according to Augustine, since on the biblical record, as he interpreted it, Adam and Eve had intercourse for the first time only after their sin, the sole instances of sinless lovemaking with intercourse in the history of the race have been those of a married saint every century or so.

All this complex judgment follows as a necessary consequence of his theory of original sin, which I shall outline in a moment. But it is clear that Augustine saw a priori only three possible motives for lovemaking with intercourse: capitulation to concupiscent passion (sinful), conception (sinless) and consent to a spouse's concupiscent demand in order to protect him or her from worse sin (also sinless). Nowhere in his writings on the subject (in none of the titles listed in note 1 of this chapter) have I found a hint that he acknowledged a middle ground of motives for which men and women who love one another make love—among others the desire to show and to feel tenderness or gratitude, the desire to comfort and console, the simple celebration of happiness, the impulse for sheer fun, the desire to give pleasure and to receive it, the sharing of intimacy, the desire to be known intimately and to know intimately.[5] Why he made no mention of these as possible motives may have been in part a consequence of the society in which he lived. The sexual arena in his twilight years of the Roman empire was as much an emotional slaughter-house as it is in our possibly twilight years of the post-Christian West. And men and women in his society did not ordinarily marry the persons they did out of love, but out of obedience to family arranging, often leaving their passion to wander elsewhere. Augustine's own experience with sexually expressed passion had for years been an agonizing struggle fought to less than a draw. Even while he was in Milan pondering baptism and had given up his mistress, taken when he was sixteen, to make way for an honorable marriage with the girl Monica had found for him, he took an interim mistress until the girl came of legal age. Somewhere in that bizarre sequence tenderness must have gotten lost and passion come to be despised.

But again his main reason for seeing almost inevitable sinfulness in marriage was his interpretation of original sin, the tragic event in the Garden of Eden and the tragic, history-long consequences of it; and joined with and doubly energizing this interpretation was that of the key portion of Chapter 5 of Paul's Epistle to the Romans.

Augustine's Interpretation of Original Sin

The narrative of the formation of the first man and woman, of their temptation and sin, contained in the second and third chapters of Genesis Augustine took without question to be a factual account of events that had transpired some four thousand years before the birth of Jesus, in a garden-like park somewhere in the Mesopotamian Valley. He would have rejected violently the suggestion that the narrative is a Hebrew parable composed in the ninth or tenth century B.C., modeled literarily on the ancient Near Eastern creation myths, and intended by its author or authors to explain imaginatively the entry of evil and suffering into human experience—and

differing from all earlier and contemporary explanations in that it insisted
that this entry was by the free choice of the first human couple.

He did reject as ridiculous the opinion of some of his contemporaries
that Adam's and Eve's sin was their having intercourse for the first time
and prematurely against God's will, since it was clear in Genesis (he said
in *De Genesi ad Litteram,* 11:41) that they had intercourse for the first
time only after their sin. In countless places and in different ways he insisted that their sin was one of prideful disobedience to God's pointed command to not eat of the tree of the knowledge of good and evil. That was
original sin the deed. What of original sin the inheritance, that with which
every human being is infected as a consequence of his first parents' sin, and
because of which Christians baptize their children? By a bitter irony that
too, in Augustine's mind, is a kind of disobedience, but a disobedience carrying a sexual name. It is concupiscence.

His thinking, imagery and nomenclature for concupiscence shift focus
constantly. I shall try to sort out their different meanings presently. For
now a central element of his theology of original sin is to be noted. The
anthropological part, so to speak, of the punishment coming to Adam and
Eve was that, just as they had sinned by disobeying God's command and
thereby upsetting the order of wills intended by him, so in just retribution
their lower powers were always to disobey reason and will in them, thereby
upsetting the order within their nature originally willed by God. Rather
than obey reason and will, these lower powers are doomed to obey the
stimulus of libido (the *incentivum libidinis,* as he named it.[6]

Augustine insisted on the hypothetical goodness and innocence of intercourse as God had originally intended it. He said that had Adam and
Eve not sinned, and had every human being therefore lived in a paradisia-
cal state, there would indeed be intercourse, since that is the natural way
for children to come into existence. But in such a situation intercourse
would take place without concupiscence.[7] This means, as part of a striking
religious psychology, that the genital organs of both men and women
would be readied for intercourse only at the calm command of the will,
itself drawn by a tranquil love.[8] These organs would obey as readily as the
hand obeys the command of an artisan. They would not, as they do now,
live a law of their own, defying the command of the will and moving into
action impelled by a surge of passion.

Again, this disobedience of the genital organs to reason and will,
which is a consequence of the one original, disobedient deed, is part of the
punishment for that deed. It is the sinfulness that Adam and Eve carried
about in their bodies until they died. Consequently only because of this
concupiscence in their bodies did they have intercourse, and inevitably this
intercourse itself was sinful. Consequently too their children, conceived by
this sinful act, contract the sinfulness in their own bodies. Augustine said
that the semen itself carries the corruption, the *vitium,* of sin.[9] This sinfulness is in every human being without exception, and would be there even

if he or she were never to commit sin personally, because all are linked by flesh (genetically, we would say) with Adam's sinful flesh.[10]

What happened in Adam's and Eve's conceiving their children has been repeated in every conception since their time. Augustine explains this in his graphic way: "But when spouses come to the dutiful work of conceiving, the very licit and good act of intercourse, which ought to be the effect of reason in them, cannot take place without the heat of concupiscence (*ardor libidinis*). And certainly this heat, whether it follow upon one's choice or precede it, stirs one's member only by a command of its own, and shows itself too to be stirred not by a free choice but by a licentious stimulus. . . . From this concupiscence of the flesh as from the daughter of sin—which is also the mother of sin when surrendered to in shameful acts—any child that is born is itself bound by original sin."[11]

Original sin thus understood is a major ingredient in Augustine's theology of salvation. By their baptism Christians are gifted with the grace of Christ merited by his death. This grace's effect on original sin is a forgiving one in the sense of a healing. (Christ himself, despite having ordinary human flesh, was born free of sin-concupiscence because his conception was not the effect of sexual intercourse.[12] Augustine explains that baptism forgives inherited original sin in such a way not that it ceases to exist in the baptized person, but that, though existing, it is not imputed to him as his guilt.[13] It remains sin in him in the mode of punishment. It does him no moral harm unless he consents to its stirring and enticement. Thus merely to feel concupiscence is not a sin,[14] though it does something to him even when he does not consent to it and even though it does not go so far as to stir up his body. That is, it stirs up evil desires in him. Indeed it is sinful *libido* that causes erotic dreams and nocturnal emissions (although this is not a sinful fault) for men and women carry this sinfulness around in their bodies.[15] And though the guilt itself of this concupiscence is washed away by baptism, the concupiscence itself remains until a man's infirmity is healed by the continual, day-by-day renewing of the interior nature through prayer and good works, even as the exterior nature grows old and crumbles. But it does not die out in those who give in to it; old men can be moved by it insanely even though it can no longer stir their bodies.[16]

Augustine says that Christian marriage has this accessory good in it— that carnal concupiscence, which is bad in itself, is rescued and turned to a good use by the spouses' doing their duty of producing children. And in marriage this concupiscence is repressed by the *feeling* of parenthood when having intercourse.[17] In their intercourse Christian spouses are affected by sinful concupiscence in the measure in which they engage in it not for the motive of conceiving but in order to take pleasure in lascivious passion. Pleasure in intercourse is without sin only if it is pleasure in attaining intercourse's primary end, which is conception.[18]

Augustine was faced with the Pelagian objection asking how an infant born of baptized parents can contract original sin, since his parents have been cleansed from this sin by baptism. His answer is that even baptized persons, although their inherited sin is no longer imputed to them as guilt but is only a punishment, nevertheless pass on sin-carrying flesh to their child. This they do because their seed is sin-carrying. Baptism cleanses the soul. But it is not the soul of the child that is passed on by inheritance; it is rather the body.[19]

A baptized person who uses his concupiscence to conceive uses this evil for a good purpose.[20] Thus because of concupiscence in spouses it happens that even from the good and legitimate marriages of the children of God there are born into the world not children of God but children of this world. This happens because even the reborn (the baptized) who procreate do so not by that wherein they are children of God, but by that wherein they are still children of this world.[21]

The Nature of Concupiscence

I suggested at the beginning of this brief examination of Augustine's thought regarding sexuality that the words he uses to explain this thought exchange meanings rather freely. There is some profit in trying to do as exact a scrutiny as possible of the sexual interior of men and women that he describes. One point of profit is that since his influence on the moral theology of the centuries following him was so overpowering, we may better understand the mood he set and the details he supplied for what preachers said from thousands of pulpits and confessors advised penitents in thousands of confessionals. More than any man, more even than St. Paul, from whom he drew so much of his thought and mood, Augustine dictated the feeling of an entire civilization about sexuality. I think it is even accurate to say that the New Testament teaching about sexuality and marriage that was understood in Christendom from the fifth century onward was that teaching filtered through the mind—and certainly through the emotions—of Augustine. His nomenclature for sexual matters became the vocabulary of Christendom. And since in such large measure language determines at least popular thought, what the Christian populace has thought of sex until this century has been the thought conveyed to it in Augustine's vocabulary.

In those of his essays I have cited he uses three words quite freely as synonyms. These are *libido, concupiscentia* and *voluptas*. They are at one and the same time (1) the residual effect in men and women of Adam's sin, (2) the punishment in all of Adam's heirs for this sin, (3) this inherited sin itself, (4) the evidence of the presence of this sin, (5) a wound in everyone's nature, (6) a sickness or infection carried in this nature, and more exactly in its flesh, and (7) the cause within persons of their sinful sexual acts—which in the concrete means virtually all their sexual acts.

Libido he describes as the *indecens motus membrorum,* the unbecoming or shameful stirring of the sexual organs. Or equally, this indecent stirring is the manifestation of *libido*. What is indecent about it is that it is beyond the control of reason and will.[22] Said another way, *libido* is a kind of rebellious law of its own in genital anatomy stirring it to activity in disobedience to reason and will. An earthy phenomenon that Augustine reports again and again in descriptive definition of *libido* is this: that whereas a man's reason and will can command the performance of his hands, his feet, his tongue, his lips, even of his bladder, when it comes to the performance of conceiving a child—a good and holy duty—he loses command over the member that was created specifically for this task. He must wait patiently as it obeys its own law. Sometimes it refuses to stir when he wills it to; at other times it stirs when he wills it not to. And he laments, "Must not the freedom of human choice blush on finding that for having despised the commanding will of God it has now lost command over members that are its own possession?" Echoing this lament is one of his incomparable epigrammatic lines: "*Ibi sumus veraciter liberi ubi non delectamur inviti*" ("Only there I am truly free where I take no pleasure against my will").[23]

Voluptas at least seems to be slightly different from *libido*. Augustine says that the semen of both men and women[24] is aroused and released by *voluptas* and with it; and *voluptas* is of course sinful. Again to the question how children could have been conceived sinlessly had Adam and Eve not sinned, his reply is that both seminations would have taken place only at the command of the will.[25]

Concupiscentia seems to be the body's tendency to rebellion, its refusal to obey the command of the will. Therefore if one would categorize it, it is more in the domain of disobedience and perverted right order than of bodily urgency or emotional compulsion.[26]

Of what exactly does the sinfulness of *libido-voluptas-concupiscentia* consist? An answer here is possible only if one notes the distinction in Augustine's mind between two kinds or states of sinfulness. One is *reatus*, actual guilty fault which is the lasting consequence of one's own sinful choices. It is this by which one is an enemy of God; it is this for which one deserves punishment. Does repentance get rid of sin understood in this sense? Yes and no. After repentance the *reatus* is still there; one is still guilty before God. But the grace of Christ coming in baptism does not let the *reatus* prevail as a cause of sinful conduct if the person does not give in to this concupiscence.[27]

The other meaning of sinfulness is *supplicium*. This too is the consequence of one's sinful choices, but unlike *reatus* it is not fault remaining in oneself. By it one is not an enemy of God but an object of his pity and mercy. The persistence of *libido* in a person is part of this *supplicium*. And what is peculiar about this part of the *supplicium* is that *libido* can become a source of subsequent sinful conduct and can again begin to rule reason and will. Of *concupiscentia* Augustine says pointedly that in those who have been baptized it is not a *reatus* if they do not consent to its "works" within their bodies. It is *called* a sin because it has been produced in persons by prior sinful conduct (Adam's) and because it in turn produces sin if it overpowers the person.[28]

He says that one of the ways in which a baptized person, a Christian husband otherwise good and faithful, lets *libido* overpower him is "to go to his wife intemperately." He offers only two criteria for the meaning here of "intemperately." One is that a man have intercourse for some other motive than to conceive. The other is that he not spare his wife even when she is pregnant.[29] He goes on to say that when a man has mastered *concupiscentia* in himself, he can use it for the one only purpose which is to conceive.[30] Thus he is not used by his concupiscence, but on the contrary he uses it. A further step in this mastery is that he not ask his wife for the marriage debt at all, but that he no more than grant it to her when she requests it.[31]

Augustine passes a kind of summary judgment on sexuality early in *De Bono Coniugali*. When discussing the nature of the good that marriage is and does, he notes speculatively that some goods, such as wisdom, are good in themselves. Others are good for the sake of another good, as a means of attaining the latter. Marriage and intercourse are this second kind of good, since they provide the good that is friendship. But it is not friendship between the spouses that he has in mind. Rather it is friendship generally in the human race. Spouses make friendship possible by propagating the race. For this reason it is good to marry. But it is still better not to marry. Enough offspring are produced by the sinful to provide persons for friendship; God draws this good from their sin.[32] Augustine urges on Christians perfect continence even within marriage; it is even better than intercourse had for the motive of conceiving. Why? Because marriage will end with the end of mortal bodies, but continence will be the permanent condition of all after the resurrection.[33]

He goes willingly with the momentum of this thought. What if all men and women, even the married, practiced continence? His answer is that this would be good, since the end of time would be brought nearer. The city of God would be filled and perfected the more quickly—as, he says, St. Paul himself wished in 1 Corinthians 7.[34]

Augustine's Marriage Ethic in Principle

One should never underestimate the degree to which Augustine took his marriage ethic from St. Paul in 1 Corinthians and from his neo-Platonic Christian predecessors. But sources aside, a likely clue for understanding this ethic is in his concept of sexual immoderation within marriage. He says that a husband goes to his wife immoderately under two conditions, which are reducible to one. In the first he seeks intercourse with her if she is already pregnant or is for some reason sterile. In the second, in which she is neither pregnant nor sterile, he seeks intercourse not in order to conceive but in order to take pleasure. In either case the immoderation consists of the same defect: seeking intercourse not for conception but for pleasure, or rather for the wrong pleasure, because if a man sought only the pleasure of conceiving a child, he would not be immoderate.

But why is it immoderate to seek intercourse for the common pleasure that accompanies the act, apart from the unlikely pleasure of conceiving? One could say it is immoderate by extension, or *in causa,* because pleasure-seeking tends to lead a man into sexual vagrancy, into adultery and fornication. But a husband could keep his sexuality faithfully within his marriage and yet be immoderate, as Augustine understands this. So the nature of immoderation must be verifiable even within marital fidelity as this is commonly understood.

The understanding of this immoderation is drawn from the Stoic ethic. For a man to act with moral rightness he must act both reasonably and in accord with reason. He acts reasonably if within himself all other faculties or powers—his emotions (such as anger and joy), his feelings (such as fatigue and hunger), his compulsions (such as to relieve genital tension), his bodily parts (such as his genital organs)—are controlled by reason and by will. He thus keeps in himself a right because natural interior order; he suppresses the ever-threatening disorder, or inversion, of letting his conduct be produced and ruled by his sub-rational and sub-volitional powers. This would be to act like the brute beasts, or at best like children and infants.

A man acts with reason when he uses his faculties in such a way as to attain the natural goals of their use. For his genital anatomy the goal is conception. The natural goal of his *libido* is to stimulate his anatomy so that it can bring about conception. These goals have been set by the designer of nature—indwelling divine Reason for classic pantheist Stoicism, God the transcendent Creator for Christian Stoicism.

But how do we know that conception is the goal for the genital anatomy and for libido? The evidence yielding the Stoic answer is threefold. First, look to the effects coming from the use of the sexual anatomy and ask which is of greatest value. Verifying it—and what is of greater value among its effects than human life?—discovers what this anatomy is for. Second, consider its structure in action. All its parts are oriented to accomplishing the result that is conception. Third, consider for what goal sexuality functions in sub-human natures where (and this is a pivotal Christian Stoic point) nature has not been perverted by sinfulness. It is here that the Stoic quickly pointed to the sexual conduct of animals as unperverted and according to nature. He took for granted that they use their sexuality exclusively to procreate.[35]

Therefore the Stoic conclusion: it is the will of nature, of nature's Creator, that human beings use their genital anatomy for no other motive than to conceive. This is its only use that is according to nature; any other is unnatural. A man making love to his wife out of the desire for pleasure differs from a fornicator only in his degree of perversion. To recapitulate what Augustine considered a sad and undeniable fact: rarely can even a devout Christian confine his motivation exclusively to conception. Concupiscence, the wound in human nature caused by Adam's sin, has brought this about. Given this fact, what is expected of him is that he keep his sinfulness as venial as possible by suppressing his pleasure as firmly as possible even while going to his wife only in order to conceive. What is hoped of him, but probably unrealistically, is that self-denial will eventually subdue in him entirely the desire for pleasure, with the consequence that he will give up intercourse for good.

The Meaning of "The Goods of Marriage"

One can define a social relationship only if one can name the goods that it is meant to attain. Such a relationship is what it *is* in the sense of what it is *for*. This is true even if its goal lies wholly within itself, such as the safety or the happiness of its members. The goal of the relationship is the good that the parties to it seek in coming together. But if its goals lie outside itself, it is an instrumental relationship; as a society it is for something other than itself and its members.

When one abstracts Augustine's three goods of marriage from their polemic context in his essays as excuses sufficient for Christian spouses' risking sinful concupiscence, one can find them serving a defining function. He uses them to define only implicitly, but when he names the three goods he does define marriage in part as a self-contained society. The fidelity and persevering commitment make it this. He defines it also in part as an instrumental society in that procreation is a good that lies beyond marriage and is for the sake of the larger societies, the state and the Church.

It is not clear that he thought of the ends of marriage when naming these goods. Nowhere in the Latin of his essays does the word *finis* appear. It is true that the ends of marriage identified later by the Scholastics are drawn in part from the three goods, and in some degree coincide with them. But they are not Augustine's formulation.

Nevertheless his goods do imply finality. Since they are the advantages marriage can bring to private persons and to their societies, they are what a person may seek to realize in marrying. The beckoning logical step at this point is to conclude that they are the advantages that marriage according to its nature is intended to realize; and therefore (now the moral step) in marrying a person *ought* to be motivated by the desire for this realization. (Eventually Catholic marriage law was to add the final step—a philosophical-juridical one—that unless a person accepts these goals in his relationship, it cannot be a marriage.)

Is the establishment of procreation and nurture as the primary end of marriage traceable to Augustine? Again no, not if one looks for an express declaration. But he did claim a primacy for procreation and nurture among the goods of marriage. In the last of his essays on marriage, *On Adulterous Marriages* (*De Adulterinis Coniugiis*), Book 2, Chapter 12, he says, "Therefore the propagation of children is the first, the natural and the principal purpose of marriage." (The Latin noun that I have translated "purpose" is *causa*.) Earlier, in his essay *Against Faustus the Manichee* (*Contra Faustum Manichaeum*) Chapter 19, n. 26, he had seemed to make procreation the only good of marriage, or if not that, at least its only end.

Only in his Latin can the near tautology he points to be seen: *Matrimonium quippe ex hoc appellatum est, quod non ob aliud debeat femina nubere quam ut mater fiat* ("For marriage is indeed called 'matrimony' from the fact that a woman ought to marry for no other reason than to become a mother").

To explain what Augustine means by each of the goods of marriage we may draw on his three statements quoted earlier in this chapter. The good that is offspring (*proles*) designates procreation, which includes not merely the bringing of children into the world but also their proper nurture. The good that is fidelity (*fides*) designates in a general way that the spouses will keep marital fidelity, but more particularly each one's honoring the other's exclusive right to the former's sexual acts. The good that is *sacramentum* designates the perseverance, the permanence of the marriage commitment, even the unbreakable character of the marital bond. (In using the word *sacramentum* Augustine did not mean to call marriage a sacrament of the New Law, a religious sign or manifestation in human conduct of God's grace-giving entry into the lives of the persons involved in this conduct. For one thing, he is here describing marriage as it is found among all human beings, pagans included. He predicates *sacramentum* of marriage according to various meanings in his essays. To date I have found that the term's principal meaning is that of a combined commitment and bond. What I have not yet found out clearly is the identity of the persons linked by the commitment-bond—whether spouse with spouse singly, or each spouse with God singly, or both spouses with God jointly while being themselves bonded to one another.)

Augustine's Secondary Goods of Marriage

However, it would be an incomplete and therefore inaccurate assessment of Augustine's understanding of marriage to say that he found no other goods in it than the three we have just examined. He found others. And as we shall see, they are, like fidelity and the *sacramentum,* goods internal to the relationship, advantages yielded to the spouses themselves.

In *The Good of Marriage,* Chapter 11, he offers a most general observation, that the husband-wife relationship is the first natural tie, or bond, of human society. Here he at least seems to set marriage in the context of friendship. He sees friendship as a primary datum, a given natural good in human association, because men and women are by nature social: ". . . because human nature is something social, because it possesses the capacity for friendship as a great and natural good."

He notes in this regard that the first man and woman did not come together as strangers. Taking the Garden of Eden parable as factual history he says that they were first of all blood relatives, since the woman was drawn from the man's body. He veers toward the Greek myth of the androgyne but reverses the path of etiological explanation in it. That is, he does not say that men's and women's craving for one another now is caused by their having been originally drawn from one another. He says rather that this attraction is evidence that the one was originally drawn from the other. He implies that Christians need invent no myths of origin to explain this power of attraction, because they have had revealed to them the history of an origin that explains it clearly. He adds that God drew all human beings from one set of parents just so that they might all be related by blood and thus might more readily take up the great natural good that is friendship.

But Augustine never takes the one more step, in developing this thought, of saying that what marriage is, is a form of friendship. On the contrary, he almost formally denies this. Later, in Chapter 9, he writes of two kinds of goods that God gives, one the instrumental good, the kind that is sought for the sake of something else that is good. The other is something good in itself, like wisdom, health and friendship. He says that marriage does not belong among the latter, It, along with sexual intercourse, is a good that is a necessary means for something else. Marriage's relationship to friendship is just this, that it is needed to provide children who may grow up to form friendships. Even so, he continues, a person does better not to wish for the (instrumental) good that is marriage. There is no danger that because of this the race will go out of existence. Illicit intercourse, given the actual state of human conduct, will assure enough human beings to form friendships. Besides, as I have noted earlier, he says in Chapter 10 that if all men and women remained continent, the sooner would come the end of history and the sooner would the City of God reach its consummation.

He does veer back toward calling marriage a friendship when, in replying to the Manichees' charge that marriage is evil, he says that it is not, because it produces good things. He says that it is valuable first of all because of its source. God created it; heterosexual attraction and union, whatever dismal things men and women have since done to them, exist by his design. (He adds a point he later repeats elsewhere, that when Jesus was invited to the wedding at Cana of Galilee, he did not turn down the invitation but accepted it. Presumably if he thought marriage were evil, Jesus would have declined.)

It is in Chapter 3 of *The Good of Marriage,* when he names the values internal to marriage making it good, that he glances again at friendship. Not the first, but the second value that marriage yields is the natural companionship of two persons of diverse sex. This is a natural good belonging in the domain of natural charity. It shows up in an especially helpful way in the care that elderly spouses, no longer capable of intercourse, can have for one another:

> One may ask justifiably why marriage is good. It seems to me to be good because of the procreation of children, but also because of even the natural association itself of the two different sexes. Otherwise one could not say that the elderly can be married, es-

pecially if they had lost their children or had simply never begotten any.

The same thought for the value of companionship appears in his essay, *On the Traditions of the Catholic Church* (*De Moribus Ecclesiae Catholicae*), Book 1, Chapter 30. He mentions there the simple association or companionship of domestic life as a good internal to marriage:

> You [the Catholic Church] subject women to their husbands in chaste and faithful obedience not for the satisfying of passion but for the procreating of children and for their sharing in family life. You set husbands over their wives not to demean the weaker sex, but themselves ruled by the law of genuine love.

Again, in his *Commentary on the Sermon on the Mount* (*De Sermone Domini in Monte*), Book 1, Chapter 15, n. 42, he distinguishes three values that a man and woman can seek for in their marriage. He all but expressly names these as motives they claim in marrying, all of them worthy. Without his taking note of it, in naming the second of these motives he touches also that good that he elsewhere identifies as marriage's (objective) primary end:

> Therefore a Christian man can live in peace with his wife. He can with her provide for the needs of the flesh—which the Apostle [Paul] sees as something permitted but not commanded. Or they can provide for the procreation of children, and this can be praiseworthy to some degree. Or they can provide a kind of brother-sister companionship, without any bodily commingling.

In these passages Augustine has enriched the source whence Catholic canonists and theologians will later draw one of their "secondary ends" of marriage, that one whose name least exactly describes its nature because the name can refer to so much—the *mutuum adiutorium* of the spouses, their mutual help, or support.

The other secondary end Augustine mentions in more than one place. It is obvious enough in Chapter 6 of *The Good of Marriage,* where he names a kind of mutual help spouses can give one another that could be deemed one of friendship's supports, but of a singular kind. They provide for one another an outlet for passion *within* fidelity, and therefore a licit outlet that protects them from fornication and adultery. Even more than this, by confining their intercourse within marriage they help one another by holding to the level of venial sin even that intercourse that is sought not for procreation but for the sinful motive of satisfying *libido*—a satisfying which outside marriage would be mortally sinful.

To return one last time to Augustine's judgment that procreation and nurture make up the principal value of marriage, and its principal reason for being chosen by men and women, I note again his axiomatic statement in Chapter 24 of *The Good of Marriage:* "These are all goods by reason of which marriage is good: offspring, fidelity, sacrament." This is a tauter summary of a looser formulation immediately preceding: two goods of marriage acknowledged among all nations and among all men are, first, that it is a source of procreation, and, second, that it is a place of faithful chastity. But among the people of God marriage has the added good that is the sanctity of the sacrament, which for them makes not only remarriage after divorce but divorce itself impossible.

Successively through the essay he advances on that formula along indirect paths. In Chapter 5 he implies that the intent to have children is so necessary to constitute a marriage that he does not see how a couple refusing to have them and taking contraceptive means to avoid conception can be married at all—although he acknowledges a marriage where the couple have the same intent against children but take no immoral means to avoid conception and therefore do not simply reject them.

In Chapter 6 he varies the earlier statement that marriage is the first association in the human race. Here he says that this association is fidelity in sexual intercourse for the purpose of procreating children. In Chapter 10 he says that that intercourse belonging to marriage is the intercourse needed for procreation. A couple having intercourse to gratify *libido* have intercourse that does not belong to marriage. In Chapter 11 he says ". . . the crown of marriage . . . is the chastity of procreation and faithfulness in rendering the carnal debt." In Chapter 17 he approximates the formula to come in Chapter 24 by offering anthropological information, saying that that which is common to marriage among all races is that it is for the one purpose of creating children; and then, going back to his biblical source, he says: ". . . marriage was instituted for this purpose, so that children might be born properly and decently." In Chapter 19 he offers another anthropological explanation: procreation is the good proper to marriage; and this is seen in the fact that men are led by an obligation, by a certain instinct of nature, to replace persons lost through death.

Such was Augustine's mind on the matter in 401, when he composed *The Good of Marriage.* As I have already pointed out, eighteen years later, when writing his *On Adulterous Marriages,* he had changed it, not at all. There again in a formula he wrote, "Therefore the propagation of children is the first, the natural and the legitimate purpose of marriage."

NOTES

1. Those of Augustine's treatises dealing formally with marriage are *The Good Of Marriage* (*De Bono Coniugali*), written in 401; *On Marriage and Concupiscence* (*De Nuptiis et Concupiscentia*), in 418–420; *On Adulterous Spouses* (*De Adulterinis Coniugiis*), in 419. He had much to say about marriage also in his *Commentary on the Literal Meaning of Genesis* (*De Genesi ad Litteram*), a work to

which he devoted himself intermittently from 401 to 414; and in *On Original Sin* (its full Latin title is *De Gratia Christi et de Peccato Originali*) written in 418.

2. "Haec omnia sunt bona, propter quae nuptiae bonae sunt: proles, fides, sacramentum" (PL 40:394).

3. "Hoc autem tripartitum est: fides, proles, sacramentum. In fide attenditur ne praeter vinculum coniugale, cum altera vel altero concubatur; in prole, ut amanter suscipiatur, benigne nutriatur, religiose educatur; in sacramento autem, ut coniugium non separetur, et dimissus aut dimissa nec causa prolis alteri coniungatur. Haec est tamquam regula nuptiarum, qua vel naturae decoratur fecunditas, vel incontinentiae regitur pravitas" (PL 34:397).

4. "Bonum ergo sunt nuptiae in omnibus quae sunt propria nuptiarum. Haec autem sunt tria, generandi ordinatio, fides pudicitiae, connubii sacramentum. Propter ordinationem generandi, scriptum est: Volo iuniores nubere, filios procreare, matresfamilias esse. Propter fidem pudicitiae: Uxor non habet potestatem sui corporis, sed vir; similiter et vir non habet potestatem sui corporis, sed mulier. Propter connubii sacramentum: Quod Deus coniunxit, homo non separet" (PL 44:404).

5. This is not to say that Augustine was blind to the possibility of dear and intimate love between a husband and wife. He speaks of this in *The City of God* where he accounts for both a reason and an effect of the first woman's being formed by being taken from her husband's side: "The fact that the woman was formed for Adam from his own side shows clearly enough how dear ought to be the union of husband and wife" (I, 12, 27). How overpowering was the bond between the first man and his wife Augustine suggests in his *Sermon* 51: "Even if it meant taking part in her sin he refused to be separated from her, his one companion." But still Augustine refuses to say that the most characteristic and strongest expression precisely of this union is sexual intercourse.

6. In *De Peccato Originali,* Lib. 2, Cap. 34.

7. *De Nuptiis et Concupiscentia,* Lib. 1, Cap. 1.

8. *De Peccato Originali,* Lib. 2, Cap. 35.

9. *De Nuptiis et Concupiscentia,* Lib. 2, Cap. 20.

10. *De Peccato Originali,* Lib. 2, Cap. 37.

11. *De Nuptiis et Concupiscentia,* Lib. 1, Cap. 24.

12. *Op. cit.,* Lib. 2, Cap. 15.

13. *Op. cit.,* Lib. 1, Cap. 25. The student of Reformation theology may recognize here a source of Luther's theory of forgiveness of sin by non-imputation of sin that remains nevertheless.

14. *Op. cit.,* Lib. 1, Cap. 28.

15. *De Bono Coniugali,* Cap. 20, and *De Peccato Originali,* Lib. 2, Cap. 39.

16. *De Nuptiis et Concupiscentia,* Lib. 1, Cap. 25.

17. *De Bono Coniugali,* Cap. 3.

18. *De Peccato Originali,* Lib. 2, Cap. 38.

19. *Ibid.*

20. *De Nuptiis et Concupiscentia,* Lib. 2, Cap. 36.

21. *Op. cit.,* Lib 1, Cap. 18.

22. *Op. cit.,* Lib 1, Cap. 5.

23. *Op. cit.,* Lib 1, Cap. 6.

24. It was commonly accepted in the ancient and medieval understanding of the sexual anatomies that the lubricating secretion of the Bartholin's glands is a semination analogous to male ejaculation.

25. *De Nuptiis et Concupiscentia,* Lib. 2, Cap. 26.

26. *Op. cit.,* Lib 1, Cap. 6.

27. *Op. cit.,* Lib. 1, Cap. 24.

28. *Ibid.*

29. *De Bono Coniugali,* Cap. 6.

30. *De Nuptiis et Concupiscentia,* Lib. 1, Cap. 8.

31. *De Bono Coniugali,* Cap. 13.

32. *Op. cit.,* Cap. 9.

33. *Op. cit.,* Cap. 7.

34. *Op. cit.,* Cap. 10.

35. The ancients had no way of knowing what Jane Goodall would one day find out, that the most "intelligent" of the primates, those closest to man, the chimpanzees, engage commonly in masturbatory and incestuous conduct.

6. MARRIAGE IN EUROPE AND THE MEDIEVAL CANONISTS

Contempt for material creation seems to be an inevitably recurring attitude in those religions that propose to raise human beings above the condition in which they first find themselves. When the attitude surfaces in a milieu already alive with cosmogonic theories, with imaginings of the spirits' manipulation of human affairs, with a mania for cabals—elite and relentlessly demanding of detachment and purity—the result is such sects as the Gnostics and the Manichees.

While the contemptuous attitude never dies but goes underground to bide its time, sects embodying it appear and disappear. Those we have examined in the preceding chapter disappeared because they were destroyed by a mixture of forces, a mixture that was not at all points an alliance. As the exercise of authority in the Christian community became more effective with the waning of the imperial persecutions, it simply emptied the community of the Gnostics by excommunicating them. Later it did the same to the Manichees. The intellectual counter-attack by Clement, Irenaeus, Origen, and Tertullian had its effect of discrediting the Gnostics intellectually. Later Basil, Gregory of Nazianz, Gregory of Nyssa, Ambrose and Augustine did the same to the Manichees. Precisely because both these sects, though conceived in emotion, grew up on speculation and appealed to intellect, they were vulnerable on the intellectual front and were defeated there by the Father-teachers. And once the emperors became Christian, and once Christianity, having become the state religion, came under imperial care, heresy became a crime. The emperors helped destroy the Manichees by persecuting them mercilessly.

But what at last brought an end to these essentially Eastern and contemplative sects was a massive change of mood in the Mediterranean basin where they had flourished. A social climate of extended stability is needed both to breed ennui with the present state of life and to allow for the bizarre speculation and cult on the edge of life. Self-denying asceticism and contempt for marriage are, in a sense, social luxuries. One can ordinarily worry about rising above the demands of the flesh only if one is not otherwise in terror of death. This is the change that came over the peoples of the Mediterranean from the fifth through the seventh centuries. Gradually from all directions vigorous and cruel peoples (barbarians in the cultured Hellenic-Roman estimation of them) invaded the Mediterranean lands, tore down their societies and governments there, uprooted their culture, and destroyed their homes and even their lives. The Goths and the Lombards invaded Italy from the east and the north. African Christianity was overrun and destroyed first by the Vandals, then by the Mohammedan Arabs. Syrian Christianity was destroyed by these Arabs. University cities and catechetical centers were wiped out; religious speculation gave way to the bare struggle to survive.

Thus when Rome, her civilization and her culture seemed finally to vanish under successive waves of invaders, her survivors held to a spare inheritance concerning the nature of marriage. From Justinian's *Digest* they had Modestinus' definition, "Marriage is the union of a man and a woman, a sharing of all of life"; from Justinian's *Institutes,* they had Ulpianus' definition, "Marriage is the union of a man and a woman, a union involving a single [or undivided] sharing of life." From the Fathers, thanks mainly to their reaction to the Gnostic and Manichee attacks on marriage, there was the conviction that was to stand unshaken far beyond the succeeding millennium, that the only sinless motive for intercourse is procreation. Linked with the equal conviction that intercourse is permitted to the married alone, it produced the conclusion about marriage's nature that it is an *officium,* a dutiful vocation to produce children for civil society and for the Church. It also, the Fathers agreed unanimously, provides a place of refuge and restraint for sexual desire untethered into lust by the inherited sin of the first parents. And lying there, close by one another but as yet unintegrated, were the elements that could be gathered into the statement that among all the goals for whose attaining marriage exists, procreation and nurture is the first and most valuable.

All these parts of the inherited perception of marriage were to surface again after a twilight of about four centuries. During these centuries historical contingency again worked its effect on this Christian perception. A conflict between another two sets of Christians demanded another resolution, and the scholars and prelates who worked out this resolution did so mainly by putting to use the inheritance accumulated within their Church's first six centuries.

But first we must take note of a major development in the formal ecclesiastical management of marriage in the West. At the same time that the Christian way of life was meeting, infiltrating, and in some degree being assimilated into the barbarian kingdoms of Europe, Roman government was crumbling. As judicial administration collapsed along with it, bishops came to occupy the resulting vacuum of authority over marriage and family life. By the end of the seventh century, in what had been the

Western empire, bishops were exercising full jurisdiction. But even by the beginning of the ninth century this was not a jurisdiction separate and distinct from the old imperial jurisdiction, which was still held by the residual civil government. What happened was that this same civil jurisdiction was more and more taken over by bishops as quasi-agents of the government. There was no conflict between two autonomous jurisdictions; the one jurisdiction came to be occupied by churchmen in default of lay magistrates.

The conflict between Christian peoples whose resolution produced the medieval refinement of the inherited definition of marriage arose from a conflict between Roman law on marriage and the laws and customs of the major ethnic groups in the West. The classic Roman interpretation of marriage as a *consortium* established by consent (and no more than that) whose interior *forma* is the *maritalis affectio* (the will to be married) spread gradually into Western society. The Roman code and its reformed version promulgated by Justinian in the sixth century was preserved and applied by the canonists of Italy and of the Midi in France. In these territories the Church lived under Roman law and usually in conflict with local tradition. This conflict was inevitable and was bound to become a conscious challenge. For each of the major ethnic groups entering the inclusive Christian community had its own traditional understanding of the nature of marriage. And most especially it had its own process by which a marriage is brought into existence. None of these groups—the Lombards, the Franks, the Germans, the Teutons—was of a mind to simply relinquish its own tradition and adopt the Roman.

They were all the less inclined to relinquish it because of what they saw to be a major flaw in the Roman practice. The latter's insistence that marriage is created by the mutual consent of the parties, a consent necessary but by itself sufficient, had the effect of validating the clandestine marriage. In the strictest legitimate use of this Roman tradition all a youth and his beloved had to do in order to become husband and wife once they were of age (fourteen and twelve years respectively according to Roman law) was to express their marital consent to one another. This they could do in perfect secrecy. They could then announce to their families and to the larger world that they were married. Much as family and civil authorities might rail at them and ecclesiastical authorities might threaten punishment by excommunication and apply the punishment, the last-named were caught in the consequences of their own Roman tradition. No one could undo the reality of the young persons' marriage nor void the general obligation to honor the marriage. In the powerfully patriarchal European societies this product of Roman permissiveness was not to be accepted without a struggle.

Lombard custom required that before the nuptial celebration the couple exchange consent in the presence of the community and before an *orator,* a layman chosen by the parents. He asked and received the spouses' consent. (This exchange of the consent creating the marriage continued in Germany and northern Italy into the late Middle Ages.) Where the *mundium,* the dowry used in negotiation of the betrothal, was in full traditional use, the marriage was contracted between the *mundoaldus,* acting as an agent for the girl's father, and the groom-to-be. But in this case the essential step in creating the marriage was the *traditio,* the handing over of the girl to her husband by the *mundoaldus.*

Where the tradition of the *mundium* was neglected, the beginning itself of cohabitation replaced the *traditio* as the moment creating the marriage. In this case it was said of the bride: *Ambulavit ad maritum* ("She has walked (or gone over) to her husband"). This practice, as well as that of the *traditio,* was discordant and even irreconcilable with the Roman marriage by consent of the parties. The point of insistence in Lombard custom was that a transfer was required for a valid marriage, either the *traditio* of the bride, or the *traditio* preceded by the transfer of the *mundium.* Thus the strong contractual element in this Lombard custom is obvious. Although the consent of both bride and groom was asked, it is not clear that this was required as essential in creating the marriage. In any case the openness and essentially public nature of the Lombard procedure in marrying made clandestine marriage impossible.

In the Frankish tradition the bride received an endowment from the groom, and her father in turn gave the *mundium* to him. Even where there was no *mundium* the endowing of the bride was obligatory. If the latter was not done, there was a strong presumption against the fact of the marriage.

Among the Germanic people too a conveyance or transfer lay at the essence of marriage. This was the transfer of authoritative guardianship of the girl from her father to her new husband. A *mundoaldus* arranged with the girl's father for the transfer. She in turn had little choice about whom she married, into whose authority she was transferred. The husband, as the one holding the *mundium* following the transfer, became his wife's *mundoaldus.* After the handing over of the bride she was led by the husband to her new home. If a marriage was to be accepted as valid, as a *matrimonium legitimum* giving to the children the right of inheritance, it had to be conducted according to this ceremony. Without the ceremony a woman could be taken as a wife, but the marriage was not considered *matrimonium legitimum.* The woman was called a *concubina* and her children could not inherit. In this Germanic tradition the notion of validity itself differed from the Roman. And again because of the public nature of the process of marrying, clandestinity was impossible.

The Roman Procedure in Marrying

It is not that the Roman tradition had failed to produce a multiphase ceremony even in face of the fact that no one was obliged to use it. By the time of Pope Nicholas I in the middle of the ninth century the ceremony consisted of these four main elements: the betrothal (*promissa foedera*), a consent given by both parties in view of future marriage, a consent which could be given only with the consent in turn of the parent or legal guardian; the *desponsatio,* wherein the wedding pledges (the *arrhae*), including the bride's ring, were exchanged and the deed of financial settlement was given to the bride; the nuptial Mass wherein the spouses received the Church's blessing; finally the departure from the church and entry into the new home to begin married life.

But Roman tradition held that within these steps it was the mutual consent of the bride and groom, however it was manifested, that created the marriage. Even if other parts of the ceremony, or even if the ceremony in its entirety, were omitted, the creation of the marriage by consent alone was accepted. A custom creating ambiguity in many minds as marriage came increasingly to be thought of as a religious reality was that where the spouses were considered old enough to make the consent but too young to begin married life, the nuptial Mass was delayed until that life began. Did the Mass have some agency in creating the marriage? If it did, what was it?

This separation of the apparently civil marriage from the religious ceremony had the effect of reinforcing in the public mind the notion that whatever a marriage is in essence, this is distinct and separable from whatever is effected in it by the religious ceremony. The separation was exaggerated in the Christianized Lombard and Germanic marriage rituals, because there the handing over of the *mundium* was done through a layman *mundoaldus,* and the same layman witnessed the marital consent of the parties. In addition there was, after this handing over and witnessing, a considerable delay until the nuptial Mass and the receiving of the bishop's or the pastor's blessing. The handing over of the *mundium* and the witnessing of the consent must inevitably have been seen as the purely civil transaction they had once been, and, in view of the clear act of conveyance in them, a contractual transaction.

But the main point of conflict between authorities in the Roman tradition and those in the central European was not that the Europeans deemed marriage a contract while the Romans did not. In the ninth and tenth centuries neither had come to these expressly conflicting judgments, however contractual the marriage transaction in the Lombard, Frankish and Germanic uses may have been. The object of Roman resistance was the European treatment of the bride as a virtual chattel conveyed in a contractual exchange to the man whose negotiation through a *mundoaldus* most pleased her father or guardian. The European resistance in turn was against the Roman concession that the consent of the parties could create their marriage apart from any witnessing ceremony—a Church-vindicated permissiveness that undermined the European father's authority over his children and voided his chance to use them to improve the fiscal and perhaps social standing of his family.

But this conflict was still only the visible surface of the disagreement between the two traditions. Beneath the surface lay the substantial issue, a quite simple one: Which act or sequence of acts is needed to create a marriage? Is nothing more needed than the parties' expression of consent to one another, as the Romans insisted? Or is some *catena* of acts, some linking of betrothal, handing over of the *mundium,* exchange of marital consent, taking of the bride into the new home, and first intercourse—all of these or a selection of them—needed to create a marriage, as the Europeans on their side insisted?

A landmark dispute and decision in the ninth century helps the student of marriage to understand the elements of the conflict. Early in the second half of the century Stephen, a noble of Aquitaine, exchanged wedding vows with the daughter of Regimund, a fellow noble. But after the solemnization of their marriage he refused to consummate it. His reason for refusing emerged in his confession that soon after the solemnization he had had intercourse with a relative of his bride and thereby incurred the impediment of *affinitas superveniens.* That is, by having intercourse with his bride's blood relative before his first intercourse with the former he had, he insisted, made the latter his wife and turned his bride into his relative-in-law—which impeded his bringing their marriage to final reality. The premise underlying his plea was the Frankish tradition that intercourse, especially when accompanied by a promise to marry, in fact creates a marriage, and in turn that the consent alone unless followed by intercourse is insufficient for creating the marriage. He had had only the latter with the daughter of Regimund and thus was, in his mind, not married to her. He had not exchanged marital consent with her relative, but he had had intercourse with her and had promised to marry her—and by dint of that combination was in fact married to her, so he insisted. He was therefore impeded from taking up as husband of Regimund's daughter.

Count Regimund asked the bishops at the Synod of Touzy in 860 for a judgment in the case. On the advice of Pope Nicholas I the bishops asked Hincmar, bishop of Rheims, to write a reply, including a theological analysis of the issue underlying Regimund's request. *On the Marriage of Stephen and the Daugher of Count Regimund* (*De Nuptiis Stephani et Filiae Regimundi Comitis*) contained Hincmar's reply. In it he took an ambiguous stand partly in favor of the European tradition, partly siding with Regimund against Stephen's claim of his freedom from the former's daughter. For Hincmar contended that consummation by intercourse is essential for creating a marriage and that without it the partners are not really married despite their exchange of vows. As he explained, ". . . there are weddings which do not effect the bond of matrimony, those, to wit, which are not followed by the union of the sexes. . . . As St. Augustine says, 'Marriage lacks the symbolism of Christ and the Church where the partners do not avail themselves of their conjugal rights, that is, where it is not followed by the union of the sexes.' "[1]

Later in the same treatise he supplied by implication a reason why, despite the exchange of consent, there is no marriage created until the first intercourse: the couple has not yet tried to realize the prime good for which they seek to marry, namely offspring: "Let anyone who doubts this know that a betrothal, a dower and a bridal, such as took place here, did not make it a marriage, since it lacked the union of the sexes, and on that account both the hope of offspring and the sacrament of faith."[2]

Hidden in the issue was a consideration logically peripheral to it but one that was to prove decisive in the eventual resolution of the disagreement about which act or acts are needed to create a marriage. It was drawn from New Testament tradition. If Hincmar was correct about the essentiality of copula in constituting a marriage, then it followed that the virginal relationship of Mary and Joseph had never been a marriage. They had lived at most only a *matrimonium initiatum* (an inchoate marriage). This was unacceptable to Catholics generally and especially to the theologians, who read in the Vulgate translation of Matthew 1 that Joseph had at first hesitated to take Mary as his wife, but then, after the angel's disclosure of the cause of her pregnancy, took her as his *coniux.* And in the Vulgate of Luke 2 the evangelist was recorded as saying that Mary was Joseph's *uxor desponsata* (his espoused wife). The combination in the divinely inspired documents of *uxor* and *coniux,* they were convinced, removed any doubt about Mary's and Joseph's fully marital relationship.

How much authority disagreed with authority, and how long the disagreement went on, is evident in the writings two centuries later of a fellow countryman of Hincmar. Yves of Chartres' statements on marriage and on the act creating a marriage are found in his letters, in his *Decretum VIII* (dating from 1093–1095), and in his *Panormia* (1095). In the last-named he favored the theory that a marriage is created by the consent of the parties, and he quoted in favor of it Pope Leo I's ambiguous dictum (in his *Epistola* 167, *Ad Rusticum*): "No woman has entered a marriage unless a man has celebrated with her the nuptial ceremony."

In his *Panormia,* Book 6, Chapter 14, he judged that the mutual consent *instaurat* (begins or creates) the marriage. From this one would conclude that intercourse is not necessary in order that there be a marriage. And this is consistent with Yves' familiarity with the Roman tradition of marriage. In the *Panormia,* Book 7, Chapter 4, he records the definition of marriage from Justinian's *Institutes* of more than five centuries earlier. It would seem from this that nothing more than the parties' mutual expression of consent is needed to create a marriage understood according to that definition—". . . the union of a man and a woman involving a single sharing of life."

Yet in the same Book 7, Chapter 32 he says there is no *true* marriage until the first act of intercourse. And in his letters Yves is indecisive. He says that prepubescent children can marry if their consent is made under oath, but he says also that a marriage is not "legitimate" before the first intercourse. But even this does not keep him from saying that a marriage is nevertheless indissoluble before the first intercourse. His vocabulary on the subject is ambiguous; it is not clear whether *desponsatio* means to him betrothal or marriage. But as he uses the term *desponsatio iurata* (engagement formed under oath) it seems to signify nothing different from a non-consummated marriage. And *pactum coniugale* (the marital pact or agreement) seems to signify the same thing. He mingles marital consent and the forming of the sacred sign: in the consent, the *pactum,* there is effected a union of souls, as necessary as the union of the bodies for the signing forth of the union of Christ and the Church. The sworn consent motivated by charity is what principally symbolizes that union. In fact Yves acknowledges a marriage only where there is this *sacramentum* of the union of Christ and the Church.

Prolongation of the Disagreement

This disagreement about the act or acts needed to create a marriage began with the conflict between cultures that already had disagreeing customs concerning these acts.[3] The debate and the confusion were bound to continue as long as all parties to both approached the question at what was logically its conclusion. That is, it was futile to try to identify this act or acts until there was agreement on the definition of marriage. If in its nature it is simply the union of a man and a woman in a single sharing of life, there is no reason why simple consent expressed mutually cannot create this union. But to find out if a marriage is this or is something more requiring complex causation for its creating, the debaters would have to think of marriage abstracted from its cultural embodiments, and abstracted too from the religious-sacramental identity it had acquired gradually in Christian Europe. That is, the churchmen and the scholars would have to speculate on something they did not meet in real life, marriage-in-itself. However much they succeeded in doing this by the end of the twelfth century when the dispute was finally resolved, the resolution was not the fruit of such speculation carried on in abstraction. As happens so often in ecclesiastically monitored disputes, it was the fruit of executive authority used powerfully—in this instance used in favor of the Roman tradition.

The differences of opinion and the consequent uncertainty among the people continued into the first half of the twelfth century. Anselm of Laon (d. 1117), replying to the question that Yves had addressed, insisted that the unbaptized can marry because they can make the marital consent. In fact their marriages are sacraments in their own way, since they too are signs of the God who instituted marriage, although they lack the *res sacramenti,* the grace of charity uniting the spouses with God. About this subject of widespread disagreement he said that the immediate agency creating a marriage is the mutual consent of the spouses. This constitutes them as truly married. However, until their first intercourse the marriage is incomplete and can therefore be dissolved. Thus even a valid marriage must pass through stages of completion. His definition of marriage in his *Sententiae: Tractatus de Matrimonio,* is prolix and carelessly worded, and it betrays the difficulty experienced by the men of his time in refining to the degree of abstraction needed in order to produce a definition of marriage. Anselm obviously saw a need to improve on the *Digest's* definition; he did so by adding details of concreteness. For him marriage is "the consent of a man and woman holding to a single sharing of life, the consent to remain with one another exclusively and to have intercourse only with one another and without barring the way to offspring, a consent that is legitimate, one that is made legitimately by legitimate persons." That intercourse is essential to marriage as the object of the consent needed to create a marriage is obviously his thought.

William of Champeaux (d. 1122) sought to get at the nature of marriage by asking, in his *Sententiae* under the heading *De Coniugiis* (On Marriage), a question not uncommon in his time: Cannot a man who has promised himself in betrothal to one woman change his mind and marry another? His answer he drew from a distinction in the meaning of the term *fides,* a commitment. There is the *fides* of engagement, and the *fides* of marriage. By the first a man promises that he will, at some time in the future, take the woman as his wife. This is only a promise and does not work the effect that is the creating of a marriage. By the second commitment the man takes the woman as his wife here and now. Consequently a man who makes only the promise to one woman, then forgets about it and marries another, must keep the latter as his wife but must also do penance for breaking his promise to the fiancée.

William here introduces, although in seminal form only, a clear distinction that could have resolved the dispute over the act that definitively creates a marriage. In his own words it is the distinction between the *sponsalia de futuro* (the marital commitment for the future) and the *sponsalia de praesenti* (the marital commitment for here and now). William's pupil, Peter Abelard, made the same distinction between a first promise, *foederatio de coniugio contrahendo* (a promise to contract marriage at some future date) and the *foederatio coniugii* (the words which express the actual creating of the marriage). He and his disciples continued the thought begun by Anselm of Laon that intercourse as the object of the marital consent is essential to marriage. In *The Epitome of Christian Theology* marriage is defined as "a legitimate union of man and wife conferring the right to have intercourse without fault."[4]

Eventually the scholars and the authorities—the canonists and the Popes—were to conclude that the second of these commitments creates the marriage; that the first is not necessary for its creation; that the first followed by intercourse does not create it; but that a marriage once created by the *sponsalia de praesenti* remains incomplete until the first intercourse after this commitment for here and now. Once the distinction was adopted definitively it would prepare the way for understanding the act creating a marriage to be a contractual act, and the future intercourse, or some facet of it, to be the object of the contract. But persistent failure to make this distinction helped delay for at least another half-century a concordant teaching on the subject. Thus, for example, Pope Alexander II held that a promise made under oath to marry in the future is equivalent in its effect to the consent creating a marriage. Answering a query in 1067 from Constantine, bishop of Arezzo, he advised him that one of his people, a man who had married a second woman after promising under oath to marry a first, was an adulterer. In a letter to the bishop of Treves in 1074 Gregory VII offered the same opinion.

The Gregorian reform at the end of the eleventh century touched the issue of marriage only lightly. It was more concerned with the truly destructive abuses of simony and lay investiture, and with the attempt to establish the universal observance of clerical celibacy. In the matter of marriage it accomplished the final vindication of the Church's exclusive authority over the marriages of Christians. It otherwise proceeded cautiously, since the reforming Popes appreciated the need to respect local custom in marrying. Hasty and forced introduction of the Roman practice of marriage by free consent alone into the patriarchal societies of central Europe in which boys and girls were married at the turn of adolescence could have undermined these societies seriously.

The Dispute and the Medieval Canonists

This then was the issue agitated by canonists, Popes and bishops, and to a lesser degree by theologians, at the beginning of the twelfth century: not the question asking what a marriage is (a forthright question apparently once answered by classic Roman law preserved in Justinian's *Digest* and *Institutes*), but the oblique question asking which among the diverse elements making up the process of marrying among the peoples of Europe, or which few in combination, actually bring a man and a woman to be spouses. Asked in the year 1000 the question would have inquired among the following elements: the betrothal (the consent *de futuro*, made under oath or without it); the handing over of the *mundium;* the parties' consent *de praesenti;* the solemnization of the marriage, including the nuptial Mass and the priest's blessing, or at least the latter; the *in domum ductio*, the leading of the bride to her new home; the first act of intercourse following the exchange of consent.

By the year 1100 it was generally agreed that intercourse with the mere intent to marry did not create a marriage, that solemnization was not essential, and that certainly the handing over of the *mundium* and the *in domum ductio* were not constitutive or even necessary. By the middle of the twelfth century the dispute was at its keenest, since its terms had been narrowed by the clear distinction made between the consent *de futuro* and the consent *de praesenti*. This distinction had simplified the disagreement to this point: granted that consent *de futuro* cannot by itself create a marriage, but when made under oath and followed by intercourse, does this combination create a marriage? Then, in turn, about the consent *de praesenti,* is it by itself sufficient to create a marriage? Or to do so must it be followed by intercourse? And then the inescapable accessory question: If the answer in either case involves more than one step, at which step does the marriage become indissoluble? For example, if one were to say that the consent *de praesenti* is sufficient by itself to create a marriage, is it also sufficient by itself to make the marriage indissoluble? If the answer to this question is affirmative, then has intercourse—the act realizing the good that Augustine had called marriage's primary end, namely procreation and nurture—no function in setting indissolubility?

Hugh of St. Victor

The two groups that carried the debate to its conclusion by the end of the twelfth century were the canonists of the University of Bologna and the theologians of the University of Paris. But there was a theologian teaching and writing at Paris in the middle of this century, Hugh of St. Victor, who merits consideration independently of the debate. To begin with, he had little to do with ending it, even though he shared the opinion of his colleagues at Paris that eventually prevailed over that of the Bolognese canonists. He was the first Christian thinker of his time—in fact the first since Augustine almost eight centuries earlier—to write an independent and integral treatise on marriage, brief though it is. This was his *The Sacrament of Marriage (De Sacramento Coniugii)*, which is Book 2, Part II of his summary treatise, *The Sacraments of the Christian Faith,* completed between 1130 and 1143.[5]

The definition of marriage that he proposed—and he did this not obliquely or implicitly, but as a formal effort to define—was in almost all its parts uniquely his own. The definition he presented in his treatise on marriage appeared in one of his earlier treatises, *On the Virginity of the Blessed Virgin Mary (De Beatae Mariae Virginis Virginitate).*[6] It lacked the exactness of the definitions in the *Digest* and *Institutes.* But it reached back behind them to long-neglected biblical sources and at the same time hinted at the distant future in proposing that a marriage is a relationship of self-giving love.

> What else is marriage but the legitimate association between a man and a woman, an association in which each partner owes (*debet*) himself to the other by virtue of equal consent? This owing can be considered in two ways, that one reserve oneself for the spouse, and that one not refuse oneself to the spouse. That is, he reserves himself in that after giving consent he does not go now to another union. He does not refuse himself in that he does not separate himself from that mutual association of one with the other.

Hugh's definition of marriage, like that of anyone who has ever tried to define it, was in some degree predetermined by his avenue of approach to it, the goal to be reached which led him to the task of defining it in the first place. The twelfth-century canonists approached it seeking the answer to the question asking which act or acts create a marriage. Augustine had approached it, spurred by the Manichee repetition of the Gnostic condemnation of marriage, asking: "Given from divine revelation that marriage is good, in what specifically is this goodness to be found?" If one may read accurately from his definition backward, Hugh apparently began with the question, "Given that marriage is by nature a sacrament, of what is it a sacrament, and what within marriage is the sacramental sign?" He was, in short, a theologian, and got his definition of marriage for having asked a theologian's question.

Like every other Christian of his time Hugh took for granted that God had created marriage, and had done so in the Garden of Eden when he gave the first woman to the first man (according to the Garden parable in Genesis 2 and 3), to help him in the propagation of the human race (according to the creation poem in Genesis 1).[7]

He pointed out that God gave the first woman to the first man not as his mistress (for he did not take her from the man's head), nor as his servant (he did not take her from his feet), but as his companion (God took her from his side, midway down his torso). Nevertheless she was to look to him as her superior, since he had come first and she had in fact been taken from him.

Hugh saw two distinct institutions of marriage, separated in time, but at each institution made a sacrament. The first took place in the Garden before the sin of the first parents. Then and there it was instituted to carry out an *officium,* a functional duty, the multiplication of the human species. In its nature it was instituted as a pact of love (*foedus dilectionis*).[8] And because it was made such it could also be the sacrament it was intended to be, a sacrament of the relationship between God and the human soul. So marriage was made to be this, a pact of love, distinct from any goods it could realize or any ends it must attain. And apart from any of these it has been made a sacrament. In saying this Hugh clearly went aside from the mainstream of Scholastic thought that did little more than repeat Augustine and the other Fathers.

But this first institution intended also that marriage fulfill its *officium* through sexual intercourse. By doing this it could also, and subsequently, become the sacrament of the relationship between Christ and the Church. In saying this Hugh joined the opinion of most of his contemporaries and anticipated that of many of his successors, that the marriage of two Christians becomes a sacrament of the new law when the spouses have their first intercourse, and only then.

Marriage's second institution took place after the sin of the first parents (although Hugh does not try to identify the time or the place of this second institution). This institution, after the parents' sin, brought no diminution of the pact of love. On the contrary, it reinforced marriage's nature as such a pact. It did so by providing a *remedium* for the weakness and the evil in the spouses, or more exactly in their sexuality, by giving it an excuse. This excuse is found in the goods that marriage yields; and here Hugh had in mind the three goods that Augustine proposed, fidelity, offspring and perseverance in the marital commitment. Thus with the second institution there comes an addition to the *officium* given marriage in the first, in that the healthy procreation (belonging to the first) becomes also the *remedium* (belonging to the second).[9]

How central Hugh thought sacramentality is to the nature of marriage—central to it even in its original state, at its first creation, before the sin of the first parents and before the coming of Christ and its second institution—is evident in his reason for insisting that this "natural" sacramentality can be present even if intercourse never takes place. For even without intercourse marriage is a sacrament in its imaging the relationship of God and the soul. The transparent implication here reiterates what he had said earlier: a marriage is a relationship of spiritual love between the spouses; it is this relationship which makes it a sacrament and, in the logical sequence of his reasoning, therefore a marriage:

> ... the very association which is preserved externally in marriage by a compact [or covenant] is the natural love of souls which is guarded in turn by the bond of conjugal society and agreement.[10]

What is the relationship of sexual intercourse to marriage thus understood? It is an act of love which is a *remedium,* a protection against the sinful effects of concupiscence.

As for the object of the spouses' consent that creates their marriage, Hugh said that this is the association itself, the companionship of the spouses.[11] He denied that for the creating of the marriage intercourse need be included within this object. It can and may be included. If it is not, neither spouse is obligated to it. But if it is, each has the obligation to not have intercourse with third parties. And even if both exclude intercourse from the object of their consent, yet they are joined in marriage—in not only marriage but sacrament, the spiritual union of souls.

About the three goods named by Augustine and lodged at the heart of the Christian understanding of marriage by Hugh's time, the latter called them blessings and said that they *accompany* marriage. He named them faith (*fides*), hope of progeny (*spes prolis*) and the sacrament (*sacramentum*). He defined their goodness to be this: that their presence in marriage limits the evil coming into it with concupiscence and turns this concupiscence into marital chastity.[12] These blessings do not remove the sinfulness of concupiscence but reduce it from grave to venial. And inevitable though this sinful concupiscence be in sexual intercourse, the blessings neutralize it by making it non-imputable to the persons.[13]

He takes care to not say that these blessings turn concupiscence to good use by employing it for procreation, and to not say that the sinfulness of the concupiscence is diminished and rendered non-imputable by reason of procreation. This is consistent with the answer he gives to the question he poses to himself in paragraph 7, "Whether or not these blessings are inseparable from marriage?" He is confident that two of the three, fidelity and the hope of progeny, are separable from it. He draws his answer from the simplest evidence: men and women advanced in years and therefore sterile can and do marry. If the blessing of progeny were inseparable from marriage, the elderly could not marry. His judgment is that these two blessings add goodness to a marriage if they are present in it; if they are absent, this absence derogates from its goodness. But their absence in no way voids the marriage.[14]

In saying, however, that the sacrament, the commitment to permanence, is necessary if a marriage is to exist, he is consistent with his earlier defining of every and any marriage as a sacrament. He does not reason that because marriage is a sacrament, the spouses are inseparable. But starting with the supposition that the partners are inseparable, he concludes from this that in their relationship there must be a sacrament. And this is found not in their carnal union in intercourse, but in their companionship, their union of souls. In short, for Hugh every marriage seems by nature indissoluble.

He touched on the debate going on around him in insisting that a marriage begins to exist the moment the mutual consent is completed—a position implicit in his having already denied that the right to intercourse need be included within the object of marital consent. He reinforced his stand by denying that a promise to marry in the future, even if it is followed by intercourse, creates a marriage. Nor does he hold that solemnization, the traditional ceremonies in whole or in any of its parts, is needed to create a marriage.

Finally, his most inclusive definition of marriage, formulated in his copious style, is this:

> Marriage is that society which is consecrated by the covenant of mutual espousal when each by free promise makes the self debtor to the other, so that from that time neither may pass into another's companionship while the other still lives, nor may either separate from that companionship which they have with one another.[15]

The Theologians of Paris and the Bolognese Canonists

By the middle of the twelfth century the debate between the Roman and European traditions had been taken over and championed, respectively, by the theologians of the University of Paris and the canonists at the University of Bologna. The master at Bologna at the time was Gratian. By 1140 or 1141 he had completed a work of research and synthesis that was monumental for his time. He himself named the work *A Concordance of Discordant Canons* (*Concordantia Discordantium Canonum*); Innocent III later called it *The Corpus of Decrees* (*Corpus Decretorum*). It has come through the history of Church law known by its abbreviated title, the *Decretum*. In it Gratian included a collection and attempted harmonization of all the major texts on marriage available to him. It was a kind of counterpart to the *Summae Sententiarum,* the summaries of patristic texts be-ing gathered and edited at Paris at the same time.[16]

Out of this effort Gratian produced his own answer to the questions making up the substance of the current debate between the canonists of Bologna and the theologians of Paris. To his mind the questions came to a point in this: Are a man and a woman who have declared their intention to marry—declared whether by consent *de futuro* or consent *de praesenti*—truly married before their first act of intercourse? He acknowledged the consequences of the two possible contradictory answers: if a man and a woman thus promised are not married before their first intercourse, Mary and Joseph were never truly married. But if they are, then a brother and sister can marry and do so innocently provided that they never have inter-course. It was in preparing for his own answer to this question that he as-sembled in dialectical fashion the pertinent texts answering one way or the other (in *Causa 27, Quaestio 2*).

To reconcile as far as possible the disagreeing texts among those he had gathered, and to propose his own solution, he borrowed a distinction that his congenial adversaries at the University of Paris had already made. This was the distinction between the *matrimonium initiatum* (the inchoate marriage) and the *matrimonium ratum* (the ratified or completed mar-riage). He said accordingly that a marriage is begun by the *desponsatio* and completed by intercourse.

Gratian did not pull this distinction out of mid-air. True to his jurist method he educed it from a typical marriage case that had been ruled on by the bishops of Toledo in council. One man kidnaps and rapes another's fiancée; he is sentenced to public penance and forbidden ever to marry. If the woman did not consent to the crime, she is not to be denied marriage. But if the partners to the rape presume to marry, they are to be excommu-nicated.

Gratian reasoned from the decision as follows: the woman could not have been a wife to anyone if while her betrothed was still alive she was not forbidden to marry another. And he asks how the betrothed could through history have been called spouses by the Fathers when they were not married. His answer to this carries his key distinction: what is to be understood from the Fathers, as also from the logic of the Toledo decision, is that by the *desponsatio* a marriage is only begun; what the first inter-course does is to complete it.

That distinction Gratian made in Chapter 34 of this *Causa 27, Quaes-tio 2.*[17] He repeats it immediately in Chapters 35 and 36, which are little more than headings taking the form of consecutive axioms: "Behold, in the *desponsatio* a marriage is begun, not completed," and "It is by the inter-course of the conjoined that a marriage is completed."[18]

This, he hoped, was the distinction that would solve two problems: that of verifying the act and the moment that begin a marriage, and that of keeping a place for intercourse in creating a marriage. With this distinction too one could say that Mary and Joseph were truly married. As to the question how their virginal marriage could be called complete, Gratian found for it another kind of completeness in that it contained all of Augustine's three goods of marriage, *fides, proles, sacramentum.*

But Gratian's use of the distinction failed at the solutions he hoped for because of the obviously ambiguous reference he leaves in his use of the term *desponsatio.* He fails to make clear whether the word as he uses it refers to the act of betrothal (the consent *de futuro*) or to the wedding vows (the consent *de praesenti*). Elsewhere in the passage he says that the *desponsatio* by itself does not create a marriage. Here he apparently means the wedding vows, because he goes on to say that these vows, insufficient by themselves to create the marriage, nevertheless have this effect: that with the ensuing intercourse the marriage does come into existence. In other words, for creating a marriage the consent and the subsequent intercourse act as necessary co-causes, each insufficient without the other, but in cooperative tandem producing their effect. His expression of this is the following:

> From all this it is evident that the betrothed are called spouses by reason of their hope of future things, not by reason of the reality of present things. But how is it that they are called spouses from betrothal if a woman deemed betrothed is not called a wife? The answer is that persons are called spouses from the time of betrothal not because in that betrothal they become spouses, but because from the commitment that they owe to one another by virtue of the betrothal, they subsequently become spouses—just as sins are said to be forgiven by faith not because they are thus forgiven before baptism, but because faith is a cause of our being cleansed from sin by baptism. . . . [19]

Then, commenting on the ancient axiom, "It is not intercourse that creates a marriage, but consent that does so," he continues:

> . . . this is to be understood in the following way: intercourse without the intent to contract a marriage, and the deflowering of a virgin without the exchange of consent, do not create a marriage. But an antecedent intent to contract marriage and the exchange of consent has this effect, that in the losing of her virginity, or in her intercourse, a woman is said to marry her husband, or "to celebrate her marriage."[20]

One consequence of his ambiguous use of *desponsatio* that Gratian almost certainly did not intend was the possibility that the act of betrothal followed by intercourse could create a marriage equally with the wedding vows followed by intercourse. But whichever meaning he intended for the term, he insisted that by itself *desponsatio* creates only an inchoate marriage. Such a marriage can be dissolved; only a marriage ratified and completed by subsequent intercourse cannot be. The reason for the latter's invulnerability to dissolution is that for two Christians intercourse is, and makes their marriage, a sign on earth of the indissoluble union of Christ and his Church.[21] Disagreeing with the Parisian Hugh of St. Victor, he insisted too that only a marriage completed by intercourse is a Christian sacrament, because only by intercourse does it become such a sign.

Gratian's Definition of Marriage and of the Object of Consent

Gratian gave a larger place to the three Augustinian goods in his defining of marriage than did Hugh of St. Victor. The reason for this is not obvious, but one may guess that as a canonist Gratian was more concerned with marriage as a problem that showed up frequently in the ecclesiastical courts. To return for a moment to his answer to the question asking which act or acts create a marriage, his reply that it is consent completed by intercourse, with neither the one nor the other sufficient of itself, was an excusable tour de force. He was trying to free marriage from a dilemma. He wanted not to admit that consent alone could create a marriage, because by leaving vague the object of this consent—especially by not making intercourse its object—one is left saying what Hugh was willing to say, that a brother and sister can marry. But on the other hand, if there is no marriage until intercourse is completed, then one must deny that Mary and Joseph were ever married. While neither of these issues worried the marriage courts, there was one consequence of the above-mentioned vagueness that did worry them and a multitude of European families. Exchange of marital consent by messenger, by letter, by the agency of proxies was done commonly in medieval Europe. Young people seeking to foil marriage plans laid out for them by their parents, and to marry instead partners of their choice, could marry securely by such means even though locked away in house arrest, if consent were all that is needed. Gratian thought to break the dilemma, and to preempt rebellious sons and daughters, by saying that it is a sequenced combination of consent and intercourse that creates a complete marriage—the only kind that could finesse parents fully and finally in becoming indissoluble by its completion in intercourse.

What Gratian did also in proposing this answer to the question was to advance the theory, first sprung up in his time, that the object of marital consent, that to which the spouses commit themselves specifically as spouses, is sexual intercourse. This was an obvious step toward the theory that was to settle in for eight centuries almost (but not quite) as Catholic doctrine: that the primary goal of marriage is procreation and nurture.

I have just suggested that Gratian's answer that a marriage is created by a combination of consent and subsequent intercourse pushed him toward the answers to two other questions, one about the ends or goals of marriage, the other about the object of marital consent. He did address these two questions. And in answering them he added impetus to another quiet movement among the canonists of his time. This was the separating of the goals (however they would finally be identified) from the long-consecrated three goods coming from Augustine.

Not that Gratian failed to make full use of these goods. I have mentioned already that he used them to explain how Mary and Joseph were fully married despite having lived a virginal marriage. He quoted Augustine's *De Nuptiis et Concupiscentia* (Chapter 11, n. 13):

> Therefore every one of the goods of marriage was fulfilled in these parents of Christ—offspring, fidelity, sacrament. The offspring we acknowledge in the Lord Jesus himself: fidelity because there was no adultery; the sacrament because there was no divorce. . . . [22]

But later, in *Causa 32, Quaestio 2,* he took away from the importance of the goods to an authentic marriage when he asked and answered the question whether a couple who marry not to procreate but only in order to avoid incontinence are truly married. His answer was confusing: he said not that such a union is invalid but that it is not evil. And despite the couple's not intending children, somehow their union may nevertheless be called a marriage:

> Perhaps it would not be absurd to call this a marriage, if they chose to live in it until the death of one of them; and if, despite their not having married for children, they were not to avoid their conception to the extent of refusing them or of even taking evil means to prevent their birth. [23]

And Gratian stayed with the full Augustinian tradition in acknowledging the two other goods. In fact he quoted Augustine's essay, *The Good of Widowhood* (*De Bono Viduitatis*), Chapter 8, in doing so:

> A good of marriage is indeed always a good. But whereas among the people of God it was at one time a matter of obedience to the law, now it is a matter of remedy for weakness, but in some too a help [*solatium*] in human need. [24]

To return to the matter of the object of marital consent as Gratian proposed this, once one says that the act of consent is necessary for creating a marriage, one is faced immediately with the question, "To what must the parties consent in order to create the marriage?" It is not enough to answer that they must consent simply to being married, because until one establishes what is essential to being married, one has no clear idea what is involved in consenting to being married. The twelfth-century canonists were not satisfied with the theologian Hugh of St. Victor's implicit answer, ". . . consent to a union of souls," because this failed to supply the specific difference between marriage and any number of other relationships that are unions of souls. Even if one were to include this union within the understanding of marriage and therefore necessarily within the object of marital consent, one would still not escape the consequence of having to admit that a mother and her son could be married, or a father and his daughter, or a brother and sister.

Here is the point at which two avenues of speculation came together productively. One is about the essential goals of marriage, the other about our present discussion, the essential object of marital consent. If one sets procreation as a goal, indeed the primary goal, of marriage, one has a convenient object of marital consent. There is solid internal consistency in saying that in order to marry, a man and woman must consent to attaining or at least trying to attain marriage's primary goal. In addition, a churchman or canonist having to decide on the validity of a presumed but questioned marriage has concrete evidence to examine: Did both parties make the consent? In doing so did they consent to intercourse? Did they leave this intercourse open to the possibility of conception? If the answers are affirmative to all three questions, the marriage is valid—at least as far as the needed consent is concerned.

This is what Gratian proposed, although hardly in as structured a formulation as I have hypothesized here. But he knew it was not enough to say that in order to be married the parties must consent to intercourse. Adulterers consent to intercourse; so too do those who fornicate. Here he was faced with a twin of the earlier question, "What must be the object of the parties' consent if it is to be marital?" Having answered "Intercourse," he now had to answer the question, "What must be the nature of the intercourse if it is to be marital?"

The answer to the second question lay ready at hand for him. The intercourse is marital if its context is the *individua vitae consuetudo,* the single, undivided sharing of life, already enshrined in the ancient definition of marriage. Gratian did in fact put this within the object of marital consent. In Chapter 3 of *Causa 27, Quaestio 2* he said of Mary's and Joseph's life that their consent to cohabit and to maintain this undivided life made them husband and wife. Given his acceptance of the tradition of their perpetually virginal marriage, he here implicitly separated, within the object of marital consent, intercourse and the *individua vitae consuetudo.*[25]

When reckoning with another biblically narrated marriage he found added reason for dividing intercourse and the *vitae consuetudo* within the object of consent. In *Causa 29, Quaestio 1* he noted the anomaly in Jacob's marrying both Rachel and Leah. For Jacob had consented to marrying Rachel, but, tricked into having intercourse with Leah, he found himself at dawn married to the latter. (Gratian never questioned the factuality of the story nor the validity of the European interpretation of it that got Jacob married to Leah by their intercourse and therefore obligated to *complete* the marriage with her, instead of only legally obligated to marrying her, as Hebrew tradition ruled.) Gratian had no difficulty getting Jacob married to Rachel. The partriarch's intent to marry her was there; he had already consented, and he needed only to have intercourse with her. With Leah the procedure followed a different sequence: Jacob had had intercourse with her, so now he needed only to consent to the marriage subsequently.[26] Thus, according to Gratian, the consent-joined-to-coitus could be retrospective as well as prospective. In either case the object of the consent creating the marriage is marriage's primary goal.

As for Gratian's own express definition of marriage, in the introductory *dictum* to *Causa 27, Quaestio 2* he simply repeated Ulpianus' definition from Justinian's *Institutes:* "Marriage, or matrimony, is the union of a man and a woman maintaining a single sharing of life."[27] He repeated this in *Causa 29, Quaestio 1.*[28]

There was nothing inconsistent in his holding to the *Institutes'* definition of marriage yet insisting that the mutual consent of the parties creates only an inchoate and incomplete marriage waiting to be completed in intercourse. The definition can be taken to say what comes into existence only when the first intercourse subsequently takes place. But the drift toward later generations of canonists' understanding marriage as a contract is under way. For if what the mutual consent does is to create an incomplete relationship waiting to be completed by a specific exchange, it is easy to take the next step and say that the mutual consent is a promise by each party to convey a good to the other in the future. Such a consent is contractual.

Had the other definition of marriage, that from Modestinus enshrined in Justinian's *Digest,* been forgotten by this time? It had not, although Ulpianus' definition from the *Institutes* had been known earlier to the medieval canonists and was thus fixed in their minds. The definition from the *Digest* appears in the *Summa* of Paucapalia, one of Gratian's first disciples at Bologna. Paucapalia accompanies this definition with that of the *Institutes,* and he explains the phrase from the *Digest, "divini et humani iuris communicatio"* ("marriage as a sharing in divine and human law") to mean that the spouses share "one church, one chorus, one home, and the like."[29]

Peter Lombard

Peter Lombard compiled his four *Libri Sententiarum* at the University of Paris during the years 1155–1158. In the language of the Scholastics *sententiae* are the statements, the opinions, the positions of notable teachers in the history of the Church beginning with the apostles and coming down to perhaps a generation before the compiler. The purpose in such compilations was to gather and in some degree arrange these sayings under headings so as to make them more available as sources and principles of — and exemplifications in—theological reasoning. Lombard's four-volume compilation became a source-book and a kind of work-book for subsequent generations of Scholastics. A compiler of *sententiae* also had the prerogative of setting forth his own interpretations and conclusions. Lombard used this prerogative generously, as is evident in his teaching on marriage, which occupies Distinctions 26 through 42 of Book 4 of his compilation.[30]

He shared the opinion common in his day that God himself positively and expressly created marriage when he inspired Adam in the Garden of Eden to say of Eve, "This one at last is bone of my my bones and flesh of my flesh." He begins his study of marriage with this, in Chapter 1 of Distinction 26.[31]

About the issue disputed by Bologna and Paris—the act or acts that create a marriage—he was unambiguous and simple. In Distinction 28, Chapter 4 he said, "What makes a marriage is not the consent to cohabitation nor the carnal copula; it is the consent to conjugal society that does so."[32] He had already said in Distinction 26 that what creates a marriage is the mutual consent of the parties, whether expressed in words or in other and equivalent signs.[33] Like Gratian he insisted that all of the traditional conditions and liturgy surrounding the marriage are non-essential, however much they may be mandated by custom and some of them by law. The consent of the parents and their ceremonial giving over of their daughter are non-essential. So too are the religious solemnities, including the priestly blessing.

In saying that the act creating a marriage is the parties' mutual consent he made the careful distinction that Gratian had not, between the *consensus de futuro* and the *consensus de praesenti.* Both are consents to marriage, but the consent *de futuro* establishes only the betrothal and not the marriage itself, even when it is made under oath. What creates the marriage is the separate consent *de praesenti,* and it creates it before and separately from intercourse. This consent is essential and, if made freely, suffices by itself to create the marriage. The consent *de futuro* followed by intercourse, with the consent *de praesenti* omitted, cannot create the marriage. The consent *de praesenti* by itself and even without the subsequent intercourse makes any other attempt at marriage invalid. What the consent *de futuro* does, to get the nomenclature correct, is to make fiancés of the man and woman (*sponsus* and *sponsa*). The consent *de praesenti* makes them spouses (*coniuges*).

Lombard continued and amplified what others such as Hugh of St. Victor and Gratian had begun: the rejection of the three Augustinian goods as the constitutive elements of marriage and the object of marital consent. In Distinction 30 he made clear that the goals, the *causae finales* of marriage, have this constituency.[34] And he distinguished three categories of goals: *principales,* the first of which is procreation, the second a refuge from fornication; *honestae* (worthy and commendable) such as reconciliation of enemies or the preservation of peace; and *minus honestae* (less worthy but permissible) such as beauty or wealth. About procreation, which he took for granted as primary among marriage's goals, he said that before the first sin it was a duty, a matter of precept for all human beings.

But since that sin it has been set under a new moral condition and been given a new goal. That is, it is not now commanded but is only permitted. And it now has the added goal of serving as a remedy for concupiscence.

Having said, as Hugh of St. Victor had, that what creates a marriage is the parties' mutual consent, and that this by itself is sufficient to do so, he had to answer the obvious next question about the exact object of this consent. Here he found himself facing the same problem that had confronted Gratian: how to establish a specific difference within the object, some element of it that would make the consent distinctly marital, would make of it a cause whose effect is a marriage and nothing else, yet not so lodge intercourse as the specific element within that object as to define the virginal marriage out of possibility.

So he had to make a crucial distinction, to find a place in the object of consent for intercourse yet not make it essential to this object. The distinction he made was not Hugh of St. Victor's between marriage as a conjugal society and marriage as a sexual union. He did distinguish these two within the object of marital consent, but he did not let the distinction lead to two different kinds of marriage, and thus not to the two different sacraments that Hugh had admitted.

He made his distinction (in Distinction 28, Chapters 3 and 4)[35] in the following way: beginning with the premise that marriage is a conjugal society, he said that the consent that creates it is not the consent to cohabitation, not the consent to intercourse, but the consent to live in this society itself:

> (Chapter 3) Here it is asked, "Because it is the consent *de prae-senti* that creates a marriage, what is the object of this consent, carnal copula, or cohabitation, or both?" If the consent is to cohabitation that creates a marriage, then a brother and sister can marry. If it is to carnal copula, then Mary and Joseph were not married. . . .
>
> (Chapter 4) Let us say then that it is consent neither to cohabitation, nor to carnal copula that creates a marriage, but consent to the conjugal society—a consent expressed according to the present moment, as when a man says "I take you as mine, not as my mistress nor as my servant-maid, but as my wife." . . .
>
> Then when they come together, so that the man says, "I take you as my wife," and the woman says, "I take you as my husband," the consent, expressed in these words or others signifying the same thing, is not to carnal copula, not to bodily cohabitation, but to the conjugal society.

This insistence that it is the relationship itself, the union or *societas* of the man and the woman, that is the object of the marital consent almost certainly accounts for some apparently minor but in reality significant additions to Ulpianus' definition of marriage that Lombard adopted. He defines it (in Chapter 2 of Distinction 27), "Marriage therefore, or matrimony, is the marital union between persons legitimate according to the law, who persevere in a single sharing of life" (*Sunt igitur nuptiae vel matrimonium viri mulierisque coniunctio maritalis inter legitimas personas, individuam vitae consuetudinem retinens*). The adjective *maritalis* is not in Ulpianus' formulation. To include it in the definition of marriage is a logical fallacy, because the intent of the definition must be to first say what *maritalis* designates, and do so by first defining marriage without it. But I suspect that Lombard interpolated the adjective in the definition because denying that intercourse belongs within the object of marital consent left him with nothing to differentiate the latter from consent to other though similar relationships. Thus he was left to invent the differentiation as best he could, and he did this by simply *calling* the union marital. This leaves the student of his thought to wonder if, had he been questioned on the point, he would have agreed with the ancient Roman tradition that what makes a relationship a marriage is a quality of the intent of the parties, their *affectio maritalis* itself, simply their wills to be husband and wife to one another. At any rate the case for including the will to procreation as an element essential to the marital consent if it is to create a marriage was not closed with Lombard, even though his claim for procreation as marriage's primary goal helped to establish it as such in the Catholic mind for the eight centuries following him.

Lombard's answer to the question about the act or acts needed to create a marriage helped, like Gratian's but in its own way, to prepare the way for defining marriage as a contract. He wisely separated the consent *de praesenti* (the consent that creates the marriage) from the first intercourse (which completes the marriage). And he separated the consent *de praesenti* from the consent *de futuro,* the betrothal promise. But if both these consents, though in different degrees, bind the parties in obligations of commutative justice to the delivering of goods in the future—in obligations having lasting effects that can be forensically verified and sanctioned—then the consents have the properties of a contract.

About the sacramentality of marriage Lombard held that at least among Christians marriage is a sacrament from the moment of the consent *de praesenti.* This is to say that it is a sign of a sacred reality. But he makes a distinction: so long as there is only a union of wills effected by the consent, the marriage is a sign of only the union of Christ and the Church. This was sufficient to make the marriage of Mary and Joseph a sacrament. But in intercourse, the union of the flesh, there is formed a more perfect image, that of the union of the two natures in Christ, and therefore of his union in nature (over and above his union of charity) with the Church. This second image is not a separate one effecting a second sacrament, but is a perfection of the first image, perfecting it as a sacrament.[36]

Resolution of the Dispute

As long as it stayed unresolved the disagreement between Bologna with its European tradition and Paris with its Roman tradition about which act or acts create a marriage could only exacerbate the practical and pastoral problems among the Catholic population. As the two positions became known and operative in different jurisdictions, such subterfuges as the following became possible legitimately within the law. A young man living under a jurisdiction of the Roman tradition could be virtually forced by the weight of family opinion and parental authority into marital consent *de praesenti,* a consent by proxy, with a girl he neither knew nor wanted. If sufficiently resourceful he and his real love, having already promised themselves to one another, could escape into territory under central European jurisdiction. There they could consummate their love in intercourse, announce accurately to both their families and to ecclesiastical authorities that they were married, and thus force a dissolution of the first but non-consummated marriage. And they could claim the support of authorities to have their right to cohabitation honored.

University faculties being then what they still are, there would have been no resolving the disagreement as long as the attempt at resolution remained only a dispute between two groups of scholars. Only intervention by some single and overriding authority acknowledged by both sides and everyone else could end the disagreement and the confusion it caused in the practical order. This resolution by authority is what took place, but not as decisively at first as modern Catholics used to unequivocal statements from Rome may expect. Only after three Popes whose pronouncements spanned about eighty years did even juridical unanimity come to the Church.

The first of these Popes, the canonist Rolando Bandinelli later to become Alexander III (1159–1181), was a model of indecision and ambiguity. In his *Summa Rolandi* he sided with Gratian. Later, in his *Sententiae,* compiled between 1150 and 1158, he swung to the side of Peter Lombard, saying that the mutual consent of the parties is sufficient to create a marriage provided that it is accompanied by the formalities that are commonly observed, for example the witnessing presence of a priest or a notary. However before consummation the apostolic authority of the Pope can dissolve the marriage by dispensation. What makes this dissolution possible from within the marriage is that it is not yet completed. Then as Pope he was presented with the case of a woman who had made her consent *de praesenti* to marriage with one man, with no solemnities and with no priest as witness, but had subsequently entered solemn espousal with a second man and, bypassing consent *de praesenti,* had had intercourse with him. Alexander's decision in this case was that she was the wife of the first man provided that their consent had been mutual and simultaneous, and provided that it had been verbalized in a formula specified post factum by Alexander himself, *Ego te recipio in meum/meam* ("I take you as my own"). The solution would have been simple and conclusive had Alexander not conditioned it by the specific formula of consent.

In another judgment in the same kind of case he decided that the first consent *de praesenti* is valid if made in the presence of a priest or notary and with the solemnities customary to the region, and provided that there are no impediments. In yet other decrees he ruled that when betrothal takes place and then is followed not by consent *de praesenti* but by intercourse, a marriage is created. His reason for so determining was that in certain places this was customary, and changing it would cause unwarranted hardship for those living by the custom. He added the reason offered by the canonist Hugucio, that when betrothal is followed by intercourse, consent *de praesenti* is justly presumed to have been given. Finally in a letter to the bishop of Norwich he ruled unequivocally that a marriage is created only by the simple consent *de praesenti*, provided that there are no impediments. He ruled also that there is no essential need for solemnities or even witnesses.

But Alexander's most lasting contribution to the history of marriage in the Church is none of these determinations of the immediate and sufficient cause creating a marriage. Where he had his principal effect is in his ruling, more doctrinal than judicial, that only a consummated marriage is finally indissoluble, and that only sexual intercourse after consent *de praesenti* consummates. Applying this in his own time to a case of *affinitas superveniens,* he ruled on the request of a woman who had made consent *de praesenti* with a man who, before consummating the marriage with her, had had intercourse with her mother. Alexander ruled that she was free to marry another following his dissolution of her unconsummated marriage. And after doing appropriate penance the man would also be free to marry another, since his intercourse with her mother had not created a marriage with the latter.

Using the same premise that an unconsummated marriage is dissoluble, he gave authoritative approval to the custom already centuries old allowing either spouse to pronounce the vows of monastic life and thereby dissolve the marriage even without the partner's approval provided that he or she did so before consummating the marriage. In this Alexander remained to a certain degree faithful to Gratian's *Decretum:* A marriage is not complete until the *unitas carnis,* the unity of the flesh, is accomplished in intercourse. In his *Compilatio Prima* (Book 10, Part 32, Chapter 7) he said: "God's command that a man or woman not dismiss the spouse refers only to a consummated marriage." He did not explain where in the New Testament or elsewhere he found the reason for attenuating Christ's command in this way.

Pope Urban II (1185–1187) confirmed Alexander's judgment on the dissolubility of an unconsummated marriage. In a letter to the bishop of Florence he dissolved by dispensation a marriage wherein one of the spouses had contracted leprosy before consummation.

Innocent III (1189–1216) simplified and systematized the teaching on effective consent and dissolubility. In cases of *sponsa duorum*—that is, where a woman exchanges marital consent with two men successively through any of various combinations of betrothal promise plus intercourse, or of marital consent without intercourse—he ruled that the first marital consent *de praesenti* alone creates the marriage and prevails against any promise to marry followed by intercourse. He also abolished the consequences to an unconsummated marriage of the *affinitas superveniens.* That is, a man having intercourse with his bride's mother or sister or cousin before consummating his marriage with the former is no longer freed from that marriage.

Gregory IX, the Decretals and Definitive Resolution

The principle, "It is consent that creates the marriage, not intercourse," dominates all of Book IV of Gregory IX's *Decretals* which appeared in 1234. With his rich contribution to and sponsorship of decretal law in the first half of the thirteenth century (he reigned from 1227 until 1241) the Roman consensual theory of the immediate cause of marriage triumphed conclusively. Thus the centuries-old dispute over the moment of a marriage's beginning was settled once for all by the first half of that century.

Another significant product came from this decretal tradition. Since the expression *contrahere matrimonium* ("to contract marriage") was already in current use in classical Roman law, and the cognate expression *contractus matrimonialis* became more common in the law being formed by the decretals and their commentators and glossators, this epoch saw the birth in the universal law of the Church of the concept of marriage the consensual contract. For the determination of the moment and the act of creating a marriage included this, that each spouse, by an exchange of consent alone, both grants and acquires full marital rights.

Thanks to Gratian and Peter Lombard the distinction between Augustine's goods of marriage and the ends, or goals, of marriage was by Gregory's time widely acknowledged. Nevertheless the former still kept a useful place in the Church's judicial decision-making. Gregory himself used them in his important decretal, *Si conditiones,* issued sometime between 1227 and 1234.[37] The decree was aimed at the abuse whereby one spouse or both sought to qualify the marital consent by making its causal efficacy in creating the marriage here and now depend on the other party's fulfilling a condition against "the substance" of marriage. Here is where the traditional goods of marriage were put to use, and to a use that leaves them only faintly distinguished from the goals of marriage and from the object of marital consent. At this point *Si conditiones* offers as an example of an invalidating condition a spouse's saying: "I contract marriage with you provided that you avoid the conception of children," that is, provided that the other party bars the good of offspring from the proposed marriage. The other two examples point directly at the sacrament and at fidelity: "... until I find someone else of more worthy character and intelligence," and "... provided that you make yourself available for prostitution."

Gregory ruled that such conditional consent, because the condition attacks these goods of marriage here understood as the object of marital consent, voids the consent of all effect. Strangely, in the same decree he ruled that conditional consent where the fulfilling of the condition requires an immoral act (such as the wife's future defrauding of her parents) is ineffective against the validity of the consent. The condition is regarded as not having been placed and the consent creates the marriage immediately. (And the spouse's promise to fulfill the condition has no binding force.)

With this decision a kind of juridical fragmenting begins to appear. Whether it lasted and grew worse or was soon noted and repaired remains to be seen. But with the goals of marriage (procreation primary among them, and the *remedium* secondary) set distinctly apart from the goods, and with marital consent now fixed as the act that creates a marriage, one would expect that the object a person must intend if the consent is to be valid would be the goals, and that the intention to exclude these would be the invalidating condition. But still they were the *goods* of marriage that were kept as the substance of marriage that one must not exclude from his or her intent. Gregory's decretal was an invitation to ecclesiastical judges of the future to use this as a criterion for verifying whose wedding had produced a marriage and whose had not.

Papal Use of the *Institutes'* Definition

In an earlier judicial ruling Alexander III had used the *Institutes'* definition to set another important precedent. The archbishop of Genoa had presented to him a case that was not untypical of an age in which the clandestine marriage was possible. This was a nettlesome by-product, we recall, of the Roman tradition's demanding nothing more for the valid creating of a marriage than the parties' mutually exchanged consent, even if made to one another in complete privacy. Since in this case the parties had lived together publicly, the question here was how to determine whether their relationship was a marriage or was no more than concubinage—and how to determine this when each one's claim contradicted the other's and was supported by conflicting evidence.

Alexander's instruction to the archbishop was to have his ecclesiastical judges inquire among the relatives and friends of the couple for evidence that could be interpreted on an essential point. That is, did the man evidently *consider* the woman to be his wife, or to be his concubine? This consideration, this intent in the man's mind was crucial since (and here the definition was put to use) "... marriage is the union of a man and a woman that perseveres as an undivided sharing of life."

How Alexander reasoned here, how he used the definition, is disclosed by this, that in all outward, judicially verifiable traits marriage and concubinage look alike. Both relationships can intend and include cohabitation, intercourse, procreation and nurture, sexual exclusivity, and permanence until death. That is, both can intend what are otherwise deemed the substance of marriage and the goals of marriage. Yet one couple can claim to be married, but the other to be only living in concubinage. By what then do the two relationships differ? (And the question was, again, pushed to the brink by the Church's demanding no observable formality for creating a marriage. Both relationships, in fine, could begin and go on as copies of the other.)

Implicit in Alexander's instruction to the Genoese judges is his acknowledgement that the *Institutes* did after all define marriage adequately as a union of a man and a woman persevering in an undivided regimen of life. He could mean only that a relationship is a marriage because a man and woman intend it to be such. Whether he meant to say it or not, his criterion for distinguishing the two relationships was not whether one of them intended the Augustinian goods of marriage as its goal and the other did not. Apparently at least his criterion was the *forma* of the couple's intent, its interior orientation to being married or not. Did this mark a return to the classic Roman principle that that which irreducibly makes a relationship to be a marriage is the partners' *affectio maritalis,* simply their will to be husband and wife to one another?

One more interpretation of Ulpianus' definition of marriage in the *Institutes* deserves attention here. In his *Summa* on the *Decretum* of Gratian, written ca. 1165, the canonist Rufinus drew his own distinction between the reference of *coniunctio* (union) and the *individua vitae consuetudo.* For him the *coniunctio* was the spiritual dimension of the relationship—not the physical commingling but the mutual and conjoined acts of will to form the marriage. The *consuetudo* he took to designate the obligation of the spouses to live permanently as man and wife.[38]

But by the middle of the thirteenth century the usual Scholastic division of reference for these terms in the definition was different from Rufinus'. *Coniunctio* was taken to refer to the union of both bodies and souls, to the marriage's double union expressed in marital consent and then in intercourse. The *individua vitae consuetudo* was taken occasionally to refer to the sharing in all of life, but was more frequently interpreted as a reference to the permanence of the union. The Scholastics' unchallenged change of Ulpianus' participle [*individuam vitae consuetudinem*] *continens* to *retinens* may have helped to generate this interpretation.

The Situation of Marriage at the Middle of the Thirteenth Century

After the publication of Gregory IX's *Decretals* in 1234 the law for marriage in the universal Church was expanded no further in the medieval era by legislation. From that point on two different kinds of work remained to be done. One was the kind of commenting, extending and applying of the law appropriate to the work of jurists and teachers composing glosses, summaries, and commentaries on Gratian's *Decretum* (Causae 27 to 36), on Peter Lombard's *Sententiae* (Book IV, Distinctions 26 to 34), and on Book IV of Gregory's *Decretals*. The jurists who worked at this first task were the Romanistici for the most part, the builders of the late medieval tradition of Roman law. The second task was to answer questions and resolve disputes about marriage. One of these resolutions we have seen, the determination that it is the mutual consent *de praesenti* that creates a marriage, and that it alone does so. But there were others that had not yet reached their climax. Principal among them was the deeply serious matter of clandestine marriage, the creating of marriages with no authorized witnessing, either civil or ecclesiastical, and virtually always against the will of the parties' families. With no small irony it was the triumph of the Roman consensual theory of the act creating a marriage that made clandestine marriage most possible.

It is worth asking as a brief parenthetical question how it came about that the Roman-Parisian consensual theory triumphed over the European-Bolognese. None of the reasons is very obscure. This was the time of the ingathering and centralizing of ecclesiastical authority in Rome, and with it the time for mandated uniformity of discipline in the Church. Given the support of the imposing papal personalities we have noted—Alexander III and Gregory IX (as well as of those we have not noted, Innocent III and Boniface VIII)—the Roman theory had an insuperable political advantage. Linked with this external drive for centralized control was a characteristic internal to the issue, that the consensual theory made marriages at least seem more controllable by ecclesiastical authority. It was not only that uniformity of procedure abetted centrality of control. Decreeing that marriage is created only by the consent of the parties in the relationship really took control away from the families once accustomed to sending their children into marriage through the instrumentality of a *mundoaldus,* through the handing over of a dowry (and earlier through the handing over of their daughters), or through the leading of the bride across the new threshold.

But to return to the irony noted just above, the consensual victory really forfeited control by everyone except the bride and groom themselves, since it validated their purely private and even secret exchange of consent. This authorized freedom and its unintended consequence became a problem that was to plague Christendom until its vigorous and somewhat arbitrary resolution four hundred years later by the Council of Trent's decree *Tametsi.*

But there is a chapter in the history of marriage's defining in the Catholic Church that calls for review before we move on to trace the development of the definition down to and into the 1917 Code of Canon Law. This chapter contains the contributions of the great thirteenth-century philosopher-theologians, with Albert, Thomas, Bonaventure and Scotus principal among them. For all the richness of their contributions on other fronts, these men had surprisingly small influence on the Catholic understanding of marriage in their own day. Why this was so was probably because they were philosophers and theologians at a time when the questions and conflicts about marriage were of a kind needing judicial resolution. What the judges needed was a definition of marriage that could serve as a criterion for resolving the judgments. Such a definition as they needed they were confident they already had.

NOTES

1. I have taken this report from G. H. Joyce, *Christian Marriage,* London, 1948, pp. 54–55.

2. *Ibid.,* p. 55.

3. Joyce, *op. cit.,* traces the history of this dispute in chapters 2 and 3, pp. 37–138.

4. Quoted in D. Fellhauer, "The *Consortium Omnis Vitae* as a Juridical Element of Marriage," in *Studia Canonica,* Vol. 13, 1 (1979), p. 44.

5. This is in Migne, PL 176. The best available version in English is *Hugh of St. Victor: On the Sacraments of the Christian Faith,* English version by Roy J. Deferrari, Cambridge (Mass.), 1951. Book 2, Part II is in pp. 324–369. Hugh himself was a canon regular of St. Augustine, born probably in the region of Ypres in Flanders.

6. PL 176:859.

7. Deferrari, *op. cit.,* p. 325.

8. This significant term appears early in Chapter 1 of Part II of Hugh's *De Sacramento Coniugii* (PL 176:481).

9. *Loc. cit.,* p. 325.

10. *Loc. cit.,* p. 326.

11. *Loc. cit.,* p. 329.

12. *Loc. cit.,* p. 339.

13. *Ibid.,* p. 340.

14. *Ibid.,* pp. 340–341.

15. "Haec ergo societas coniugium est, quae foedere sponsionis mutuae consecratur, quando uterque voluntaria promissione debitorem se facit alteri, ut deinceps neque ad alienum altero vivente transeat, neque se ab illa quae ad invicem constat societate disiungat" (PL 176:485).

16. Graziano de Clusio was a Camaldolese monk of the monastery of St. Felix in Bologna. He began the gathering and arranging of extant canons in 1127, during the papacy of Eugene III. The synthesis that became the *Decretum* he divided into 101 Distinctions, each of which is subdivided into its own chapters; and into 36 Causes, each of which is subdivided into its own questions and chapters. The entire work is divided into Parts I and II; the canons on marriage are in Causes 27–36 of Part II. (The entire work is in PL 187, the causes on marriage in cols. 1371 through 1520.)

17. PL 187:1406.

18. PL 187:1407.

19. *Loc. cit.,* Chapter 43 (PL 187:1410).

20. ". . . ita intelligendum est: Coitus sine voluntate contrahendi matrimon-

ium, et defloratio virginitatis sine pactione conjugali non facit matrimonium, sed praecedens voluntas contrahendi matrimonium, et conjugalis pactio facit, ut mulier in defloratione suae virginitatis vel in coitu dicitur nubere viro, vel nuptias celebrare" (*ibid.*).

21. In *Causa 32, Quaestio 7,* Chapter 2 (PL 187:1495.

22. In *Causa 27, Quaestio 2,* Chapter 10 (PL 187:1395).

23. PL 187:1470.

24. In *Causa 27, Quaestio 1,* Chapter 41 (PL 187:1388).

25. PL 187:1393.

26. PL 187:1431–1432.

27. PL 187:1392.

28. PL 187:1430.

29. In Fellhauer, *op. cit.,* p. 39.

30. I have used the Second Revised Edition of Lombard's *Sententiae* published in 1916 by the Collegio di San Bonaventura, Florence.

31. *Op. cit.,* p. 912.

32. Chapters 3 and 4, *op. cit.,* pp. 927–928.

33. Chapter 6, *op. cit.,* p. 914.

34. Chapter 2, *op. cit.,* pp. 935–937.

35. *Op. cit.,* pp. 927–928.

36. Distinction 26, Chapter 6, *op. cit.,* pp. 914–915.

37. Denzinger-Schönmetzer, *Enchiridon Symbolorum,* Editio 32, Barcelona-Freiburg-Rome-New York, 1963, n. 827, p. 269.

38. In Fellhauer, *op. cit.,* pp. 41–42.

7. THE THEOLOGIANS AND THE NATURE OF MARRIAGE

The unforewarned student searching through the great thirteenth-century teaching on marriage—that of Albert, Thomas, Bonaventure, and Scotus—would probably be surprised to find how large a portion of these theologians' thought is pre-theological. It is accurate to say that these men have produced rather a philosophy of marriage and, because of the elements of psychology, history and sociology in it, almost an anthropology. I see the following reasons for this phenomenon.

These were theologians of an age that took for granted that doing theology is impossible unless one can do philosophy first, because philosophy provides the indispensable language and conceptual system without which theologizing is impossible, in the same sense that doing physics is impossible without mathematics. They worked out a philosophy of marriage because they sought to do a theology of it.

A second reason was that for a century before them and even into their own, the Church in and for which they labored had, as we have just seen at some length, struggled to bring order to a chaotic marriage situation by working out a coherent law of marriage. But a law is functionally valid, as distinct from merely efficient, to the degree that it understands its object accurately. Somewhat after the fact and indeed in a sense too late the medieval theologians labored to define the object of marriage law ever more exactly. On the way to defining marriage the sacrament, which is the proper object of *ecclesiastical* law, they could not bypass the defining of marriage the natural relationship. The natural relationship is to the sacrament as its matrix.

But the most obvious reason for the theologians' working out first a philosophy of marriage was the same reason that had ignited the minds of Clement and Irenaeus in the third century and Augustine's in the fifth. This was marriage's apparently unending need to be defended against its doctrinal enemies. Here I mean doctrinal not in the sense of religious orthodoxy or heterodoxy, but in the sense that the ascetic Gnostics and the Manichees were doctrinally committed to destroying marriage because

176

they believed it to be an evil. This time they were the Albigensians and the Cathars of the twelfth century and early thirteenth century who had condemned marriage and sexuality as degradations of the person.

They made two charges against them. First, starting from the premise that every pleasure of the flesh is sinful, they saw marriage as a kind of systematic debauchery because in nature it is a permanent carnal bond, because its characteristic expression of itself is a work of the body. Being pious Christians they were able, like the Gnostics ten centuries earlier, to cite in their favor St. Paul counseling Christian males, as they thought, "It is better not to touch a woman," and to cite even Jesus himself saying: "The children of this age marry and are given in marriage, but those judged worthy of a place in the age to come and of resurrection from the dead do not." Secondly, this sinful carnal mingling has as its effect the worst evil of all, and in this it does the devil's work. For in conception a soul until that moment happy in God's presence is dragged down into the misery of the flesh. For the Albigensians even the libertine and the prostitute are better than the married, since they ordinarily take care to avoid conception.

The bishops, the canonists and the preachers who fought back in the second half of the twelfth century did so mainly with three weapons: with the Scriptures, the texts of the Fathers, and the punitive power of the law (part of Gregory IX's counter-attack was to establish the Holy Office of the Inquisition in February 1231). As I have already said, the Albigensians' challenge was not new. It continued the Manichean pessimism of seven centuries earlier. The Pelagians' accusation against Augustine that he taught Manichean doctrine had drawn from him the apologia, *The Good of Marriage,* which, though an essay in defense of marriage, was a qualified defense, as we have seen. He stuck by his earlier teaching that bodily concupiscence is the carrier of the most universal sin, Adam's sin now become the common inheritance of every human being. And since marriage is in fact, if not in God's intent, all about bodily concupiscence, it is also for virtually every husband and wife in history an arena of sin. He insisted that marriage is not evil in its nature. It is good. And though by Adam's sin it is made in every spouse's life an occasion of sin, marriage can be rescued from this sinfulness, or at least excused from it, by the spouses' securing the goods available in it.

In the Stoic and in the Scholastic way of understanding natural human relationships, when one finds what good things can come from them, one has found what they are for. One has verified their natural goals. And in naming these ends one states the substance of their definitions—definitions that would have stopped at the generic if one had gone no further than to call them relationships. In naming the good things that can come from marriage, Augustine gave his definition of it, albeit informally and implicitly. In defending marriage against the Albigensians and the Cathars, the Scholastics defined it again, using Augustine's definition.

Albert the Great

Albert, the Dominican scientist-philosopher-theologian who was
Thomas Aquinas' teacher, wrote a treatise on the seven sacraments whose
Tractatus IX is *De Matrimonio*.[1]

In replying to the sixth objection under Question I he said that the
principal good coming from marriage is the *multiplicatio prolis*, the conceiving and bearing of children. In Question 2 he became more detailed
about the goods coming from marriage and said the following things pertinent to this point. In Article 4 (replying to Objection 1 of Question 1 within
this article) he said that generically considered a marriage is a *coniunctio*, a
union of a man and woman. The question he asked and answered in this
Article 4 inquires about the most valuable goods coming from a marriage.
In answering the question he revealed his perception of the heterosexual
union underlying these goods and producing them. Returning to the notion of marriage as the union of a man and a woman, he said that there are
three areas of union unique to it, of sharing in which only a man and a
woman in this kind of union can have part. There is the unique union or
sharing of life (out of this comes the *sacramentum*, the permanence in
union). There is the unique union of the flesh (from this comes the *proles*,
the child). There is the unique union of the consent of wills (from this
comes the *fides*, the fidelity). Then he answered the question about the
most valuable good. If one compares all these goods *within* the domain of
goods unique to marriage, the conceiving and bearing of children is the
most valuable of them because procreation was God's intent in instituting
marriage.

But if one compares the goods *outside* the domain of those unique to
marriage, fidelity is the most valuable of them because the union of wills in
love is man's final goal. Finally, if one compares them according to the criterion of useful goods helping men and women to their goal, perseverance
in union is the most valuable.

About the causes creating a marriage in real life, after naming God as
its principal cause Albert added that its immediate causes are the man's
and the woman's consent of the heart joined to the consent of their words
(*consensus cordis coniunctus consensui verborum*). He did not hint that this
consent is contractual. The closest he came to saying this was in Article 2
of this Question 1, where he said that since marriage is meant to fulfill a
dutiful vocation in society (*est in officium*), it must be ruled according to
instituta patriae—that is, according to the laws and traditions of one's
country. For, he added—and the choice of words is significant—every *pactio* (every agreement or covenant) must take place according to the *instituta* designed for this covenanting.

Thomas Aquinas

On St. Thomas Aquinas' teaching on marriage I want to dwell at some length and for particular reasons. One is that in this quarter he so well represents the thinking of high medieval philosophy and theology because his teaching is set out in his commentary on Book IV of Peter Lombard's *Sentences,* Distinctions 26 through 37.[2] This he completed before his thirtieth year, when much of his thinking was still only the partly criticized and partly assimilated thinking of not only the Church Fathers but also of the Scholastics a generation older than he. We find much of their thinking assembled in Thomas' commentary.

In Distinction 26, Question 1, Article 1[3] Thomas gives an implicit answer to the Albigensian charge that marriage and sexuality are by nature evil. Beginning with the supposition that anything natural to human beings is the effect of creation by a good God, he insists that marriage is indeed natural. But he makes a distinction. It is natural not in the sense that it is essentially necessary in order that a person be and act as a human being, but in the sense that there is in human beings an inherent inclination to marriage that can become active by free choice—choice for marrying or against it. What nature in men and women inclines them to in inclining them to marriage (as distinct from merely sexual activity) is twofold: to a primary end, namely that good which is the procreation and nurture of children, something not possible outside a stable and obligatory union of the father and mother; and to a secondary but conjoined end, which is the help that father and mother need from one another in doing the nurturing. The marital relationship is in itself naturally good for the reason just given. The human race, created by God, is also in its nature good. Since there is no other way to keep it in existence than by sexual intercourse, this too must of its nature be good.

In Article 2 of the same Question 1 Thomas asked whether marriage ought to have been instituted by God before the sin of Adam and Eve.[4] In his *solutio* of this article he discloses other details of his thinking about marriage the natural relationship. He says that other helpful features of marriage such as the friendship and mutual help of the spouses (a mutual help distinct from that needed in nurturing offspring) have their *institutio,* their causative origin, not in nature nor even in the old law, but in civil law.

At this point a caution is in order. "Nature" as Thomas understands it here designates that which is needed essentially. For this reason he says that of itself marriage is *in officium naturae*—it is meant to be a dutiful vocation in the service of nature in human beings in order to preserve the race. But friendship and mutual help of husband and wife he says are *in officium civilitatis*—they are a subsequent dutiful vocation in the service of the society first set up by marriage. Hence his meaning of civil law as the term is used just above: not secular positive law, but that which is necessary for human beings if they are to survive and do so in society. He is of one mind with the other great medieval teachers in saying that friendship between the husband and wife is not a primary need of nature, and therefore one in mind with them in denying implicitly that marriage is one of nature's forms of friendship. I think it is clear enough that his fundamental reason for these denials is his way of understanding nature in human beings this early in the history of his thought.

In Distinction 27 he digs down to the generic level of his definition of marriage. He says here that marriage is a *coniunctio,* a conjoining or union. Even more generic than this is his statement that conjoining or union involves an *adunatio,* a bringing of plural elements into oneness for the sake of some goal or goals. In the conjoining that is marriage the goods for which it takes places are those named earlier: children and the mutual help of the spouses. He also attends to the meanings of some words current in his time. Because the essence of marriage is a *coniunctio* it is named *coniugium.* Because it is caused by *desponsatio* (nuptials) it is named *nuptiae.* Because its principal effect is *proles* it is called *matrimonium* (maternal function, care, duty).

Aquinas and Marriage as Contract

It is in Article 2 of this Question 1 of Distinction 27 that the term "contract" appears for the first time.[5] The issue here is whether the agency creating a marriage is the partners' consent. Thomas notes the common opinion that marital consent ought to be expressed verbally because in forming a contract there should be such an expression. But it is significant that in answering his own question Thomas does so in terms of the demands of marriage as a sacrament, and that within this context he suggests for the first time the contractual nature of marriage. His reasoning proceeds as follows. In every sacrament there is some spiritual operation that goes on through the medium of a material, sensate operation that manifests it, as in baptism corporeal washing manifests interior spiritual cleansing. Since in marriage there is a joining that is spiritual because it is a sacrament, and since this is also a sensate joining in that it is meant to fulfill a duty of nature as well as of life in society, it follows that the spiritual joining must be accomplished through material means. Therefore since the joining done in material contracts is accomplished through the sensately manifested consent of those taking part, the conjoining in marriage ought also to be by expressed mutual consent.

Does Thomas imply here that one of the features of marriage is that it is a material contract? Or does he say that because it involves a material joining of two persons, this ought to be done in the same way as the material contract? I think the answer can at best be only inferred from other parts of his consideration of the nature of marriage.

It is in the third Solution of this article that he comes closest to predicating the term "contract" explicitly of some element in marriage. Here he answers the question asking whether the *verba de futuro*—in the idiom of the time, the words of promise to marry in the future—themselves create a marriage. He says they do not. In his reply to the second objection he says of betrothal that the *verba de futuro* do not here and now transfer authority over oneself to another person, which transfer is needed if a marriage is to be created. In saying this he makes a comparison: "... even in other contracts using *verba de futuro* these *verba* do not transfer to other persons authority over one's own possessions." It is the making of the engagement by the betrothed that he here implies is the contracting.

A contractual notion appears in Article 3 of Distinction 27, Question 1, where Thomas poses the question asking if one spouse even after consummation can enter religious life against the other's will.[6] His answer in Solution 1 here is that no one can make to God an offering of that which belongs to another. But in a consummated marriage the spouses' bodies belong not to themselves; they have given them over into one another's authority. In answering the second objection under the second Solution here he returns to the same thought in answer to the objection which urges, against the Catholic use common in his time, that not even *before* consummation by intercourse can one spouse enter religious life against the other's will. His reply is that before intercourse the spouses have not given over their bodies completely into one another's authority, but only conditionally—that is, provided that neither decides to seek a higher state of life. But with intercourse the giving over is completed because then each enters into the bodily possession of the authority handed over to him or her.

However, in Distinction 28, Question 1, Article 4 he again moves away from the notion of marriage as a contract, apparently because he returns to generic defining.[7] Here he asks and answers a question that will be the object of much keener interest centuries later; it is the question about the object of the consent that creates a marriage. Thomas' formulation of the question has it ask whether this is consent to intercourse. His reply is that the effect proportioned to marital consent as to its cause is the marriage itself. But marriage is not in essence the act of intercourse; it is a specific association of man and wife oriented to intercourse and to the other traits which belong as a consequence to a husband and wife from their granting to one another authority over their bodies. Thomas makes an interesting division here that is later quite forgotten. It lies in this, that in making their marital consent a man and a woman grant to one another authority over their bodies for sexual intercourse; yet this exchange is not itself the object of their consent making it specifically marital. This object seems, as Thomas explains it in this passage, to be the summary marital relationship with its essential orientation to intercourse and to other plural rights and duties natural to husband and wife.

Aquinas on Marriage as Friendship

Thomas did not say that friendship is a good belonging to the essence of marriage. He did not say that what a marriage is, is a specific kind of friendship, however much the spouses may also be friends. He makes this clear in his reply to the second objection in Article 1 of Question 1 under Distinction 31.[8] This objection urges that since the friendship usual between man and wife is natural and includes therefore the good as well as the useful and the pleasurable, it needs no excusing. His reply is that whatever renders marriage worthy should belong to it by its nature, because the goods of marriage making it worthy should come to it not from causes outside it, but from within the marriage itself. But, he insists, friendship is not a good coming from within the essence of marriage. Therefore it is not of the goods making a marriage worthy.

He says equivalently the same thing in Article 2 under this same Question 1 when asking whether, in naming *fides, proles* and *sacramentum* as the goods of marriage, one has named all its goods.[9] He insists that this is so. He reinforces this opinion in replying to the first objection, which has it that these three goods are not an exhaustive list, since men and women marry not only for procreation and nurture but also in order to join in a life together for the sake of sharing their duties and labors. Thomas answers that within the comprehension of the good that is *proles* there is included not only procreation but also nurture. All other sharing in duties and labors by the man and woman insofar as they are married is ordered to nurture as to its end. That is, he implies, the specific good making the relationship to be a marriage is the reason for all the other goods possible within it.

Finally, the second objection under this Article 2 contains Thomas' clearest reference to the contractuality of marriage.[10] The objection is that a marriage signifies Christ's union with the Church, which is perfected by charity, and that as a consequence charity rather than *fides* should be included among the goods of marriage. His reply is that the word *fides* in this case does not designate the theological virtue of faith, but a feature of the virtue of justice, the keeping of a promise, because in marriage, since it is a certain kind of contract (*cum sit quidam contractus*) there is a kind of promise through which a specific man and woman are joined.

Thomas wrote commentaries on both the treatises in which Aristotle offered his interpretation of marriage, *Politics* and *Nicomachean Ethics*. But he broke off his commentary on the former at the end of Book 3, Chapter 6, just before Aristotle takes up marriage formally in Chapter 7. On the *Ethics* his commentary is characteristically succinct. And consistently with the character of his commentaries Thomas nowhere suggests that he disagrees with Aristotle.[11]

In Paragraphs 1719 and 1720 he comments on Aristotle's notion of the friendship proper to a husband and wife.[12] He notes that Aristotle says that between husband and wife there is a natural friendship, and this because man is by nature a political animal, and much more naturally a conjugal animal. In support of this claim Aristotle offers two points of evidence. The first is that those relationships which are prior by nature and more necessary to human welfare are more natural to men; and the domes-

tic society, to which marriage belongs, certainly antecedes the political society on both these counts. The ground on which the domestic society is
more necessary than the political is that it provides procreation and nutri-
tion, which are first in necessity.

The second point of evidence is that procreation, to which the union
of husband and wife is ordered, is common to all the animals, and hence
procreation belongs to the more basic element of man, that which is generic to him, while (by implication) political society belongs to his particular
species alone.

Thomas points out in Paragraph 1721 that Aristotle then goes on to
assign that trait of conjugal friendship which belongs to human beings
alone.[13] This is that unlike the couples among other animals, which stay
together only to generate offspring, human couples stay together in order
to secure the necessities of life. Hence the conjugal friendship of human
beings is not only natural in the sense that this is found in the other animals, as oriented to the work of nature that is procreation, but it is also
economic (or domestic) because oriented to providing for domestic life.

In Paragraph 1723 Thomas notes Aristotle's acknowledgement that
the three characteristic traits of friendship are to be found in the friendships of spouses. First there is usefulness (*utilitas*) in that this friendship
provides for the necessities of life. It has pleasure (*delectatio*) in the act of
procreating. Finally, if the spouses are virtuous, with each having the virtues proper to husband and wife respectively, marital friendship can be
maintained for the sake of a virtuous life and for the delight that comes to
the spouses from this virtue.

In Paragraph 1724 he acknowledges the crucial part children play in
both the nature of marriage and in the marital friendship. *Because* the
marital union is for children, these are the shared concern of both spouses.
And where a serious concern is truly shared, the partners tend to persevere
in their union.

Hence in this commentary (presuming that at every point Thomas
agrees with Aristotle) we have a much tighter statement of the former's
mind on marriage. He does not say here that it is a friendship in essence; it
is in essence something more generic, a heterosexual union. By nature this
union is fundamentally for children, but it is also for providing the necessities of life. It can *also* produce friendship between the spouses; it tends by
nature to do this because of what they share by nature in their union. And
this friendship can for distinct reasons be a source of help, of pleasure and
of moral delight.

Bonaventure on Marriage

Bonaventure, Thomas' Franciscan contemporary, friend and amiable
adversary at certain points, set out his thought on marriage, as did Thomas, in his commentary on Distinctions 26 through 37 of Book 4 of *The Sentences.*[14] Unlike Thomas Bonaventure dealt with marriage the natural

relationship within his treatment of marriage the sacrament. As a consequence one must in reading him continually sift and distinguish what he says about marriage *qua* Christian sacrament from what he says about marriage simply. A possible reason for this superimposed consideration is that Bonaventure regarded even marriage the natural relationship as a sacrament. In his *Conclusio* to Question 1, Article 1 of Distinction 26[15] he suggests that from the beginning marriage was a sign of the soul's need for God's conserving action in that it is both the sign and the effective cause of the bodily conservation of human beings. He confirms this in his *Conclusio* to Question 2, noting that Adam was divinely inspired to utter the words, "This one at last is bone of my bones and flesh of my flesh." The reason for the institution of marriage—and even of its institution as a pre-Christian sacrament—is that it be *in officium*, a dutiful service to provide for the preservation of the race.

In Distinction 27 he offers his definition of marriage. It is that of the *Institutes* plus one added element: it is a union of persons who are legitimately capable of this union. In the same distinction he names as the act creating a marriage the mutually expressed consent of the parties—and this is the *consensus de praesenti*, not the betrothal promise, the *consensus de futuro*.

About the nature of marriage he makes a distinction (in the *Conclusio* of Distinction 27, Question 1, Article 1)[16] inspired, it appears, by his understanding of even marriage the natural relationship as a sacrament. He proposes it as the fruit of an analogy. As there is in baptism both an exterior and temporary reality which is the washing with water, and an interior and lasting reality which is the baptismal character in the soul, so too in marriage there is the passing exterior reality that is the *coniunctio* or joining in marriage effected by the mutual consent, and also the lasting interior reality, which is the *vinculum*, the marital bond. Both the joining and the bond, he adds, are called marriage. (This distinction would not be forgotten in the history of Catholic marriage. Seven centuries later Pope Paul VI used it to defend the permanence of marriage the bond in the face of the fallibility of marriage the union. And he insisted that the true essence of marriage is in the bond.)

What does Bonaventure hold to be the essential object of marital consent? To what relationship and what conduct in the future do the spouses consent in their vows? In the *Conclusio* to Article 2, Question 3 of Distinction 26 he answers the question obliquely in answering another question, whether intercourse is needed for the *integritas*, the complete reality of the *sacrament* of marriage.[17] His answer to this question is a distinction: for the integrity of the sacrament's *esse necessitatis* intercourse is not needed. (The Latin terms are beyond literal translation into English. They signify that which belongs to the irreducible and essential minimum of the nature of marriage.) But Bonaventure says that intercourse is needed for the reality of the *esse completionis* of marriage, its full and complete nature. Thus he holds that a man and woman are truly married by consent and before their first intercourse, but they are completely married only after the latter. Hence the irreducible object of marital consent is, by elimination, the *vinculum,* the marital bond. Thus a couple could consent to forming this bond while at the same time agreeing never to have intercourse.

Bonaventure offers a fuller understanding of this distinction within the object of marital consent in his *Conclusio* to Question 6 of the single article in Distinction 28.[18] This question asks forthrightly: "Whether the marital consent is to intercourse?" After rejecting the opinions which he finds unacceptable answers he offers his own: marital consent has as its object each spouse's *potestas* (his and her power or right) over the body. Each gives to the other this right over his or her own body. But immediately he makes another distinction. The right over one's body is given one way in the consent, another way in the act of intercourse itself. In the first case the right is so given that while the spouse lives the same right cannot be given to a third party. And it is given to the spouse also in such a way that the latter has perpetually the right to ask for intercourse and one has the obligation to accede to this request. But in the act of intercourse this right is given over completely, so that once it is given there can be no justifying reason for denying the other's exercise of this right. Given this distinction Bonaventure could explain how Mary the mother of Jesus could both give her marital consent and maintain her virginity. She could give Joseph the right over her body, the right to demand intercourse of her, but she knew in advance (from divine revelation made privately to her) that he would never ask for the exercise of this right. Thus one can say that Mary and Joseph were truly married.

Thus too Bonaventure fully agrees with, and is an ample contributor to, the tradition that the object of marital consent is the right over one's sexual acts, and that the consent, given mutually by the man and the woman, transfers this right each to the other. Because, according to this theory, marital consent has only this transfer of rights as its irreducible object, and because in the last analysis the spouses can agree never to claim the use of this right—leaving as their only obligation that they not grant the right to a third party—this theory has been said to leave marital consent really a camouflaged vow of virginity. In addition, because Bonaventure holds that marital consent is consent to an exchange of rights, he also contributes to the now (by his time) burgeoning opinion that this consent is contractual and that its object is a contract.

Duns Scotus

A generation later than Thomas and Bonaventure the Franciscan philosopher-theologian Duns Scotus wrote his treatise on marriage in the same format they had used, as a commentary on Book 4, Distinctions 26 through 37 of Peter Lombard's *Book of Sentences.* With the distinction between the right to sexual intercourse as the object of marital consent and the use of this right now fastened in the scholars' consciousness, he devel-

oped this useful precision to its fullest. This appears in his definitions of
marriage, which are singular at three points. They do not simply repeat the
classic Roman definition from Justinian's *Institutes.* They unambiguously
set the exchange of the parties' right to their own sexual acts as the object
of marital consent. And he names marriage explicitly a contract. About
the last-named feature, in one place—in his commentary on Distinction
26, Quaestio unica, Article 8)—he even played on the Latin noun in order
to make clear what he meant: *Matrimonium dicitur contractus, quasi simul
contractus duarum voluntatum* ("Marriage is called a contract in the manner of a drawing together of two wills").[19]

But he stated the contractual nature of marriage, along with the exchange of sexual rights as the object of marital consent, more clearly yet.
In Distinction 30, Question 2 he offers a formal, two-part definition:

> Marriage is an indissoluble bond between a man and wife arising
> from the mutual exchange of authority over one another's bodies
> for the procreation and proper nurture of children.
>
> The contract of marriage is the mutual exchange by a man
> and wife of their bodies for perpetual use in the procreation and
> proper nurture of children.[20]

Thus in defining marriage he sets at the heart of the definition the
bond (the *vinculum*) as Bonaventure had done. This seems to replace the
coniunctio, the union, that is there in the Roman definition. The juridical
notion thereby supersedes the anthropological. And in defining the act creating a marriage Scotus sets at the heart of the definition the mutual exchange of rights. Here again the juridical notion—or at least the notion of
a juridically verifiable feature—settles in at the core of marriage's meaning.

Marriage Understood as Contract

From the evidence we have reviewed here we see that the medieval
canonists did not come easily to the conceiving of marriage as a contract,
and that the philosophers and theologians were even more hesitant about
doing so. Only Scotus seems to have found this instantly congenial. How
did it come about that in the face of this hesitation marriage was, by the
middle of the fourteenth century, nevertheless thought commonly to be a
contract and was so defined in the universal law of the Church in Boniface
VIII's *Liber Sextus Decretalium?*[21]

Classic Roman law never defined marriage as a contract. Neither did
the European tradition, which was in any case not a philosophic or juridical and therefore not a defining tradition. The answer to the question lies
in the history of Roman commentary on the earlier classic law beginning
in the late eleventh century as part of the Gregorian reform, one of whose
major concerns was to produce a single and central body of law that would

help bring order out of the disorder of Christian life in Europe, a good part of which disorder was blamed on regional and discordant systems of law.

An a priori, deductive theory of law begins with the definition of the object to be ruled by the law. If what is wanted by persons in authority is effective regulation, it behooves the designers of the law to so define its object as to render regulation most effective and even easy, even when they have multiple models of definition to choose from. It takes no keen insight to see that marriage is most easily and effectively regulated by a central authority if it is defined as a contract.

The early medieval Roman commentators on the classic law defined marriage as a contract even before the renaissance of legal studies in the University of Bologna. And in order to specify marriage more exactly among the several kinds of contracts—material, real, solemn, consensual—they designated it a consensual contract in order to stay with the classic tradition saying that to create a marriage nothing more is needed than the mutual consent of the parties. The glossators on the post-classic Roman code, the reform code of Theodosius in the fifth century and of Justianian in the sixth, treated marriage as a *contractus de societate,* a contractual union of persons.

The victory of the Roman side, that of Peter Lombard and the University of Paris, in the twelfth-century debate over the act creating a marriage, favored the defining of marriage as a contract. It did so "by contagion," as some historians have described it. What they mean is that once it was generally admitted that the *sponsalia per verba de futuro* (the betrothal, created by a promise to engage in a future act) has the nature of a contractual consent and the binding effects thereof, it was difficult not to say also that the *verba de praesenti* actually creating the marriage are anything less.

There was a special reason of interest to the theologians of the time favoring the defining of marriage as a contract. They took for granted that marriage in general had been instituted by a positive and specific act on God's part in the Garden of Eden. This act was identified either in his inspiring Adam to say of the woman taken bodily from his side, "This one at last is bone of my bones and flesh of my flesh" (Genesis 2:24), or it was seen also, by combining Genesis 1 and Genesis 2 into a single historical account, in God's creating man in his own image as a sexually reciprocal pair, male and female; and then (according to the creation poem in Genesis 1) commanding them to "be fertile and multiply, fill the earth and subdue it." It was also a part of the commonly accepted theological teaching of the time that God is the first cause active in constituting every marriage down through history. He it is who brings every man and woman together who marry. What function then is left to them and their free choice? How can their entering the sacrament, where the marriage is that, be meritorious as it must be if they are to in fact enter a sacrament? For there is no merit without free choice. An available answer was that the man and woman make an act of free contractual consent. Thus a role was provided for their wills, an inherently meritorious role on condition they make their consent in order to realize obediently God's intent in originally instituting marriage, namely to be fertile and fill the earth.

St. Albert the Great, in his commentary on the *Sentences,* when answering the question why, as an exception against the rest of the sacraments, the consent of the recipients is required in marriage, gave this reason, that this sacrament consists in a certain exchange (*commutatio*) or contract of the persons receiving it.[22] But such an exchange cannot be made without the consent of the persons doing the exchanging.

All, canonists and theologians alike, said that although to marry is not itself an obligation, the consent creating a marriage sets obligations of spouse to spouse. The question concerning the nature of marriage, put in words to fit the issue of obligation, asked: "What manner of obligation? By what name shall we call the obligation of marriage?" As we have seen, Duns Scotus supplied the clearest answer to the question, naming the contract as marriage's first intelligible characteristic: "Marriage is called a contract, as though it were the drawing together of two wills." But he defined marriage as a contract more formally than that: "The contract of marriage is the mutual exchange by a man and wife of their bodies for perpetual use in the procreation and proper nurture of children."[23] He emphasized the element, the clearly contractual element, of the exchange of the same good by both parties: "This contract can be nothing else than that of a mutual exchange of or—what is the same thing—a permutation of the power over one's body for perpetual use for the end in question."[24]

With all the canonists agreeing by the end of the thirteenth century that a marriage is in essence a contract, and with most theologians agreeing but none disagreeing energetically, it remained only to determine which kind of contract it is among the several kinds commonly acknowledged. The glossators of Roman law and of the imperial codes had said that it is a *contractus de societate,* a contract about life together, about living in a society. Their successors, the *Romanistici,* wished to specify further and say that a marriage is a *stipulatio,* a verbal contract. No one insisted that it is a *contractus realis,* a real contract in the sense of an exchange of rights to goods that are alienable and consumable. The object of the contractual consent, that which the parties exchange by their consenting, is not their bodies, not their acts of intercourse, *but their right to the use of their bodies* for intercourse as well as for all other acts oriented in some degree to accomplishing this intercourse. The proper term to designate this is *contractus personalis.*

There was still one feature of the essential contractual nature of marriage that was for another two and a half centuries to continue a world of trouble for Church authorities, for Christian princes and magistrates, and for heads of families. This was the admission that marital consent is not made in a *solemn* contract. That is, of its essence the contract requires no writ, no dowry, no solemnizing either religious or secular, no witnesses, no ceremony at all. As a consensual contract it can be formed by the consent alone of the contracting parties. Ecclesiastical and civil authorities might demand, and demand under severe penalty, that for purposes of verification the consent be solemnized before authorized witnesses. But for those two and a half centuries until the Council of Trent and its decree *Tametsi* they refused to say that the witnessing is required for the validity of the contractual exchange. Despite all the misery and confusion brought by clandestine marriages the Church insisted on honoring the freedom of the parties and the nature of a consensual contract.

Disagreement about the Object of Marital Consent

By no means was there unanimity among the thirteenth-century theologians that the mutual consent creating a marriage is consent to the right to sexual acts. William of Auxerre (d. 1231), a master at Paris a generation earlier than Thomas and Bonaventure, wrote his own commentary on Peter Lombard's fourth book of the *Sentences* as a part of his *Summa Aurea.* In his comment on Article 6 of the one question in Distinction 28 he asked whether it is consent to intercourse or consent to cohabitation that creates a marriage. He replied that it is consent to neither of these:

We say first of all that neither consent to cohabitation nor consent to carnal copula is the efficient cause of marriage; but it is consent to the conjugal union [*in coniugalem copulam*]. And the conjugal union is composed of a number of things, such as cohabitation and carnal copula, and a mutual service [*mutuum adiutorium*], and the mutual power over the body. . . . [25]

Obviously this statement of the object of consent lacks the narrow, manageable exactness of that coming from Scotus. But it has the virtue of reflecting what men and women think in real life that they consent to when they marry—to the entire marital baggage, so to speak. Cohabitation and intercourse are only part of this. Do we have here a faint echo of Modestinus' "sharing in all of life," and a harbinger of the same phrase in *Gaudium et spes?*

There was another man who drew from a rudimentary phenomenology of married life in offering his definition of it, and who as a consequence produced the most copious descriptive definition of marriage that we have yet seen. This was William of Auvergne (d. 1249), also a master at Paris. He called marriage "the bond of the perfect or complete society," and he found the following to be its constituent parts:

. . . it remains for us to determine the elements (*partes*) of this society. The first of these is [communion] in the true religion itself, which is the right worship of the divinity. . . . The second element of the conjugal society is a communion of bodies for the conjugal task, namely generation. The third is a communion of temporal goods, in which it is not lawful for one [spouse] to defraud the other. The fourth is a communion of physical presence (*communio corporum propriorum*), which is to care for and serve each other, and to provide for each other in health as well as infirmity. The fifth is a communion of offspring, and of the entire family, which is to bring up, to educate, to govern, and to provide for the future. [Marriage] is therefore a perfect society from these five communions; and it consists integrally and totally in these; and whoever bind themselves to each other by the bond of matrimony oblige themselves to this society and to all its parts.[26]

Like William of Auxerre before him, William of Auvergne appears to have tried to be descriptively inclusive in finding all these communions in a marriage. His most consequential reflection on them is in the last clause of this passage: ". . . whoever bind themselves to each other by the bond of matrimony oblige themselves to this society and all its parts." No doubt the jurists of his time found this copious statement of the five *communiones* essential to marriage and necessary objects of marital consent to be diffuse and unmanageable. How could they be used as criteria for a judgment concerning the sufficiency and validity of a person's marital consent? Given the rules of evidence and the capacity for judgment native to a court, some criterion verifiable empirically and much more exactly defined would have to be selected. The consent having as its proper object the right to sexual acts offered these characteristics.

NOTES

1. This treatise is in Alberti Magni, *Opera Omnia,* Westfalorum in Aedibus Aschendorff, 1958, Tomus 26, *De Sacramentis . . .* pp. 154–170.

2. There is a short treatise on marriage in the *Supplementum Summae Theologiae* bearing Aquinas' name. But this is no more than Reynaldo of Piperno's adaptation of the material in Thomas' *Commentary on the Sentences* arranged according to the method of the *Summa,* and published after Thomas' death along with the rest of the *Supplementum.*

To my knowledge the best available edition of the *Commentary* is in the Parma edition of the *Opera Omnia* of Aquinas, published first in 1852–1873, and again in 1948 with a general introduction in English by Vernon J. Bourke. Thomas' commentary on Distinctions 26 through 37 of Book 4 is in Volume 7.2 of this edition.

3. The *Solutio* to this question is *op. cit.,* p. 918.

4. *Loc. cit.,* p. 919.

5. *Op. cit.,* pp. 927–929.

6. *Loc. cit.,* p. 930.

7. *Op. cit.,* p. 940.

8. *Op. cit.,* p. 954.

9. *Loc. cit.,* pp. 954–955.

10. *Ibid.,* p. 955.

11. This commentary is available in the Pirotta edition, *In Decem Libros Ethicorum Aristotelis ad Nicomachum Expositio,* Taurini, 1934.

12. *Op. cit.,* p. 552.

13. *Loc. cit.,* p. 553.

14. In S. R. E. Cardinalis Bonaventurae *Opera Omnia* . . . cura et studio A. C. Peltier, Tomus VI, Parisiis, 1866, pp. 206–369.

15. *Op. cit.,* p. 211.

16. *Op. cit.,* p. 221.

17. *Op. cit.,* p. 218.

18. *Op. cit.,* p. 246.

19. *Quaestiones in Quartum Librum Sententiarum,* in *Opera Omnia,* Vol. 19, p. 176.

20. *Op. cit.,* p. 186.

21. *Liber I, Titulus xix, De Procuratoribus* (Paris 1549 edition, p. 101, col. 4)

22. *Opera Omnia, loc. cit.,* p. 158.

23. *Op. cit.*

24. *Loc. cit.*

25. Fol. 286 (in Fellhauer, *op. cit.,* p. 67).

26. *De Sacramento Matrimonii,* Caput 6, in *Opera Omnia,* Vol. 1, pp. 520–521 (in Fellhauer, *op. cit.,* pp. 67–68).

8. THE DEFINITION OF MARRIAGE AND THE CODE OF CANON LAW

Those who are used to taking for granted that Catholics live their religious life within a system of law that is centuries old must inevitably be surprised to find that this law has been worked into a code only once in its history, and this within the last sixty-five years. This first and only codification was promulgated on Pentecost Sunday, 1917 (and formally adopted a year later). A revision of the entire code was completed by the summer of 1980 but has not yet (at this writing) been promulgated. The revised law on marriage, completed in the spring of 1978 as a sub-section of the law on the sacraments, is to be promulgated as a part of the entire revised code.

But the editing of collections of the Church's laws, short of inclusive codifications, is an enterprise that has gone on from the time of the Roman emperors. These were regional collections of limited geographical inclusion, decrees of local councils, of individual bishops. Some of the earliest collections were inauthentic in the sense that they were ascribed to the authorship of persons who had long antedated them. The Apostolic Constitutions, a collection in eight books done in Syria toward the end of the fourth century, was one of these. It was for centuries credited to Clement I, a disciple of the apostles and bishop of Rome. Another was the pseudo-Isidorian Collection, the "False Decretals," assigned, as the collection's name designates, to the seventh-century bishop of Seville, but coming in reality from France in about the middle of the ninth century.

In the preceding chapter we examined a minuscule fraction of the most used of all the collections, Gratian's *Decretum,* completed in 1140 or 1141. Its value lay in part in its character as an attempt to gather and put in order the entire mass of ecclesiastical legislation which had accumulated until his time. This value lay, *post factum,* in larger part in its serving as a kind of foundation for a series of collections that built on it in succeeding centuries. Gratian had brought the first order to the universal juridical chaos; others could then use his *Decretum* as foundation, matrix, center-point in expanding the law and refining it. It became the first and most fundamental element in what was subsequently and gradually through the centuries built up into the Corpus Iuris Canonici, the corpus of Church law.

Four great collections drew on and added themselves to the *Decretum* during the four centuries until the Council of Trent (1545–1563). In succession they were the *Decretals* of Gregory IX (A.D. 1234), composed by the Dominican canonist Raymond of Pennafort but promulgated by Gregory. Then came Boniface VIII's *Liber Sextus Decretalium* (The Sixth Book of Decretals) in 1298, getting the adjectival name it did because it added a sixth book to Gregory's five books of decretals. John XXII promulgated a body of laws in 1317 that has the name *Clementinae* because it was taken mostly from the Constitutions of Clement V decreed in the Council of Vienne, 1311–1312.

Finally in 1500 the canonist John Chapuis edited a collection that because of its inclusiveness merited the title *Corpus Iuris Canonici*. It contained the *Decretum* of Gratian, the *Decretals* of Gregroy IX, the *Liber Sextus* of Boniface VIII, and the *Clementinae* of John XXII. To these Chapuis added two more sub-collections, the *Extravagantes,* the decretals of several popes from Boniface VIII to Sixtus IV (d. 1484), and the *Extravagantes Communes.*

These were not steps in the development of the law. They were infrequently spaced collections of what had developed up to their time. The specific development of the law on marriage during the centuries following Gratian moved forward along two paths, and these paths converged only infrequently. One path was that laid by the commentators on the law. These were the scholars and teachers: decretalists (commentators on Gratian's *Decretum*) and glossators (those who taught the law and wrote their interpretations and applications onto the margins of the texts as glosses). It was not the character of these commentators to broaden the law and to innovate in it, but rather to repeat, preserve, refine and interpret. These were "the custodians of the definition" of marriage, so to speak. The greater part of this chapter will examine the results of their preservation of the definition, as also the significant changes they worked in it by their interpreting and refining. But for a moment we shall look at the other path of the law's development, that of the *ad hoc* decisions, the decrees by Popes and councils that were intended to resolve serious conflicts in the conduct of marriage among Catholics. Our attention will center on two or three of the major decrees.

We have already seen that the dispute between the Bolognese and the Parisian schools on the nature of the act creating a marriage was resolved in favor of the latter's teaching that the consent *de praesenti*, the mutual consent here and now to be man and wife, is both needed and suffices to create a true marriage. Alexander III first, in his *Summa Rolandi,* sided with Gratian and the Bolognese that consent followed by intercourse was needed. But in his later *Sententiae* (1150–1158) he adopted the Parisian theory. Urban III (1185–1187) confirmed Alexander's judgment. Innocent III did so in 1198 explicitly when asked to rule whether two deaf-mutes can marry one another. His reply was that since for the creating of a marriage there suffices the consent of the parties, and deaf-mutes can indicate their consent clearly, there is no reason why they cannot marry.[1]

Boniface VIII emphasized the centrality of consent in creating a marriage when he issued a decretal in 1299 regarding marriages by proxy. He ruled that where one of the parties, after having given his or her consent and commissioned the proxy to manifest this mutually with the proxy of the betrothed, withdraws the consent before the proxies' exchange, there is no marriage.[2] This was contrary to the general rule regarding the acts of a proxy, which were held to be valid unless he had been told of the withdrawal of his commission. But it follows with logical necessity from the premise that the parties' mutual consent is the immediate cause creating the marriage. If even one consent has been withdrawn, there is no causation sufficient to create the marriage.

The Problem of Clandestine Marriages

The problem of clandestine marriages could enter the history of the Catholic defining of marriage only indirectly, but enter it it did. How it did so may become clear if we get at the exact meaning of the term "clandestine marriages." In its simplest signification the term refers to a marriage whose existence cannot be proved before the law. The marriage exists; the parties know they are spouses to one another. But the judicial person of the Church does not "know" this because it cannot verify it. The marriage is hidden or secret (*clandestinum*) in the face of the Church.

Such a marriage was possible in the Catholic Church for centuries because her authorities refused for centuries to require as a condition for the validity of the marital consent that its expression by the parties be witnessed. Clandestine marriages took place because men and women—and boys and girls—took advantage of this refusal and exchanged consent wholly outside the presence of third parties, or in the presence of third parties sworn never to verify their witness of the exchange. In Western Christian history men and women did this no doubt for a variety of reasons. But principal among the reasons was their desire to marry the partners of their choice instead of partners chosen for them by their families.

Not that the Church's refusal to require witnessing as a condition for the validity of the consent bespoke approval of clandestine marriages. From the first appearance of clandestinity in the West with the advent of the Roman tradition making mutual consent sufficient for creating a marriage both ecclesiastic and civil officials condemned and punished it. (The Eastern Church ended the possibility of it in the ninth century when Emperor Leo IV decreed that marriages attempted without ecclesiastical witness were null and void.) One form of sanction applied as early as the middle of the ninth century in the West (it appeared among the pseudo-

Isidorian decretals and is included in Gratian's *Decretum, Causa* 30, *Quaestio* 5, *Cap.* 1) was the determination that marriages attempted without ecclesiastical witness were to be treated as null and void in the external forum. But as a sanction it was weak, of course, because it could never gainsay the fact of the marriage. And the presumption of nullity had to yield to subsequent counter-proof where the man and woman chose to come out of their clandestinity already securely married to the spouses of their choosing.

Penances were assigned to couples who married clandestinely. But because the imposition of them sprang from the acknowledgement of the marriage, the penances could not be of a kind to separate the spouses, and thus were never severe enough to deter them from marrying clandestinely in the first place.

Another sanction was for the ecclesiastical courts to declare illegitimate the children born of clandestine marriages. But this too failed because the civil courts regularly presumed the legitimacy of children until the contrary was proved, and the ecclesiastical courts had to accept legitimacy once a couple verified the validity of their clandestinely created marriage.

From the ninth through the fifteenth and on into the sixteenth centuries authoritative persons and groups in the Church sought to end clandestine marriages by legislating and decreeing the severest penalties. Alexander III ordered excommunication. The Fourth Lateran Council in 1215 decreed that a priest who blessed a clandestine union be suspended from office for three years and that the parties be punished as circumstances warranted.

The modern student inclined to side with the parties and their freedom against the medieval authorities' effort to suppress clandestine marriages should, on second thought, recognize that there were other serious moral matters at issue. It is true that for couples marrying at the early age customary to the times (Romeo and Juliet, seeking to marry at fifteen and fourteen years, were not untypical) the only alternative to clandestinity was marriage to a partner selected by the parents. But the clandestine free choice led to seriously damaging abuses on its side. A man who had in fact consented to marriage with a girl clandestinely could later abandon her all the more easily while ecclesiastical law presumed the nullity of clandestinely formed marriages. A man could falsely claim clandestine consent with a woman about to be married, and block this marriage permanently by getting friends to perjure themselves as witnesses to the fictional clandestine exchange. Or a man could solemnize marriage, exchanging marital consent formally and publicly with a woman, but then claim, again with the help of perjured witnesses, that he had already formed a marriage clandestinely.

The consequences of this truly criminal conduct in planned for but blocked marriages, in abandoned spouses and children, in embittered parents and feuding families called for the most serious efforts at control by

Church and state. But for centuries, as I have said, the Church refused to apply the one really effective control, the refusal to accept as valid any marriage whose creating consent had not been exchanged before her own and the state's authorized witnesses.

Why this reluctance and even refusal? They came from the Church's sense of limitation in her own authority. To marry is a man's and woman's most fundamental right. Not only must any reason for limiting the exercise of this right be a surpassingly serious one, but there was the question whether, if it were agreed to set conditions to the right to marry, the conditions could be guarded effectively. The Church acknowledged that no one but the spouses can create the marriage, and this by their own acts of consent. Should she—indeed could she—invent a new condition for the validity of the consent, one that admittedly came not from divine revelation, not from Catholic tradition, and certainly not from legal precedent? Voiding the efficacy of otherwise sufficient marital consent as a punishment for violating the law would be a disproportionate sanction. Decreeing persons to be legally incapable of creating a marriage only because they refused to have a positively imposed form of witness also seemed disproportionate, since all declarations of legal incapacity had until that time been grounded in either positive divine law (for example, the incapacity of a married man to marry bigamously) or in natural law (the incapacity of an impotent man for marrying).

The long-sought and long-delayed effective action was finally taken in November 1563, in the twenty-fourth and last session of the Council of Trent. It was spurred significantly by the charge coming from the Lutheran reformers that Catholic authorities had been remiss in permitting the abuse of clandestine marriages to continue. This is one of the principal themes in Luther's essay, *On Marriage Matters*.[3] What he, Melancthon and others insisted on in addition was that ancient tradition be acknowledged and even established in Church law, namely that marriages attempted without the approval of both sets of parents be null and voild. And, more than that, Luther demanded that where a marriage had been attempted without the parents' approval, these should have the authority to declare it null, even after intercourse and even after children had been born of it.

The council debated its proposals regarding marriage during five meetings of its last session in the summer and autumn of 1563, on July 20, August 7, September 5, October 13 and November 11. What were approved in the last meeting were a doctrinal preamble, twelve canons, and the decree *Tametsi* that sought to end the possibility of clandestine marriages.[4] The last-named took its title from its first word, as was common with such ecclesiastical statements. What the decree said and established were the following:

1. Clandestine marriages created by the free consent of the parties are true and ratified marriages as long as the Church does not invalidate them. Hence (in reply to the Reformers) those who say that marriages attempted

without parental permission are invalid, or who say that parents can invalidate such marriages, are wrong.

2. The Church has always condemned and forbidden such marriages. But now it is evident that condemnation and prohibition have not overcome disobedience, and grave sins and harm have come from continued clandestinity.

3. The decree of the Fourth Lateran Council that the banns of marriage be published on three consecutive days of public worship in the parish of the engaged is renewed; and if no legitimate impediment is found, the marriage is to take place, with the man and woman declaring their vows before the pastor.

4. If the announcing of the banns on three occasions would probably bring harm upon any person, the marital consent could, with the permission of the ordinary, be witnessed after only one announcement, or the announcements could be made after consent but before consummation.

5. In any case, the council declares and makes incapable of contracting marriage any persons who attempt to do so without having as witnesses the pastor of the place, or some priest delegated by this pastor or by the ordinary, along with two or three other witnesses. The council declares marriages attempted without these witnesses to be null and void.

From the first debate on the proposed decree about sixty of the ablest bishops at the council opposed it. They did so for the reasons indicated above, in addition to the reason that for Christians marriage is a sacrament, and Christ himself has fixed the conditions for its valid administration. What is more, those who favored the decree could not agree about the ground of the Church's authority for promulgating it. Some said that though in Christian marriages the contract and the sacrament are inseparable, nevertheless they are distinct. Thus though the Church has no authority to set conditions for the valid administration of the sacrament, it can set them for the valid forming of the contract. Others said that Church authority can inhabilitate the persons attempting a clandestine marriage, making them incapable of marrying in the same way that she inhabilitates a man for marrying certain of his close kin. But others criticized this reasoning, pointing out that inhabilitation traditionally attaches to something in the person making him or her incapable of carrying out a certain act. But *Tametsi* would inhabilitate for the novel and unheard of reason that certain conditions external to the parties were not fulfilled, because a certain formality in marrying was omitted.

A crucial provision in the decree was that it would become effective thirty days after its promulgation in any particular parish. Along with this went a wise and compassionate qualification. The decree was not to be promulgated in territories where Protestantism was the established religion, nor in those where Catholics would find serious difficulty in having a priest witness. Without this exception the decree would have the effect among Protestants of declaring thousands of otherwise valid and sacramental Christian marriages invalid, and among Catholics unable to find a priest witness of leaving them with only the alternatives of either living in prolonged celibacy or of settling into concubinage.[5]

The Definition of Marriage

The other path of development in marriage law that we glanced at in the beginning of this chapter was that of the scholars—the commentators and the glossators—who developed the *substantialia* of this law, including marriage's definition. This was a path heavily traveled from the fourteenth down through the twentieth centuries, with a seeming halt finally called at the promulgation of the Church's first universal code of law in 1917. A tendency and a shift in the defining of marriage during these six centuries was obvious. Ulpianus' definition of marriage from the *Institutes* held its place; a marriage was deemed a *coniunctio,* a union of man and wife persevering in a single sharing of life. Occasionally Modestinus' definition from the *Digest,* the *consortium* or sharing in all of life, was repeated. But these definitions were gradually added to, or others were substituted for them, as we saw in the case of Scotus' definition in his *Commentarium Oxoniense.* The goal of marriage that is procreation came under gradually more frequent emphasis until by the nineteenth century commentators and scholars spoke of marriage almost exclusively as a contract in which a man and a woman give over to one another, and claim from one another, exclusive and perpetual right to use of their sexual acts that are apt for procreating.

But this came on only gradually. In 1566, three years after the adjourning of Trent, Pope Pius V published the Catechism of the Council of Trent.[6] Its Chapter 8, "On the Sacrament of Matrimony," shows inclusiveness and flexibility in defining marriage.

> Matrimony . . . is defined as "the conjugal and legitimate union of man and woman, which is to last during life." In order that the different parts of this definition may be better understood, the pastor will teach that, although a perfect marriage has all the conditions, viz. internal consent, external assent expressed by words, the obligation and tie which arise from the contract, and the marriage debt by which it is consummated, yet the obligation and tie expressed by the word "union" alone have the force and nature of marriage. The peculiar character of this union is marked by the word "conjugal," distinguishing it from other contracts by which persons unite to promote their common interests.
>
> Hence it is evident that in that tie consists marriage; therefore marriage is not a simple donation but a mutual contract. . . . As then the marriage contract is not a mere promise, but a transfer of right, by which the man yields the dominion of his person

to the woman, the woman the dominion of her person to the man. . . . [7]

What I mean in citing the inclusiveness of this defining of marriage is evident if we note all the substantives used in doing so. Marriage is called a union, a contract, a tie and its obligation, a contract, a transfer of right. These are not correlated; the only derivative association hinted at is that "the obligation and tie" arise from the contract.

Continuing this inclusiveness the writers of the Catechism moved on to give due place to the goals of marriage in understanding its nature. By this time such goals were clearly distinguished and even separated from the traditional goods. So much is this evident that later in the chapter the three traditional goods are described as advantages to be gained from marriage. What would come as a mild surprise to a nineteenth or twentieth-century student of marriage used to finding procreation and nurture listed first and emphatically as the primary good and goal of marriage is that the Catechism lists the personal good of the spouses first in sequence. But in the end, as the following quotation shows, the authors leave no doubt that the propagation of the race is the primary natural goal intended for marriage.

> The original institution of marriage, as a natural contract, had for object the propagation of the human race; its subsequent elevation to the dignity of a sacrament is intended for the procreation and education of a people in the religion and worship of the true God, and of our Lord Jesus Christ.[8]

Tomás Sanchez

Possibly because he was as much philosopher as canon lawyer, the Spaniard Tomás Sanchez (1550–1610) centered attention on an unfamiliar element when he proposed his definition of marriage. This is the category of being under which marriage is to be understood. Apparently confident that a single answer to it is possible, he asked himself the question simply, "What is marriage; in what does its essence consist?"[9] His first answer was faithful to the tradition of Roman law and repeated its tautology: "Marriage is the marital union of a man and a woman legitimately capable of marrying, who persevere in an undivided sharing of life." To his mind the definition obviously needed analyzing in the literal sense of being broken down into its parts. Sanchez did this, saying it is supposed that there are seven constituent elements of a marriage. They are mutual consent; the external contract; the mutual handing over of each partner's right to the body (which is the immediate effect of the contract); the obligation that follows immediately from the foregoing, namely the obligation to render the marriage debt, a debt that is of each to the other; and finally the use and consummation of the marriage.[10]

Sanchez saw that listing these seven components obliged him to choose among them for that which is essential. And this is where the philosopher in him sought for the category of being under which to more exactly understand marriage. So he said that the essence of marriage consists not in its consummation, not in the parties' internal consent, not in their external contract (these are the efficient causes of the marriage), not in the mutual giving over of the right to their bodies, nor in the mutual obligation to render the marriage debt. He said that the essence of marriage, that which remains when all else is abstracted from, is the bond whereby (or in which) the spouses are united. This bond is the formal cause of the marriage. And—to note a most significant point in his analysis—the bond arises from (*oritur ex*) the mutual giving over of the right to the parties' bodies. He specified even more reductively, assigning the bond to one of the traditional ontological categories. It is a real relationship because it is grounded in the real, external action of plural persons, which action is the external contract (the internal consent being by itself insufficient to create the relationship).[11]

Having been that detailed and exact he then turned back to explaining what he *called* the definition of marriage. Again it is Peter Lombard's version of the definition in the *Institutes*. Marriage is called a union (*coniunctio*) because it is in this that the essence of marriage resides. It is called marital (*maritalis*) because it arises from the mutual giving over, and in order to make clear that the bond is not created by the betrothal promises. It is said to be of a man and a woman (*viri et feminae*) in order to identify the parties to the union. It is said to be between persons legitimately capable of marrying (*inter legitimas personas*) so as to make clear that only those free of invalidating impediments can marry. Finally it is said to be a union persevering in a single sharing of life (*individuam vitae consuetudinem retinens*) in order to indicate that it is a lasting union, and thereby to make clear the end or goal of marriage, which is the carrying on of life together, and that it cannot, like other contracts, be dissolved by the mutual consent of the parties to it.[12]

Did Sanchez agree with the by then congealing opinion that procreation and nurture constitute the primary goal of marriage? He did, and he made the point clearly in answering the question, "When was marriage instituted by God?" He answered that it is more probable that marriage was simultaneously both instituted and commanded by God in his words recorded in Genesis "Increase and multiply . . ." because then it was that he manifested his will to the first man and woman that they unite and that they do the mutual giving over of their bodies in which marriage consists, and because in these words is suggested (*intimatur*) the principal end of marriage, the increase of the human race. Thus through these words was instituted the marriage by which this end is attained.[13]

Nevertheless he wanted considerable weight given to the shared life as an end or goal of marriage. Going back to his quoting the definition of marriage from the *Institutes* we find him giving a key clause a unique meaning: "[Matrimony] is said to be *individuam consuetudinem vitae retinens* [persevering in a single sharing of life] in order to explain the goal of marriage, which is mutual habitation."[14] Fellhauer has the following to say of this unusual interpretation:

> It was Sanchez' opinion that the permanent exclusion of this mutual habitation (which was more than mere living together) rendered the marriage invalid. While he cannot be accused of having ever lost sight of the procreative finality of the conjugal union (as well as its function *in remedium*) the aspect of *mutuum adiutorium* [mutual help] is very much in evidence in the thought of Sanchez. It [the mutual help] is a dimension of his notion of "cohabitation" from which the obligations of love and friendship are not absent, obligations which derive from the very nature of marriage.[15]

In a refusal, such as Sanchez', to narrow the goals of marriage to an exaggerated exclusiveness in procreation, and to insist instead on a significant place for the function of helping friendship among these goals, we find a hint of a debate among Catholic scholars and authorities that was to occupy the distant future. Three and a half centuries of refining and emphasizing the primacy of procreation were to follow Sanchez. Modulated into the question of marital consent and its necessary object, the primacy of procreation became the exchange of rights to the parties' sexual acts as such object. Refining and emphasizing this juridical interpretation until it was made virtually a first principle of juridical explanation and judicial decision became perhaps the main project of canonical commentators during these centuries. This project was to produce as its fruit in 1917 Title VII (*De Matrimonio*) of the Code of Canon Law. Before examining the key canons of this Title it will help to review the thinking of a few of the most influential commentators who worked during these intervening centuries.

Goals of Marriage and Object of Consent: The Fixing of a Position

As the canonists worked through the seventeenth, eighteenth and nineteenth centuries at refining the definition of marriage, they gradually pushed off into secondary consideration the concept of marriage as a union, a society, a sharing (yet never denying that it is any of these), while at the same they were fixing two cognate ideas at the center of the definition. Both of them we have seen repeatedly in the documents, emerging there with gradual clarity. One is that marriage, taken universally and in abstraction, has natural goals or ends, and that primary among these, because the most valuable, is procreation and nurture. (Thus the good of marriage that Augustine said to be offspring settled at the head of the definition even though its designation as a good was mainly abandoned.) The other is that the object of the consent creating a marriage, that which the man and woman must intend and will if they are to create a marriage, is the exchange of the right to their sexual acts. The canonists came to decide that for a man and woman to consent in a verifiable way to exchange this right is to marry. Whatever else they will to share, and however exclusively and permanently, if they fail to will this exchange of this right, they do not marry.

We shall see too, I think, how the inherited concepts of marriage that were pushed toward the periphery of significance—the society, the union, the sharing—were absorbed into these two concepts and interpreted in terms of them. Thus if one wishes to include the *consuetudo vitae,* the sharing of life, in the definition of marriage, he must be ready to explain at what point this sharing differs from others quite similar to it. One explanation ready at hand is that this sharing is one whose main ingredients are the parties' use of each other's right to their sexual acts, and the use of this right for the purpose of bringing children into the world—while admittedly including such secondary purposes as releasing concupiscence legitimately and helping one another in the ordinary business of living.

It will help to look at some examples of the canonists' refining and confining and at this absorbing, and to do so in the writings of four scholars working during the last decades before the formulation of the Code of Canon Law began in 1904.

J.-P. Martin wrote his *De Matrimonio et Potestate Ipsum Dirimendi Ecclesiae Soli Exclusive Propria* (On Marriage and the Church's Rightly Exclusive Power to Declare It Invalid) in 1844. He said that there is a definition of marriage *in fieri* (in the process of being formed). It is " . . . a legitimate contract, whereby a man and a woman who are legally capable give to each other the right to one another's bodies for the sake of acts apt of their nature to produce children, and who obligate themselves to an undivided sharing of life."[16]

His conviction of the need to include this by-then-acknowledged primary goal of marriage in the definition shows up immediately as he observes the following:

> But in place of this definition, which is otherwise true, another can be substituted, which more correctly expresses the essence and primary property of marriage considered in this way [*in fieri*]: "A contract whereby a man and a woman, legally capable, unite with each other and are joined in a single and unidivided principle [*principium*] for the procreation and upbringing of children."[17]

Martin takes note of the ancient definition of marriage coming down from Peter Lombard six centuries earlier than his own, and suggests courteously at what point it is deficient and how this deficiency may be supplied for.

> Marriage *in facto esse* [in its abiding existence] is commonly defined: "The marital union of a man and woman between persons legitimately joined, persevering in an undivided sharing of life." But [and here he notes the fallacy of redundancy in this definition] since this marital union is the very marital union that needs defining, marriage can be defined more clearly if we view it in this way: "A permanent union of a man and a woman in the unity of undivided purpose [*individui principii*] to procreate and nurture offspring."[18]

It is obvious that Martin saw the necessity of finding a specific difference for the marital union that distinguishes it from all other *coniunctiones*. He found it in the union's natural orientation to procreation and nurture.

Fifty years later M. Rosset published his six-volume *De Sacramento Matrimonii* (in 1895–1896). Typically for such treatises he discussed the various definitions of marriage that tradition had passed down to him. Implying that not all of them touched what he regarded as the essence of marriage, he urged the obvious, that the most accurate definition is that one which expresses the essence of what is defined. What he says next makes quite clear that he finds the essence of marriage in this heterosexual union's inherent orientation to procreation and nurture. So he chooses the definition from the *Institutes* as the best of those he has inherited. He also makes a transparent and unexplained addition to it.

> . . . it explains the essence of marriage *in facto esse* and its own characteristics, namely the bond [*nexus*] whereby a man and woman are joined to each other in a single and undivided complete principle for the generation of offspring, while at the same time it explains the indissolubility of the bond.[19]

Rosset's insertion of the term "bond" in his preferred definition suggests that he shared the concern that we saw in Sanchez to locate marriage within one of the categories of being.

By the first decade of the twentieth century the definition of marriage had become the product of a reductionist process. Simplicity and univocity had been secured. Marriage itself was distinguished into *matrimonium in fieri* and *matrimonium in facto esse*. Two major elements from the ancient inheritance were the core of the definition, namely the primary goal of offspring, and the essential object of marital consent, the exchange of the parties' rights to their sexual acts. And marriage's category of being was the contract-bond. All these are exemplified by F.X. Wernz in his *Ius Decretalium* published in 1911–1912:

If marriage is considered *in fieri*, it can be defined: "The lawful and undivided *contract* of man and wife for the generation and education of offspring."

If on the other hand marriage is taken as the *bond* or permanent society, as in common speech and even that proper to theologians and canonists, it is defined: "The lawful and undivided *union* of man and wife for the generation and education of offspring, or, more briefly, the undivided conjugal or *marital society* of man and wife."[20]

It may be that in including the last clause here he meant it to be in apposition with what immediately preceded it, with the union oriented to generation and education explaining the more generic "conjugal or moral society." If this is so, it is another example of the ancient definition absorbed into the later definition in order that the latter may reduce the inexactness of the former.

Cardinal Gasparri and the Code of Canon Law

The process that produced the Catholic Church's Code of Canon Law lasted for about seven centuries. It reached its goal in the sense of going as far as it could, given the assumptions underlying it, in the work of Cardinal Pietro Gasparri. He was the principal designer of the Code, promulgated on Pentecost Sunday, 1917, and supervised its writing. He also wrote extensively on marriage legislation during the years before and after the Code's promulgation.[21]

His most influential work was his *Tractatus Canonicus de Matrimonio,* first published in 1892 while he occupied a chair in the newly formed faculty of canon law at the Institut Catholique. It clearly served as a sourcebook for Title VII in the Code, *De Matrimonio.* He published a second and revised edition of the *Tractatus* forty years later, in 1932, *ad mentem Codicis Iuris Canonici* ("according to the mind of the Code of Canon Law"), reflecting the Code and the jurisprudence on marriage resulting from it in the fifteen years since its promulgation.

The 1932 volume is a summary intended for student use and shows clearly its filiation vis-à-vis the Code. In the 1892 volume Gasparri introduced Article I defining marriage with the classical definition in Justinian's *Institutes.* But immediately he began the series of distinctions long since introduced by the medieval canonists.

Marriage in general is defined . . . as the union of a man and woman persevering in a single sharing of life. But for the sake of clarity marriage can and should be considered both *in fieri* and *in facto esse.* Marriage *in fieri* is a legitimate contract producing the man's and woman's single sharing of life. Marriage *in facto esse* is the sharing of life resulting from this, namely the marital bond.[22]

In the 1932 and briefer edition of the *Tractatus* he alters this defining slightly:

> Marriage *in fieri* is the act of creating a marital contract accurately manifesting internal consent on the part of persons bound by no invalidating impediments. Marriage *in facto esse* is the abiding marital contract itself with its attendant natural rights and obligations.[23]

The concept of marriage as contract is now front and center in the definition. In the 1892 edition Gasparri called the mutual consent, the act of creating the marriage, a contract. In the 1932 edition he omits this but says that the product of the consent is a contract—which in the 1892 edition he had called the bond (*vinculum*). He is sensitive to the criticism this has evoked. He admits that the term *contractus* was predicated of marriage nowhere in either Roman or Gallic law, and he notes that some contemporary writers reject the term as either degrading to marriage or offering an inadequate concept of it. He calls these writers temerarious and misguided. His reason for calling marriage a true contract is mainly that it is formed by the legitimate consent of two parties to one and the same agreement, a consent creating in each of them an obligation in commutative justice to either perform or to omit certain acts. He specifies further that the contract can be made between only a male and a female, since of itself it is oriented primarily to the procreation and nurture of children.

Gasparri's interpretation of the clause from Ulpianus' definition in the *Institutes* finds a double meaning in it.[24] He goes far beyond the original meaning of the *individua vitae consuetudo* by filling the generic semi-vacuum with what he thinks it should mean in order to be juridically effective. He brings it to exact focus to mean the couple's mutual right to one another's body in its capacity for intercourse—their exclusive and perpetual right. After that he acknowledges the phrase's second meaning. This is the spouses' sharing (*communio*) in "bed, board and dwelling," in a union of spirit through mutual love and in some sharing of possessions. Marriage brings to both parties a right to have these as well as the mutual obligation to provide them. There is a particular name for this right once it is created by the marital consent. It is the marital bond (*vinculum seu ligamen matrimoniale*).[25]

Like every contract marriage has both its material and its formal objects. The material object is the contracting parties themselves, who are also the subjects of the contract. The formal object is identical with the *vitae consuetudo* as Gasparri understands it just above: it is the permanent and exclusive mutual right of the parties, with corresponding obligation, to one another's body in its capacity for intercourse, the act oriented *in se* to procreation. He attends carefully to the locating of the union of spirits and of possessions. This does not belong to the marital contract, but is a condition necessary to the happy living out of the contract and to the bearing of its burdens.

In the earlier edition he offered a more complex and revealing division among the objects of marital consent. He distinguished first of all the material object of the consent, which consists of the persons themselves, the contracting parties. Then there is the formal object, which is the sharing of life, the *vitae consuetudo*. But he added a third category of object of marital consent, the *essential* formal object, that which makes the sharing of life specifically marital. This is the bond, the *vinculum*. But this bond has a most specific and characteristic content, making it to be not just any kind of bond but exclusively the marital bond. This is "the mutual right and correlative obligation to the other's body for the procreation and education of offspring."[26]

Note how Gasparri sorted out and classified for their essentiality and non-essentiality the several elements of the object of marital consent. The only element he deemed essential, the only one that the parties need consent to on the condition that rejecting it would invalidate their consent, is the object he calls *essential formal*. This is the parties' right to one another's sexual acts.

What of the other traditional objects of marital consent, the union of wills, the mutual love, life lived together, mutual support in the ordinary business of living? While acknowledging that these are ordinarily to be found in the object of men's and women's consent when marrying, Gasparri denies that they belong within the essence of that object. That is, one or both parties could exclude them, but provided that they mutually granted and accepted the right to the sexual act, they would create the marriage. The other elements, he insisted, thus belong not to the essence of the marriage contract but to its integrity, its completeness. In fact he added that the union of souls and of goods is not an element of the object of marital consent at all, but rather a necessary condition for marital happiness.[27]

He willingly followed to its extreme the logic implicit in his position. What if both parties should positively exclude from their marital consent any life together, any cohabitation, and do so *in perpetuum*, so that never would they live together? What if, in addition, they agreed in advance never to exercise the exchanged right to their sexual acts, so that they lived celibately all their lives as well as apart? Could they still be husband and wife? Gasparri's answer was that they could.[28]

In the 1932 edition his final distinctions and definitions are the traditional ones. The ends or goals of marriage he divides into *fines operis*, the goals of the contract itself prior to and apart from any intent on the part of the contracting parties, and *fines operantis,* which are the parties' particular and personal motives for marrying. The former, he says, are fixed and immutable. The primary *finis operis* is procreation and nurture; the secondary is twofold, namely the spouses' mutual help and the remedying of concupiscence. He names also the accepted essential properties of marriage, its unity or exclusivity (which corresponds to the *bonum fidei* named by Augustine) and its indissolubility (corresponding to the *bonum sacramenti*).[29]

The Code of Canon Law

In the sense of a formal, taxative definition—a distribution of the elements of the thing defined into the generic and the specific—the Code of Canon Law, in its Title VII, contains no definition of marriage. But a student with even no more than a surface awareness of the history of the Catholic understanding of marriage can detect what of this history has been left out of the marriage law. So he need not guess that the necessary excluding function of a definition has been at work in the writing of this law.

In the introductory chapter of this study I pointed out that the first canon on marriage in the Code is a product of historical circumstances. This is not singular; none of the canons is not in some degree such a product. But this first canon, 1012, looks to a bitter conflict between the Catholic Church and the governments of Europe that began as early as the fifteenth century. Let us note first how the canon is worded.

1. Christ our Lord elevated the contract itself of marriage between baptized persons to the dignity of a sacrament.
2. Therefore it is impossible for a valid contract of marriage between baptized persons to exist without being by that very fact a sacrament.[30]

The conflict grew out of the fact that by about the thirteenth century ecclesiastical authority in Europe—which meant Roman Catholic authority—exercised a final and decisive rule over all that is substantial in marriage. This was not yet, as it was to become later, a claim to exclusive authority. But the claim was final and overriding. It is significant that this was an authority that during approximately her first six centuries the Church had claimed hardly at all. Popes and bishops had been content to have Catholic marriages ruled judicially by the civil courts—if only, perhaps, because so many of these courts in turn conceded to bishops the function of deciding in marriage matters.

But with the growth of the national states in Europe and the attendant shrinking of the effectiveness of centralized Roman authority, the heads of these states sought to get back at least in some degree the authority over marriage they thought to be rightly theirs. The Popes resisted, and the conflict was on. It was not a conflict born of or peculiar to the Protestant reform. Through all its history some of the bitterest opponents to the papal claim were Catholic heads of state, such as the Bourbon kings of

France and the Hapsburg heads of the Holy Roman Empire, all of whom remained at least nominally Catholic.

To establish their claim philosophically and juridically, and even theologically, these heads of state had to prove that every marriage has a non-ecclesiastical and secular dimension to it, even the marriages of Christians and even the marriages of Catholics. With the reality and the separateness of the secular dimension verified, the purview of their secular authority would be established. They found in marriage as it is understood among Catholics during those four centuries a convenient division between the contract and the sacrament. The former is secular, they said, and belongs by nature and necessarily under their secular authority. The sacrament is religious and belongs naturally under ecclesiastical authority.

The fundamental secularity of the marriage contract they sought to verify on two points of evidence. First Christ had come admittedly at a middle moment of time in the history of the human race and of marriage. But marriage has been in the race from its very beginning—as the theologians, bishops and popes never tire of repeating. Therefore marriage was secular for centuries before being made a sacrament by Christ. And there is no evidence that he annihilated its nature when he made marriage among Christians a sacrament. He did not annihilate it but elevated it and graced it. To grace it he had to leave it intact.

The second point of evidence is that even now a majority of human beings are not Christian. Consequently they form marriages that are not sacraments but only secular contracts. Therefore the contract and the sacrament in marriage must still be separable.

Obviously then, if the contract in marriage and the sacrament are separable, if it is the contract that is secular and belongs under secular authority, and if the essence of marriage is in the contract (as Catholic jurists were insisting more and more), then the state gets the marriage and the Church is left with the nuptial Mass or at least the blessing, which are the only unambiguously sacramental features of marriage according to this point of view.

The reply of Popes and theologians was that although in a marriage of two Christians the contract and the sacrament are distinguishable, they are not separable. This Catholic counter-position is stated succinctly in Canon 1012, and is there turned into an assertion about a presumed event in history: "Christ our Lord elevated the contract itself of marriage between baptized persons to the dignity of a sacrament." (Since a code of law is not an historical interpretation, there is nothing here in explanation of when or where Christ did this.) To read the statement and get from it the meaning intended in it, one could add the explanatory note, "That is, in making the marriage of two Christians a sacrament Christ did not simply add a religious garnishing to an otherwise untouched secular contract."

Paragraph 2 of the canon adds the consequence of this historical event: "Therefore it is impossible for a valid contract of marriage between baptized persons to exist without being by that very fact a sacrament."

Understood in its historical context the paragraph means to say these things: first, that any marriage of two baptized persons is a sacrament, whether they know it or not and whether they will it or not; second, that as soon as the marriage is contracted it is a sacrament; finally, that what makes the contract to be also a sacrament (paragraph 1 said this) is the historical event of both parties' baptism and the sacramental baptismal character abiding in each of them. A consequence of all these in the juridical and judicial domains is that the contract cannot be dealt with by civil authority separately from the sacrament. And since in the order of values the sacrament supersedes the contract, ecclesiastical authority has priority over civil authority in dealing with the marriage as a single whole. Finally, the conclusion that was so offensive to the secular authorities in Europe, as well as in Latin America from the sixteenth century onward: ecclesiastical authority has an *exclusive* right to rule all Christian marriages in what is substantial to them, while to civil authority is left only what is non-substantial, such as dowries, rights of succession and patrimonies.

The Ends of Marriage

The first of the canons contributing to the defining of marriage is Canon 1013. Its paragraph 1 makes a familiar statement.

The primary end of marriage is the procreation and nurture of children; its secondary end is mutual help and the remedying of concupiscence.[31]

The paragraph means to say what marriage is for, the ends for whose realization God instituted it. It arranges these ends in order of value: the highest is procreation and nurture; the others are secondary to this. Contained virtually in this asserted hierarchy is the conclusion that if the realizing of the two strata of ends should come into conflict, the realizing of the primary must by moral necessity override the realizing of the secondary. The lesser value cannot suppress the higher.

Paragraph 2 of the canon states two essential properties or characteristics of marriage. By naming them distinctly from the ends it means either that the ends are not characteristics of marriage, or, if they are, that unity (meaning monogamy and sexual exclusivity) and indissolubility are characteristics distinct from them.

The essential properties of marriage are unity and indissolubility, which acquire a unique firmness in Christian marriage by reason of its sacramental character.[32]

One would think that in this statement the very possibility of polygamous marriage and of dissolution of a marriage are defined out of existence. But here the law performs under historical duress. It wants not to deny that the holy men of old, the patriarchs of Israel, had polygamous marriages that were truly both marriages and polygamous. And it wants not to contradict and cancel what has been going on in the Catholic Church for four centuries, namely the dissolving, by papal authority, of marriages that are not sacraments. Nor does the canon want to touch an even older practice, the dissolving of sacramental but non-consummated marriages by entry into religious life and the pronouncing of the vows of this life. The canon saves a place for the radical possibility of polygamous marriage and of dissolution by adding that monogamy and indissolubility gain a unique firmness in the marriages of Christians by reason of their sacramental character. In other merely natural marriages the monogamy is exceptionable and the indissolubility is dissoluble.

The first of three other canons from which the elements of the law's definition of marriage are to be drawn is Canon 1081. In its two paragraphs are concentrated the recognizable end-products, the resolutions of a centuries-old debate and just as ancient a process of refining and focusing.

> 1. Marriage is created by the consent of the parties lawfully expressed between persons who are capable according to the law; and for this consent no human authority can substitute.
> 2. Marital consent is an act of the will by which each party gives and accepts a perpetual and exclusive right over the body for acts which are of themselves suitable for the generation of children.[33]

The canon specifies three things: the act that alone can create a marriage; who are capable of the act; what the nature of this act of consent is, and this in two senses. The first names which of the human faculties immediately performs the act; the second names to what the consenting persons commit themselves. All the parts of these paragraphs except the last-named have to do with matrimonium *in fieri,* the act of creating a marriage. The last-named touches matrimonium *in facto esse,* marriage in its existence.

Gasparri's mind is evident in what is not included in the object of marital consent as this is stated in paragraph 2. Absent from it are mutual help, union of souls, cohabitation, even the remedying of concupiscence. A man and a woman need commit themselves to none of these in order to become husband and wife. After seventeen centuries Gasparri's precision has finally displaced Modestinus' vagueness in saying that a marriage is a man's and a woman's sharing in all of life, and Ulpianus' vagueness in calling it an undivided sharing of life. Gasparri did not mean to get rid of these ancient and almost axiomatic definitions. More probably he meant finally to provide the exact and specific content of these generic statements. To the extent that he included them incognito he meant that the union and the sharing that constitute marriage as distinct from any other possible union and sharing are a contracted exchange of each party's right to his and her sexual acts.

The same precise specification of the goal of marriage and of the object of marital consent comes back in two subsequent canons. Canon 1082 simultaneously says what minimum degree of understanding a person needs in order to be capable of marital consent, and implies what degree of ignorance makes a person incapable of it.

> 1. In order that marital consent be possible it is necessary that the contracting parties be at least not ignorant that marriage is a permanent society between a man and a woman for the procreation of children.
> 2. This ignorance is not presumed after puberty.[34]

Presuming that the minimum a person must understand of the object of marital consent in order to make the latter is exactly equal with the minimum object he can consent to and yet create the marriage, this canon seems to add an element to the object of marital consent that is stated in canon 1081.2. This is "the permanent society."

The second of the canons is 1086.2. It states those elements whose exclusion from the object of marital consent invalidates the latter.

> But if either party or both parties by a positive act of the will exclude marriage itself, or all right to the conjugal act or any essential property of marriage, the marriage contract is invalid.[35]

Where Canon 1081.2 names as the object of marital consent only the perpetual and exclusive right to the parties' sexual acts, according to this canon one could bring invalidity upon his consent by excluding from its object more than just that right. It is self-evident that if a person excludes marriage itself from the object of his consent, the latter is invalid.[36] If he or she excludes the right to intercourse, the consent is invalid in virtue of Canon 1081.2. But beyond this, Canon 1086.2 specifies that if a person excludes sexual exclusivity or indissolubility from the consent, the latter is invalid. In other words, though the latter two qualities do not, according to the law, belong to the object of consent, nevertheless excluding them from the consent invalidates the latter and renders the attempted marriage null and void.

About these four canons—1013.1, 1081.2, 1082.1 and 1086.2—Fellhauer offers the following comprehensive interpretation:

> The element which is dominant in all four of these formulations is procreation and the right to its physical prerequisite, acts which are suitable for generation. It seems fair to say that in the Code of Canon Law the juridical essence of marriage is therefore the right to carnal copula which is ordered to procreation. This right has the qualities of permanence and exclusivity, as succinctly stated in Canon 1081, n. 2, the canon which stipulates the ob-

ject of consent and which likewise is the Code's most concise statement of the canonical nature of marriage. Canon 1013, n. 1, stating that procreation and education are together the *finis primarius*, is a parallel declaration to Canon 1081, n. 2 and partially explains it, although it is not identical; rather it looks at the same object from a different viewpoint and within a different schema. Together these two legal statements determine what *essentially specifies* marriage, distinguishing it from all other societies, and they determine the *essential formal* object of matrimonial consent.[37]

Cardinal Gasparri's Use of the Sources

The degree to which the formulation of these four crucial canons defining the nature of marriage according to Catholic law is the product of Cardinal Gasparri's innovating mind and supervising will is the object of a brief examination by the contemporary canonist, Urbano Navarrete.[38] This examination appears in Part 1 of a long and thorough study titled "Structura Iuridica Matrimonii Secundum Concilium Vaticanum II" (The Juridical Structure of Marriage According to Vatican Council II).[39] The examination at this point is brief enough to be quoted in full.

If we examine the documents of the Church's [magisterium] on marriage, or the documents of the Holy See in general, and the *Corpus of Canon Law* itself, that touch this subject in some way, we find—and by no means without surprise—hardly a thing said about the ends of marriage precisely as goals, until the formulation in 1917 of Canon 1013. [Footnote 9 at this point reports that in the preliminary formulation of the canon reached by 1913 there is no indication of a hierarchy of ends: "The end of marriage is not only the procreation and nurture of children, but also mutual help and the remedy for concupiscence."]

16. It will suffice to examine the sources that Cardinal Gasparri supplies for this canon [1013]. Those he draws from the *Corpus of Canon Law* are nothing other than the texts from St. Augustine which deal not with *ends* under the formality of ends, but with goods. The one text which is not from Augustine [taken from the *Corpus*] says anything about ends only in a distantly implicit way. The Council of Florence spoke not of ends but only of goods, of which "the first is the bearing and educating of children for the worship of God."

Benedict XIV in his constitution *Dei miseratione* says only this: "Indeed the marital covenant instituted by God, insofar as it is a dutiful vocation of nature, is for the nurture of offspring and for the gaining of the other goals of marriage." Leo XIII in his encyclical *Arcanum* [of 1888] reckons as an end [of marriage] only the propagating of the human race and the raising of progeny for the Church. The other elements of which he writes—the most complete love, the unfailing fidelity, the adroit and resourceful help—he locates in the category of rights and duties.

Two instructions that are cited as sources—one of December 9, 1874 from the Holy Office to the bishop of St. Albert, the other from the Sacred Congregation for the Propagation of the Faith to the Romanian-Greek bishops in 1858—contain nothing new about the ends of marriage.

17. Strange as it may seem it is nevertheless certain that Canon 1013.1 is the first document of the Church that lists these ends and arranges them hierarchically: "The primary end of marriage is the procreation and nurture of children; its secondary end is mutual help and the remedying of concupiscence." This canon is also the first document of the Church to use the terminology "primary" and "secondary." In addition this peculiarity is worth noting, that under the "secondary end" (singular in number) are listed both mutual help and the remedying of concupiscence, even though these are quite diverse ends.

Fellhauer has subjected Gasparri's use of the sources for his Canon 1081.2 to the same kind of examination. He reports the following results:

Of the eight *fontes* [sources] adduced, six make no mention of the copula or the *ius in corpus* [the right to the use of the body] as the object of matrimonial consent. The other two sources (the first and third in the footnote), both from Gratian—c. 3, C. 27, q. 2; and C. 29, q. 1—deal respectively with the marriage of the Blessed Virgin and with the Old Testament union of Jacob and Leah. Carnal copula does indeed figure in these passages, but in a nuanced way. . . .

Thus, while both these sources present copula as part of marriage, they do not identify the two nor attempt to specify the right to sexual relations as the sole object of consent. And a reading of the *fontes* for Canon 1082 and 1086.2 likewise shows no source which presents the juridical essence of marriage as the *ius in corpus* for procreation or which identifies the object of consent in similar terms.

What did the formulations of these canons contribute to the history of the Catholic understanding of marriage? Despite the apparently deliberate intent to write no formal definition of marriage into the law, Canons 1013.1 and 1081.2 (with the help of Canons 1082 and 1086) in fact provide a definition of it containing precisely identified specific differences. Moving from the most general to the irreducible specific these canons say that marriage the institution (marriage *in facto esse*) is a permanent society (Canon 1082), whose primary end is procreation and nurture (Canon 1013.1), a society that is in species a contract that is unitary and indissoluble by nature (Canon 1012 and 1013.2), whose substance is the parties' exchanged right to their sexual acts (1081.2).

Canonists say constantly of this definition that it designates the "juridical essence" of marriage. Leaving aside for now the question asking if the adjective in this compound term hints that there are other essences of marriage deserving equal recognition by the Church and her people, what it has in practice meant is that in the juridical regulating and the judicial ruling of marriages, the latter are dealt with just as these canons define them. For example, as long as this definition of marriage functioned as the criterion of judgment in the Catholic marriage courts (it has now been displaced in most of the courts in the United Kingdom, Holland, Germany, the United States and elsewhere), the judgment could be drawn from no point of evidence that could not be subsumed under one of the categories in this defintion. Even the judgment by some courts that refusal to cohabit is evidence of invalid consent was subsumed as evidence against consent to the specific object of marital consent, namely the right to sexual acts.

Put succinctly, thanks to these canons marriage became, in the judicial sector of the Catholic Church, a juridical entity. (And since, according to Canon 1012.2, the sacrament of marriage is naught but the contract elevated to sacramental status, the sacrament too was treated as a juridical entity.) If the reader suspects that the Church's magisterium has, in the years since the Second Vatican Council, moved beyond thinking of marriage as a juridical entity, an inspection of Pope Paul VI's discourse of February 9, 1976 to the officers of the Roman Rota will correct this mistaken impression. (We will inspect this discourse in a later chapter.)

Another effect of these canons is the reduction of meaning of a term and a concept that I have already mentioned. Gradually across centuries canonists had sought to reduce the meaning of "conjugal society" to fine specificity in order to legislate for and rule marriage more exactly. They sought not to abandon this term but to fill in its semantic semi-vacuum. In these canons Gasparri finally did so by bringing the term down to refer to the mutually exchanged right to sexual acts.

Bits and pieces of the long-established inclusive but less precise concepts remained in the marriage law. "Permanent society" (*societas permanens*) stayed in Canon 1082, although its meaning there is that marriage is a society and is permanent for the sake of procreation. Canon 1111 retains "conjugal life" (*vita coniugalis*) but with no intent to use it in defining marriage. Canon 1129 has "sharing of life" (*vitae communio*) but in a context indicating that it refers to cohabitation. Canon 1130 has *consortium vitae,* but with the same reference. And Canon 1131 has *vitae consuetudo,* again with the same reference.

Pius XI and Casti connubii

On December 31, 1930 Pope Pius XI sent his encyclical letter, *Casti connubii*, to the Catholic bishops throughout the world.[40] His motive for doing so he revealed in his words of explanation to the bishops. It is little different from the motive which had produced Leo XIII's *Arcanum divinae sapientiae* fifty years earlier. Pius explained, "We observe—and you, Venerable Brethren, cannot but share Our sorrow as you also observe—that there are many unmindful of this divine work of renewal, who are totally ignorant of the sanctity of marriage, who imprudently deny it, who even allow themselves to be led by principles of a modern and perverse ethical doctrine to repudiate it with scorn. As these pernicious errors and degraded morals have begun to spread even among the faithful. . . ."[41] The immediate occasion for the letter is said to have been the declaration by the Anglican bishops in Lambeth Conference in the spring of that year that the members of that church were free to follow their own consciences about using contraceptive means for birth control.

Part Two of the encyclical is a brief encyclopedia of the evils Pius had in mind: denial of the origin of marriage in God's creation and claim for its arrival through an evolutionary process resulting in marriage the social contract, companionate and trial marriages, contraception, abortion, sterilization, adultery, the emancipation of women, religiously mixed marriages, and divorce.

His first step in passing moral judgment on these evils was to establish his criteria for judging. These he reduced to substantially one, but a criterion presenting itself to men in two ways, as the will of God revealed in the nature itself of marriage, and as the same will revealed in marriage the Christian sacrament. To declare the nature of marriage is, of course, to define it at least informally. And in doing this Pius was without novelty, except in a qualified way I shall note in a moment. He said that marriage is by nature a contract established by the free consent of the parties. The object of their consent is the specific marital right, which each both gives and receives. This is the parties' right to their sexual acts. With their consenting the parties' freedom in regard to the contract ends; they have taken on themselves the unchanging nature of marriage and its correlated rights and duties.

Pius leaves no doubt that he regards procreation as primary in marriage. Early in the encyclical he insists that among the goods of marriage offspring hold first place.

> Among the blessings of marriage offspring holds the first place. The Creator of the human race Himself, who in His goodness has willed to use human beings as His ministers in the propagation of life, taught us this truth when in instituting matrimony in the Garden of Eden He bade our first parents, and through them all

married persons who should come after them: "Increase and multiply and fill the earth." St. Augustine rightly draws the same conclusion from the words of the Apostle St. Paul to Timothy: "The Apostle testifies that procreation is the purpose of matrimony when, having said, 'I will that younger women should marry,' he adds immediately, as though he had been asked the reason, 'so that they may bear children and become the mothers of families.' "[42]

Pius goes beyond saying merely that offspring are the primary good of marriage. He changes the term easily from "good" to "end" and quotes Canon 1013.1. "The primary end of matrimony is the procreation and education of offspring."[43]

It is somewhat surprising that when Pius comes to his moral judgment on contraceptive intercourse, deeming it contrary to nature and intrinsically immoral, he does not say that it is against nature because it blocks the attaining of marriage's primary end. He says rather that the use of contraceptives is against nature because it voids the natural finality of sexual intercourse, which is procreation.

But no reason whatever, even the gravest, can make what is intrinsically against nature become conformable with nature and morally good. The conjugal act is of its very nature designed for the procreation of offspring; and therefore those who in performing it deliberately deprive it of its natural power and efficacy, act against nature and do something which is shameful and intrinsically immoral.[44]

Shortly afterward he repeats the same judgment. Although this time he refers to contraceptive intercourse within marriage, he still condemns it because it voids not the primary end of marriage but the natural finality of intercourse.

... the Catholic Church ... through Our mouth proclaims anew: that any use of matrimony whatsoever in the exercise of which the act is deprived, by human interference, of its natural power to procreate life, is an offense against the law of God and of nature.[45]

The special value of *Casti connubii,* to my mind, lies in its calling back onto center stage elements of marriage which had been quietly ignored by the canonists in their work of refining the definition of marriage. One could list them under the category of "the good of the spouses," or one could say that they are Pius' brief spelling out of what is implied by "mutual help" as an end of marriage. In any case he develops descriptive definitions of conjugal fidelity (albeit as honoring the contractually exchanged right to sexual acts), of the monogamy and sexual exclusivity as preservers of the marriage and the family.[46]

And at this point he brings to the forefront an element that had once been named clearly in The Catechism of the Council of Trent, but which had since then been almost entirely forgotten. This element is a kind of love specific to marriage, called in the Latin of the encyclical first *amor* then *caritas*. Pius locates this love fully in marriage; it pervades all the duties of married life. It has a primacy in marriage—not juridically as an end of marriage, but a primacy of honor. More exactly this love is charity, of a kind drawn from its model which is Christ's love for the Church. Said most exactly, this charity " . . . is not an attachment founded on a mere carnal and transitory desire, or limited to words of affection; it is a deep-seated devotion of the heart, which, since love shows itself in works, is manifested in action."[47]

At this point Pius opens the door just a bit (and probably unknowingly) into a new chapter in the history of the Church's thinking on marriage. For he finds it necessary to state more accurately just what he means by married love's manifesting itself in action. This love and the action it impels have a much higher and fuller goal than mutual help as this has been traditionally understood. Their goal is to bring the spouses toward the fulfillment of the potential in them that is interior and most characteristically human.

> This action in the home is not confined to mutual help; it must have as its higher and indeed its chief objective that of shaping and perfecting the interior life of husband and wife. Their life-partnership must help them to increase daily in the practice of virtue, and above all to grow in the true love of God and their neighbor, in that charity on which "depends the whole Law and the Prophets."[48]

Then comes the statement that pushed the door open to stay.

> This mutual interior formation of husband and wife, this persevering endeavor to bring each other to the state of perfection, may in a true sense be called, as the Roman Catechism calls it, the primary cause and reason of matrimony, so long as marriage is considered not in its stricter sense as the institution designed for the procreation and education of children, but in the wider sense as a complete and intimate life-partnership and association.[49]

Since the last clause here echoes the definitions of marriage in the *Digest* and the *Institutes* of seventeen centuries earlier,[50] the suggestion that marriage may be considered a life-partnership and an association is hardly novel. Where the entire statement begins, though faintly, a rethinking of the nature of marriage, just thirteen years after Cardinal Gasparri had seemed to think the most refined possible thing about it, is at two points that are inseparable. The first is the suggestion that marriage even be thought about not in its stricter sense (which is obviously within the limits of juridical categories), along with the hint that there may be good reason for doing so (such as to gain an understanding of marriage in its human completeness). The second point is that, given the good reason for considering marriage in this wider sense, this consideration produces evidence that the primary cause and reason of marriage (*primaria causa et ratio matrimonii*) is "this mutual interior formation of husband and wife, this persevering endeavor to bring each other to the state of perfection."

Pius was careful. He did not so word that paragraph as to make it interfere with his earlier quoting of Canon 1013 to the effect that procreation and nurture are the primary end of marriage. And since he nowhere offers a formal definition of marriage, nor does he write of the "juridical essence" of marriage, one cannot draw from this passage the conclusion that a unique love impelling a man and woman to work together for their own and the partner's perfection belongs to the essence of marriage. But again, what Pius has done here is to extend a quiet invitation to ponder marriage outside the limitations of a juridical and reductionist definition. In fact there were already Catholic thinkers in Europe thinking of marriage more or less as Pius suggests here—"not in the stricter sense." The book that was to have the most decisive effect in the 1930's and 1940's in opening Catholic minds to a change of teaching about marriage's nature very nearly borrowed Pius' own words for its title. This was the German theologian Heribert Doms' *Vom Sinn und Zweck der Ehe* (On the Meaning and End of Marriage) published in 1935.[51]

In addition these Catholic thinkers were asking a question that appears not to have occurred to Pius, at least not in the composition of the encyclical. This question asks whether the primary end of marriage and its primary reason and cause (presuming the latter differ from the end) could stand simultaneously as accepted Catholic understandings of marriage, or whether they are necessarily in conflict so that one or the other must yield. Or did that question in its more fundamental form occur to Pius: Can both the meanings of marriage that he proposed—the stricter or narrow, and the wider—be kept simultaneously? And there grow out of this two derivative questions: If both meanings can be kept, can they be held in equal value, or must one be subordinated to the other? And if one must be subordinated, which shall it be?

The Hierarchy of Ends and Controlling Subordination

To say with Canon 1013.1 only that the primary end of marriage is procreation and nurture, and its secondary end mutual help and the remedying of concupiscence, is by itself to leave unsaid some things important for the juridical regulation of marriage. For one thing this does not state exactly the relationship of the secondary end to the primary—for example whether, if realizing simultaneously the two strata of ends becomes impossible, the primary must override the secondary *because* it is primary, and must do so in every case. It does not say what place the secondary end has in the constituting of a marriage—for example, whether a prior refusal to bring mutual help or to remedy concupiscence invalidates the marital consent.

But the careful formulation of the other canons we have examined above—1081.2 (the object of consent), 1082.1 (the knowledge of the object requisite for making the consent), and 1086.2 (intentions that invalidate the consent)—prepared the answers to these questions. For example, making the right to sexual acts the one irreducibly necessary object of marital consent puts all other possible objects in their place. Granted that they are the objects of consent but are unnecessary, what other function can they have except to be tributary to the necessary exchange of the right to sexual acts? Or to draw the same kind of inference using different terms and concepts, if procreation and nurture are exclusively the primary end of marriage, what function can the secondary end have other than one tributary to procreation and nurture? Mutual help must be *for* these, to make them possible and to assist them. So too must the remedying of concupiscence.

This relationship of secondary to primary in the mode of controlled subordination waited for its elaboration, after the promulgation of the Code and after *Casti connubii*, for the jurisprudence of the marriage courts and for declarations by the Church's magisterium. This jurisprudence reached a kind of apex, found its most thorough explanation, in a decision on a petition for nullity handed down on January 22, 1944 by the Roman Rota.[52] It was written by the auditor (the Rotal judge) Arthur Wynan.[53] The declaration by the magisterium took its most comprehensive form in Pope Pius XII's discourse of October 29, 1951 to the Association of Italian Catholic Midwives. A review of this discourse will occupy a sizable part of the following chapter.

That the Rota's decision of January 1944 was published unabridged in the official pontifical record, *Acta Apostolicae Sedis*, suggests the importance it had in the minds of the Church's appointed judges. The judgment was on the petition by a young Italian male that his presumed marriage of September 19, 1931 be declared null on the two grounds of simulated marital consent by his partner and of consent on his part invalidated by force and grave fear. The court of first instance denied his petition on December 10, 1942. The Rota accepted the case on December 11, 1943 on appeal, but on the single ground of simulated consent. It is important, when examining the decision written by Wynan, that this last fact be kept in mind.

The young man had had sexual relations with the woman before their wedding. He found out that she had an incurable and contagious disease, and that he had got her pregnant. He fled to a different city, but at the pleas of his own mother and under the threats from the girl's relatives he returned to Rome and married her. He claimed subsequently that he had never intended to consummate the marriage; the two of them were able to prove that they had never cohabited following the wedding. The Rota denied the petition for nullity on the one ground it considered, simulated consent. But it did secure from the Pope a dissolution of the marriage after satisfying itself that it had never been consummated.

Wynan's argument in denying the petition for nullity makes up the valuable jurisprudence that interests us here. The *turnus* of Rotal judges did not challenge the petitioner's claim that he and his bride had never lived together after the wedding. The crucial point it did make—and its denial of the petition sprang from this—was that the couple's decision not to cohabit had been a mutual one, and most especially that there was no evidence that in making their marital consent in 1931 they had denied one another the right to intercourse—even though they had intended never to use this right and had in fact not had intercourse as husband and wife. Their not denying this right had kept their consent valid and had got them married.

The *in iure* portion of the Rota's decision (the explanation of the causes of the decision drawn from the law) draws heavily on the primacy of procreation as an end of marriage and the subordination to it of any other ends. It says that procreation is the *finis operis* of marriage, the objective and natural reason for its existence, its "formal cause."

The explanation then looks to marriage's secondary end, especially to "mutual help." Under this category it acknowledges such elements as " . . . cohabitation . . . *communio mensae*, the use of material goods, the earning and administration of the means of support, a more personal assistance in the physical and emotional spheres of life, and even in spiritual matters."[54]

The explanation then poses the crucial question: What is the relationship between the secondary end of marriage ("mutual help" understood according to the details just above) and its primary end? To prepare an answer to this question it pointed out that these kinds of "help" can be found in relationships other than marriage—for example, between siblings or between dear friends. Hence there must be some specific feature or situation of this congeries of helps that makes them marital.

This special feature is precisely the relationship of their subordination to the primary end of marriage. That is, what makes cohabitation, use of material goods, emotional and physical sustenance, etc., marital is their being employed in the service of procreation and nurture. Indeed all that is significant in marriage must, if it is to be marital, be in the service of procreation and nurture. Said another way, the secondary end is an end of marriage only in virtue of this subordinate and tributary status.

Yet another distinction was in order, one needed to maintain logical consistency. Just as the spouses' appropriation of the primary end is not in the domain of use and conduct but in the contractual domain of exchange of rights (they don't have to have intercourse with one another, but need only grant one another the right to it), so too their appropriation of the secondary end is in the contractual domain. They need not actually ask or offer help, but only grant one another the right to it. And again the tributary-subordinated relationship: the right to intercourse necessarily entails the *right* to mutual help; the right to mutual help is, in turn, marital in that it subserves the right to intercourse.

However—and here the subordination of secondary to primary shows a crucial consequence—the secondary right is not a constitutive part of the primary right. They are distinct, different, separable. It is not even a necessary condition for the exchange of the primary right. And here is the core of the Rota's logic in denying the young Roman's petition for nullity. A valid marriage can be created as long as the primary right is given even if the secondary right has been explicitly refused. The judges granted that in this case this explicit refusal had been made by both parties, but insisted that there was no evidence that the primary right had not been granted by both. Hence there was no evidence for nullity.

But what juridical significance, if any, can be drawn from the parties' explicit refusal to grant the right to the secondary end of marriage? From this refusal can nothing be inferred about their intent to create a marriage at all? The answer to this is a kind of parallel though asymmetric judgment. Suppose it became evident from inquiry sometime after the wedding that a couple had intended never to have intercourse. From this discovery judges could infer the likelihood of their having denied one another the right itself to intercourse. But from it alone the judges could never *prove* the denial of this right. So too from the discovery that a couple had from before the wedding denied one another the right to mutual help in all its facets (the subordinate object of consent), the judges could infer the likelihood of their having denied one another also the right to their sexual acts (the primary object of consent). But from the first denial alone they could not prove the second denial.

This decision of 1944 denying a petition for a declaration of nullity was not sequentially the last Roman word on the subject. As I have already mentioned, seven years later Pius XII was to speak at almost equal length in reply to the Catholic scholars who, he thought, were denying that procreation and nurture are the primary end of marriage. But this decision is logically a conclusion in the sense that it is the furthest point to which logical ratiocination starting from one or two methodological premises can lead. One of the premises here was that for the sake of good order in the Church, it *must* be possible to verify forensically who is married and who is not, and who is married to whom. The second premise evolves from that one: the criterion for this verification *must* enable the Church's judges to do three things. The first is that they be able to find with certainty among the kinds of familiar heterosexual relationships at least one characteristic that differentiates one of them from all the others. The second is that they be able to make that characteristic one that can be intended to serve, intrinsically and of its own nature, the traditional primary end of marriage. The third is that they be able to judge, in forensic examination and empirically, the presence or absence of this characteristic. Thanks mainly to the juridical genius of Cardinal Gasparri, this act with this characteristic was isolated and identified. It was the expressed consent to the exchange, with a heterosexual partner, of both parties' right to his and her sexual acts apt of their nature for conception. Thus a judicial need subserving a pastoral need produced this definition of marriage we have seen distributed in the four key canons of the Catholic marriage law, and gathered tightly in the decision written by the Rotal *turnus* presided over by Arthur Wynan.

NOTES

1. In Denzinger-Schönmetzer, *op. cit.*, n. 766.
2. Reported in G. H. Joyce, *op. cit.*, pp. 69–70.
3. In *Luther's Works*, J. Pelikan and H. T. Lehmann, general editors, Vol. 46, Phila., 1967, pp. 259–320.
4. These are in Denzinger-Schönmetzer, *op. cit.,* nn. 1797–1816. The decree *Tametsi* is under the last four of these numbers.
5. But *Tametsi* scored no decisive victory over young Catholics in their campaign to marry partners of their choice. Many took to the practice of "the surprise marriage." By careful plotting they could arrange, with two or three sympathetic friends, to break into the pastor's residence in the small hours of the morning, shake the pastor awake and quickly pronounce their wedding vows in his hearing. They thus fulfilled the requirement of *Tametsi:* they had declared their consent *in facie Ecclesiae,* and the pastor would afterward have to admit that he had heard their vows. Amazingly nothing effective was done in Catholic marriage law to close off this route of escape from *Tametsi* until its 1978 revision (when clandestine marriage had long since vanished from Catholic experience). This revised law, when it is promulgated, will require in Canon 311 that for the validity of the marital consent this be not only declared in the presence of an authorized priest, but that it be declared in his presence *after* he has requested it. The proposed canon is worded carefully. Paragraph 1 rules that only those marriages are valid that are contracted before an "assisting" bishop, priest, deacon or other person delegated to witness the contracting. Paragraph 2 states the conditions under which the witness "assists": he must be physically present, request the consent of both parties and receive it in the name of the Church.
6. Its full title is *Catechismus ex Decreto SS. Concilii Tridentini ad Parochos, PII V . . . Iussu Editus.* An English translation is available: *Catechism of the Council of Trent*, trans. by the Rev. J. Donovan, N.Y., n.d.
7. *Catechism* . . . pp. 226–227.
8. *Op. cit.*, pp. 229–230.
9. *De Sancto Matrimonii Sacramento Disputationum, Liber Secundus, De Essentia et Consensu Matrimonii*, Venetiis, 1726, p. 91.1.
10. *Loc. cit.,* p. 91.2.
11. *Ibid.* p. 91.6.
12. *Ibid.,* p. 91.8.
13. *Op. cit., Disputatio* 4, "Quando matrimonium institutum sit in lege naturae et evangelicae," p. 92.3.
14. *Disputatio* 1, n. 8 (quoted in Fellhauer, *op. cit.,* p. 53).

15. *Ibid.*

16. In Fellhauer, *op. cit.*, pp. 73–74.

17. *Ibid.*, p. 74.

18. *Ibid.*

19. *Ibid.*

20. *Loc. cit.*, p. 75.

21. Gasparri was a superb scholar and organizer. He taught at the Institut Catholique in Paris until called back to Rome in 1901, and in 1904 he began supervising the codification of the entire corpus of Catholic law as secretary of the commission of cardinals guiding the work as well as president of the two groups of scholars doing the work. The codifying was expected to take twenty-five years. But Gasparri delivered the completed project to Pope Benedict XV twelve years later on December 4, 1916.

22. Vol. 1, p. 117.

23. P. 12.

24. *Op. cit.*, p. 58.

25. *Op. cit.*, p. 16.

26. Vol. 1, p. 119.

27. *Ibid.*, pp. 119–120.

28. I think Gasparri's logic can be taken one step further. Since all that a man and woman need essentially do in order to get married to one another is to exchange the right to their sexual acts, could they not also hate one another bitterly and perpetually, and after their exchange of consent never again set eyes on one another, yet be husband and wife?

29. P. 18, paragraph 9.

30. "1. Christus Dominus ad sacramenti dignitatem evexit ipsum contractum matrimonialem inter baptizatos.

"2. Quare inter baptizatos nequit matrimonialis contractus validus consistere, quin sit eo ipso sacramentum."

31. "1. Matrimonii finis primarius est procreatio atque educatio prolis; secundarius mutuum adiutorium et remedium concupiscentiae."

Elsewhere in these pages I have translated *finis* as "goal." Here in the discussion of the marriage law in the Code I prefer to use the word "end" because virtually all Catholic discussion of the matter uses it. I intend the two English substantives to be in this context exactly synonymous.

32. "2. Essentiales matrimonii proprietates sunt unitas ac indissolubilitas, quae in matrimonio christiano peculiarem obtinent firmitatem ratione sacramenti."

33. "1. Matrimonium facit partium consensus inter personas iure habiles legitime manifestatus; qui nulla humana potestate suppleri valet.

"2. Consensus matrimonialis est actus voluntatis quo utraque pars tradit et acceptat ius in corpus, perpetuum et exclusivum, in ordine ad actus per se aptos ad prolis generationem."

34. "1. Ut matrimonialis consensus haberi possit, necesse est ut contrahentes saltem non ignorent matrimonium esse societatem permanentem inter virum et mulierem ad filios procreandos.

"2. Haec ignorantia post pubertatem non praesumitur."

35. "2. At si alterutra vel utraque pars positivo voluntatis actu excludat matrimonium ipsum, aut omne ius ad coniugalem actum, vel essentialem aliquam matrimonii proprietatem, invalide contrahit."

36. If the reader wonders how a person could make the marital consent in the

wedding but nevertheless exclude marriage itself from the object of the consent, the following real-life example will show how it can be done. Shortly before a wedding at which I officiated in 1964 the bride-to-be said to her sister, who was helping her dress for the wedding, that she really had no intention of marrying in the ceremony. She did not want the groom for a husband; she preferred another man who was then awaiting the final decree of civil divorce. She intended that her ceremony be only make-believe. I found out about this only after the ceremony. Had I found out about it beforehand, the ceremony would have been cancelled.

37. *Op. cit.*, p. 80.

38. Navarrete has taught in the Faculty of Canon Law at the Gregorian University in Rome for more than two decades and is now dean of this faculty. He is also a consultor of the pontifical commission that completed the revision of the Code of Canon Law from 1966 to 1978.

39. The entire study is in *Periodica,* Volumes 56.1 (1967), pp. 357–383, 56.2, pp. 554–578, 56.3, pp. 131–167, and 56.4, pp. 169–216. The examination of Gasparri's sources is in Vol. 56.1, pp. 366–368.

40. A satisfactory English translation of the encyclical is in *Papal Teachings: Matrimony,* translated by Michael J. Byrnes, Boston, 1963, pp. 219–291.

41. N. 3 (p. 220).

42. N. 11 (pp. 224–225).

43. N.17 (p. 228).

44. N. 54 (p. 247).

45. N. 56 (p. 248).

46. Nn. 31–37.

47. N. 23 (p. 231).

48. *Ibid.*

49. N. 24 (*ibid.*).

50. In fact the Latin substantives here are *totius vitae communio, consuetudo, societas.*

51. It was translated into English in 1939 as *The Meaning of Marriage,* thereby losing some of the cutting edge of the German title.

52. The name "Rota" was in use in papal government as early as the Avignon residency in the fourteenth century. Whatever the judicial body designated by the term at that time, since Pius X's reform of the papal curia in 1908 it refers to an ordinary court whose work is to rule on appeals that are brought before it. In 1980 it had twenty-four functioning auditors from eight different countries. Since it is a court authorized by the Apostolic See, it has no territorial limits to its competence. Most of the decisions it has rendered have been in matrimonial cases, although it can and does hear all kinds of ecclesiastical cases, even cases criminal according to Catholic law. Marriage cases get to it on appeal from courts of first instance in dioceses around the world, since it is a second-instance appellate court. The auditors ordinarily render their decisions functioning as a *turnus* of three court members. The decision is always governed by a majority vote among the three auditors making up the *turnus* in a particular case.

53. My outline of the decision will be a paraphrase of Fellhauer's analysis of it in his essay, pp. 89–92.

54. *Op. cit.*, p. 90.

9. THE MODERN CATHOLIC CHALLENGE TO THE CANONICAL DEFINITION

It is difficult to know whether what took place in the Catholic defining of marriage between the two world wars was a purely coincidental irony or a fractional example of the dialectical movement of history. From the beginning of Gasparri's work, through the drafting of the Code of Canon Law and on into the ever more precise uses and interpretations that flowed from these, the Catholic magisterium settled into the most fixed and unambiguous definition of marriage it had ever had. But simultaneously this definition, with all the explicit juridical and implicit philosophical reasoning that produced it, began to be undermined by thinkers who were themselves active and loyal Catholics. They put a radical challenge to the received definition. The challenge drew a powerful riposte from the magisterium in the persons first of the Congregation of the Holy Office and then of Pope Pius XII. But eventually the challenge won out in the Second Vatican Council, in a somewhat changed but in a fundamentally unchanged form of its original self. Did the triumph of juridicism, exemplified in the Code's definition of marriage, function as a dialetical thesis to produce the challenge, the antithesis that was psychological, anthropological and philosophical in spirit? The exact cause-effect nexus of the two is difficult to verify. It is more profitable to examine the challenge itself.

Those who raised it were German and French scholar-writers deeply influenced by the phenomenology of Edmund Husserl, Max Scheler and Maurice Merleau-Ponty. Of these the best known to English-speaking Catholics were Dietrich von Hildebrand and Heribert Doms. The former's essays still retain some currency in the United Kingdom and in the United States. Doms' popularity in these and other countries waned once his most influential work, *The Meaning of Marriage,* was withdrawn from publication in the early 1940's by order of the Congregation of the Holy Office.

225

Hardly known at all among English-speaking Catholics, probably because they entered the challenge-become-debate almost a decade later than von Hildebrand and Doms, were Bernardin Krempel and Ernst Michel.[1]

These writers' interpretation of marriage was given a name borrowed from their own philosophical stance—"Christian personalist." The interpretation was developed thoroughly and intricately. Presuming that it is possible to isolate their most fundamental thesis about marriage, it seems to have been the following.

A marriage's richest value is not instrumental. It is not an institution whose greatest value is in gaining some goal outside itself, such as the continuing of the human race and the prolonging of civil or ecclesiastical societies. It can and does serve these goals. But it is a community of persons with a meaning and therefore a value within itself. This is the becoming-one of two persons (Doms called this *Zweieinigkeit,* two-in-oneness), the creating of the I-Thou in which the man and woman can be brought to completion as human beings. Again this is not to deny that a marriage can serve ends outside itself, nor that among those ends procreation may be primary. But the first intelligible, the first value in marriage is this meaning, this person-completing union—a meaning and a value which are there and give a "reason" for marriage distinct and even separable from procreation.

That this thesis was already some decades in preparation is evident in the quotations from his antecessors that Doms included in the introduction of *The Meaning of Marriage.* He notes that von Hildebrand first advanced the distinction between the meaning and the ends of marriage in his essay *Reinheit und Jungfräulichkeit* (which antedated *Die Ehe* and has been translated into English as *In Defense of Purity*). But von Hildebrand drew this in turn from Otfried Ebertz' *Vom Aufgang und Niedergang des Männlichen Weltalters* (The Rise and Fall of the Masculine Age). As early as 1850 Ferdinand Probst had written in his *Katholische Moraltheologie:* "This union is bound to remain the basis of marriage . . . this union finds its highest expression in the marriage act. This gives us reason for saying that the principal purpose of marriage is undivided community of life."[2]

In 1878 F. X. Linsermann wrote in his *Lehrbuch der Moraltheologie,* "Sexual intercourse should be subordinated to the higher purpose of marriage which is spiritual. . . . From the *subjective* point of view the child is only a secondary purpose of marriage. If it were the first purpose, we should be right in forbidding married people to have sexual intercourse when they could no longer hope to have children. . . ."[3] And in 1905 Anton Koch in his *Lehrbuch der Moraltheolgie* added: "It is reasonable to suppose that the purpose of marriage is a sexual community ordained to quieten concupiscence and produce children. But the highest and principal purpose of marriage is undivided community of life between a man and a woman."[4]

Much of what von Hildebrand and Doms were to say was at least suggested in an essay written in 1933 by the Franciscan, Fidelis Schwendinger:

> Unless we are prepared to maintain that the Church consecrates sacramentally an institution which has no meaning (i.e., an unfulfilled marriage like that of Joseph and Mary), we are bound to admit that marriage has some other meaning besides procreation and that this other meaning is essential to marriage. Community of personal life between husband and wife is the only possible other meaning. If we consider the psychological process which leads up to marriage ("falling in love," etc.), we must see that community of life is the first thing which the man and the woman desire. . . . The Me-You community still remains the first thing when one looks at marriage objectively. The first thing that husband and wife want to do is not to create a third thing distinct from either. The third person is not that which unites them and makes them say We, nor do they fulfill and consummate each other through it. No, the first and the most obvious characteristic of marriage is the direct union in love between a Me and a You. The object of their desire is *the whole person.* And when marriage is consummated each person gives and receives *an entire personality.* And this complete giving of the whole of a person to a person is for both human beings concerned the primary value and meaning of marriage union.[5]

Because von Hildebrand's brief essay, *Die Ehe,* was published six years earlier than Doms' lengthy analysis, and because it is most likely that Doms drew from and was influenced by von Hildebrand, a précis of the latter's thought is first in order.

Von Hildebrand made a fundamental change in the very mode of thinking about marriage. He refused to ask about its goals or purposes, and insisted especially on not defining it as a means of gaining some good or goods outside itself. He thought and wrote rather of the *meanings* of marriage. About this he said at first simply that the primary meaning of marriage is love. The reason for getting married is to live in love, just as the reason for being born is to exist humanly. He built up this nuclear thesis. The meaning of a marriage, its reason for existing, is the partners' building and living in a community of love. He interpreted the biblical ". . . and the two shall become one flesh" to refer to this communion. The social function of marriage and its importance for civil society and the state are secondary and are subordinate to the experiencing of the community of love. They exist to serve this community; it does not exist to serve them.

Marriage is an I-Thou relationship, a face-to-face relationship, a becoming-one of two persons. It is not a side-by-side relationship ordered to the reaching of some goal outside itself. The relationship of conception and of the child to marriage is this, that the latter comes from this fully realized meaning. The child is the natural flowering of this love-making when it is fully realized. But even in those marriages in which procreation is impossible the love-union has its fundamental meaning and value. The words of God in Genesis 2, "It is not good for the man to be alone. I will make a suitable partner for him," suggest this without any hint of cooperation in procreation. The woman was given to the man rather as his love-partner.

As a marriage is in its nature fundamentally a community of love, so too the physical consummation-expression of this love is not to be interpreted fundamentally as a means to procreation. Procreation is neither the only meaning nor the primary meaning of intercourse in marriage. Its primary meaning is to be the most complete expression of the parties' love for one another, its fullest embodiment. And since marital love is one in which the partners give over their whole persons to one another, intercourse is the act in which this self-giving can be at its fullest.

Thus every mature and fulfilled marriage is *intrinsically* fruitful. This fruitfulness is found in the forming of the new love relationship, in its continual enrichment and in the partners' growth of soul.

Von Hildebrand developed a rudimentary psychology of married love. This love involves a unique because total giving of the partners' selves one to the other. This completeness it is that makes true marital love both exclusive and permanent. This is why true marital love cannot be polygamous: a complete self-giving cannot be divided. Completeness is in this love in another sense as well, because the "I love you" that is marital is unique in its meaning. It sees not some one or few desirable features of the beloved, but his or her total person and accepts all of it. And since it takes in the total person, it takes in the uniqueness of him or her.

Marital love is heterosexual. Male and female designate more than biological differences; they are different metaphysically. They have a unique capacity for complementing and completing the other's incompleteness. They can together form an interiorly complementing and completing unity. Indeed only by and between the two sexes can *full* human complementing be found. Here is another rich aspect of the meaning of marriage. Thus too married love is not, as some have said vulgarly, merely friendship plus sexuality.

Von Hildebrand links this interpretation of marriage, so new for its time, to already established values. He comes close to accepting what his more traditional contemporaries were saying is the core of marriage: "The act of voluntary surrender of one's own person to another, with the intention of forming a permanent and intimate union of love, creates an objective bond, which once established is withdrawn from the sphere of arbitrary decision of the persons concerned."[6] He does not say whether in marriage there is an identity of community and bond, whether the marriage *is* the bond, whether the union of love and the bond are identical or in some way distinct. What he clearly *intends* to say is that the self-giving that creates the union creates an objective reality, the marriage bond, which is invulnerable to any subsequent decision to destroy it by those who had once created it. What von Hildebrand offers in explanation of this is an analogy. As a promise once made creates a moral obligation binding its maker, an obligation from which the latter cannot withdraw, so the marital commitment creates a bond that its creators cannot destroy. He does not say if he thinks that the bond is more than a moral obligation, albeit an objective one.

The Critique Implicit in the Challenge

Before examining Doms' development of von Hildebrand's thought a consideration of certain criticisms unexpressed but implied within the thought of both these authors will help to understand their interpretation of marriage. Among other things that one finds them saying between the lines is that the canonical understanding of marriage is phenomenologically empty. This understanding was intended to be a definition of marriage because the Catholic judicial processes needed an exact definition. But a definition is such only if it describes accurately the reality it seeks to define. And here is the glaring weakness of the canonical definition: it has no referent "out there" in reality, in marriage as men and women experience it in the twentieth century. It would have seemed flippant but it would have been accurate to say that where the referent of the canonical definition exists is nowhere but in the minds of the definers. This is the only place where marriage is experienced according to the definition.

For whatever else a marriage is, it is first of all a relationship of persons; it is a more or less stable and structured interaction of a man and a woman. But it is not likely that many men and women in Western society in about 1930 would have replied affirmatively to the question asking if they experienced their marriages as contracts in which they exchanged the right to the sexual use of their bodies. Nor probably would they have answered affirmatively if asked whether what they experienced in their sexual intercourse was the exercise of the exchanged right with its inherent orientation to conception. At least in the tiny and crowded apartments of Europe's working people, who made up the great majority of the European Catholic population, what men and women experienced in their lovemaking more likely included an explicit rejection of this orientation to conception.

Thus the married do not find in the real-life conduct of their marriages a subordinated-ends structure. They do not ordinarily make love principally for the motive of conceiving a child. But what the married do only infrequently, by its very infrequency brings compelling evidence against its claim to be the primary orientation of sexual intercourse. It does not strengthen the traditional Catholic case for the natural orientation of intercourse to procreation that for most spouses to act *according* to such an orientation they would have to act *against* their spontaneous inclination to have intercourse for a variety of other reasons—such as to offer and re-

ceive pleasure, to strengthen their love, to console, to relieve tension, to be
erotically artistic. In short, to verify inductively the accuracy of the definition, the verifiers would have to contradict a tidal wave of evidence denying this accuracy.

Doms and von Hildebrand imply that the canonical definition fails to
describe reality at another point. This definition has no place within itself
for love; love is excluded from the essence of marriage. It can find at best
only a supporting function for it within the secondary goal that is mutual
help. But at least since the beginning of the romantic era in Europe in the
early decades of the nineteenth century the overwhelming portion of men
and women in European society, and among its heirs in the two Americas,
have chosen their partners in marriage because they had come to love
them in some way, with one of the multiple forms of love. Without expecting that a definition could decide which form of love is appropriate to marriage, one could yet expect that a definition purporting to describe the
reality of marriage would find within itself a place for an entire society's
motive for marrying appropriated consciously for at least a century. Doms
makes much of this. He says that it is simply a fact that the heterosexual
love of men and women is a stronger and more universal motive for marrying, at least in the West, than is the desire for children. This is true during
courtship, true in the wedding, and true in sexual intercourse. But if procreation were, because of the sexual nature of men and women and from
the nature itself of marriage, the primary value of marriage and therefore
its primary goal, this experience of love as the stronger and more universal
motive would be an enormous evil because such a universal and unrelenting deception.[7]

Also just under the surface of these critiques is a rejection of Plato's
and Aristotle's utilitarian evaluation of not human sexuality, but of human
genitality fragmented from the full human person and dealt with as a function of animal nature. In both the Greek masters sexuality is the reproductive capacity, and this capacity is, in turn, for the service principally of
civil society to provide members for it. Enough of the Scholastics accepted
this to drown out the medieval voices insisting that it is in sexual intercourse that the union of a husband and wife is most like the love-union of
Christ and the Church. And the later canonists accepted it without significant hesitation.

Doms implies that only a rudimentary and even crude psychology can
accept this. Such a psychology sees a man's and woman's sexuality confined to the reproductive anatomy. Then observing the obvious, that this
anatomy supplies society's most fundamental need, its very prolongation
in existence, the Scholastics and the canonists could conclude that a man's
and woman's sexuality is mainly the servant of society, and this at nearly a
sub-personal level. And since it was easy to synonymize society's most fundamental need with its most universal good, the conclusion came readily
that procreation and nurture are sexuality's primary natural end.

As we shall see, Doms, as a representative of the personalist Catholic theologians, rejected this thinking at two points. He denied that sexuality is a sub-personal accessory to the person of a man and woman confined to their reproductive capacities. He insisted instead that it is an integrating element of their persons that suffuses them totally. Therefore (his second point of disagreement) he denied that when the values of sexuality's function are measured, the good of society overrides the good of the persons. Persons are for one another if they are *for* anyone. Their greatest value is as partners in love-unions (which are inescapably sexual in some degree). They are not for civil society (a thesis with which no Scholastic philosopher or canonist would disagree); therefore the ingredient of their persons that is their sexuality is at least not primarily for this society.

The Sexual Nature of Human Beings

Doms' positive exposition of his own thesis begins with an examination of the sexual nature of human beings. He insists first of all that what is natural or unnatural in it is not to be judged by what is natural or unnatural in irrational animals. Nature, indeed the animal nature, in human beings transcends that in other animals because its vitalizing principle, its *forma,* is the spiritual soul. A manifestation of this that is not negligible is that sexuality in human beings is not bound to nature's cyclic rhythm. Men and women are not sexually subject to a rutting period. They can want to express themselves to one another sexually according to the direction of time-transcending spirit. They can want to do so even during pregnancy.

There is no understanding human sexuality at all unless it is first understood in its real-life context. The first element of this context is that every human being begins life as an incomplete, unfulfilled being and will remain such if he or she goes through life in psychological isolation. The second element is that every human being is fundamentally sexual, and is either masculinely sexual or femininely sexual. The two sexualities are diverse and they need one another as their correlates. This sexuality suffuses everyone's spirituality, just as one's spirituality penetrates one's sexuality. The human spirit lives in, is conscious in, and expresses itself in a needful sexuality.

Thus human nature exists in two incomplete but correlated sexual types, the masculine and the feminine. Therefore only through the mutually completing masculine-feminine union can human beings come to the completion of all that is potential in them. No one can be completed in sexual solitude. Doms offers virtually a definition of sexuality. It is the desire and capacity for fusion of personalities with a person of different sex. This desire rises from instinctual drive as from one source; it rises also from the source that makes the man or woman a person, namely from spirit. This enables the persons to make free gifts of themselves to one another, and thus to form a union. By this union the incomplete persons can be completed.[8]

The need for this completion and the task of it last a lifetime. For the sexual union to be completing it must involve the totality of both persons. But they can continue to grow through their entire lifetime. Therefore the entire lifetime must be put into the union.

The sexual intercourse of men and women is far more than the activity of their genital organs. It is more than physical and it is more than spiritual. It is a fusion of the two with each determining the other. Because of the spiritual component of the act it is the meeting of two persons. Indeed because of the intimate union within each of the persons of spirit and matter the sexual act can express the spiritual with exceptional force and clarity.

In all other interactions of person and person they meet not *within* the act itself but in the middle-ground effects of each one's acts—for example, in art work, in speech, in teaching. But in sexual intercourse the persons meet within the act. Intercourse thus has a unique power for giving the self and accepting the other. And this power and function it has in and of itself, not from any symbolism added to it by the partners, not by any meaning coming to it from outside itself. The directness of bodily-spiritual expression in intercourse gives it a power to convey its meaning that surpasses all other human conveying of meaning.

Genital Anatomy, Intercourse and Reproduction

To begin with, one must distinguish the reproductive anatomy from the organs of copulation. The latter are to the former as parts to the whole. Long after the reproductive anatomy has ceased to be able to attain its goal copulation is both possible and desired. This suggests that copulation has no exclusive orientation to reproduction.

There is a *catena* of biological evidence that conception is not the inherent *primary* goal of intercourse. First of all, the production of spermatozoa and of ova and their release are activities totally separate from conception.

Sexual intercourse's immediate goal is not to conceive but to put spermatozoa and ovum in immediate proximity. From there these two autonomous cells are capable in and of themselves of performing the genetically predetermined function on their own, apart from the intention and will of the man and woman. In most instances the activity of the reproductive anatomies naturally fails to attain its goal. Therefore conception cannot be the *immediate* goal of the act of intercourse. (The only such immediate goal is the union of the two persons.) Therefore too conception must be seen as a contingent effect of intercourse, one dependent on conditions not under the partners' control. These conditions cannot be fulfilled during pregnancy nor after menopause, when—to repeat an earlier point of evidence—both the desire and the capacity for intercourse remain strong.

The medieval philosophers and the later canonists interpreted the physiology of conception erroneously because they simply lacked the method for informing themselves accurately about it. Doms makes much of the consequences of this inaccuracy for the ethical premise that the primary end of intercourse is procreation. He deems the accuracy of the premise to depend on the accuracy of the assumption that conception is an immediate effect of intercourse, that it can be intended as such, and that the refusal to intend it as such is a moral disorder. The medievals, he charges, forced the matter-form model on conception. Accordingly they considered that the woman contributes no active agency to conception, but only the menstrual flow, which serves as a passive *materia*—which is informed, vivified by the active semen of the male. The forming of the combined sperm and the female *materia* into a human being, the medievals thought, is the effect immediately of a spiritual energy or force in the semen coming from the man's soul. In this spiritual energy there is also heat coming from the sun. These two energies co-work, so that conception is the effect of both the man and the sun. The energy the man gives to his semen educes from the female *materia* one form of life after another, which forms dispose the developing organism to finally receive the rational soul which is created directly by God.

Again, in all of this the biological source of the moral premise that conception is the primary goal of intercourse is the assumption that in intercourse the man and woman act so as to unite immediately the formal and material causes of conception. And again this is an erroneous interpretation of the physical facts of conception.

The Meaning of Marriage and the Goals of Intercourse

Because sexual intercourse in marriage of its nature effects the union of the spouses, there is no need to distinguish two goals of this intercourse, both procreation and the completing of the union of persons. It is accurate instead to say that intercourse has one immediate goal, which is to realize the union in which the spouses give and accept one another's entire persons. This is intercourse's first meaning, its first value. The realizing of this union is in turn oriented to two ulterior goals: the fulfilling of the husband and wife as persons, and the conceiving of the child. This meaning is realized objectively in every normal act of intercourse. But not in every case are the ulterior goals attained, despite intercourse's natural orientation to them.

To express this relationship of meaning and goals in married intercourse still more precisely, marriage attains its goals in and by realizing its meaning. That is, this meaning which is the union of the husband and wife is not *for* some goal apart from itself; it is not a means to such a goal. The conception of the child is related to the uniting of the husband and wife as the latter's natural completion. It is the full flowering of their giving themselves to one another completely.

The child is first of all a gift from both husband and wife to one another. Their personal sexual fulfillment leads them to give this gift. Its giving is the most *specific* completion of their union; it is the visible expression of their distinct but conjoined sexual natures. Their child enriches their union, their self-giving. It also completes them as persons; its prolonged need for nurture matures them as man and woman.

It is also true that the sexual union in marriage is a good for the larger societies even before and apart from procreation. This is so because this union is more than a physical coupling. It brings men and women into union and completes them. Since their union is realized most completely in intercourse, the latter does not directly and in the first place serve the good of the species and of the larger societies—although it surely serves these goods. If one is to speak of marriage in the language of goals, it is better not to try to say that any one goal is primary. Each is primary from a different point of view, from a different center of need. Only for the preservation of the race and of society is procreation the primary goal of marriage and sexual intercourse. And in the end the persons of the spouses are not for society, but society is for them, for their happiness and completion.

As he offered a reasonably careful definition of sexuality, so too Doms offered such a definition of marriage.

> To sum up:—the *immediate* purpose of marriage is the realisation of its meaning, the marital two-in-oneship. In the process of this realisation a community of fundamental importance for human society is formed. This intimate community is marriage. As a result of marriage two human beings come to live a life single in everything from religious community to sexual. But the presence of sexual community is what expressly constitutes marital community, for every other community can be realised outside marriage. By marriage we mean the enduring love-relationship of two grown-up persons of different sex, who come together to form one indivisible and indissoluble community of life in which they can fulfil and help one another. The supreme point of intimacy in this community occurs when they become one in the marriage act. This two-in-oneship of husband and wife is a living reality, and the immediate object of the marriage ceremony and their legal union. This vital two-in-oneship is to some extent a purpose in itself. But it also acts powerfully on the personalities of husband and wife, though in such a way that the individuality and independence of each is not lost in the union. It is for them a source of health and sanctity, and becomes for them the door to every natural and supernatural consummation. It tends also to the birth and education of new persons—their children. The

child assists their own fulfilment, both as a two-in-oneship and as separate individuals. But society is more interested in the child than in the natural fulfilment of the parents and it is this which gives the child primacy among the natural results of marriage.[9]

Reaction of the Church's Magisterium

As I have already pointed out, this interpretation of marriage did not go unnoticed in Rome. But the Congregation of the Holy Office's order halting the publication and distribution of Doms' essay did not halt the tide of disagreement among European philosophers and theologians. The essay was read the more widely by Catholics around the world because of its publication in French translation in 1937, and in English in 1939. By the spring of 1944 the same Roman congregation was sufficiently alarmed to apply a far more vigorous braking action against the change. On April 1 of that year it published a decree that is brief enough to be quoted in full.[10] With the help of four decades of hindsight one can appreciate the irony that the very conceptual development and vocabulary condemned here by the Holy Office were adopted in 1965 by the drafters of the Second Vatican Council's statement on marriage in *Gaudium et spes* and approved by an overwhelming vote of the Church's bishops.

In recent years a number of books and articles have been published treating of the ends of marriage, of their mutual order and relationship, which deny that the primary end of marriage is the generation of offspring, or that the secondary ends are subordinate to the primary, but are instead independent of it.

In these lucubrations[11] the primary end of marriage is designated differently by different authors. Some say it is the mutual fulfillment and personal perfection of the spouses through their total sharing of life and conduct. Others say it is the spouses' mutual love and union developed and perfected in the psychological and physical giving of themselves to one another.

At the same time these writings take the terms used commonly in Church documents, such as "end," "primary," "secondary," and give them meanings discordant with the meanings commonly attributed to them by the theologians.

This novel way of thinking and writing is prone to breed error and uncertainty. In view of this the Most Excellent and Reverend Fathers of this Supreme Congregation, charged with the defense of faith and morals, met on Wednesday, March 29, 1944, to consider the following question: "Whether the opinion of some current authors is admissible which either denies that the primary end of marriage is the generation and nurture of offspring, or teaches that the secondary ends are not essentially subordinate to the primary, but are independent of it and equally primary." Our response to this in decree: *negative.*

And in the audience of Thursday, March 30, 1944, requested by the Most Excellent and Reverend Lord Prefect of the Holy Office, His Holiness Pius XII, by divine providence Pope, deigned to approve this decree and ordered it promulgated.

This decree too was ineffective in ending the intramural challenge to the established Catholic teaching on the ends of marriage. Seven years later Pius XII himself was to condemn the challenge even more vigorously and in finer detail. Meanwhile the reason for anxiety in the Church's magisterium, hinted at in the decree's phrase, "prone to breed error and uncertainty," was clear enough. At issue was a change in the Church's very understanding of marriage, an understanding consecrated for centuries in a carefully thought through and precisely worded though informal definition. If the doctrinally dissident Catholic writers were to win what was by then certainly a theological and probably a doctrinal dispute, the method and valence of magisterial teaching would themselves be brought into question. The Congregation of the Holy Office in 1944 and both Pius XII and the Congregation in 1951 stared full in the face one of the questions that was to confront Paul VI in 1965–1968 as he meditated the composition of *Humanae vitae:* Can the Church change her teaching? And if she can, what are the theological and moral-pastoral consequences for common Catholic belief and practice?

Furthermore there was at issue not only the definition of marriage but also the morality of conduct within marriage. *Casti connubii*'s ethical reasoning in condemnation of contraceptive intercourse drew its conclusion from the principle that the primary end of intercourse in marriage is conception. In the encyclical's own words, "The conjugal act is of its very nature designed for the procreation of offspring; and therefore those who in performing it deliberately deprive it of its natural power and efficacy act against nature and do something which is shameful and intrinsically immoral."[12]

But in recognition of the serious hardships more pregnancies and more children could bring upon spouses locked into poverty or illness or both, Pius reminded them of the possibility and the permissibility of periodic abstinence, "the rhythm method" permissible in that it attains the subordinated secondary ends of the marriage act without frustrating directly its primary end.

> Both matrimony and the use of the matrimonial right have secondary ends—such as mutual help, the fostering of reciprocal love, and the abatement of concupiscence—which husband and wife are quite entitled to have in view, so long as the instrinsic nature of that act, and therefore its due subordination to its primary end, is safeguarded.[13]

But what would happen to this moral logic if the magisterium should decide finally that procreation is not related to the other ends of marriage as primary,[14] and that therefore when the attempt at attaining both primary and secondary ends becomes an irreconcilable conflict—for example, in trying to sustain marital love while allowing pregnancy, perhaps an eighth or ninth in twelve years—the erstwhile primary end need not prevail but could be suppressed for the sake of the other ends? For if the plural ends to be attained are equal in value, no compelling reason for having one rather than the other rule the moral choice could be found within the ends themselves. The choice could and would then have to be made according to the real needs of the spouses as persons trying to sustain a love relationship. It is no exaggeration to say that the challenge to the morality of inherent ends of the physical act of intercourse was a challenge to an entire moral system.

The Reaction of Pius XII

It was in the best-remembered of all his discourses on marriage, delivered to the Union of Italian Catholic Obstetricians on October 29, 1951, that Pius XII reaffirmed what the Holy Office had said in its decree of April 1, 1944.[15] But having the time and the place to do so, he went into greater detail. I quote him here at length.

> "Personal values" and the need to respect such are a theme which, over the last twenty years or so, has been considered more and more by some writers. In many of their works even the specifically sexual act has its place assigned, that of serving the "person" of the married couple. The proper and most profound meaning of the exercise of conjugal rights would consist in this, that the union of bodies is an expression and the realization of personal and affective union.
>
> Articles, chapters, entire books, conferences, especially dealing with the "technique" of love, are composed to spread these ideas, to illustrate them with advice to the newly married as a guide in matrimony, in order that they may not neglect, through stupidity or a false sense of shame or unfounded scruples, that which God, who also created natural inclinations, offers them. If from the complete reciprocal gift of husband and wife there results a new life, it is a result which remains outside, or at the most on the border, of "personal values"—a result which is not denied, but neither is it desired as the center of marital relations. . . .
>
> Now if this relative evaluation were merely to place the emphasis on the personal values of husband and wife rather than on that of offspring, it would be possible, strictly speaking, to put

such a problem aside. But, however, it is a matter of a grave inversion of the order of values and of the ends imposed by the Creator himself. . . ."[16]

From this précis of the dissent and from this evaluation of its seriousness as a departure from the established teaching of the Church Pius moved on to an exact statement—or more accurately restatement—of that teaching. I think it is accurate to say that this stands as his definition of the nature of marriage.

> Now the truth is that matrimony, as an institution of nature, in virtue of the Creator's will, has not as a primary end the intimate and personal perfection of the married couple but the procreation and upbringing of new life. The other ends, inasmuch as they are intended by nature, are not equally primary, much less superior to the primary end, but are essentially subordinated to it. This is true of every marriage, even if no offspring result from it; just as of every eye it can be said that it is destined and formed to see, even if, in abnormal cases arising from special internal or external conditions, it will never be possible to achieve perception.[17]

Pius then located the personal values of marriage in what he considered their right relationship to procreation.

> Would this lead, perhaps, to our denying or diminishing what is good or just in personal values resulting from matrimony and its realization? Certainly not, because the Creator has designed that for the procreation of new life human beings made of flesh and blood, gifted with soul and heart, shall be called upon as men and not as animals deprived of reason to be the authors of posterity. . . .
> All this is therefore true and desired by God. But on the other hand, it must not be divorced completely from the primary function of matrimony, the procreation of offspring. Not only the common work of external life, but even all personal enrichment—spiritual and intellectual—and that in married love as such is most spiritual and profound, has been placed by the will of the Creator and of nature at the service of posterity.[18]

In short, not only does marriage exist first and principally for procreation and nurture, but everything else of value in it is for them. The spouses' love for one another is there for the sake of offspring; their striving for maturity as husband and wife is for offspring. The subordinate and tributary status of the "everything else" could not have been stated more clearly.

The Conflict on the Eve of Vatican II

Eleven years passed between that address of Pius XII and the convening of the Second Vatican Council in October 1962. During that time his declaration and that of the Holy Office did little to quiet the dispute about the ends of marriage and its meaning.[19] New voices began to be heard, those of theologians, philosophers and psychologists—Schillebeeckx, Häring, Janssens, Fuchs, Oraison, Michel, Philips, Moeller, and a voice that was to be most influential in the near future, that of Leo Joseph Suenens, cardinal-archbishop of Malines-Bruges in Belgium. These men were building up a counter-position to that of the traditional Church teaching. But they were not drawing it from the continuum of juridical teaching coming down from the twelfth century and trying to revise it. They were building rather anew a theology drawing from the Scriptures and from a Christian anthropology of heterosexual love. And they were effecting what amounted to a seismic shift in methodology. Instead of continuing the centuries-long use of the canonical understanding of marriage to interpret its biblical-religious character among Christians (calling it, for example, a sacred contract), they were doing the reverse. They were making marriage the religious covenant among Christians become a sign of Christ's love for his people interpret marriage the natural relationship and institution.

The main elements of their position I understand to be the following. In the domain of methodology the Church's magisterium had engaged in a kind of tour-de-force in establishing its normative definition. As late as the end of the first thousand years of Christian history there were two understandings of marriage available to this magisterium each carrying an equal weight of tradition. These were the Roman and the central European traditions. Out of the conflict of choice between them was fashioned a compromise victory. This determined that marriage is a consensual relationship, one created by the consent alone of the parties (the Roman element of the compromise). The relationship is, however, incomplete if there is no more than consent. But it is brought to completion by sexual intercourse after the exchange of consent (the European element). The consent is contractual. It creates a contract whose contractual good is each party's right to his or her own sexual acts (an added element from the later canonists). The contractual consent has as its object the exchange of these rights.

To indicate in one minor way how this was a tour-de-force, there was another tradition at the beginning of Christian history, the Jewish tradition in which Christianity was born. It saw marriage as a covenant between families made in order to perpetuate the paternal family. Accordingly it saw a marriage as complete only when it had in fact produced a child, a male child, who could guarantee this perpetuation. According to rabbinic law, if a marriage had within ten years produced no child, the couple was obliged to dissolve it by divorce so as to free the husband to marry another and, he hoped, fertile woman.

From the Roman-European compromise the magisterium drew the norm that a marriage remaining incomplete—incomplete not in the Jewish sense of failing to produce a child, but in the sense that it had not been consummated by intercourse—could be dissolved in such a way as to free both parties to marry again. But having decided that a marriage is a contract, the magisterium committed itself to deciding that consummation is effected by the first exchange of the contractual good. But how different the consequences for the married lives of Christians would have been if the Church had kept the Jewish tradition. Consummation would then have been understood in the Jewish sense. Sterility would have become a ground for dissolubility. Partly out of compassion for the divorced and abandoned sterile wife—a compassion mandated by Christ's forbidding that a wife be dismissed even for her sterility—the Church's magisterium set the boundary of dissolubility much farther out. It was set not in a physical disability of which a wife herself might be the victim, but in an episode of conduct over which both spouses have a measure of control. This is the act of sexual intercourse. And it was made the pivot of dissolubility-indissolubility because it is the delivery or not of the contractual good of the marriage. But something most valuable could have been kept from the Jewish tradition. Consummation could have been defined as the sustaining and the fulfilling of a covenantal commitment made out of love for the spouse and the family. A consequence of keeping this would have been that the refusal or even the failure to work at fulfilling this familial covenant would be judged a failure to consummate the marriage.[20]

Marriage the Sacrament as Normative

Other consequences for the understanding of marriage followed from this new insistence on interpreting the natural institution in light of the sacramental covenant instead of vice versa. Hints that contractuality and sacramentality may be incompatible began to be heard. It is the nature of a contract that it puts both parties in a mutual relationship of commutative justice. By the contract each gains the right, a claim in justice, to the good the other has promised. But if, as the Church's magisterium has insisted repeatedly since the end of the eighteenth century, the contract and the sacrament are inseparable because the sacrament is simply the contract elevated to the capacity to give grace, then do the contract's obligations in commutative justice also get taken up into the sacrament? If they do, how can the sacrament survive? That is, how can the marriage be an image of the love of Christ and his Church—an image in which the magisterium had agreed for centuries that the heart of marriage's sacramentality resides? Does one say that Christ and the Church have claims in commutative justice on one another?

The need to find a place for the covenantal love essential to the sacrament brought still another difficulty to the canonical definition. Virtually by design the latter had no place for love among either its ends or its essential properties. But what marriage the sacrament is, to say it again in the accepted formulation, is the contract itself elevated to be a grace-giving sign. But grace involves love; Christ's work of gracing by and in the sacrament is a work of love. But if in the contract there is no matrix-love that becomes the sacramental love in a way consistent with the claimed contract's becoming the sacrament, serious consequences follow. If love enters the contract-become-sacrament only and exclusively via the sacrament, how can one still say that what the sacrament is, is the contract elevated to sacramental condition and efficacy?

The adamant exclusion of love from a place among the ends and even the properties of marriage led to anthropological anomalies. Evidence for this is found again in the glaring example first pointed to in the Introduction to all these chapters. It was about a sacramental marriage of two Catholics that the Congregation of the Sacraments ruled in its decision of August 2, 1958. The issue was whether the marriage had ever been consummated, and therefore whether it were dissoluble by papal action. In every instance of intercourse the wife had had to drug herself so heavily to endure what she regarded as a vile experience that she was senseless when the act took place. The Congregation's decision was that the marriage—the sacramental marriage—had indeed been consummated. The criterion appropriate to a contract and its completion had been met. Her husband's penis had penetrated her vagina sufficiently and had deposited semen there. Neither had taken contraceptive measures to block this. With this mechanical consummating of the contract the sacrament too was mechanically consummated, presumably as a grace-giving experience for both spouses. And presumably too this act had, in virtue of its sacramentality, imaged the love of Christ and his Church.

The Effect of the Changed Image of the Church

The canonical definition of marriage fit ill in the Church's vision of her own character freshly regained just before and during Vatican II. As long as the Church had been seen as a self-contained and perfect society structured pyramidically, with bishops and clergy guiding the laity in holiness and ruling them in obedience, the understanding of marriage as a contractual union whose principal function is to supply members for this society jarred but little.

But once the vision of the Church changed to that of the people of God, a people on pilgrimage toward a final union with God in response to his call made in paternal love and conveyed to men and women through a fraternally loving Christ, that understanding jarred violently. How could marriage the contract, with its primary and secondary ends, have a place in the pilgrim response and journey? By men and women contracting to produce an ever-renewed supply of pilgrims, and remedying one another's concupiscence along the way? Or if a part could be assigned them under the title of mutual help, how realistic would it be to keep assigning this help a secondary place among pilgrims who, of all people, grievously need help because they have not yet come to their true home but are struggling to do so? Pilgrims' greatest needs are for faith, trust, courage and caring love for one another. One would think that the vision of a pilgrim Church would produce an understanding of marriage as a kind of sub-community within the Church whose work is to create and sustain these qualities of soul.

The canonical definition of marriage had at least made possible, and at worst encouraged, a judicial procedure in the Church's marriage courts one of whose possible effects is injustice to the persons of men and women initiating the procedure. The injustice in this procedure has been made possible by a flawed interpretation of the justice appropriate to the petitions for nullity and dissolution.

A Church tribunal action in response to a petition for a declaration of nullity, for example, is structured according to the law as an adversary action. But unlike divorce procedures still current in many civil courts in the United States, the adversaries in the tribunal procedure are not the two spouses, one of them the plaintiff and the other the defendant. It is the marriage that is the accused, the defendant; one or both spouses the accuser and plaintiff. In the language of the tribunal the spouse(s) are said to "accuse the marriage" of nullity. A quasi-adversary relationship between the two spouses may arise where only one of them petitions the annulment but the other opposes it. In any case the petitioner is designated just that, the petitioner. The other is called the respondent.

Since the marriage is treated as the defendant, it must be reified. For the sake of the procedure it is dealt with as a fictitious person. The court assigns it a counsel for defense, the Defender of the Bond. The procedure is in form understood to be a search for justice in the case, and a determination of the demands of justice in view of the petitioner's accusation. Since the defendant is the marriage, turned into a person fictitiously for the sake of the adversary procedure, the dominant concern of the court, at least in principle, is to defend the marriage against an unjust accusation by the petitioner. A secondary concern is that injustice not be done the respondent if he or she contests the accusation. The accused, the marriage, is presumed innocent—which is to say valid—until proven guilty, or null. The burden of proof of nullity rests on the petitioner. Thus, what is in reality a finding of fact, the fact of validity or of nullity, is dealt with as an accusation of delinquency. And in principle the court's main concern that harm not be done is that it not be done to the juridically reified marriage, the fictitious person. The real, flesh-and-blood persons are secondary objects of this concern.

What makes possible the structuring of the procedure in this way is what makes easy the reifying of the marriage. We have seen the long tradition in the West, antedating the birth of canon law and surviving it, that a marriage is fundamentally a relationship, a relationship rooted in a reciprocal condition or quality adhering in the persons of those who so interact as to create the relationship. If marriages in the Church had been regularly thought of and treated as such relationships, the make-believe involved in turning them into fictitious persons for the sake of adversary court procedure would be more obvious. But the make-believe has been easy to ignore because marriages have been thought of and treated as contracts.

It is ironic that tribunal procedure has long given the marriage a greatly overweighted advantage as a defendant versus its accusers where it is a sacrament and because it is a sacrament. That is, because as a sacrament it is "a sacred thing," even a sacred person, it has an extraordinary claim on survival. The irony lies in the fact that it is a sacrament in that it images the love of Christ and his Church, which is a love relationship, not a contract.

Thus it was until recently even in the tribunals I mentioned in the introductory chapter that in order to render justice to the claims of the fictitious person, the marriage, the real needs and claims of the real persons trapped in a destructive relationship were often overridden. But if the Church's tribunals had universally treated marriages not as fictitious persons but as they really are, love relationships intended for the happiness of the spouses and their children, their concern for justice would presumably have looked not to the defense of the fictitious person but to that of the real persons just named. The alternative concern for justice, namely to protect the fictitious person of the marriage from its real-person attackers, is itself a product of the defining of marriage according to juridical categories: in essence it is a contract; and the object of its contractual consent is the parties' right to their own sexual acts, and their exchange of these rights. If one accepts this definition it is not inconsistent that Church authority in her courts weight their procedure to defend the offspring-producing contract against its attackers, since offspring are the most fundamental good that the contract can produce. Granting the assumed definition, neither is it inconsistent to overweight the case for the contract additionally in order to "protect the sacrament," provided that one also admits the other assumption that the sacrament is nothing other than the contract elevated to an effective sign of grace.

Happily this criticism of the traditional tribunal procedure and the injustice to which it has been vulnerable gets progressively more out of date in certain countries in the Western world because most tribunals in the United States, Canada, the United Kingdom and elsewhere more and more weight their procedure in favor of justice as a concern for the petitioners' right to happiness in marriage. I think it can be shown that this change has itself come in great part from the Church's changed understanding of marriage given to her by *Gaudium et spes* and *Humanae vitae*.

The Case for the Defense

Those are a few of the main elements of the case against the accepted canonical understanding of marriage fixed in the Catholic law and judicial procedures by the middle of this century. But those who defended its fixed position had a counter-case against the changes they knew were being urged by the bishops, philosophers and theologians mentioned earlier. For one thing, serious consequences for the moral teaching of the Church would follow from accepting Doms' and the others' understanding of marriage according to its meanings instead of its ends.

Thus if the first value of marriage is in its meaning as a fulfilling union of the spouses, if conception and nurture are the fruit of this union, and if conception is subordinated to this union (not as a secondary end subordinated to a primary but as a non-necessary effect to its cause), what moral judgment is acceptable if the union and conception come into conflict in a marriage? For example, the love union of a husband and wife can be damaged seriously if they conceive and bear yet another child, perhaps the sixth or seventh in their marriage. Sexual abstinence is a morally unacceptable alternative for them because this would in its way damage their union seriously. Caught in this conflict of values they would find no compelling reason for not using contraceptives to avoid conception while preserving the sexual heart of their union. For it would be a conflict of unequal values, between the essential meaning of their marriage and one of its effects, and a non-necessary effect in their real-life circumstances at that. For the sake of preserving the greater value they could suppress the realizing of the lesser value.[21]

If the essence of marriage is in the union of love, not in the bond-contract in in which the couple have exchanged the right to their sexual acts, there can surface a serious difficulty about the coming into existence of a marriage in real life (with *matrimonium in fieri*). This may no longer be an act as simply verifiable as a contractual exchange of rights. It is the creating of a union of love encompassing the entire persons of the spouses and all their lives. But can this be done in a single and non-repeatable moment in time? Can one exchange of consent early in the history of a potentially rich relationship really bring it into existence? If the Church were to accept this union, this sharing as the essence of marriage, what kind of verifiable act would be said to create it? What criteria could be established for verifying that the act had in fact created the union.

Then there is the question of ability to form a marriage. Verifying who has this ability, when the matter comes up infrequently, has never been very difficult as long as the ability is proportioned to the understanding that marriage has procreation as its primary goal, mutual help and the remedying of concupiscence as secondary goal, and that its essential characteristics demand fidelity and perseverance in the relationship. If a person can make an act of consent that is a contractual commitment to realizing the goals and sustaining the characteristics, he or she can marry.

But if creating a marriage comes to be understood as the creating of a love-union meant to fulfill the spouses as persons, with children the natural flowering of this fulfilling union, what imaginable criterion would be possible for judging a man's or woman's ability to marry? What kind of love and what degree of it would be needed? Fulfillment in what sense and in what measure? With only the vaguest criteria possible for judging these, what man or woman couldn't escape a marriage in which he or she was unhappy by alleging inability from the beginning to form the essential love union?

Such, in outline, were some of the most serious of the questions and conflicts about marriage that the Catholic bishops took with them into the Second Vatican Council in October 1962.

NOTES

1. As I noted earlier, Doms' essay bore the original German title, *Vom Sinn und Zweck der Ehe.* He was a Privat-Dozent at the University of Breslau when he published it in 1935, a priest and a doctor of theology. It appeared in its first French edition in 1937 under the title *Du Sens et de la Fin du Mariage.*

The first substantial development of von Hildebrand's thought appeared in 1929 in his essay, *Die Ehe,* published in English in 1942 as *Marriage.* Krempel's major contribution was his essay in 1941, *Die Zweckfrage der Ehe in Neuer Beleuchtung* (A New Perspective on the Question of the Ends of Marriage). Michel's *Ehe, Eine Anthropologie der Geschlechtsgemeinschaft* (Marriage: An Anthropology of the Sexual Community) was published in 1948 and placed on the Index of Forbidden Books in December 1952. To my knowledge neither Krempel's nor Michel's essay has been published in English.

As I have hinted, the essays of Doms, von Hildebrand, Krempel and others stirred up a debate that continued in Europe, and to a minor degree in the Western Hemisphere, for over two decades, until the eve of the Second Vatican Council. I note here, in the sequence of their appearance, some of the major essays contributing to the debate (the magisterial documents that entered the debate I shall consider separately): Erich Przywara, "Psychologie oder Theologie der Ehe," *Stimmen der Zeit,* 131 (1937) 253ff; A. Robillard, "L'amour et l'enfant (Les fins de mariage—le 'sens' ou valeur absolue de mariage)," *Vie Intellectuelle* 60 (1938) 9ff; B. Lavaud, "Sens et fins du mariage. La thèse de Doms et sa critique," *Revue Thomiste* 44 (1938) 737ff; "The Interpretation of the Conjugal Act and the Theology of Marriage. A Propos of Recent Essays," *The Thomist* 1 (1939) 360ff; Doms again, "Amorces d'une conception personaliste du mariage d'après S. Thomas," *Revue Thomiste* 45 (1939) 754ff; R. Boigelot, "Du sens et de la fin du mariage," *Nouvelle Revue Théologique* 66 (1939) 5–33; Francis J. Connell, "Recent Theology," *Ecclesiastical Review* 101 (1939) 179ff; A. Lanza, "De fine primario matrimoni," *Apollinaris* 13 (1940) 57–83: 14 (1941) 12–39; John C. Ford, "Marriage: Its Meaning and Purposes," *Theological Studies* 3 (1942) 333–374; F. Carney, *The Purposes of Christian Marriage,* Washington, 1950; Louis Lochet, "Les fins du mariage," *Nouvelle Revue Théologique* 73 (1951) 449–465; 561–586; Bernard F. Lonergan, "Finality, Love, Marriage," *Theological Studies* 4 (1943) 477–510.

2. In Doms, *op. cit.,* p. xix.

3. *Ibid.*

4. *Ibid.*

5. *Ibid.,* pp. 20–21.

6. *Ibid.,* p. 18.

7. *Op. cit.,* p. 26.

8. *Op. cit.,* p. 32.

9. *Op. cit.,* pp. 94–95.

10. This is in *Acta Apostolicae Sedis,* Vol. 36 (1944), p. 103.

11. The Latin of this evaluative phrase is ". . . hisce in elucubrationibus." The decree is wide of the mark at a number of points. For one, Doms' principal challenge was not so much that procreation and nurture are not the primary end of marriage, but that marriage is not to be interpreted primarily in terms of its ends, but of its meanings. In fact, as we have seen, when one talks of the ends of marriage, after first verifying its meanings, he admitted that procreation is primary among them. (Paul VI apparently agreed substantially with Doms fourteen years later. In his encyclical letter, *Humanae vitae,* he wrote of the ends of marriage not at all, but interpreted it solely in terms of its meanings.) Again, the personalists did not say of mutual fulfillment and personal perfection of the spouses that these are the primary end; they said they are the first and fundamental meaning of marriage. Finally, this way of thinking, if it was novel, was no more so than the thinking that subordinates all other ends in marriage to procreation and nurture, since, as Navarrete pointed out, this interpretation was introduced at the earliest by Gasparri. In fact the case could be made that the interpretation of marriage according to its meanings goes back to classic Roman law and even to whoever first wrote "It is not good for the man to be alone. . . ."

12. N. 54.

13. N. 87.

14. This the bishops of Vatican II did deliberately and explicitly, after long and arduous debate, in their key phrase in *Gaudium et spes,* ". . . while not putting the other ends of marriage at less value . . ." (*non posthabitis ceteris matrimonii finibus*) (par. 50).

15. An English translation of this discourse is in *Papal Teachings: Matrimony,* pp. 405–434.

16. *Op. cit.,* pp. 422–423.

17. *Ibid.,* p. 424.

18. *Ibid.,* pp. 426–427. Other statements of Pius XII repeating the same instruction are found in his discourse to members of the Roman Rota on October 3, 1941 (*op. cit.,* pp. 331–338), in a discourse to newlyweds on March 18, 1942 (*op. cit.,* pp. 339–340), and in a discourse to the members of the Second World Congress on Fertility and Sterility, May 19, 1955 (*op. cit.,* pp. 482–492).

19. A few exemplary authors, and their essays, continuing the challenge during these years are the following: Doms again, *Dieses Geheimniss Ist Gross,* Köln, 1960; Bernard Häring, *Ehe in Dieser Zeit,* Salzburg, 1960; Jacques Leclercq, *Le Mariage Chrétien,* Tournai, 1949 (translated as *Marriage, A Great Sacrament,* N.Y., 1950); Marc Oraison, *Union in Marital Life: Its Physical and Spiritual Foundations,* N.Y., 1958; Henri Rondet, *Introduction à l'Etude de la Théologie du Mariage,* Paris, 1966; Gertrude Reidlich, *Die Hierarchische Struktur Der Ehe* München, 1953; Friedrich von Gagern, *L'amour des Epoux,* Paris, 1956 (translated as *Union in Marital Love,* N.Y., 1958).

20. On this issue see my essay, *Consummation: Of Contract or of Covenant?* in *The Jurist,* Vol. 32.1 (Spring, 1972), pp. 103–117, and 32.2 (Summer, 1972), pp. 330–354.

21. Those familiar with Pope Paul VI's moral logic in *Humanae vitae* will recall how he sought to avoid this logical consequence of understanding marriage not

according to its subordinated ends but according to its meanings. Understand it according to the latter he did. Nowhere in the encyclical did he mention ends at all, much less hierarchically subordinated ends. What he did was to assert two meanings for sexual intercourse in marriage, the unitive and the procreative, and to assert also that these two meanings are equal in moral value and morally inseparable in conduct. From this asertion he intended two conclusions: first, that since they are equal, neither value can claim to override the other; second, that any suppression in marital intercourse of one of the values (*in casu* the procreative) is inescapably a suppression of the other—with the result that this double suppression renders the act altogether valueless and therefore immoral. For reasons not explained he did not offer evidence verifying the accuracy of this premise in his moral logic that the two meanings of sexual intercourse are both equal in value and morally inseparable in conduct. Lacking the verifying evidence his premise remains hypothetical; and by the rules of logic a hypothetical premise can produce only a hypothetical conclusion.

10. THE SECOND VATICAN COUNCIL AND THE NATURE OF MARRIAGE

A major part of the preparation for the Second Vatican Council consisted of the gathering, by the Central Preparatory Commission planning its agenda, of suggestions from persons and groups of persons from around the Catholic world. This was done early in 1960, a little more than a year after Pope John XXIII had, on January 25, 1959, announced the convening of the council. (It is important to keep in mind that the full council met in four approximately ten-week sessions, with the first convening on October 11, 1962 and the last adjourning on December 8, 1965.) Bishops and other prelates were asked to submit suggestions (*consilia*) and make known their recommendations (*vota*), the Catholic universities and faculties their studies (*studia*) and recommendations. The congregations of the Roman curia were asked to submit their recommendations and advice (*monita*).[1]

Two of these congregations proposed that the general council treat of marriage, and they named the elements of marriage they wished the bishops in council to deal with. The Sacred Congregation for the Discipline of the Sacraments was one of these. Its recommendation for marital matters to be dealt with went into considerable detail.[2] In outline the recommendation worked its way through Title VII of the Code of Canon Law, urging special attention to the preparation of couples for marriage, to the impediments listed in the law, to other conditions invalidating marital consent, to the form of marriage, and to the dissolution of marriages. Nothing in this lengthy recommendation was said about the ends of marriage nor about the object of marital consent. In fact it stated clearly that nothing in the early canons on marriage in the Code (1012 through 1018) ought to be changed.[3]

The Preparatory Commission made no recorded use of this recommendation. In March 1962 this Congregation for the Sacraments wrote an even more detailed plan for the council's treatment of the sacraments.[4] Part 6 is a statement on marital consent. It repeated the phrases of Canon

1081.2 about the nature of this consent and its object, but with one exception. It said that the consent is a free act of the will by both partners, but instead of repeating that for its object this act of will has the exchange of the right to sexual acts, it said only that this object is the exchange of the right proper (*proprium*) for creating a marriage.[5] Of this document too the Preparatory Commission made no recorded use.

The other Roman congregation that recommended to the council that it take up marriage was the Congregation of the Holy Office. This it did in its *Schema Pro Concilio Oecumenico*,[6] which was in substance and in mood an exhortation to the bishops of the council to condemn the new errors against reason and against the Catholic faith that had gained currency since the First Vatican Council's condemnation of the errors current in 1870. What it recommended that the council say about marriage is in its Part 4, Paragraph 24.

> It is most opportune to recall, clarify and reconfirm the main headings on the doctrine of marriage: its origin, its end, its essential properties, its use. Then it should examine and define in the matters of birth control, periodic continence, *amplexus reservatus,* artificial insemination, consummation (penetration and semination), impotency, therapeutic abortion, mixed marriages, and the Petrine privilege, so called. There should be a careful examination of the validity of marriages in general of the baptized, and of the conditions of this validity.[7]

This brief paragraph proved to be the seed of a quite comprehensive text that almost certainly had as its principal author the prefect of the Holy Office, Cardinal Alfredo Ottaviani. And as the paragraph gained length by being expanded into a full schema, it also doubled its juridical valence relative to the council. For Cardinal Ottaviani was not only the prefect of the Holy Office (which produced the brief paragraph). He was also president of the Theological Commission set up to help prepare agenda for the council. It was this group which produced the lengthy schema that had been born in the brief paragraph above.[8]

This Theological Commission submitted its schema to the Central Preparatory Commission early in 1962. Its title was *De castitate, virginitate, matrimonio, familia.* In a prenote the authors of the schema pointed out that a chapter, *De castitate et pudicitia christiana* (On Christian Chastity and Modesty), written earlier as part of a constitution, *De ordine morali,* had been removed from the latter and included in this schema along with a proposed constitution, *De matrimonio et familia.* The schema was thus a combination of the two previously independent parts.

The Central Preparatory Commission examined and discussed this combined schema in its sixth session, from May 3 to 12, 1962. The Commission eventually rejected it after substantial protest by a number of its members against its content and its attitude. But it is profitable to examine parts of it here just because it was a chapter—a kind of closing chapter—in the history of the Catholic understanding of marriage. It will be profitable too to record the protests from within the Preparatory Commission that got the schema shelved permanently.[9]

In preparation for the Preparatory Commission's first discussion of this schema, on May 7, Cardinal Ottaviani had sent to it a *relatio* in which he pointed out that the constitution was to be "... pastoral, but pastoral and doctrinal, not pastoral-disciplinary. Consequently the Theological Commission has set out the objective order, that which God himself has willed in instituting marriage. Only in this way can the modern errors that have spread everywhere be vanquished."[10]

The purpose of the constitution, the Theological Commission's intent for it, was made clear in its Prooemium: "... the Holy Synod [the council] has decreed that in one and the same dogmatic constitution it extols and defends the nobility of both chaste continence and its loveliest flower, consecrated virginity, as well as chaste marriage and its heavenly fruit, the Christian family."[11]

In Part 2, Chapter 1, "The Divinely Established Order of Marriage," the Theological Commission set forth the interpretation of marriage it intended for the entire council to establish in the Church by dogmatic decree. The interpretation is encapsuled in the last paragraph (no. 16) of this chapter, "Errors Condemned," where, in a method imitating that of earlier councils, it proposed to teach doctrine by anathematizing exactly phrased contradictions of the doctrine in question.

> The Holy Synod knows how greatly the health of the Mystical Body of Christ depends on a right acceptance of the divine order ruling marriage. In order to protect this health it is constrained before all to condemn those radical errors according to which marriage, in its order and constitution, is a mere social phenomenon undergoing continual evolution: those errors that deny it comes from God and from Christ, and deny that it is subject to the power of the Church.
>
> It likewise condemns those errors holding that the marriage of Christians is not a sacrament or that the sacrament is only something accessory to and separable from the contract itself. It condemns the opinion asserting that marriage is a specific means of attaining that perfection by which man is truly and properly an image of God and of the Blessed Trinity. Likewise it condemns the opinion of those who hold either that the marital state is in the objective order superior to the state of virginity or to celibacy taken up for the kingdom of God. ...
>
> It condemns severely the errors and theories denying that there is an immutable divine order regarding the properties and ends of marriage. And it rejects explicitly as a supreme calumny the assertion that the indissolubility of marriage comes not from

God but is something invented cruelly by the Church and cruelly held to. What is more, it condemns the theories which subvert the right order of values and makes the primary end of marriage inferior to the biological and personal values of the spouses, and proclaim that conjugal love is in the objective order itself the primary end.[12]

Earlier in this same chapter, in paragraph 10, "The Origin, Nature and Dignity of Marriage," two footnotes spelled out more in detail the interpretation of marriage that the Theological Commission intended for the council to establish as doctrine. Note 19 reads, "It is of supreme importance to affirm that the ends themselves of marriage are to be understood according to the teaching of Pius XI in his encyclical *Casti connubii.* . . . For the institution, the ends, the law, the goods of marriage are from God himself. . . ."

Part II, "On Marriage and the Family," contains the Theological Commission's statement that comes closest to a formal definition of marriage. It is in paragraph 13, "The Ends of Marriage." Given the vigorous, lapidary quality of its clauses, it must have had Doms and the other personalists in mind.

What is more, marriage has in itself—that is, independently of the intention of the contracting parties—its own objective ends that have been established by God. Among these ends—and this we know from the plan of its divine institution, from nature itself, as well as from the Church magisterium—the one and only primary end is the procreation and nurture of children, even if in a particular instance a marriage is infertile. It follows therefore that procreation, even though it be not the object of marital consent, is in itself so connatural to every marriage, even to the point of being essential to it, that no human will can by acts contrary to nature exclude it from the marriage. It is essential in the sense that in any valid matrimonial consent the exchange of the perpetual and exclusive right to those acts naturally apt for generation must be included in its object. So much is procreation primary and overriding (*praevalens*) that it in no way depends on any of the other intended ends, even though these are natural to marriage; nor can it be reduced to equality with them or confused with them.

The other objective ends of marriage, rooted in the character itself of marriage but still secondary—such as the spouses' mutual help and the remedying of concupiscence—constitute genuine (even if subordinate) rights in marriage when they are rightly intended. Hence these secondary ends are in themselves not to be rejected and devalued, but promoted rightly and in true charity.

The paragraph concludes with a placing of the two secondary ends of marriage in what is regarded as their rightful function.

> But inasmuch as this mutual help and the remedying of concupiscence are to be sought for within marriage itself, they partake of the specific nature of the marital union, in that they differ specifically from any other kind of help, even if it is bestowed by friendship. Any other subjective goals that frequently bring persons to marry as their first and immediate goals are no obstacle to marriage as long as they do not contradict the ends indicated by nature itself but are subordinated to them.

Note 29, from the middle of this statement, explains how the relationship between the primary end and the secondary end of marriage is to be interpreted and decreed by the council.

> For the secondary ends to be attained in marriage share, even though in a secondary way, in the specific nature of the marital union, a union differing specifically from any other, even from a union of friendship. This marital union thus differs by its intrinsic and essential relationship to the primary end. And these objective but secondary ends are therefore also ordered of their nature to this primary end.[13]

Most of the cardinals making up the Central Preparatory Commission found this draft of the proposed constitution substantially satisfactory. They suggested a few minor amendments, additions and subtractions.[14] But there were four of the prelates who did not find it substantially satisfactory. These were Cardinal Julius Döpfner of München-Freising, Cardinal Emile Léger of Montreal, Cardinal Bernhard Jan Alfrink of Utrecht, and Cardinal Leo Joseph Suenens of Malines-Bruges. Quoting their criticisms of the schema at some length will show the mentality strikingly different from that of Cardinal Ottaviani and the Theological Commission that these men brought to the preparation of the council.

Cardinal Döpfner's critical comment was by far the longest (it occupies twelve pages in the *Acta*). It objected at the most fundamental level and in greatest detail. It also included the most significant of the objections voiced by the others. The heart of it follows here.

> The schema of this constitution deals in a clear and for the most part constructive doctrinal way with questions that are truly current and in some degree urgent. The things it teaches and the way it does so are acceptable in general.
>
> However, since it deals with a most serious issue that has stirred the souls of many, one which will have a special resonance in public opinion, satisfaction with it will not come easily.

The bishops of the Church surely cannot be ignorant of how many damaging mistakes have been made in our pastoral practice under the inspiration of those textbooks treating this matter in an exclusively negative and juridically analytic way rather than in a spirit of charity and concern. We need not be surprised that so many of the faithful have been scandalized by the practice of confessors (so many of whom disagree with one another) interpreting sexual intercourse in a way looking only to the animal nature of men and women, while either ignoring the aspect of personal union in it or relegating it to a secondary status.

Our faithful, who must give and want to give witness to the Christian life in marriage, but in most difficult circumstances, seek from the council above all a synthesis that is truly constructive and attractive, in which marital love consecrated by the sacrament has a visible role. For such love it is that bears the fruit that is chastity and fertility for this life and the next. It is this love which sustains fidelity and all the marital virtues.

The draft says a number of things in a beautiful way about the mystery of marriage, and about charity and love. But from a first reading of some parts of it one gets the impression that what it must say of marital love it says in a grudging way, more in order to warn against its dangers (which are, of course, not to be ignored), and more to point out its falsifications than to present it in its authentic nature. For example, in the entire chapter, "The Divinely Established Order of Marriage," nothing more is said about married love than the condemnation, at the end of the chapter, of the opinion of " . . . those who claim that marital love is the primary end in the objective order."

One must be grateful that the draft does not insert marital love into the order of marriage as a secondary end, as some have done, and to the considerable scandal of the educated faithful. But does not marital love, in the objective order itself and according to God's intent, somehow constitute the very form and soul of marriage, in such a way that without true marital love the ends themselves of marriage can neither be conceived of nor be rightly attained?[15]

Cardinal Alfrink continued and expanded the negative criticism of the Theological Commission's schema. (His intervention occupies almost three pages in the *Acta*.) I quote here the most significant part of it.

What the constitution says about the ends of marriage, specifically in its Part II, paragraph 13, "The Ends of Marriage," is in general true. But it will bring little light to the contemporary discussion of the subject. There are a certain confusion and disagreement in these discussions because so many of today's

Catholics think and speak in a way quite different from those who talk in traditional terms of the primary and secondary ends of marriage. They do not understand one another because they speak different languages—one of them a juridical language which considers marriage merely as a contract, the other a language of psychology—a human and, unless I am mistaken, also a theological and biblical language. This second group understands marriage primarily as a sharing of life by two human beings who love one another and seek to bring children into the world.

One senses a most urgent need that through this constitution the council bring light into this quite confused discussion. But I am afraid that this constitution will deceive and disappoint many because it does nothing else than set forth the traditional way of thinking.

Without doubt it ought to present an uncompromised Catholic teaching on marriage. But the question is whether this juridical way of thinking really belongs to Catholic doctrine. Marriage is, to be sure, a contract. But is it only a contract? Or does it have other very important components? And is it not possible to set forth Catholic teaching in some other mode of thought?

If, on page 8, lines 22ff, the constitution is condemning those theories according to which marital love is the primary end in the objective order, I doubt that the terminology used here really touches the ideas that it seeks to refute.

For the question here asks about the place and the function of marital love in marriage. Perhaps Holy Scripture can teach us something about this. The Book of Genesis says: "Therefore a man shall leave father and mother and cling to his wife." And Christ himself later quoted this passage.

The term "he shall cling"—in the Hebrew *dabaq,* and in Greek *kolláo*—denotes a physical, bodily, sexual union. But it indicates in addition a psychological union that takes place in the bond of marital love, as is evident from other passages wherein the same verb is used to indicate a union of friendship or to indicate the relationship between a master and his disciple. In these relationships there is obviously a psychological rather than a physical union. The passage in Scripture to which I refer implies this in comparing the marital relationship with the parent-child relationship, which is surely psychological and which supposes a mutual love.

This passage speaks of a marital love which surpasses the love of parents and drives a man to his spouse. Here marital love seems to be understood not as a consequence of marriage but as its cause. Men and women who are about to marry do so *because* they love one another. Marital love is rather an element making up marriage itself than a consequence of a marriage.

Precisely because of this marital love marriage is universally in the Old Testament and in the New Testament a symbol of the relationship between Christ and his Church. Surely this is because of marital love which is the image of the love of Christ for his Church.

Sacred Scripture sees this bond of marital love not as the end of marriage—neither as its primary nor as its secondary end. It sees it rather as a constitutive element of marriage itself, not in the sense that without it the marriage would be invalid, but in the sense that it would be in some way defective, imperfect, incomplete. Marital love belongs to marriage itself, at least if marriage be considered not merely as a juridical contract. And the primary end of this bond of marital love remains in the objective sense the offspring conceived of this love, even though in the conjugal act the spouses do not have the child as their primary intent.

Unless I am mistaken, this is the modern Catholic's way of thinking, a way of thinking that is more psychological, more human, as well as theological-biblical.

If the proponents of this way of thinking oppose the traditional way, they are not challenging Christian teaching but the merely juridical way of considering marriage.

There seems to be much confusion on both sides, and it would be good if the constitution we have in mind could bring some light to the situation. Consequently this constitution ought to free itself from the merely juridical and traditional way of thinking and treat more profoundly the role of marital love itself in marriage. Perhaps it could include something on the subject from Pope Pius XI's encyclical, *Casti connubii,* which contains a number of beautiful statements on marital love. It seems certain that many of the Catholic faithful await urgently some statement of this kind from the council.[16]

The remarks of Cardinal Michael Browne, himself a member of the Congregation of the Holy Office and of the Theological Commission, offer a glimpse at the philosophy which underlay this draft of the constitution that we have seen Cardinals Döpfner and Alfrink challenge. This is a Scholastic philosophy. And Cardinal Browne insisted that the constitution's theory of primary and secondary ends was not juridical but a product of this philosophy.

Regarding the comments of Cardinals Döpfner, Alfrink and Suenens, they touch many points that would be difficult to discuss in the Central Commission or in the council itself. Hence they ought to be taken up in this commission. This text could perhaps be improved. But I note in general that this teaching, which is Catholic doctrine, namely that procreation and nurture are the primary end of marriage, is not a juridical teaching. It is an expression of the law of nature itself, of the philosophy of nature concerning the basic social entity that is the family. Hence when it is said that procreation and nurture are the primary end of marriage, the reference is to its *finis operis*. Then the other ends are mutual help and the remedying of concupiscence.

Now the question of love as an end [or the end] of marriage, as His Eminence the Cardinal of Mechlin has said, according to the statement of the Supreme Pontiff Pius XII, if we are to understand it at depth and hold to it firmly, we must also hold firmly to the truth that the *finis operis* of marriage is the procreation and nurture of offspring. For this society, established according to its true nature, is surely constituted between two human beings in order that life may be given to yet other human beings. This is then perfected by the sacrament. And all these are components of love, so that love itself is established in its own place of primacy, in the sense explained by the Supreme Pontiff and by the Cardinal of Mechlin. It is truly necessary that we hold to this teaching most strictly and rigorously. I would never admit that this is said according to a merely juridical concept, for then we would be seeking something less than a philosophical or theological statement. But in itself it is an application of the philosophy of nature. It is an expression of the philosophy of nature itself, and it is taken into sacred theology in order to explain the nature of the "social contract," so that the sacramental nature of marriage itself may be understood correctly. Hence we may say this for certain: much can be said about the primacy of love, in the same sense that there is a primacy of love in the social virtues, because the first demand of love among men is that they treat one another justly. Hence in order to explain the love of husband and wife the social nature of their union must be made clear. But this cannot be done except in terms of the *finis operis* of marriage—which is primarily procreation and nurture, and secondarily mutual help and the remedying of concupiscence.[17]

Cardinal Ottaviani's comments at the meeting contained this animadversion about marital love:

As to the question of marital love, about which so many and endless things have been said—things that tell of the environment in which Cardinals Döpfner, Alfrink and others live—it seems to me that it must all be taken with a grain of salt [*cum mica salis*]. Surely what Cardinals Döpfner, Alfrink and Suenens have said will be taken into account, but we must accept it carefully and on secure ground. For today the aspect of marital love is exaggerated to the point where it is set in the front rank, ahead of the nature itself of the marriage contract and ahead of the primary end of marriage. We have therefore included in the constitution a paragraph on the moral necessity for the spouses' loving one another. For, rather than being of the nature of marriage, this love is one of its duties. When in his exhortation St. Paul writes of obligations, he commands husbands, "Love your wives," as a kind of duty, not as stating the nature and the supreme characteristic of marriage itself.

Finally, we ought not forget that there can be a marriage without love, and that sometimes the love that shows itself in marriage is only a kind of physical attraction that is taken for marital love. Consequently we ought not provide ammunition for those who seek to promote divorce by urging: "Marital love is essential to marriage; therefore when it ceases, the marriage itself should be ended." So we must proceed with caution. To be sure, we shall later take into consideration what has been said here, and shall develop certain points about marital love. But as I say, it seems to me that it ought all be taken with a grain of salt. We ought to pay careful attention to what Cardinal Browne has said so well, and especially to what Cardinal Larraona has said.[18]

When a vote was taken at the end of this sixth session it became obvious that the document could not be sent to the full council with the approval of the Central Preparatory Commission. Of its sixty members only ten voted unqualified approval (a vote of *placet*). While only one voted unqualified disapproval, the other forty-nine so hedged their approval (*placet iuxta modum*)—some with substantial amendments, others with the request that the schema be rewritten entirely—that the commission had in effect rejected it. What is more, thirty-five of the sixty members of the commission sided expressly with the criticisms leveled by Cardinals Döpfner, Frings, Alfrink and Léger. Cardinal Bea's summary comment following his vote suggests where the deeper dissatisfaction lay: "The text ought to be less juridical—more positive and constructive. Let it use Sacred Scripture more fully and let its language be less technical."[19]

In the end this document was simply abandoned, but after at least serving the valuable function of showing how minds in the Church, and among the Church's appointed teachers, were divided.

The Debate and the Compromise in the Council

From this point on, following this meeting of May 7, 1962, the project of producing a conciliar document on marriage and family idled for several months. Nothing was done about it during the summer before the council's first session, and little during that session itself. But a much larger and more inclusive statement on the social and international orders had been Pope John's intent from the beginning. Toward the end of the first session a small number of council fathers, Bishop Helder Camara and Cardinals Montini, Suenens and Lercaro among them, urged that steps be taken to produce it.

On December 4 Cardinal Suenens' discourse proposing a new structure for the statement on marriage and family aroused enough enthusiasm that in January 1963 he himself brought together two commissions to begin working on the larger document dealing with the social and international orders. These were the Theological Commission and the Commission for the Apostolate of the Laity. The proposed document carried the name *Schema 17* until July 1964, when with the rearranging of plans for all the conciliar documents, it was renamed *Schema 13*. According to Cardinal Suenens' intent the statement on marriage and family was to be one of the document's six chapters, and was to carry the title "On Marriage, the Family and Demographic Problems." This mixed commission in turn appointed a subcommission to write this chapter. (Hence the steps of authority through which the chapter would have to move upward toward acceptance or rejection: from the *ad hoc* subcommission appointed to draft it to the mixed commission organized by Cardinal Suenens, to the Central Preparatory Commission, and finally to the full council of bishops.)

Meanwhile another attempt was being made at composing a statement on marriage. In January 1963, after the close of the first session at the end of the previous November, the Central Preparatory Commission became aware that different persons and groups were contemplating and had begun statements on marriage. So it ordered their work to be reduced to a single document, and turned over the work of combining them to the Conciliar Commission for the Discipline of the Sacraments.

From the six drafts that it received this commission produced and turned over to the Central Preparatory Commission a *Decretum de Matrimonii Sacramento,* which it sent to the bishops in July 1963.[20] It contained next to nothing of the teaching on the ends of marriage that had been in the Theological Commission's *De castitate, virginitate, matrimonio, familia* that had been examined and abandoned a year earlier. It consisted of an introduction, five chapters and a concluding pastoral instruction. Its only mention of the object of marital consent was a reference to "the right proper to marriage."

The reactions of the bishops to this text were gathered, and the text itself was discussed toward the end of the second session. But the Central Preparatory Commission, dissatisfied with the results, requested that the proposed conciliar statement on marriage not have the dimensions of a decree. It asked that the document be shortened to a simple *votum,* a kind of brief recommendation. Back to the Congregation for the Discipline of the

Sacraments went its decree-length draft, to be reduced to the status of the desired *votum*.

The congregation finished this second stage of its work and its reduced document was circulated to the bishops at home between the second and third sessions, in April 1964. When their dominant reaction showed that they considered the *votum* too brief, the same congregation enlarged it. It came to deal mainly with the impediments to marriage, with the problem of mixed marriages, with the form of marriage, and with the pastoral preparation for marriage. This enlarged version of the *votum* was eventually distributed to the bishops in council, on November 10, 1964, when they were already well into the third session. The fate they dealt the document was their vote on November 20 that it be remanded to Pope Paul for consideration by the yet-to-be-formed commission that would eventually revise the *de matrimonio* section of the Code of Canon Law (whose summary revision John XXIII had announced at the same time he announced his intention to convoke the council). Nothing more was heard of the document—the second on marriage to be worked up, discussed, revised, discussed again, and finally abandoned.

The Constitution on the Church in the Modern World

While that *votum* on marriage was making its way to oblivion the document that was eventually to be promulgated by the bishops of the council as Chapter 1 of Part 2 of *Gaudium et spes,* the Pastoral Constitution on the Church in the Modern World, was going through its long and painful gestation.[21] The subcommission appointed to draft it (under the supervision of Cardinal Suenens and his mixed commission preparing the entire *Schema 17*) first met in the spring of 1963, between the council's first and second sessions. Conflict attended this work from the beginning. Some of the subcommission's members wanted a document that would very nearly repeat the traditional teaching and censuring attitude of the earlier production by Cardinal Ottaviani and the Theological Commission. Others wished for a pastoral document, sympathetic to the difficulties of spouses in the modern world, encouraging them, and above all else telling of marriage in a context of love, and defining marriage, even if informally, as a community of love.

Since the entire text of *Schema 17* was, in the judgment of the Central Preparatory Commission, not ready for distribution to the bishops by the summer of 1963, it was not discussed in the council's second session in the fall of that year. It was reworked during the winter and spring of 1964, and finally distributed to the bishops in July of that year—but now, following the reordering of the council's documents, as *Schema 13,* "The Church in the Modern World."[22]

It treated of marriage at two different places within itself. In its Chapter 4, "The Special Tasks to be Accomplished by Christians in the Modern

World," paragraph 21 is titled, "The Dignity of Marriage and the Family." I will note here just a few of its crucial statements on marriage, so different from those in the Theological Commission's abandoned document as to alarm, and to draw the severe criticism of, Cardinals Ruffini, Browne, Ottaviani and others.

A statement early in the paragraph seems to demote procreation and nurture, as ends of marriage, to parity with more personal goals.

> For God, in the wisdom of his love, designed marriage not only for procreation and nurture and for the husband's and wife's mutual help in earthly matters [the remedying of concupiscence is not mentioned], but also for the mutual sanctification and shared glorifying of God. Thus through them their children, even their neighbors and the environment in which the family finds itself are helped along the road to holiness and salvation.[23]

Then comes recognition of the centrality of love in modern marriage, and the recognition is a cue to an assertion of the true nature of this love.

> Since in our time so many exalt the love of husband and wife, it is the work of Christian spouses to show the world the true nature of this marital love. . . . True marital love is a mutual and free gift of the self made by each spouse to the other into one spirit and one flesh. It is a mutual interior conformation of one to the other. It is proved by tender affection; it far exceeds mere passing infatuation.[24]

Finally the statement makes an effort to relate marital love to procreation.

> Marriage is no mere instrument of procreation. Rather the nature itself of the indissoluble covenant between the persons, and most especially the good of the children, demand that the spouses truly love one another. And even if the marriage has no children, it is in no way deprived of its fundamental value or its indissolubility. But such is the character of marital love that marriage is of its nature oriented to the procreation and nurture of children.[25]

One can understand the anxiety of the conservative members of the subcommission and of the mixed commission on reading the last clause here. For centuries procreation had been said in and by the Church to be the natural end of marriage, and said in recent decades to be its primary end. But here the necessity of children is grounded not in the nature itself of marriage but partly in marital love and partly in an orientation of marriage. The hint is there too that the love is the source of the orientation.

But the cardinals and bishops knew that marriage the contract can do without love, and that in real life love is absent from many marriages.

The other place in the text that speaks of marriage is in one of the *adnexa,* or appendices, to the body of the schema. This is Adnexum II, "On Marriage and the Family."[26] What it said about the centrality of married love, on the place of this love as the source of marriage's orientation to children, and finally about love in the object of marital consent, all helped to create the anxiety and hostility mentioned above.

Paragraph 2 of this *adnexum* is "A Brief Description of the Marital Vocation."[27]

> God, seeing that it was not good for the man to be alone . . . created them male and female from the beginning. He joined them in a covenant of love [a defining term that will lodge at the heart of the final draft of this document]. He blessed them and said, "Increase and multiply and fill the earth." By blessing them he called them, so that "in one flesh"—joined, that is, in a single and indissoluble union—they might co-work with him and glorify him in the procreating of the human race.

Note again that it is not the nature of marriage in its ends that is the source of the centrality of procreation, but God's call to the first man and woman. And again marital love itself is said to be the source of marriage's natural orientation to children: "Marital love is of its nature ready [*promptus*] to accept and care for children."

When the statement turns to marital consent and its object, another radical change is evident. Its object is in no sense the exchange of rights. It is taken entirely out of the domain of contract and located in that of covenant.

> Marital consent of its essence intends the unity of this covenant, its indissolubility and the love that is devoted to the service of life. The stronger and purer the marital love, the more strongly and perseveringly will the spouses accept and realize marriage's specific traits and its essential goods. . . . No one is unaware of how seriously necessary it is that love be fully present in the act of consent, and increase throughout the entire married life. For love will fulfill and cause to be fulfilled what the consent has said and has promised.[28]

But lest it be concluded that procreation has been reduced to a secondary and subordinate status in marriage, or can even be omitted from it, the *adnexum* makes two points clearly. First, "Let all acknowledge, before all else, that procreation and truly human nurture are an innate and a most specific orientation in marriage." Second, "The assertions of those who deem procreation and nurture to be something secondary which one can subordinate to its other goods, or even radically separate from them—these contradict the very nature and orientation of marriage."[29]

It was inevitable that even with these last and apparently mitigating clauses a text containing such radical departures from the patiently elaborated and hard-won formulations of the Code of Canon Law and of recent jurisprudence must stir up long and even bitter debate in the council. It was criticized for being at best unclear on the place of procreation in marriage, at worst (by Cardinal Browne) for ignoring what was by then the certain doctrine of the Church (he must have had in mind especially the 1944 decree of the Holy Office and the 1951 discourse of Pius XII). On the other hand the progressive cardinals and bishops— again Léger, Suenens, Alfrink, Döpfner and Reuss principal among them—urged the personalist formulation of the text. Cardinal Léger even wanted it to say that love is one of the ends of marriage.

The upshot of all this was that the text was, in this third session of the council in the fall of 1964, approved in principle but sent back to its authors for substantial revision.

Final Debate on the Council's Statement on Marriage

As part of this revision during the winter and spring of 1965, between sessions 3 and 4 of the council, a major structural redrafting was completed. The *adnexa* chapters of the entire *Schema 13* were put into the body itself of the text. This body was divided into two parts. Of the second part Chapter 1 became "On Fostering the Nobility of Marriage and the Family." As a statement on marriage it had been thoroughly revised from what it was a year earlier, but it still retained its personalist conceptualization and language. It refused to say that procreation and nurture are the primary end of marriage. In fact it avoided any discussion of the ends of marriage and therefore mentioned no hierarchy of ends. It refused to call marriage a contract and thus called into doubt the exchange of rights to sexual acts as the object of marital consent. It gave a central place in marriage to marital love and again seemed to ground marriage's natural orientation to procreation in this love. Aware of the criticism and debate it had already stirred up, the *relatio* (or covering letter) that came with the full text of *Schema 13* at its introduction in the fourth session on September 21, 1965 insisted that those who had drafted the chapter on marriage had been guided by the serious concern "to unite the two principal goods of marriage, procreation and love."

With absolute predictability the document's treatment of the ends of marriage, or rather its neglect of them, caused long and again bitter debate. The same conservative prelates criticized it severely for ignoring the traditional conceptualization and vocabulary of primary and secondary ends. Again they urged their opinion that this hierarchy of ends is the accepted Catholic doctrine and *cannot* be changed. The debate on the entire text of *Gaudium et spes* continued until October 8. The fruits of this debate, the *modi,* or recommended amendments, were turned over to the subcommissions assigned to revise its several chapters. Subcommission 6, revising the chapter on marriage and family, had as its chairman Archbishop Charles Dearden of Detroit.[30] It worked under the authority of the Mixed Commission, which supervised the drafting of the entire document. It was assisted by theological experts, or *periti,* brought to the council by individual bishops.

By October 17 this subcommission had finished the revision of its chapter, incorporating the *modi* coming from the bishops in the full council. It then sent the revision to the Mixed Commission, which in turn submitted the entire *Schema 13* to the full council once again on November 12. By now this was the sixth version of the full document.

The voting on the document in its several parts occupied three days, November 15, 16 and 17. The greatest number of *non placet* (rejecting) votes by the bishops bore upon Part II, Chapter 1. But even so this chapter was approved by an overwhelming majority. The exact tally of the voting on November 16 was the following (using the paragraph numbering of the final and promulgated draft):[31]

Paragraph 46, Preface: *Placet* 2106; *Non placet* 39.

Paragraphs 47–49; On the Nature of Marriage and Conjugal Love: *Placet* 2052; *Non placet* 91.

Paragraphs 50–51: Responsible Parenthood: Placet 2011; *Non placet* 140.

The sharpest points of criticism remained what they had been from the beginning. It was at them that the largest number of *non placet* and *placet iuxta modum* votes was directed. These points included an apparent change of teaching concerning the nature of marriage and its hierarchy of primary and secondary ends—the issue provoking such earnest debate, as we have seen, from the first session of the Theological Commission, on May 7, 1962. The other point was the refusal of the *schema* to repeat the magisterium's earlier explicit condemnations of contraceptive practice, especially as these were contained in Pius XI's encyclical, *Casti connubii,* and in Pius XII's discourse to the Union of Italian Catholic Midwives.

This brought on the final round of the document's history, a round witnessing a manipulation of the council's rules of procedure that was both delicate and exciting. For one of these rules held that once approval of a document had been voted by the full council, no substantial changes could afterward be made in it. But still within the purview of this rule the bishops were told that the deadline for submitting their *modi* in written form for any part of *Schema 13* was extended beyond the deadline set by the rules, to midnight of that Wednesday, November 17, the last day of the voting in full conciliar session.

Exactly a week beyond that deadline, on Wednesday, November 24, while the Mixed Commission was busy with the final revision of the *schema,* including the written *modi* submitted by the deadline indicated above, Cardinal Ottaviani asked Fr. Tromp to read to the Commission two communiqués. The first, from Archbishop Pericle Felici, Secretary General of the Council, stated that the completed revision, including the latest *modi,* was to be ready for the printer by the following Monday, November 29— which left the Commission just two days, Thursday and Friday, to respond to the second of the communiqués and take action on it.

This was a letter from the papal Secretary of State requesting the Commission, "in the name of higher authority," to include in the text of the chapter on marriage and family explicit reference to Pius XI's condemnation of contraceptive intercourse in *Casti connubii* and to Pius XII's condemnation of it in his 1951 discourse. Since Pope Paul was the only authority higher than the Secretary of State, the letter was clearly presented as an expression of his will. Attached to the letter were four *modi* to be included in the final modified text of the chapter. The first and third of these concerned the morality of contraception (and are not germane to this review of the chapter's history). The second had to do with the definition of marriage. But before getting to it a brief explanation of what was done about these *modi* is appropriate.

The conservative members of the Mixed Commission that had just received the two communiqués insisted that the group had no choice but to do as the letter requested, since, as they said, holy obedience required it. For his part, the chairman, Archbishop Dearden questioned the authenticity of the letter.[32] But what he and the other members saw as crucial was to find out exactly whether Pope Paul was really commanding the insertion of the two older papal condemnations of contraception, or whether his letter and the attached *modi* were to be treated according to the rules of the council—that is, as recommendations to be dealt with at the bishops' discretion. For this purpose Cardinal Emile Léger went on Thursday, November 25, to Pope Paul to get a personal clarification of his will in the matter.

Paul's answer came back the following day in the form of a second letter from the Secretary of State. It specified four points: (1) Pope Paul considered the *modi* attached to the first letter to be of great importance; (2) the method of formulation was not obligatory; (3) certain things could be added to the *modi* provided the latter's meaning were retained; (4) the Pope himself would decide subsequently whether the Commission's decision was acceptable. The majority of the Commission seized on point 3 and followed out its obvious implication that the *modi* were to be dealt with according to the rules of the council.

What the second *modus* requested (the one which touched the essence of marriage) was that a one-word modification be made in the following passage from paragraph 50 of the text of the chapter on marriage and family.

> Marriage and conjugal love are by their nature ordained toward
> the begetting and educating of children. The God himself who
> said "It is not good for man to be alone," wishing to share with

man a certain participation in his own creative work, blessed the male and female, saying, "Increase and multiply." Hence the true practice of conjugal love and the whole meaning of family life which results from it also have this aim, that the couple be ready with stout hearts to cooperate with the love of the Creator and Savior, who through them will enlarge and enrich his own family day by day.

The requested modification was that the word "also" (*etiam*) be deleted from the first clause of the last sentence. The intended effect was obvious: to reassert the ancient moral philosophy that the primary end of marriage is procreation and nurture, and to reinforce it by aligning the very meaning of marital love and family life as tributary to this end.

The Commission's way of dealing with this *modus* was to propose a compromise. It would delete the "also" as requested. But it would add to the paragraph a new and crucial clause making clear beyond doubt what the majority of the Commission wished to propose to the full council. This clause is in italics in the paragraph below and was readied for the final discussion and vote on December 3.

Marriage and conjugal love are by their nature ordained toward the begetting and educating of children. Children are really the supreme gift of marriage and contribute very substantially to the welfare of their parents. The God himself who said "It is not good for man to be alone," wishing to share with man a certain special participation in his own creative work, blessed the male and female, saying "Increase and multiply." Hence, *while not making the other ends of marriage of less account,* the true practice of conjugal love and the whole meaning of family life which results from it have this aim, etc.[33]

The intent of the added clause is either one of two: to decisively demote creation and nurture to a level of equality with the other ends of marriage (which are unnamed in the statement), or to reopen the question of hierarchy of ends after its having been apparently closed by the earlier magisterial statements we have already seen. Whichever the intent, when the entire revised text was shown to Pope Paul over the weekend of November 27–28, he approved it for final deliberation by the full council in its one hundred and sixty-sixth meeting that occupied December 2 and 3.

Detailed Statement in *Gaudium et spes*

I said in an earlier chapter that the Catholic magisterium has never tried to formulate a definition of marriage in the strict sense of this term. I have in mind here again the ancient, classical definition of "definition," an identifying of the thing defined according to its genus of existence, then according to its specific difference of existence. The neglect or reluctance or refusal to define marriage in this rigorous way is surely evident in *Gaudium et spes*. Apart from any identifying of genus and inclusion within it of specific difference, the document's description of marriage is too abundant, too diffuse, at points too imprecise in its predicating to qualify as such a definition.

That said, the question still remains whether the bishops intended in *Gaudium et spes* to give the Church and the world their understanding of marriage, and have it serve at least in the Church as a norm by which to measure heterosexual relationships, especially those thought to be marriages. There is compelling evidence that they had exactly that intent. All the argument beginning from May 1962, all the in-and-out, round-and-about of council stratagems from that time until December 3 over the crucial clauses to be kept in or kept out of the chapter on marriage and family, argue for such intent. The text whose acceptance the bishops voted on December 4 was a fifth revision. In the meeting of December 2 and 3 the bishops discussed and disposed of amendments numerous enough to occupy thirty-six pages in the *Acta* of the council.[35]

One party, the smaller and conservative one, wanted marriage to be understood in an exact way as having a hierarchy of fixed, inherent ends, with procreation and nurture primary among them, and with an exactly and traditionally designated object of marital consent, the right of the parties to their sexual acts. The other party, the majority, wanted that if marriage was to be understood still according to such inherent ends, no priority among them was to be assigned. And it insisted that marital consent be called an exchange of gifts, of the entire selves of the spouses. This was a dispute about what marriage is, about the goods it can bring to human beings, about the kind of act that creates it. Such a dispute about a functional relationship in society is a dispute about this relationship's nature.

Before beginning a kind of exegesis of *Gaudium et spes* it will be helpful to report on the kind and degree of valence the bishops of the council meant the constitution to have. Verifying this has become most significant because of some quasi-epistemological evaluations of it that have been made in the years since its promulgation. These have come mainly from canonical writers and from judges of the Church's marriage courts, including the two highest appellate courts, the Roman Rota and the Signatura.

They have argued that *Gaudium et spes* has changed little or even nothing of the Church's teaching about marriage. Their evidence for this claim is that the document is titled a *pastoral* constitution, in contradistinction to a dogmatic constitution, such as, for example, the Dogmatic Constitution on the Church, *Lumen gentium*. Therefore one cannot conclude from the nature of *Gaudium et spes* as a conciliar document that it teaches what must be accepted if one is to be a faithful Catholic. Moreover it is addressed to the entire world, not only to those who hold to the Catholic *corpus* of belief. Finally, it is not written in the language of theological or even canonical statement. It has not the exactness, the precise predication that must be used to change elements of this *corpus*.

There is a footnote to the Prooemium of the document in the *Acta Synodalia* that speaks to this point. It explains that part of its title that is "pastoral constitution," with particular attention given to the word "pastoral".

> The Pastoral Constitution on the Church in the Modern World consists of two parts but forms a single whole.
>
> The constitution is called "pastoral" because, though rooted in doctrinal principles, it intends to explain the relationship of the Church to the world and to modern man. Consequently the pastoral intent is present in Part I, as the doctrinal intent is present in Part II.
>
> In Part I the Church sets forth its teaching on man, on the world in which man is situated, and on its relationship to both. In Part II it considers in finer detail different aspects of modern life and of human society, especially questions and problems that seem more urgent in our time. As a consequence the material in this Part II, while grounded in doctrinal principles, consists not only of fixed elements but also of those that are contingent.
>
> Therefore the constitution is to be interpreted according to the general norms of theological interpretation, while keeping in mind, especially in Part II, the naturally changeable context of the material that is dealt with.[36]

But the thirty-year dispute about the ends of marriage and about the object of marital consent was by no means the principal concern of the bishops in writing this constitution. They sought to describe marriage as it is lived, and urge how it ought to be lived, by men and women in the second half of the twentieth century. In the course of this description and urging they said things that can be used in resolving the disputes. In a sense they described the characteristics of a happy marriage.

I will try now to examine these characteristics, and do so in a tight, schematic way in order to gather in the diffuseness that I mentioned above. I will limit myself to those characteristics that seem to belong to marriage's nature, or to manifest this nature as either causes or effects of it, or at least necessary conditions for this nature's realization. The first part of the examination will be of the text itself of the constitution. A second part will look briefly at some important amendments to those paragraphs in the text that express these characteristics, and at what the council did with these amendments. Finding out the last contributes much to understanding the mind of the bishops in writing and promulgating *Gaudium et spes*.

The first and most nuclear evidence of the bishop's understanding of the nature of marriage is in the inventory of substantives they used to describe it.[37]

They first refer to it (in paragraph 47) as a community, and a community of love (*communitas amoris*).

Then (in paragraph 48) they designate marriage an intimate partnership—or community, or sharing—of married life and love (*intima communitas vitae et amoris coniugalis*). They call it an institution (*institutum matrimonii*); they refer to the marital vocation (*vocatio coniugalis*); they call marriage (in paragraph 49) a Christian vocation (*vocatio Christiana*), and a marital covenant (*foedus coniugale*).

In paragraph 50 the bishops repeat the notion of covenant, calling marriage an unbreakable covenant (*foedus indissolubile*). They add that it is a sharing of the whole of life and a communion of life that are indissoluble (*totius vitae consuetudo et communio perseverat, suumque valorem et indissolubilitatem servat*).

More revealing than this simple list of the substantives the bishops used to designate marriage are their statements about the kind of act that creates a marriage. It is here that the notion of covenant is continued and expanded. Interwoven with these statements about the consent creating a marriage is, inevitably, a disclosure of what the bishops think is the object of marital consent.

They say first (in paragraph 48) that marriage, which they have already called an intimate community of married life and love, is formed by "a conjugal covenant of irrevocable personal consent" (*foedere coniugii seu irrevocabili consensu personali instauratur*).[38] Here is the biblical notion of the act of covenanting; it is this that creates a marriage. It is a personal act that can be placed only by the parties themselves to the covenant.

The text here goes on immediately to say that this covenanting is a human act in which the spouses "mutually bestow and accept one another" (*actu humano quo coniuges sese mutuo tradunt et accipiunt*). Each spouse gives; each spouse accepts. And here the text reaches a crossroad in the history of Catholic thought on marriage. Where it had been appropriate for centuries to complete the thought by adding that it is the right to their sexual acts that the spouses give and accept, *Gaudium et spes* says rather that it is their own persons that they give and accept (*sese tradunt et accipiunt*).

By this mutual giving and accepting an institution (*institutum*) is created which is not a temporary one, but permanent (*firmum*). And such is the nature of this institution that once created by the self-giving consent, its existence is invulnerable to any subsequent acts of choice by the spouses or by any other merely human agent (*non ex humano arbitrio pendet*).

The bishops come back a second time to the notion of self-giving. Referring again to marriage as an intimate union, they call it a mutual gifting of two persons (*mutua duarum personarum donatio*). The notion of gifting is a charged one. It is biblical, it is pre-juridical and pre-contractual. In fact it must be antithetical to contractuality. For precisely what an act of contracting is not is an exchange of gifts. What is given under contract is not a gift; it is something owed in commutative justice.

Marital love has its function in this self-donation, although the bishops do not say exactly what this is. They do say of it (in paragraph 49) that such love leads the spouses to a free and mutual gift of themselves and pervades the whole of their lives (*talis amor . . . coniuges ad liberum et mutuum sui ipsius donum . . . conducit totamque vitam eorum pervadit*). What they do not determine here is whether the love in question is indispensably necessary to the self-donation that creates a marriage, whether as a necessary cause of it, a necessary trait, or a necessary effect. This innocent lack of precision left an opening for argument about the essentiality of marital love which we saw come to life in the May 1962 meeting of the Theological Commission, and which we shall see (in the following chapter) has been the source of unceasing disagreement since the council.

What do the bishops say marriage as a mutual self-donation requires that the spouses do *within* the marriage? The question is crucial because it asks about the more specific and inclusive object of the spouses' consent when this seeks to create a marriage. It also asks, but less explicitly, what is required of a man or woman in order to be able to make the marital commitment.

Borrowing the biblical affirmation that their covenanting makes the spouses "two in one flesh," the bishops say (in paragraph 48) that this covenant engages them in an intimate union of their persons and their actions (*intima personarum atque operum coniunctione*) in which they help and serve one another. They say too that in living this covenant, and as an effect of it, the spouses come to experience the meaning of their oneness and to grow in it day by day (*sensumque suae unitatis experiuntur et plenius in dies adipiscuntur*).

Procreation and Nurture in Marriage

I have already traced the history of the dispute in the council's last session, the dispute about the place of procreation, that ended in the bishop's rejecting procreation and nurture as a *primary* end of marriage while retaining it as one essential end among others. But that much was only a minimum expression of their thought. Early in paragraph 48 they say that of its very nature marriage is oriented to the procreation and nurture of children. They compound the assertion by saying that marital love too has this orientation (*indole autem sua naturali . . . ad procreationem et educationem prolis ordinantur*).

This is not the same as to say that marriage and marital love are a means to the end that is procreation and nurture. It does not say that they are instrumental realities. Rather, they are developmental realities. They move from an inchoate state, grow, flower in a completion internal to themselves. What the bishops mean is that procreation is an essential element of this completion. The last clause in the paragraph expresses the same idea under a different figure. It says that marriage and marital love reach a kind of culmination in children (*iisque veluti suo fastigio coronan-tur*).

Two implications here are worthy of notice. Presuming that the love the bishops have in mind is a compound of affection and of the will to self-giving they spoke about earlier in the chapter, they here propose a love that naturally desires children in the giving of the selves. This is what love that is marital contains.

Their other implication is that unless a man and woman love with this love, and unless they intend a marriage that contains and tries to realize the orientation to children, they do not form a marriage. Or at least this *seems* an implication in their statement. How they attenuate the essentiality of the orientation to children we shall see presently.

The bishops begin paragraph 50, titled "The Fruitfulness of Marriage," by repeating the thought noted just above: marriage and marital love are by their nature oriented to the begetting and nurture of children. They come slightly less close to repeating the notion that children are the flowering of marriage's naturally developmental process as they say that "children are really the supreme gift of marriage" (*praestantissimum matrimonii donum*).

The essentiality and the naturalness of children to marriage come back yet again in a slightly different form. The bishops say that the peculiar and the characteristic mission of spouses (*propria eorum missio*) is found in the work of transmitting human life and nurturing it. This is a substantial part of what it means to be a husband or a wife—to carry out this mission. The bishops add that in doing so the spouses co-work with the love of God in his creation, and in doing so mediate this love on earth (*cooperatores . . . amoris Dei Creatoris eiusque velut interpretes*).

What is said thus far leaves the troubling question asking whether the orientation to children is so essential that without it a relationship cannot be a marriage. To this question, although it is never posed explicitly in the document, the bishops devote the last paragraph of paragraph 50.

> To be sure, marriage is instituted not solely for procreation. Rather, its very nature as an unbreakable covenant between persons and the good of the children both demand that the mutual love of the spouses be expressed and grow and mature in a rightly ordered way. Consequently even when children are lacking, frequently despite the intense desire of the spouses to have them, the marriage persists as a regimen and sharing of all of life, and holds its value and indissolubility.

The logic of the passage seems to be this, that the internal meaning, the value, the impulse toward personal fulfillment, the holding power of a marriage do not vanish or even weaken if the natural conceiving, bearing and nurturing of children can never take place. Marriage has other elements of meaning and value. It can flower in other forms of fulfillment. The happiness toward which it strives by nature demands by itself that it be an indissoluble relationship.

The *Expensio Modorum*

The general assembly of December 3 was devoted to the *expensio modorum* of the chapter on marriage and family—the explanation and disposition of the amendments to it urged by different bishops. Among the general *modi* was one recommending that the entire chapter be dropped, since its material would be dealt with by the Pope with the help of a pontifical commission. Another observed that love is so emphasized in the entire chapter that one could infer from it that if the love in a marriage should die, the marriage would go out of existence. The Mixed Commission simply rejected the first of these *modi*. About the second it pointed out that the indissolubility of marriage is stated clearly and forcefully in the document.[39]

The most severe of these general *modi,* proposed by two bishops, came to the core of the disagreement that had festered since 1962. It criticized the chapter as theologically immature, as either equivocal or silent on some essential points, and as speaking predominantly and almost uniquely of marital love and of the personal gifting of the selves—ways of speaking that are discordant with the way the Church had taught continually from its earliest centuries down to *Casti connubii,* Pius XII, John XXIII and Paul VI. (However accurate this terse historical assessment, the *modus* did make clear how momentous was the change in Catholic thinking on marriage proposed in *Gaudium et spes.*) If the chapter is to be approved, let it at least be revised to state clearly the hierarchy of ends in marriage, the intrinsic evil of onanism (twenty bishops approved this), the immorality of certain kinds of birth control, the validity of marriage even where love is absent, and the personal and mutual exchange of the rights and duties proper to marriage.[40]

The reply to this was that the particular points of the criticism in the *modus* would be answered in the responses to later *modi,* and that the document already states clearly the sacred character of marriage, of love, of fertility, of the rights and duties proper to marriage and family life. It added that the notion of love is emphasized in *Casti connubii.* And finally it pointed out that the chapter had no intent to resolve all difficulties and answer all questions. It sought only to shed more light on certain points of Church teaching. A full treatment has been remanded to the Pontifical Study Commission on Population Control.

The next *modus* touching seriously the nature of marriage and marital consent was directed at the passage early in paragraph 48 that designates the act creating a marriage: "The intimate community of marital life and love . . . is created by a conjugal covenant of irrevocable personal consent. Thus from the human act by which the spouses mutually bestow and accept one another. . . ." Thirty-four bishops joined in proposing an alternative formulation of the second of these clauses: ". . . by the human act in which the spouses mutually and according to the law give to and accept from one another (or between their persons) the specific rights and duties . . . they are constituted before society in a legitimate marriage, joined by a divine bond."[41]

The reason offered for this *modus* was this—that the object of marital consent is not persons but the acts of persons. Therefore the expression "bestow and accept one another" should be avoided, as the Congregation of the Holy Office warned in its decree of April 1, 1944.

Immediately following this *modus,* one hundred and ninety bishops motivated by the same consideration and in addition by the desire to retain Catholic doctrine—especially that concerning the hierarchy of ends in marriage—proposed this reformulation of the crucial clauses:

> Thus by an act of will manifested according to the law, by which each party gives and accepts the perpetual and exclusive right to his or her body for acts *per se* apt for generation, an institution is created that is perpetual by divine ordination. Thus this sacred bond, in consideration of the good of both the persons and of society, once freely contracted in no way depends on any human decision. For God himself is the author of marriage which has in itself various goods and ends that are structured hierarchically. . . .[42]

Immediately on the heels of that *modus* came one from ten bishops who asked that the following addition be made to the same clauses: "Thus that human act by which the spouses personally give and accept one another in the communion of life and love. . . ."[43] Their intent was that married life be understood as fully human, not locked within biological categories.

The proposed reformulation by the one hundred and ninety bishops was part one of the obvious final attempt by the small group of conservative prelates to have the understanding of marriage fixed in the Code of Canon Law written into *Gaudium et spes.* The *modus* coming from the ten bishops seems just as obviously a move to block that attempt. (The *expensio modorum* leaves anonymous the authors of the *modi.*)

The reply to and disposition of the *modus* coming from the one hundred and ninety bishops was one of the most significant in all the debate on *Gaudium et spes.* It was to be remembered, and has been used by ecclesiastical judges continually since the council, and interpreted in divergent ways according to the assumptions that the judges bring to the writing of their decisions. The reply said first that the canonical precision requested in the *modus* is not called for in a pastoral statement. As for asking that the object of marital consent be declared an exchange of rights, a right does not exist without its object—which in marriage is the persons of the spouses. The expression "the giving over of the persons" was in fact not interdicted by the Holy Office in 1944. Moreover *Casti connubii* had used exactly this expression: ". . . the generous giving over of their own persons" (*generosa propriae personae traditio*).

The reply continued that in a statement that is pastoral, that seeks to start up a conversation with the world, these juridical details are not called for.

As for the inclusion of a statement of the hierarchically ordered ends of marriage, these can be considered under different aspects. Here the response pointed to the passage in *Casti connubii* saying that if marriage be considered in its fuller sense, the fulfillment and sanctification of the spouses can be considered its principal end.

And again to the point of the style appropriate to a pastoral statement: ". . . in such a document excessively technical terms (such as 'hierarchically') are to be avoided. And beyond this, the primordial importance of procreation and nurture is stated at least ten times in the text; it speaks frequently of the sacrament; fidelity and indissolubility are demanded clearly at least seven times."[44]

Part two of this last attempt to write the thinking of the Code into *Gaudium et spes* came in a *modus* to the clauses in paragraph 48 that express the natural orientation of marriage and marital love to procreation. One hundred and seventy-nine bishops asked that the words "by their nature" be added to the following clause after its first set of substantives: ". . . the institution of marriage and marital love . . . reach a kind of culmination in the procreation and nurture of children." The stated reason for the *modus* was that the passage might express more clearly that procreation as an end of marriage is its primary end. Fourteen bishops wanted to revise the statement to read: "The institution itself of marriage, which exists for the service of life and love, reaches a kind of culmination in the actual procreation and nurture of children, joined with the practice of a conscious and generous virtue of marital love".

The disposition of both *modi* came in the formulating of the statement as it now reads in the published text: "The institution itself of marriage and marital love have, as a natural characteristic, an ordination to procreation and in them find their natural culmination."[45]

It is significant that in the end *Gaudium et spes* was given the canonical-theological title of *Constitutio*. This itself was the product of a brief debate between the majority of the bishops, who wanted this title, and the minority who sought as a last-ditch defense to give the entire document the title *Declaratio*, or at least to reserve *Constitutio* for Part I, and to label Part II, containing the chapter on marriage and family, a *Declaratio*. Their intent was obvious. Since in conciliar nomenclature a *declaratio* indicates a

statement less important then a *constitutio,* they sought to diminish the
doctrinal and juridical value of the statement on marriage and family.

The Encyclical Letter *Humanae vitae*

Two years and seven months after Vatican II had adjourned Pope
Paul VI completed the task he had taken away from the council and had
promised to tend to on his own. This was to declare, in virtue of his ordinary teaching authority, on the moral permissibility of the artificial limitation of fertility. He did this in his encyclical letter *Humanae vitae* of July
25, 1968.[46] It is clear that he saw an explanation of the nature of marriage
to be a necessary step in making this moral declaration. For this reason he
came to his explanation, in its character as a definition of marriage, with
two assumptions—one of which he acknowledged, but the other he did
not.

First, about the assumption he acknowledged. In Paragraph 7 of the
encyclical he begins the *processus* of his moral logic at a point of dialectic
already reached by the philosophers and theologians with whom he eventually disagrees in the conclusion of this *processus.* He says that they appeal to the demands of marital love and of responsible parenthood in order
to justify artificial means of birth control. Therefore in order to join issue
with them he begins the encyclical with his understanding of "these two
great realities of married life." And he acknowledges his first assumption
implicitly when he adds that in setting out this, his understanding of marital love and of responsible parenthood, he will keep in the forefront of his
memory what the Second Vatican Council has with highest authority
taught in *Gaudium et spes.*

By making this first step in his logic an explanation of marital love
and of responsible parenthood Paul commits himself to explain marriage
as a reality made up of at least these two components. This becomes evident in the first two logically linked statements in Paragraph 8.

> . . . Conjugal love reveals its true nature and nobility when it is
> considered in its authentic origin, God, who is love. . . .Marriage
> is not, then, the effect of chance or the product of evolution or
> unconscious forces; it is the wise institution of the Creator to re-
> alize in mankind his design of love.

The logical linking here is clear enough: *because* God is the ultimate
source of the love that is marital he is the author of marriage itself. (One
may note here that unlike his predecessors Paul does not explain God's authorship of marriage by citing Genesis 1 and 2 as factual sources.) And
what kind of love marital love is, is understandable from its source taken
as both its model and its *telos,* its goal of accomplishment. That is, marital

love and therefore marriage are intended by God to accomplish what he is seeking to accomplish in human beings in history. They are intended by him to accomplish their specific subset of his plan.

Taking this assertion as a kind of *fons* or principle, Paul sets forth in a single complex statement what one may fairly take to be his informal definition of marriage.

> By means of the reciprocal personal gift of the self, proper and exclusive to them, husband and wife tend toward the communion of their beings in view of mutual personal perfection, to collaborate with God in the generation of new lives.

Paul says that in marrying, a man and woman make to one another a gift of their selves. Although he does not say that they do not enter a contract, the word *contractus* appears nowhere in the text of the encyclical. As with the bishops of Vatican II, so with Paul this cannot have been oversight, because he surely knew the consequences for all future Catholic jurisprudence of marriage of his omitting the word. He must have known too the consequences of his naming the mutual gifting of the persons of the spouses for the sake of forming a communion of their beings as the object of marital consent, and of including procreation and nurture in his formulation not as a primary end of marriage, not as an end at all, but apparently as the goal and culmination of the communion of their beings.

The second assumption at work in Paul's explanation of marriage is his judgment that it was absolutely necessary for him to repeat the standing magisterial condemnation of contraceptive intercourse. Evidence for this is Paul's treatment of the recommendation given to him in the spring of 1966 by the Pontifical Study Commission on Population Control. Readers whose memories span the last decade and a half will recall that an opinion subscribed to by a significant majority of that commission advised that it is possible to modify the magisterial teaching to permit contraceptive intercourse. Paul rejected this recommendation. His reasons for doing so he details briefly in Paragraph 6 of the encyclical. The first was that ". . . within the commission itself no full concordance of judgments concerning the moral norms to be proposed had been reached"; the second, that ". . . above all because certain criteria of solutions had emerged which departed from the moral teaching on marriage proposed with constant firmness by the teaching authority of the Church."[47]

The second of these reasons indicates clearly that before writing the encyclical, and consequently before setting out in it his understanding of the nature of marriage, Paul had already made up his mind to not contradict the proscriptive judgment his predecessors had passed on artificial means of birth control. This put at least a negative control on his understanding of marriage. He could not define it in such a way as to make the definition a premise whence a moral conclusion permitting artificial methods could be drawn. Rather, since he wished to reason logically to the established moral condemnation from a premise valid by natural law in human beings, that premise had to consist of a self-evident fact about marriage, a fact needing no prior proof. Therefore this fact had to be established in his definition of marriage. At the end of paragraph 10 Paul himself implies this point of method in the moral logic needed for his reiteration of the condemnation. In explanation of what is involved in the exercise of truly responsible parenthood he says, "In the task of transmitting life, therefore, they [the married] are not free to proceed completely at will, as if they could determine in a wholly autonomous way the honest path to follow; but they must conform their activity to the creative intention of God, *expressed in the very nature of marriage and its acts* . . . (italics added)."

None of the elements of Paul's understanding of marriage contained in the brief passage I have quoted above contains and asserts this fact needed by his moral logic. And apparently Paul agreed that the fact had not yet been established. For he makes clear that it is not enough simply to say (as he did) that the reciprocal personal gift of the self proper and exclusive to a husband and wife, by which they tend to a communion of their beings in view of mutual personal perfection, is a gift given *in order to collaborate with God in the generation of new lives* (again italics added). It was in his mind not sufficient because it is not this assertion that he uses as the premise whence he draws his conclusion repeating the condemnation of artificial birth control.

What seems surprising is that where, in paragraph 12, he asserts this fact-used-as-premise, it is a fact not about the nature of marriage itself but about the act of intercourse (which he calls the "conjugal act"). The fact is ". . . the inseparable connection, willed by God and unable to be broken by man on his own initiative, between the two meanings of the conjugal act, the unitive meaning and the procreative meaning".

Paul does not say where God's will linking these two meanings inseparably is revealed—unless one can infer from his earlier words that this revelation takes place in the very nature of marriage or of marital intercourse. And taken only this far, his predetermined conclusion about the immorality of artificial birth control does not quite yet predetermine his understanding of marriage. The predetermining appears when he makes this fact-asserted-as-premise work to produce his conclusion. He does so where, in paragraph 13, he reasons *a pari* (by parallel, or equivalency).

It is a fact justly observed that a conjugal act imposed upon one's partner without regard for his or her condition and lawful desires is not a true act of love and therefore denies an exigency of right moral order in the relationship between husband and wife. Hence one who reflects well must also recognize that a reciprocal act of love which jeopardizes the disponibility to transmit life which God the creator, according to particular laws, inserted therein is [*a pari*] in contradiction with the design constitutive of marriage. . . .

That is, just as loveless and coerced intercourse offends against the nature of marital intercourse, and therefore apparently against marriage itself, since one of its essential meanings is the unitive, so too does intercourse with contraceptive intent offend against this nature. This can be only because another of the meanings in marriage's nature is the procreative. What is more, since the two meanings are assertedly inseparable, it is impossible to offend against the one without also offending against the other. In short, the unitive meaning of marriage is also procreative, just as the procreative meaning is also unitive.

Thus from an examination of this moral logic in *Humanae vitae* it seems accurate to infer these added elements in Paul's understanding of marriage: not that it has primary and secondary ends, but that it has two meanings, the unitive and the procreative, which are equal in value and morally inseparable in conduct as well as in intent.

That in *Humanae vitae* Paul truly abandoned the understanding of marriage according to primary and secondary ends is further evident in the difference of moral logic used in his condemnation of contraceptive intercourse from that which Pius XI had used in his condemnation of it thirty-eight years earlier in *Casti connubii*. Both used as a premise of their logic the nature of marriage; both drew the conclusion that contraceptive intercourse violates the nature of marriage (although Paul says this indirectly by saying that it violates the nature of sexual intercourse). But the difference in the way the two Popes understand this nature is evident in the difference in their understandings of its violation. And this in turn is evident at two points in *Casti connubii*. Early in his encyclical Pius explained the nature of marriage according to the Augustinian goods of marriage, and of course named offspring as primary among these goods: "Among the blessings of marriage offspring holds first place."[48] Paul nowhere in *Humanae vitae* mentions these goods.

But the place of the hierarchically subordinated ends in Pius' moral logic surfaces much more clearly when he explains why the practice of periodic continence, or rhythm, does not violate the nature of marriage or of sexual intercourse. Although the couple do not positively seek to realize the primary end (and in fact seek to avoid it although having intercourse whose very nature is ordered to this end), they do seek the secondary ends of marriage and intercourse, and keep the latter in subordination to the primary end.

Nor are husband and wife to be accused of acting against nature if they make use of their right in a proper and natural manner, even though natural causes (due to circumstances of time or to certain defects) render it impossible for new life to originate. Both matrimony and the use of the matrimonial right have secondary ends—such as mutual help, the fostering of reciprocal love, and the abatement of concupiscence—which husband and wife are quite entitled to have in view, so long as the intrinsic nature of that act, and therefore its due subordination to its primary end, is safeguarded.[49]

In short, periodic continence is not immoral because it preserves the nature of marriage and intercourse by keeping their secondary ends subordinated to the primary. Paul, in contrast, reasons not from subordination but from parity—and from the parity not of ends but of meanings. That is, contraceptive intercourse is immoral because it seeks to destroy a parity that is natural to marriage.

NOTES

1. In *Acta et Documenta Concilio Oecumenico Vaticano II Apparando,* Series I (Antepraeparatoria), Vol. 3, 1960. See the title page for this division of contributions by bishops *et al.*

2. *Op. cit.,* pp. 93–102.

3. *Ibid.,* p. 93.

4. *Op. cit.,* Series 2, Vol. 3, Pars 1, pp. 499–557. The proposed marriage matters are on pp. 519–547.

5. *Ibid.,* p. 528.

6. *Op. cit.,* Series 1, Vol. 3, pp. 3–17.

7. *Ibid.,* p. 13.

8. This document is published twice in the *acta* of the council, and in perfect synonymity. It is in pages 40–134 of Series II (Praeparatoria), Volume 3, Pars 1, which contains the *acta* of the Preparatory Commission's secretariates. It is also in pp. 893–937 of Series II (Praeparatoria), Vol. 2, the *Acta* of the Central Preparatory Commission, Pars 3.

9. The schema was a labor of considerable research and scholarship. Within its forty-four pages it had one hundred and seventy-six reference footnotes filling almost two-thirds of those pages. An outline of its headings and sub-headings tells much about its content, its attitudes and its intent.

Prooemium

Paragraph 1: The Church as Exemplar of Both States of Life (consecrated virginity and marriage).

Part I: On Chastity and Virginity

Paragraph 2: Prenotes

Chapter 1: Prenotes on the Nature of the Two Sexes

Paragraph 3: The origin and nature of the sexes (or of sexuality). *Paragraph 4:* Man has not absolute dominion over his body.

Chapter 2: On the Chastity of the Unmarried and on Virginity

Paragraph 5: On the chastity of the unmarried. *Paragraph 6:* On virginity. *Paragraph 7:* On the defense and care of chastity. *Paragraph 8:* Certain errors are censured.

Part II: On Marriage and the Family
Chapter 1: On the Divinely Established Order of Marriage
Paragraph 9: Prenotes. *Paragraph 10:* The origin, nature and dignity of marriage. *Paragraph 11:* Marriage and consecrated virginity. *Paragraph 12:* The properties of marriage. *Paragraph 13:* The ends of marriage. *Paragraph 14:* The power of the Church. *Paragraph 15:* The competence of civil authority. *Paragraph 16:* Errors condemned.

Chapter 2: On the Rights, Obligations and Virtues Proper to Marriage
Paragraph 17: The rights and duties of individual persons. *Paragraph 18:* Rights and duties regarding the good that is offspring. *Paragraph 19:* Rights and obligations regarding the good that is fidelity. *Paragraph 20:* On conjugal chastity. *Paragraph 21:* Obligations regarding indissolubility (the *bonum sacramenti*). *Paragraph 22:* On civil divorce. *Paragraph 23:* Mixed marriages. *Paragraph 24:* Errors condemned.

Chapter 3: On the Divinely Established Order of the Christian Family
Paragraph 25: The origin and dignity of the Christian family. *Paragraph 26:* The family as a true society. *Paragraph 27:* Authority in the domestic society. *Paragraph 28:* Condemnation of certain errors.

Chapter 4: On the Rights, Obligations and Duties Proper to the Christian Family
Paragraph 29: The responsibility of parents regarding the number of children. *Paragraph 30:* The fear of over-population. *Paragraph 31:* The rights and duties of parents regarding their children's education. *Paragraph 32:* The rights and duties of children. *Paragraph 33:* The duties of others and of civil society toward the family. *Paragraph 34:* The family and the schools. *Paragraph 35:* The family and the Church. *Paragraph 36:* Some errors condemned.

Epilogue
Paragraph 37: A brief admonition

10. Series II, Vol. 2, Pars 3, p. 937.

11. *Loc. cit.*

12. *Loc. cit.*, p. 910. Footnote 50 to the text at this point reads, "See the various erroneous positions concerning the ends of marriage, among them those of H. Doms, *Vom Sinn und Zweck der Ehe* (Breslau, 1935). See also E. Michel, *Ehe, Eine Anthropologie der Geschlechtsgemeinschaft* (Stuttgart, 2nd edition, 1948)."

13. *Op. cit.*, p. 909.

14. Their comments on it and recommendations fill pages 939–970 of the *acta* of this session.

15. *Op. cit.*, pp. 947–948.

16. *Op. cit.*, pp. 960–962.

17. The cardinal of Mechlin is Cardinal Suenens, Mechlin being the Flemish name of the city whose French name is Malines. The term *finis operis* refers to the natural goal of a kind of conduct considered in abstraction from the particular goal intended by the person engaged in it. The latter goal is the *finis operantis*.

18. *Loc. cit.*, pp. 977–978. Cardinal Larraona's brief remark was this: "May I note that the Romans had precisely this conception about which we have said so much here, the conception that from two lives there is formed one— *individuam vitae consuetudinem retinens.* As is obvious, this is a juridical concept. But we should understand the term 'juridical' correctly; otherwise we shall not understand the 'life' in question here. The term indicates something more than an external feature, although it is often thought and said to be nothing more. Why in fact has the

contract of marriage been worked out in Christian law exactly *as* a contract? Only in this negative sense, not that other elements be excluded in any way, but so as to exclude a marriage of mere event (*matrimonium factum*), an effect produced only when two wills are joined, in the way that light is produced only when the positive and negative poles are actually joined. This concept is not a Christian one. I mean in this sense, that since there is the union of the two wills, even if they should later be separated, they have produced their effect. Thus the concept of contract by no means touches all that has been said here so wisely, so beautifully, so edifyingly" (*loc. cit.,* pp. 964–965).

19. *Op. cit.,* p. 978.

20. This is in *Acta Synodalia,* Vol. 3, Periodus 3, Pars 8, pp. 1068–1083 and 1147–1149.

21. For a detailed history of the document's production see Heribert Vorgrimmler, editor, *On the Documents of Vatican II,* Volume 5, "The Pastoral Constitution on the Church in the Modern World": "History of the Constitution," by Charles Moeller, pp. 1–76, and "Part II, Chapter 1," by Bernard Häring, pp. 225–245. Translated by W. J. O'Hara, London and N. Y., 1969.

22. The entire *schema* is in *Acta Synodalia,* Vol. 3, Periodus 3, Pars 5. This paragraph is on pp. 131 and 132.

23. *Ibid.,* p. 131.

24. *Ibid.,* p. 132.

25. *Ibid.*

26. *Op. cit.,* pp. 158–168.

27. *Ibid.,* p. 159.

28. *Ibid.,* p. 161.

29. *Loc. cit.,* pp. 164–165.

30. The other members of this subcommission were Monsignors C. Colombo, Heuschen, Petit, van Dodewaard, Géraud, Lambruschini and Prignoni; Canons Delhaye and Heylen; Fathers Schillebeeckx and van Leeuwen; and Messrs. Work, Minoli, and Adjakpley.

31. The voting on November 17 covered the rest of the chapters of this Part II of the *schema.*

32. In Xavier Rynne, *The Fourth Session: The Debates and Decrees of Vatican Council II,* September 14 to December 8, 1965, N.Y., 1966, p. 213.

33. The following explanation of this *modus* was offered in the general assembly of December 3: "The Commission admits that the word *etiam* is somewhat ambiguous. It was included in the text, as is explained clearly in the *Relatio* . . . not in order to settle the question of the hierarchy of ends, but in order to emphasize that procreation is not the sole end of marriage. But if the word *etiam* is simply deleted, the clause could then seem to some to suggest that the other ends of marriage are not to be considered. In order to avoid this the Commission proposes that *etiam* be deleted, but at the same time there be added, after the words *indole oriens,* the clause "While not making the other ends of marriage of less account." In order to emphasize the importance of children let there be inserted at the beginning of the paragraph . . . the following addition: 'Children are really the supreme gift of marriage and contribute very substantially to the welfare of their parents." (In *Acta Synodalia,* Vol. IV, Periodus 4, Pars 7: Congregationes Generales CLXV-CLXVIII, Sessiones Publicae IX-X.)

34. This chapter on marriage and the family is in English translation in *The Documents of Vatican II,* Walter M. Abbott, S.J., general editor, N.Y., 1966, pp.

249–258. Outside the *Acta Synodalia* the Latin text is available in *Sacrosanctum Oecumenicum Concilium Vaticanum II: Constitutiones, Decreta, Declarationes,* Città del Vaticano, 1966 and 1974.

35. This *expensio modorum* is in pages 469–509 of the volume of the *Acta Synodalia* recorded in Note 33 just above.

36. *Op. cit.,* pp. 235–236.

37. In the long view of the history of Catholic thinking on marriage it is striking that the bishops treated the notion of marriage as contract at least with simple neglect or, to stay closer to the facts of the case, with calculated rejection. Nowhere in the chapter is the term "contract" so much as suggested, either in its nominal form (*contractus*) or in its verbal form (*contrahere*). This cannot have been a consequence of oversight. An assembly of over 2,400 bishops, hundreds of them canonists by education and avocation, cannot without deciding to do so have discarded the word and concept that had for the preceding seven centuries been predicated universally of marriage.

38. The English-language edition's translation (p. 250) of *instaurare* as "*rooted in* the conjugal covenant of irrevocable personal consent" misses first of all the signification of the Latin verb. I have found no Latin lexicon which even hints that "rooted in" is the signification of this verb. It also misses the meaning in the minds of the authors of the draft, and of the bishops, because the passage's purpose is to name the kind of act that creates a marriage.

39. *Acta Synodalia, loc. cit.,* p. 471.

40. *Ibid.,* pp. 471–472.

41. *Op. cit.,* p. 476.

42. *Ibid.*

43. *Ibid.,* p. 477.

44. *Ibid.*

45. *Op. cit.,* pp. 479–480.

46. The authentic Latin text of the encyclical is in *Acta Apostolicae Sedis,* Vol. 60 (1968) pp. 481–503. It is available in English translation in the Paulist Press edition, *Encyclical of Pope Paul VI, Humanae Vitae, On the Regulation of Birth . . .* 1968.

47. This second reason for rejecting the commission's recommendation raises two questions about the commission's goal in doing its work. Early in the encyclical (paragraph 5) Paul says: "That commission . . . had as its scope the gathering of opinions on the new questions regarding conjugal life, and in particular on the regulation of births, and of furnishing opportune elements of information so that the magisterium could give an adequate reply to the expectation not only of the faithful but also of world opinion."

If the charge given to the commission was first to gather opinions and then to furnish information, why did it go so far beyond this charge as to make a recommendation? And why, in rejecting the recommendation, did Paul not do so because it had gone beyond its charge instead of doing so because its recommendation disagreed with traditional teaching?

I have had the opportunity to discuss these questions with Fr. Josef Fuchs, a member of the commission and one of the writers of its report containing the recommendation. In his explanation to me he intended to account for no one but himself. To the first of these questions he replied that he simply must have misunderstood the charge given the commission. To the second he had no answer.

48. *Papal Teachings: Matrimony,* p. 224.

49. *Op. cit.,* p. 250. A person examining Pius' logic would expect to find him explaining that periodic continence's maintaining the subordination of the secondary end to the primary consists of a couple's never having intercourse for the sake of the secondary end with the intent to void the primary end. But this is not his explanation, as it cannot be, since the couple does intend to void the primary end of intercourse. They do so by intending to have intercourse but to avoid conception while having and despite having it. Pius' explanation of their safeguarding the subordination is that the couple does not interfere with the act of intercourse itself. Safeguarding the subordination seems thus to be a matter of not preventing the meeting of sperm and ovum when they could otherwise meet. Does one conclude then that Pius did not consider the subordination of the ends in intent immoral provided the ends are not subordinated in the technique of performing intercourse? If this conclusion is consistent with Pius' reasoning, what is immoral about the use of the oral steroid, the "pill"? It involves no interference with the act of intercourse. And the woman using it has the same intent as a woman practicing 'rhythm: to avoid conception despite having intercourse.

11. THE DEFINING OF MARRIAGE SINCE VATICAN II AND *HUMANAE VITAE*

It is obvious that with the Second Vatican Council's promulgation of *Gaudium et spes* and with Pope Paul VI's publication of *Humanae vitae* two major instruments of the Catholic regulation of marriage had to be changed. One of these was Title 7, *De matrimonio,* of the Code of Canon Law. The other was a derivative of this law once it was revised, the jurisprudence at work in the Church's tribunals, the use of the law in adjudicating petitions for nullity and for ecclesiastical dissolution.

This chapter will consist mainly of an examination of the changes made, or at least under way, in these two instruments, the marriage law and the jurisprudence in the marriage courts. The examination of the latter will consist of an inspection of a few select decisions handed down by the Roman Rota, of a critical ruling by the Sacred Signatura, and of a discourse by Pope Paul VI already mentioned a number of times in this study. (It is interesting, although not uncommon in the history of law, that with the Catholic marriage law the revision of the jurisprudence has run on ahead of the revision of the code of law. Or to put it more exactly, the law's revision has got under way in its jurisprudence before doing so in its code. Many tribunals in Western nations have, since the late 1960's and early 1970's, been using the informal definition of marriage in *Gaudium et spes* and *Humanae vitae* as their functioning criterion for judging validity or nullity in marriage cases. To do this they must set aside the definition still in effect in the incumbent Code.)

The Definition in the Revised Marriage Law

When a society revises its code of law it does so presumably because it judges that its incumbent law does not serve its members satisfactorily in directing them to that society's goals. By 1959 Pope John XXIII had come to this judgment about the Catholic Church's Code of Canon Law that had been promulgated forty-two years earlier. On January 25 of that year, in the same homily delivered in Rome's basilica of St. Paul during which he announced the future convocation of the Second Vatican Council, he announced also that the Church would revise the entire Code.

This examination will confine itself, among the canons concerning marriage, to those containing the "defining clauses"—those clauses in Canons 1012, 1013, 1081, 1082, and 1086, according to the numbering of the Code, all of which have received a new numbering and a new arranging in the revision.[1]

It is important to know that three interlocked groups worked at revising the Code. A commission has supervised the revision of the entire Code. It has Cardinal Pericle Felici as its president. Under this commission's supervision several subcommissions (*coetus*) worked on the sub-sections of the Code. These were each managed by a secretary and a *relator,* or sub-secretary who organized the subcommission's work. These subcommissions worked under the supervision of Cardinal Felici, who attended and presided at their most important sessions.

Overseeing the commission itself was a *plenarium* of cardinals, about thirty in number, with Cardinal Felici presiding here too by reason of his office as president of the revising commission.

The work of revising took the following path and sequence. First the subcommission formulated the revision of the title of the Code assigned to it. This piece of revision was sent, via the president of the commission, to the Pope for his judgment on its initial suitability for inspection by other agencies in the Church. If it was judged suitable the president then sent it out to these agencies—to the national conferences of bishops around the world, to the faculties of canon law in pontifical universities, to canon law societies in several nations, to the officers (dicasteries) of the papal curia, to the superiors general of religious orders.

These agencies were invited to send to the commission their criticisms of the revised section. The commission turned these criticisms over to the subcommission, which reworked the revised formulation in light of the criticisms. The reworked formulation was then sent to the *plenarium* of cardinals for their inspection, criticism and reformulation, if needed. The *plenarium* then sent it back to the subcommission for final rephrasing.

The *plenarium* of cardinals met in Rome during the week of May 22–28, 1977 to review and amend the revision of the marriage law completed to that date by the subcommission. The subcommission had completed its own preliminary revision in 1975, and had sent it, via the president of the commission, to the critical agencies named above. To understand what the cardinals did at their 1977 meeting we must first review briefly what the subcommission had done in its work until 1975.

Recall that the Code of Canon Law has no definition of marriage in the formal sense of this term. It identifies marriage within no category of being; it does not locate its essential elements under genus and species. Recall too that the first canon of the marriage law, Canon 1012, is not even an attempt at an informal definition, but an assertion of an event in the history of marriage and of a religious fact resulting from the event.

1. Christ Our Lord has elevated the contract of marriage to the dignity of a sacrament.

2. Therefore it is impossible for a valid contract or marriage between baptized persons to exist without being by that very fact a sacrament.

It seems clear that in both its paragraphs the canon takes for granted that a marriage anywhere at any time was, is and will be a contract. Only slightly less clearly does paragraph 2 take for granted that nothing more is needed to make a marriage a sacrament than that both parties to it have been baptized.

In its 1975 proposal for the revision of this canon the subcommission saw no reason to change it at any point. (An exception to the apparent consensus among the subcommission's consultors was Fr. Peter Huizing, the *relator,* who was so dissatisfied with the group's entire revision of the marriage law that he later wrote and published his own recommended revision of it.[2])

During the ten months that the subcommission's proposed revision was in the hands of the national conferences of bishops, of the regional canon law societies, *et al.,* this refusal by the subcommission to see any need for reformulating Canon 1012 came under severe criticism. This bore mainly upon two points. The first was the assumption that any and every marriage is a contract, and its attendant ignoring that the bishops of Vatican II had abandoned this concept and replaced it with the biblical image of marriage as a covenant. The second was the assumption that any marriage of two baptized persons is a sacrament by the mere fact of their having been baptized.

About the subcommission's insistence on referring to marriage as a contract, the Canon Law Society of America had the following to say:

The draft repeatedly refers to marriage as a "contract." This is contrary to Vatican II as well as to the traditional sources of faith. These have used such terms as "covenant," "communion," etc. In fact, Vatican II uses a variety of terms precisely because no one term adequately expresses the richness of the mystery of marriage. It might be better to use no category but simply refer to *matrimonium.* The issue is not simply a matter of terminology. The "contract" emphasis colors the draft's entire approach to marriage. The sacrament appears to be more of a juridical entity than a theological-pastoral one.[3]

The subcommission's reaction to this and other criticisms of its refusal to alter Canon 1012 was a relaxed one. How it proposed to deal with these and seven other comprehensive criticisms of its *schema* of revision it explained in this way:

> The consultors [in the subcommission] made some comment on each of the general issues touched [in the criticisms], but determined to make no decisions of a general nature because of them, since these criticisms have come from only a very few of the groups reviewing the *schema,* while on the contrary the majority of them was pleased with it. The consultors will keep these general criticisms in mind so that when examining individual canons they may propose changes in them—if such proposals they have—which may take the criticisms into consideration.[4]

On the second point, the sacramentality of every marriage of baptized persons, the American group voiced one of its most trenchant criticisms.

> An area of profound theological-canonical investigation today is the identity of the sacrament and every marriage relationship among the baptized. . . . This identity is a fundamental principle underlying the draft. Yet such automatic sacramentality of marriage among the baptized is questioned because of a renewed sense of the sacraments as actions of faith within the Church . . . . In Aquinas and other medieval theologians there was a strong sense of a real distinction between marriage as *officium naturae* [a dutiful office of nature] and marriage as *sacramentum novae legis* [a sacrament of the new law]. This issue of automatic sacramentality needs further study, wider consultation and authentic teaching by the College of Bishops before it is "frozen" into new law.[5]

But despite its initial reaction to the American and other criticisms, the subcommission did in the end modify the revision of Canon 1012 substantially at one point, while leaving it at another just as it had proposed it in 1975. This appears in the final draft of the proposed revision given to the Pope in the spring of 1978, which we shall examine presently. What had happened in the meantime to bring about the change? While the subcommission worked, between February 1977 and February a year later, at producing this final draft in light of the criticisms of the 1975 draft received from around the world, the *plenarium* of cardinals met, as I have mentioned earlier, in Rome in the last week of May 1977 to put its hand to the revision. Since this was a supervisory group, the subcommission was answerable to it. And among the cardinals enough challenged the retention of the Canon 1012 formulation so vigorously that their peers in the *plenarium* voted with them to send the latter back to the subcommission to rework it according to the mind and vocabulary of *Gaudium et spes.* By February 2, 1978 the subcommission completed the mandated reworking not only of this canon but of others in the revised marriage law.

The result in the final draft shows that the subcommission yielded on one point of criticism of Canon 1012 but resisted on another. In the canon now renumbered as Canon 242 there are still two paragraphs. But the first of them begins with a quasi-definition of marriage that is taken not quite verbatim from the first words of Paragraph 48 in *Gaudium et spes.*

> 1. The marital covenant, by which a man and a woman create between themselves an intimate sharing in all of life, a sharing which of its nature is oriented to the good of the spouses and to the procreation and nurture of children, has been raised, where it is of baptized persons, to the dignity of a sacrament.[6]

Paragraph 2, where the subcommission resisted even the criticism of the cardinals in the *plenarium,* remains unchanged from its wording in Canon 1012: "Therefore it is impossible for a valid contract of marriage between baptized persons to exist without being by that very fact a sacrament."

Reading paragraph 1 of new Canon 242 carefully one finds, I think, that although the biblical notion of covenant (*foedus*) has been accepted into the new understanding of marriage, marriage as a relationship has not yet been called a covenant. Rather, the term "covenant" is limited to designating the consent that creates a marriage. Thus "... *foedus quo vir et mulier... constituunt... communionem*" ("The covenant by which a man and a woman ... create ... a sharing"). Clearly the creating of the communion is called the covenant, not the communion itself.

Does this formulation, on the other hand, admit that what a marriage is, is a man's and a woman's intimate sharing or communion in all of life? I think it does. But this becomes evident only if one reasons inferentially and compares the clause here with earlier magisterial statements. That is, here the sharing or communion in all of life is said to be oriented to procreation and nurture, and to be thus oriented as a trait of its nature (*indole sua naturali*). In earlier documents, for example in the 1917 Code itself, the equivalent of this orientation, namely the primary end of marriage, is said to be procreation and nurture. The conclusion: if that of which procreation and nurture were said to be the primary end is marriage itself, then that of which they are said in the new canon to be a natural orientation is marriage itself.

To be noted too is the choice of the subcommission to call marriage a *communio* rather than the *communitas* that *Gaudium et spes* calls it. And the subcommission repeated Canon 1012's assertion of the historical fact that Christ has raised marriage the natural relationship, when it is formed by two baptized persons, to a sacrament. However, here in the new Canon 242 it is the covenant, the *foedus,* that Christ has thus raised, not the contract. But if what I suggest just above is accurate—that the term *foedus* here refers not to the marriage as a relationship or institution, but to the act of consent creating the marriage—then the canon falls short of saying that Christ has made marriage among Christians a sacrament.

About paragraph 2 of Canon 242 the subcommission did a strange thing. After having banished the term "contract" from paragraph 1 and substituted for it "covenant," in paragraph 2 it restored the term "contract" by repeating it in paragraph 2 of Canon 1012 without change. Thus, "Therefore it is impossible for a valid *contract* of marriage to exist without being by that very fact a sacrament" (italics added).

One can only guess that the reason for the subcommission's doing this in its last reworking of the canon, late in 1977 and early 1978, was identical with the reason it gave in 1976 to criticisms for its having persisted in referring to marriage as a contract in its original revision of 1975. The reason it offered was this, that the canon deals with marriage as a natural institution, and as such marriage is a contract.[7] Thus it appears that the consultors of the subcommission really thought not only that a marriage could be both a contract and an intimate sharing in all of life, but that what the covenanting act creating a marriage creates is a contract. We shall see in a few pages the subcommission's more exact statement of the nature of this act creating a marriage, while remembering that its consultors have said that as a natural institution a marriage is a contract.

The Revision of Canon 1013

It is in Canon 1013, become Canon 243 in the revision, that the most consequential change has been made. Canon 1013 comes closest, among all the canons of the incumbent Code, to a definition of marriage, and does so by stating its ends in paragraph 1, and its essential properties, or characteristics, in paragraph 2.

> 1. The primary end of marriage is the procreation and nurture of children; its secondary end is mutual help and the remedying of concupiscence.
> 2. The essential properties of marriage are unity and indissolubility, which in Christian marriage gain special firmness from its being a sacrament.

During their meeting in May 1977 the cardinals of the *plenarium* gave long and serious attention to the reformulation of this canon. They knew that its destiny was to serve, along with new Canon 242, as the Church's functional definition of marriage. Judgments of nullity, even decisions for and against ecclesiastical dissolution, would be determined in great part by the wording of this canon.

But to understand how they eventually worded it, and why they did so, we must trace backward through the history of the canon's revision to about 1971.

The following is the proposed formulation that the subcommission sent to the president of the commission in 1975, to be distributed for the general criticism I have described above.

> 1. A marriage, which is created by the consent described in Canons 295 and following,[8] is a man's and woman's (intimate) joining in all of life, which of its nature is oriented to the procreation and nurture of children.[9]
>
> 2. The essential properties of marriage are unity and indissolubility, which in Christian marriage gain special firmness from its being a sacrament.

Paragraph 2 here is unchanged from the wording in Canon 1013. The major change is obviously in paragraph 1, which makes no mention of ends of marriage. It says rather what a marriage is, almost but not quite repeating verbatim the first clause of Canon 242. And in place of procreation as a primary end it locates it where *Gaudium et spes* has it, as a natural orientation of marriage.

In its own earlier report of 1971 the subcommission had explained what it regarded as its most significant task in formulating this new canon as a revision of Canon 1013. This was to express in one and the same paragraph the personal relationship of the spouses and marriage's natural orientation to procreation as the latter is stated in *Gaudium et spes*. The idea of this natural orientation is taken from the first clause of Paragraph 48 and the first clause of Paragraph 50 in the conciliar document, and is in fact a conflation of the two. Actually both clauses include marital love in this orientation. Paragraph 48 begins: "*Intima communitas vitae et amoris coniugalis....*" Paragraph 50 begins: "*Matrimonium et amor coniugalis indole sua naturali... ordinantur.*" The exclusion of love from the concept taken otherwise whole from *Gaudium et spes* was consistent with the general unwillingness to find a place for marital love in the Church's marriage law, for the reason, as so many Roman canonists were to explain, that there is no place for it in the law.

What the subcommission strove to do during its early reworking of Canon 1013 was to incorporate the council's resolution of the doctrinal dispute about the ends of marriage that had exercised Pius XI, Pius XII, the Congregation of the Holy Office, and the bishops of Vatican II themselves, and had brought on the striking intervention by Pope Paul on the eve of the council's final vote and adjournment. What they did the consultors of the subcommission explained simply in their 1971 report.

> Following the council's lead the subcommission decided not to include the concepts of primary end (the procreation and nurture

of children) and of secondary end (mutual help and the remedying of concupiscence).[10]

But this report does not explain why, in borrowing from *Gaudium et spes* the new understanding of marriage as a personal relationship, the consultors omitted the conciliar document's marital love. Nor does it explain why it made a significant change in the key substantive of the conciliar formulation. For where the bishops had said that a marriage is an intimate *communitas,* the formulation of the new canon said that it is an intimate *coniunctio.*

The reason for the subcommission's refusing to follow *Gaudium et spes* by omitting from this defining canon any reference to marital love was almost certainly the foreboding with which this love was discussed virtually from the moment the revision of the marriage law got under way. In one of his meetings with the subcommission Cardinal Felici expressed his opinion that if love were included in the revised Code's understanding of marriage, there is hardly a marriage in existence that could not be suspected of nullity.[11]

Six years later than this first report of the subcommission, during the *plenarium's* meeting in May 1977, Cardinal Pietro Palazzini urged first that the revised Code either contain no definition of marriage at all, or that it contain the quasi-definition of it in *Casti connubii.* But he was especially insistent that in any case the term "love" not appear in the Code's understanding of marriage—especially not as modified by the adjective "intimate." He warned of the serious consequences (*gravia consectaria*) that would come of including these terms in the Church's marriage law.[12]

Lacking the subcommission's own explanation one can only guess at why it changed *communitas,* the key substantive in *Gaudium et spes'* defining statement about marriage, to *coniunctio* in the revised canon. But it can be an informed guess. And when we look at the deliberations by the *plenarium* in May 1977, the guess passes into certitude. Both groups meant to state the nature of marriage not *in facto esse,* marriage as an existing state, but the nature of marriage *in fieri,* its coming into existence, which is not a state but an event. The noun *coniunctio,* as its last three letters indicate, designates an action. *Communitas* on the other hand, as also its last three letters indicate, designates a state of existence.

The cardinals of the *plenarium* proceeded in their deliberation on this canon in May 1977 by putting to themselves the following three *quaestiones de natura matrimonii:*

(a) Whether a concept of marriage ought to be included in the code. If so . . .

(b) Whether the definition ought to include the element of "conjoining of life" (or "communion," or "sharing" of life) as an expression of the personal aspect of marriage (*Gaudium et spes,* no. 48). If so . . .

(c) What should be the valence of this element in determining the validity of a marriage?[13]

They voted that, yes, a concept of marriage ought to be included in the revised code. But they urged that it take there a form both oblique and descriptive, presumably in preference to a formal definition.[14] They added the qualification that explains their keeping the substantive *coniunctio* instead of *communitas*. They wished the defining concept to refer to a marriage *in fieri*, to a marriage in its creation at the moment of consent. But what a marriage is in its nature as an abiding state they apparently wished the law not to say. Knowing what the Code's definition was likely to be, they meant it to refer only to the act which creates a marriage. With this vote went the admonition that expressions leading to false interpretations be kept out of the canon.

In their second vote the cardinals drew that much definition to a finer focus. They agreed, although with a weaker majority, that the element "conjoining of life" (or "sharing" or "communion" of life) be included in the definition. But again a kindred caution was urged, namely that in the final phrasing of the canon expressions be avoided that could open the way to false interpretations of the canon in the jurisprudential practice of the Church's marriage courts.

Answering the third and last of their own questions, about the valence of the element of communion, or sharing, in determining the validity of marriages, the cardinals voted by a still smaller majority that this element have valence in so determining. But again they urged their earlier qualification that this valence be limited to judging the validity of the consent creating a marriage, but that it have no valence in judging the validity of a marriage *in facto esse*, once it is established in existence. They wanted nothing in the Church's law vulnerable to the interpretation that once the "intimate sharing in all of life" disappears irretrievably from a marriage, the marriage dies out of existence.

Such was the long, painstaking and anxious deliberation that went into the reformulation of the first two canons of the law (1012 and 1013) that contribute to the defining of marriage. In the end, as we have seen, what the deliberation produced was the new Canon 242.1 with its significantly modified near-quotation of the first paragraph from *Gaudium et spes*, paragraph 48.

Kept also from Canon 1013 was its paragraph 2, which was renumbered Canon 243: "The essential properties of marriage are unity and indissolubility, which acquire a unique firmness in Christian marriage by reason of its sacramental character."

The Consent That Creates a Marriage

We have already seen that the consultors of the subcommission revising the marriage law agreed to move the erstwhile new Canon 295 specify-

ing the nature of marital consent backward in sequence to become Canon
244. In the 1917 Code this specification is in Canon 1081.2. The entire
canon is the following:

> 1. A marriage is created by the legitimately manifested con-
> sent of the parties to it, who are persons capable according to the
> law; this consent is one for which no human power can substi-
> tute.
>
> 2. Marital consent is an act of the will by which each party
> gives over, and accepts, exclusive and perpetual right to the
> body, a right ordered to those acts which are in themselves suit-
> able for the generation of children.

No paragraph in the 1917 Code sets out so clearly the contractual
conceptualization of marriage as does the second paragraph of this canon.
It names the object of the act of consent by which a man and a woman
create their marriage, that upon which their minds and wills bear in consenting. This is not their persons in any inclusive sense. It is a right that
each one has by nature, the right to his or her own body in its sexual acts
capable by nature of conceiving. In the consent each gives this right over
to the other, gives it permanently to the other and exclusively to the other.
From the moment of consent each owes sexual intercourse to the other by
an obligation in commutative justice. Their mutual act of exchange is contractual; the exchanged right is the contractual good; their subsequent exercise of the exchanged right in intercourse is the use of the contract, itself
an act of commutative justice—the giving of something owed. (Two
strangers can make this exchange, and can do it through proxies.) The
conditions essential for their making it are borrowed from the essential
properties of a marriage. Both must will exclusivity and permanence for
the exchange. (To create their marriage they need love one another in no
way other than being willing to make the exchange and hold to these conditions.)

In its proposal sent to the commission in 1971 the subcommission left
paragraph 1 of Canon 1081 unchanged. In paragraph 2 it made a significant change when naming the object of marital consent. But first it explained its reason for recommending this change.

> Here, as in Canon 1013, the teaching of the Second Vatican
> Council on marriage and marital consent demands several
> changes in the canons dealing with consent. This is true both in
> regard to the object of consent and in regard to defects of consent
> by exclusion of an essential element of this object.[15]

The second paragraph of this explanation contains the first and tentative reformulation of this paragraph 2.

> The subcommission recommended by majority vote that this
> consent be defined as an act of the will by which a man and a

woman by a mutual act of covenanting establish a perpetual and exclusive *consortium* of married life oriented of its nature to the procreation and nurture of children.[16]

The most significant elements of the Code's Canon 1081.2 omitted from this first formulation of new Canon 244 were contractual in nature, those that had been the last and irreducible refinement of the object of marital consent at the hands of Cardinal Gasparri and the other canonists of the first half of this century. The parties' exchange of the right to their sexual acts was abandoned. The act creating a marriage was still said to be volitional; it is the act of consent. It must also be mutual. But instead of being in substance a contractual exchange, it was called in the reformulation a covenanting. Further, instead of the exchange of rights, the object of the covenanting consent is a *consortium vitae coniugalis,* a community or sharing of married life.

The essentiality of procreation and nurture, no longer fixed (as in old Canon 1013.1) in the inherent principal end of marriage, is here (as in the new Canon 242.1) relocated in an orientation said to be natural to the kind of *consortium,* or sharing, that a marriage is.

But the draft of Canon 295 that finally went into the proposed revision of the Code in February 1978 as Canon 244 was both somewhat simpler and significantly different. Paragraph 1 remained unchanged from paragraph 1 of old Canon 1081. But the simplification appeared in paragraph 2, which differs from the 1971 formulation in two ways. The clause expressing the orientation to procreation and nurture is omitted, apparently in view of its already established presence in Canon 242. And instead of saying that the marital consent produces the *consortium* or sharing of married life, it has as its effect a mutual giving of the selves in order to create the marriage. And in adding the adjective "irrevocable" to characterize the consent, the canon repeats what *Gaudium et spes* had said in its paragraph 48, that the unbreakable holding power of a marriage is in the irrevocability of the act that creates it (rather than in the indissolubility of the contract, as the Code implies in Canon 1013.2).

Marital consent is an act of the will by which a man and a woman give themselves to and accept one another in an irrevocable covenant in order to create a marriage.[17]

The most striking difference of this formulation from that of 1971 is, I think, in what is named as the effect of the covenanting act of the will. There it was the *consortium* of married life, the relationship of the spouses to one another, perhaps no different from the *communitas vitae* of *Gaudium et spes,* or even from the ancient *consuetudo vitae.* Here it is the very persons themselves of the spouses—or more accurately the giving and accepting of their persons. That the Latin verb expressing this giving is *tradunt* rather than simply *donant* may not be without meaning. The former carries the sense of self-surrender, of a giving over of the self for the sake of another. In the Latin versions of the New Testament it is what Christ did for those he loved: *Tradidit semetipsum* . . . (Galatians 2:20).

The removing from this paragraph of the *consortium* of the 1971 formulation as the effect of marital consent leaves to Canon 242.1 to supply the one new substantive designating what a marriage is. This is a *communio,* a sharing, and, be it noted, a *communio omnis vitae,* a sharing of all of life.

Students of this revised law must be curious at the insistence on continuing to call marriage a contract in certain clauses, as happens in the unchanged second paragraph of Canon 1012 now become Canon 242: "Therefore it is impossible for a valid contract of marriage between baptized persons to exist without being by that very fact a sacrament." The vocabulary and the conceptualization in these new canons are so thoroughly from *Gaudium et spes,* which nowhere calls marriage a contract. And singular consequences emerge from this insistence where it meets the new formulations. The marital consent in the latter is a covenanting act, yet what it is apparently thought to produce is a contract. The consent is said in the new canons to have the persons of the spouses—these persons given and accepted—as its object. Are they, in virtue of the contract, themselves the exchanged contractual good? The other substantive in Canon 242.1 designating the marriage as a state (*in facto esse*) is *communio.* Is this *communio* identical with the contract?

This perplexity is not lightened when one comes upon the proposed revision of the other two canons contributing to the definition of marriage. The first of them, old Canon 1082 become new Canon 298, is a statement of the minimum understanding that a person may have of the nature of marriage in order to be capable of marital consent. Canon 1082.1 states it in the following way:

> In order that marital consent be possible it is necessary that the contracting parties be at least not ignorant that marriage is a permanent society between a man and a woman for the procreation of children.[18]

New Canon 298 makes two changes in this wording. It says that what a person must know about marriage *ad minimum* is that it is a permanent *consortium.* This brings back into the Code's repertory of nouns designating marriage one that had been in the 1971 revision of Canon 1081.2 (become at that time Canon 295), but banished from the 1975 reformulation (renumbered Canon 244). This was done in order to have this canon say that the effect of the marital consent is not to establish a *consortium* of married life, but to have the spouses give themselves to and accept one another. Presuming that this substituting of nouns was done carefully, reintroducing *consortium* here into Canon 298 appears to result in this, that the giving and accepting of persons in the marital consent creates a *consortium* (called earlier in Canon 243 a *communio,* a sharing in all of life). And whether one calls it a *communio* or a *consortium,* both Canons 243 and 298 say that it is of its nature oriented to procreation. Thus Canon 298:

> In order that marital consent be possible it is necessary that the contracting parties at least not be ignorant that marriage is a permanent *consortium* of a man and a woman oriented to procreation by some kind of physical cooperation.[19]

Why the second change from Canon 1082.1, the addition of the phrase "by some kind of physical cooperation"? I have found no explanation for this. But one reason at least for the addition seems to be a demand that the marital consent be a more aware and mature consent. The requirement in Canon 1082.1 that this consent demands only the knowledge that marriage is for procreation is an echo from a European society in which pre-adolescents and even children were put into marriage, and had to make the marital consent; but only the most rudimentary knowledge of conception could be expected of them.

The fourth and last canon making up the defining section of the law is old Canon 1086.2 become new Canon 303. Its intent is to specify those elements of marriage whose exclusion from the object of marital consent invalidates the latter. Canon 1086.2 reads as follows:

> But if either or both parties by a positive act of the will exclude marriage itself, or all right to the conjugal act or any essential property of marriage, the marriage contract is invalid.[20]

The new Canon 303 both makes an expected change here and fails to make one that could also be reasonably expected. Quite expectedly it says: ". . . if either or both parties by a positive act of the will exclude marriage itself or the right to those things which enter essentially into the sharing of life . . ."[21] replacing "the right to the conjugal act" at this point with "the right to those things that belong essentially to the *communio vitae*"—which is what Canon 242 says is created by the spouses' covenanting act. This reasonable substitution in the new canon would lead one to expect that "the right to the conjugal act" would simply disappear from it. But surprisingly it survives as the next phrase. Thus the entire new canon reads as follows:

> But if either party or both parties by a positive act of the will exclude marriage itself or the right to those things which enter essentially into the sharing of life, or the right to the conjugal act, or any essential property of marriage, the marriage contract is invalid.

Two things are perplexing about this new formulation. First, it seems to imply that the right to sexual intercourse is not included in the right to those things that enter essentially into the intimate sharing of all of life. It implies this by naming the two rights in separate phrases divided by the disjunctive particle *aut*. But if sexual intercourse is not one of the elements making up marriage's intimate sharing, what is? Is this a faint, lingering echo of the ancient dispute about what is contained in marriage's *consuetudo vitae?*

Second, it is no less perplexing that whereas Canon 295 says that the effect (or object) of marital consent is the spouses' covenantal giving over and accepting of their persons, here Canon 303 has it that the object of marital consent is, as old Canon 1081.2 reads, the *right*—or rather two rights. For it is the exclusion from marital consent of these rights, to intimate sharing and to intercourse, that invalidates the consent. This is retrograde. It leaves the way open to thinking of marriage still as a contract. It is still vulnerable to the legal logic which concludes that a man and a woman can be husband and wife provided that they exchange the rights to intercourse and to cohabitation, even though they intend from the beginning never to exercise either right. In the wording of this canon the essence of marriage still belongs among the legal categories.

The significance of these preliminary drafts—and of the reasoning behind them—of the new canon law of marriage is not difficult to appreciate. For one thing, the hierarchy of the ends of marriage, asserted in the Code of Canon Law and so strongly reaffirmed in subsequent papal and jurisprudential statements, is completely avoided. Secondly, the concept of marriage as a *consortium omnis vitae* has been given juridical import in the proposed new canons. The compilers of the new law justify the canonical status accorded the *consortium* by pointing to *Gaudium et spes;* and in a real sense they are correct. It might not be inaccurate to observe, nevertheless, that there is a slight difference of meaning between the concept as it appears in the teaching of *Gaudium et spes* and the *ius ad vitae communionem* [the right to the sharing of life] of the proposed law. In the conciliar document the notion first of all describes marriage as a *whole* while, secondly, highlighting its personal dimension. In the proposed law the same concept designates primarily a specific *ius matrimonii* [right of marriage], distinct from the *ius in corpus* [right to the body] and even from *matrimonium ipsum* [marriage itself]. As U. Navarrete has remarked, the *ius ad consortium vitae* [the right to the sharing of life] of the proposed law can be viewed as the practical equivalent of a *ius ad mutuum adiutorium* [a right to mutual help] if this latter expression is understood to refer to "mutual aid" not in a superficial and merely external manner, but in a more profound (and even biblical) sense; it is not, for instance, simply a question of the *communio mensae, lecti et tori* [sharing of table, bed and body] as is pointed out in the *schema*. The immediate problem raised—a problem clearly recognized by the compilers of the law—is the issue of determining concretely the rights and obligations encompassed by the *ius ad consortium vitae,* since it is proposed that this *ius* involve the very validity of marriage. Such a determination is the task not only of the law, but also—and perhaps chiefly—of ecclesiastical jurisprudence.[22]

Marriage Jurisprudence Since Vatican II

Thus far the agents of the gradually changing Catholic understanding of marriage since about the middle of this century that we have examined have been, in sequence, the bishops, philosophers and theologians who prepared the mind of the Second Vatican Council; the bishops of the council themselves; Pope Paul VI; the subcommission that drafted the revision of the Catholic marriage law; the many who criticized the draft; and lastly the cardinals of the *plenarium* who ordered and supervised the law's final formulation.

There is another group of persons making up a source of development that will be in the future more continually at work than any of those named just above. These are the judges of the Church's marriage courts. Their contribution is to develop the jurisprudence coming necessarily from the changed understanding of marriage, the developing of what still needs developing in it, whether by interpretation, by application, or by extension of it. This they do in writing decisions, as judges of the courts, in cases brought to their courts for adjudication. And the decisions they write are virtually all in response to petitions that supposed marriages be found null.

These judges have had to work in an unusual, and unusually difficult, jurisprudential situation. Ordinarily jurisprudential interpretation is of statutes in a code of law. The Catholic Church has a coherent system of statutes on marriage in her Code. But the judges of these courts, along with everyone else, know that crucial statutes in the marriage law have been at least put in juridical limbo, and more probably displaced and even superseded by what the bishops of Vatican II taught about marriage. (A few of the judges disagree about this displacing and superseding, as we shall see, but they are in a minority.) Consequently the jurisprudential interpreting under way is of a definition of marriage not in a code of law but in an apostolic constitution, in a formal and authoritative teaching document. And this interpretation must encompass two main tasks, it seems to me: it must understand the bishops' statements about the nature of marriage in *Gaudium et spes;* and having understood them it must use them in the *de iure* portions of the decisions regarding petitions for nullity or for ecclesiastical dissolutions of marriages.

As I understand the judges' jurisprudential enterprise since the council, they have worked mostly at answering three questions. The first has been asked by only a few and briefly. It is whether their interpretation, their informal definition of marriage, was intended by the bishops of Vatican II to go into the revision of the marriage law they had been told was to be done after the council. (I am convinced that this question has been answered once for all by the use of the very vocabulary itself of *Gaudium et spes,* paragraph 48, almost verbatim at some points, in the defining canons of the proposed revision of the law that we examined above. This was done by the *plenarium* of cardinals, most of them participants themselves in the council, and, as bishops, authorized teachers of the Church in a way that none of the disagreeing judges is.)

The second question asks whether the most nuclear elements of the bishops' understanding of marriage in *Gaudium et spes* belong to its essence—whether marriage is in fact "an intimate community of marital life and love," an "intimate union." As asked by jurists this question has a peculiarly juridical meaning that is not easily grasped by the non-jurist. In face of the fact that the bishops named marriage by these predicates, the jurist yet asks whether they are predicated of the *juridical* essence of marriage. And if one reads certain decisions rendered since Vatican II by a few judges of the Roman Rota, one detects that they asked whether these names are even *predicable* of marriage's juridical essence, which reveals that before and apart from *Gaudium et spes* these judges hold in mind a juridical definition of marriage that they use to judge the predicability of these names of marriage coming from the council. (I hope to show in the final chapter in virtue of which assumptions they bring an apostolic constitution of a general council of the Church under the judgments they do.) A sub-set of this same question asks whether the forming of the intimate community of marital life and love belongs to the essence of the object of marital consent, whether the man and woman in consenting commit themselves essentially to the forming of this community—with the consequence that if they are unable to do so with one another, or refuse to do so, their consent is invalid and the ensuing union is null as a marriage.

The third of these questions at which the developing jurisprudence has worked starts from the conclusion that the answer to the second question immediately above is affirmative—yes, the intimate community of marital life and love is of the juridical essence of marriage, and the commitment to forming it does belong to the object of marital consent. It asks thence what are the necessary and essential components of this community, of this union. If they can be verified, this consequence follows: that if a person cannot or will not produce one or more of them, at least with his partner, he cannot form the union with her, and his marital consent is invalid. For example, if interpersonal, heterosexual affective union is essential, or if the ability to parent effectively is essential, but he cannot provide either or both of these elements with this woman, his consent in attempting to marry her is invalid.

The decisions I will examine have been handed down by judges of the Roman Rota (decisions in courts of first instance, the diocesan tribunals, are reported sparsely, and they by nature have less jurisprudential value than do those coming from the higher and appellate court). I will divide the decisions according to three post-conciliar periods: the early years, 1966–1968, during which *Gaudium et spes* was for the most part ignored by the judges; the years 1969–1972, which saw the beginning of a jurisprudence drawing on the conciliar document, the period during which disagreement about the value and the use of it first appeared; and the third period, 1973–1978 (the last year of which record is available as this is being written), the period during which the disagreement has become controversy.[23]

Early Post-Conciliar Jurisprudence, 1966–1968

For the three years immediately following the adjournment of Vatican II on December 8, 1965 the thinking of the Rotal judges was still ruled unquestioningly by the quasi-definition of marriage worked out in the Code of Canon Law, the 1944 decree of the Holy Office, the discourses of Pius XII and the jurisprudence already established by such decisions as that of the judge Arthur Wynan in 1944. These simply took for granted that the essence of marriage is a contract whose good to be exchanged contractually is the two contractants' rights to their sexual acts—an understanding drawn necessarily from the premise that marriage's primary end is procreation and nurture. Given this interpretation it was impossible to find an essential place for the intimate community, or sharing, of marital life and love. But since *Gaudium et spes* valued them seriously, they must be given some place in marriage. What may this be? A decision written by a *turnus* of judges (*coram* Bejan)[24] on March 1, 1967 answered the question simply: the terms *consortium vitae* (the decision's version of *communitas vitae*) refer to nothing other than cohabitation, which does not belong to the essence of marriage.[25]

This same insistence on interpreting the *communitas vitae et amoris* as simply Vatican II's terms for what had for centuries been known as cohabitation surfaced in a Rotal decision of November 30, 1968 (*coram* Fiore). Of the juridical value of the key concepts from *Gaudium et spes* about the nature of marriage the decision had this to say:

> ... although today there are many who believe that in the light of the constitution *Gaudium et spes* (n. 48) the *intima communitas vitae et amoris coniugalis* is of the essence of the matrimonial contract, the Fathers of the Rotal *turnus* are of the opinion that this is to be completely denied; the reason is that the communion of habitation, bed and table belongs to the essence and integrity of the *individua vita* rather as an effect of validly given consent.[26]

Like the cohabitation that the judges appear to identify it with, the intimate community or sharing of life belongs not to the essence of marriage but to its completion or perfecting.

First Juridical Recognition of the *Communitas Vitae,* 1969–1972

That the *communitas vitae* of *Gaudium et spes* has a place in the essence of marriage even as this is understood juridically was first acknowledged in the Rota by the judge Lucien Anné. His decision written early in 1969 and handed down on February 25 was, in legal language, a landmark decision.[27] It marked the entry of *communitas vitae* into Catholic jurisprudential decision-making; it started a discussion and a controversy that still continue.

The decision was rendered in a petition for a decree of nullity made by a man whose presumed wife had begun a pattern of homosexual conduct with her lesbian lover at seventeen years of age, had interrupted this during the first years after the wedding, but had resumed it after the birth of their first child. It is significant that in the homosexual relationship, as she reported, she consistently and compulsively took the masculine, phallic role. The issue, the question, was whether her deeply rooted sexual inversion had rendered her incapable of marital consent because it had made her incapable of willing effectively the object of this consent. During the years that the presumed marriage survived she bore three children, and this was later taken as evidence that she did have the needed capacity to consent.

But in his *de iure* analysis of the law pertinent to the issue Anné reasoned that what Canon 1081.2 identifies as the object of marital consent—the perpetual and exclusive right to sexual acts—does not name the entirety of this object. It names only what is most specific to marriage within the total object, especially when the right to sexual acts is taken only in a physical sense. *Gaudium et spes,* he insisted, names other elements of this object.

> This formulation of Vatican Council II [*"Intima communitas vitae et amoris coniugalis . . . instauratur . . . actu humano quo coniuges sese mutuo tradunt et accipiunt"* ("The intimate sharing of marital life and love . . . is created . . . by a human act in which the spouses mutually give over and accept one another")] has juridical significance. For it looks, not to the mere fact of inaugurating a community of life, but to the *right and obligation* to this intimate community of life, which has as its most specific element an intimate union of persons by which man and woman become one flesh, a union to which, *as its summit,* that community of life tends. This points out that marriage is a *most personal relationship* and that matrimonial consent is an act of the will whereby the spouses "mutually hand over and receive *each other.* . . ."[28]

Anné went on to make a crucial point that, intentionally or not, contradicted an equally crucial claim in the decisions of Bejan, Fiore and Fagiolo. They had taken for granted that the intimate community of life of *Gaudium et spes* refers to nothing more than what is already understood in traditional jurisprudence as cohabitation. Anné insisted that it designates something more and something essential to marriage. To explain what he meant he offered his own interpretation-definition of marital consent.

> ... an act of the will whereby a man and a woman establish, by a mutual pledge or irrevocable consent, a *consortium vitae coniugalis* which is perpetual and exclusive and which of its very nature is ordered to the generation and education of offspring.
> Thus the formal substantial object of this consent is not only the *ius in corpus* [the right to the body], perpetual and exclusive, ordered to acts naturally suitable for the generation of offspring, to the exclusion of any other formal essential element; rather it comprises also the *ius ad vitae consortium seu communitatem vitae* [the right to the sharing of life, or the community of life] which is properly considered matrimonial; and it comprises likewise corresponding obligations, that is, the *ius ad "intimam personarum atque operum coniunctionem"* [the right to the intimate joining of persons and of actions] by which [the spouses] "perfect each other in order to collaborate with God in the procreation and education of new lives" (Enc. *Humanae vitae*).[29]

Having said that Anné addressed the difficulty which has forced itself inevitably and justly on all Catholic jurists who demand that the essentiality to the object of marital consent (and therefore to the capacity to marry) of the intimate community of life and love be acknowledged. This difficulty lies in identifying which exactly are the ingredients of this intimate community or sharing. What is it that a person must be capable of sharing if he or she is to be capable of making valid marital consent?

Anné prefaced his answer to these questions by acknowledging that it is indeed difficult to list those traits which are essential to the sharing of life that is in turn essential to marriage. He suggested that there are three aspects of marriage that have always to be kept in mind: the natural law element, in which the essential comes from the Creator's primeval design for marriage; the cultural element, where there is clear evidence that the sharing of life has taken strikingly different forms in different cultures; and finally the particular, real-life, existential situation of the man and woman in question. This is the territory proper to the ecclesiastical judge. And here the latter must be alert to two fundamental psychic deficiencies that make persons incapable of marital consent (apart from obvious mental deficiency preventing a person from making the act of consent at all). One of these deficiencies is a paranoid disorder of affectivity preventing a person's giving himself into union with another in any sense. The other is a serious deflection or perversion of the sexual instinct.

It was in virtue of this second deficiency that Anné seems to have wanted to rule affirmatively on this petition for nullity. He reasoned that the woman's emotional perception of herself as the male partner in her lesbian relationship kept her from giving herself into her marital relationship emotionally as a woman and thus as a wife. Being incapable of doing this she could not, in her attempted marital consent, commit herself to the feminine side of the heterosexual marital community. (But the other two judges of the *turnus* disagreed with Anné, apparently because of added evidence of the wife's jealousy born of other women's attraction to her husband. And the petition for nullity was finally denied.)

But what was significant about this decision was the place within the juridically verifiable essence of marriage—a place acknowledged for the first time in judicial reasoning at the Rota level of the intimate sharing of marital life and love. By the end of 1972 Anné had handed down four more decisions in which he reaffirmed his conviction that this sharing belongs to the juridical essence of marriage. In a decision of July 22, 1969 he refined his thinking to this point: that for a person to have the capacity to commit himself to marriage as *Gaudium et spes* understands it, he himself must be able to understand it as a relationship of interpersonal communication, and in order to have this understanding he must have reached sufficient intrapersonal and interpersonal integration by the time he attempts marriage.

> Conjugal life, that is, marriage *in facto esse,* is lived out most particularly in interpersonal communication, underlying which, for both parties, is a healthy interpersonal orientation (*sana ordinatio interpersonalis*). And so if the life-history of the one who marries is judged by experts to indicate clearly that even before the marriage he seriously lacked intrapersonal and interpersonal integration (*graviter deficere integrationem intrapersonalem et interpersonalem*), then that person should be deemed incapable of understanding adequately the very nature of the communion of life which is ordered to the procreation and education of offspring—that is, marriage. . . .[30]

In this decision Anné pointed to a fact of life that was to be noted frequently by judges in the lower courts: that a person may be able to commit himself to other enterprises and other relationships, such as those in the business world, and sustain and bring them to success, while yet being incapable of forming and sustaining a marriage.

Another judge of the Rota, Mario Pompedda, in a decision of December 22, 1969, borrowed from the principle in *Humanae vitae* that the two meanings of marriage, the procreative and the unitive, are inseparable. Referring to the unitive meaning under the heading of "secondary end of marriage," he gainsaid some illustrious predecessors by insisting that this too belongs to the juridical essence of marriage. He concurred with Anné's judgment of February 25 of that year that the object of marital consent cannot be restricted to the physical realm. Because of the inseparability of the procreative and unitive meanings of marriage, the love-union too must be included in the object of consent.

A decision almost as significant as Anné's for opening up hitherto untouched juridical territory was one of the judge Vincenzo Fagiolo of October 30, 1970. In it he affirmed that marital love must have a necessary place in the making of marital consent. He seems to have said that this place is that of a cause necessary for the forming of the sharing of life and therefore for making the marital consent. But more than that, he saw love as a formal cause of marriage, one of its essential *internal* components, without which the relationship cannot be a marriage. The substance of this love, he seems to say, is the spouses' mutual self-giving and accepting that are oriented by nature to children.

> In order that matrimonial consent attain its object, the person must know and will the *consortium of life,* i.e., the community of life, between a man and a woman in accord [with] the essence peculiar to its institution. This *consortium* supposes a mutual giving of a man and a woman. This giving is done by a true and authentic and unfaked consent, and in this is conjugal love.
>
> If, with St. Thomas (Summa Theol. q. XLV, art. II [sic] and Vatican II, in *Gaudium et spes,* nn. 48, 49, we say that matrimonial consent is the act of the will by which each party willingly consents to give and receive each other in a community of life which by its very nature is ordered to the procreation and education of children, then it is not difficult for us to have a more profound knowledge of marriage questions and in making laws to follow it, a knowledge which admits that conjugal love is an element proper to marriage, and has force and effect both in its efficient cause and in its formal cause, that it is the truth and the authenticity of the consent, and the integrity of the object of consent.[31]

In a decision of November 27 of that year Fagiolo added his own to the gathering judgment that the sharing of life is to be included in the object of marital consent: ". . . matrimonial consent looks not only to 'acts which are naturally suitable for the generating of offspring,' but the total object of marriage (unity, indissolubility, the intimate community of life, etc.)."[32]

Early Opposition to the *Communitas Vitae*

It is to be expected that during the first post-conciliar period, from 1969 to 1972, Rotal decisions denying an essential place in marriage to the *communitas vitae* would be few. These would not appear until decisions giving it a place had established themselves on record and the judges, perceiving this as a threat, had begun to react. But the judges José Pinto, on July 20, 1969, and Giuseppe Palazzini, on June 2, 1971, wrote decisions in which they denied that love is a juridical element in marriage, although they said nothing decisive about the place of the *communitas vitae* in the object of marital consent. Palazzini wrote his decision on a routine appeal by the Rotal Defender of the Bond in the same petition for nullity in which Fagiolo had decided favorably on October 30, 1970. He confirmed Fagiolo's decision for nullity but disagreed thoroughly with the place that the latter had given to marital love in his sentence. Palazzini acknowledged that *Gaudium et spes* speaks of marriage within a dominant context of love, and that love runs as a kind of thematic melody through its entire chapter on marriage and family. But his judgment on the place of love in marriage was the following:

> The appellate judges of that *turnus* concentrated so intently on the place accorded marital love [in *Gaudium et spes*] that in writing their extremely elaborate opinion they seem to have given an exaggerated value to this love. They ranked it almost equally with marital consent itself. They even produced a novel interpretation of this court's jurisprudence in giving excessive weight to the defect of marital love in judging the nullity of marriage.
>
> Since a marriage is created by the consent of the parties . . . the judges [of this *turnus*] are of the opinion . . . that the importance of marital love cannot be so magnified that deficiency in this love is ranked equally with defect of intent in judging the validity of a marriage.
>
> In other words, we have decreed that it is impossible to depart from the old and constant teaching, sanctioned by the Church's *magisterium,* that a marriage depends wholly on the consent not only as its *materia* but also as its *forma* (which latter is more in conformity with marriage as a sacrament).
>
> Indeed we consider the interpretation that the sacrament of marriage consists essentially in the contract itself—in the covenant of marriage, the irrevocable personal consent—to be Catholic doctrine and expressly acknowledged and confirmed in the constitution *Gaudium et spes* itself, n. 48.
>
> And though a marriage is ordinarily contracted for motives of benevolence and love, so that a lack of love may be a kind of sign of simulation of consent, yet a lack of love cannot be said to be of itself and absolutely incompatible with true marital consent, which can be motivated by other considerations than love.[33]

In short, according to Palazzini's appellate judgment, love is needed for the forming of a marriage in no really essential way at all.

The Accelerating Jurisprudential Controversy, 1973 to the Present

A decision written by the Rotal judge J. M. Serrano on April 5, 1973 took the *communitas vitae* another step deeper into marriage—into the object of marital consent. Serrano discussed thoroughly the trait of marriage that is so unique to it, that puts it in significant ways beyond comparison with any other juridical entity. This is its interpersonal character. Thus it is not enough to say that in a marriage the spouses give and receive rights. If one is to talk of marriage "rights," these are in a real sense the persons of the spouses themselves: ". . . it must at least be maintained that matrimonial consent is given by persons insofar as these persons are themselves not completely distinct from the rights and obligations which are given and received."[34] In arguing for the essentiality in marriage of the interpersonal relationship Serrano expressly denied what had been said for decades and even centuries before him: that the interpersonal relationship belongs only to the *bene esse* of marriage, to its fullness, its ideal completion secondary to its substantial essence. He hedged a bit, apparently wary of saying that the marriage exists only if the interpersonal character exists, by confining the essential demand for this only to the *matrimonium in fieri*, the act of consent creating a marriage. This it is, this marital consent, that must be the giving and accepting of the spouses themselves.

> While it must be concluded that an "inter-personal" relationship can reach greater or lesser perfection for different spouses, it is in no way admissible to claim that it belongs entirely to the "more perfect" or the "desirable" ideal marriage, because, as has been said, it constitutes an "essential property" of each and every marriage "in fieri." If [this relationship] is totally lacking, the marriage itself is non-existent.[35]

Serrano took a second step in this jurisprudential development of interpersonality in his decisions of April 30, 1974 and July 9, 1976. The first of these ruled in a case involving apparent hyperaesthesia and homosexuality. His most significant opinion here was that the interpersonal relationship demanded essentially by marriage demands also that the partners be capable of engaging in sexual relations in a way "worthy of human dignity." He drew this statement in part from *Gaudium et spes,* Paragraph 49:

> The actions within marriage by which the couple are united intimately and chastely are noble and worthy ones. Expressed in a manner which is truly human, these actions signify and promote that mutual self-giving by which spouses enrich each other with a joyful and thankful will.[36]

Serrano insisted that this passage proposes more than a moral ideal. Granted that there are in even a stable marriage occasional failures in this

domain of intimacy, yet spouses must always be fundamentally capable of
a responsible and "human" sexual relationship with one another.

In his 1976 decision Serrano broke into jurisprudential territory that
had been until then almost untouched. He did this not so much in equating
the by then acknowledged *communitas vitae* with the interpersonal relationship in marriage. But he insisted that the rights and duties of marriage
are essentially relational in concrete circumstances. A man's or woman's
ability to sustain marital obligations cannot be judged while taking the person in isolation. It must be judged in his or her relationship with the intended spouse. It is their marriage attempted in real life that is at issue, not
some hypothetical marriage with just any hypothetical spouse. Thus a person's incapacity for marriage is always a relative incapacity, as his or her
capacity is also relative.

> In his insistence upon the interpersonal character of marriage,
> Serrano has stressed even more emphatically than Anné the per-
> sonal dimension of the *consortium,* and has explicitly extended
> the notion of "interpersonality" to sexual relations themselves
> (although by no means limiting it to this). He has expressed the
> opinion that it is often less profitable to concentrate on the objec-
> tive *iura matrimonii* [the rights of marriage] than on the subjec-
> tive condition of the parties themselves, specifically with respect
> to each other. At the same time Serrano has emphasized that
> only a serious and truly incapacitating psychic defect (regardless
> of how it might be medically classified) can radically prevent one
> from assuming the obligations of the *consortium vitae.*[37]

Lucien Anné, the judge who did so much in 1969 to begin the locating
of the *communitas vitae* in the essential heart of marriage, continued to
write decisions that added to the momentum of this jurisprudence. On
February 6, 1973 he decided in a petition for nullity of a union one of
whose partners was homosexual and in a degree ambisexual. He reasoned
that the *communitas vitae* must not only be heterosexual, and this not only
to the point of capacity for heterosexual intercourse. The union must also
be one in which there is a substantial and dominant affectivity, an affective
sexual orientation to the partner precisely insofar as he or she is of the other sex. If a person's deepest affectivity is oriented homosexually, he or she
is incapable of marital consent.

In a sentence of March 11, 1975 Anné found nullity because he
judged the psycho-moral character of the male partner to be so immoral,
so egoistic and hedonist that affectively and in effect he could not distinguish between marriage and concubinage. Lacking this ability he lacked
the "due discretion" about marriage and about himself vis-à-vis marriage
needed for the marital consent. He had not excluded the marriage itself or
fidelity or the *communitas vitae* by a deliberate act of will. Rather his con-

duct and his habitual attitude manifested a character incapable of forming and sustaining a marriage.

In a third decision, on December 4, 1975, Anné urged the consideration Serrano was to emphasize in his 1976 decision. This was to identify the *communitas vitae* with the interpersonal marital relationship. He cited Navarette's opinion that the right to the *communio vitae* is an essential marital right distinct from all other rights of marriage and separate from its three goods.

> At the core of this interpersonal conjugal relationship inherent in the heterosexuality of human beings—marriage *in facto esse*—is the state of mind of husband and wife, by which the spouses, despite human frailty and the grave, even very grave faults of one or the other, constantly strive, in their concrete circumstances, to bring into effect "that undefined and indefinable sum of attitudes, of behavior and of actions—varying in its concrete expressions in different cultures—without which it would be impossible to bring into being and keep in being that communion of life . . . which is necessary for the achievement, in a truly human way, of the ends which marriage is destined to achieve."[38]

In an unpublished decision of April 14, 1975 the judge Ignace Raad insisted that the personal dimension is part of the essential object of marital consent, and that the *communitas vitae* has juridical value in judging the reality or nullity of a marriage. The ability to live this *communitas* includes the ability of both spouses to live married life in a truly human fashion.

Raad's decision is noteworthy for its severe criticism of the attempts of some American and Canadian canonists to answer too exactly a question that hovers unavoidably over this developing jurisprudence of the *communitas*. It is a simple question, asking which exactly are the human capacities a man or woman must have in order to form this *communitas* and thus a marriage. One especially detailed attempt at listing these capacities was made by Fr. Germain Lesage of the Canon Law faculty of St. Paul University of Ottawa.[39] He listed thirteen characteristics of an integral capacity for forming a marriage that is the intimate community of life that *Gaudium et spes* and *Humanae vitae* describe. In the sequence he presents they are the capacity for oblatory love, a love that is not egoistic but which seeks the happiness of the partner; respect for conjugal morality and for the partner's conscience in sexual matters; respect for the partner's heterosexual sensitivity; responsibility in establishing conjugal friendship; responsibility in providing for the material necessities of the home; moral and psychological responsibility in conceiving children; parental responsibility in love and care of the children; maturity of personal conduct in the ordinary affairs of life; self-control and temperance; stability and the ability to adapt to changed circumstances; gentleness and kindness of character and manner; willingness and ability for mutual communication and consultation in important matters; objectivity and realism in evaluating events that are a part of married life.

In a later essay[40] Lesage reduced these elements to five major and inclusive categories: (1) the balance and maturity required for a genuinely human form of conduct; (2) the relationship of interpersonal and heterosexual friendship; (3) the aptitude for adequate collaboration with respect to conjugal assistance; (4) the mental equilibrium and sense of responsibility required for the material well-being of the family; (5) the psychological capacity of each partner in his or her own normal way to see to the well-being of the children.

Raad denied the possibility of identifying components universally necessary for the essence of marriage. He argued that each person must be judged in his unique situation, and concluded that if his or her personality is basically healthy the capacity to exchange marital rights is there. He demanded a serious psychic defect as evidence of inability to give and receive the right to the *communitas vitae.*

Denials of the Juridical Relevance of the *Communitas Vitae*

By no means were the judges of the Rota unanimous in accepting the *communitas vitae* and the capacity for a heterosexual, interpersonal love relationship within the juridical essence of marriage. Two of them especially, José Pinto and Sebastiano Masala, have argued seriously against them in certain of their decisions since 1973. Pinto has been especially insistent in his counter-position. His decision written on November 12, 1973 contains an excellent précis of the traditional canonical case against the jurisprudence that we have seen Anné, Fagiolo *et al.* develop.[41] In its parts the case is the following:

> (1) That marriage is to be understood according to its hierarchically ordered ends, and that the essential formal object of marital consent is the parties' right to their sexual acts, is the established teaching of the Catholic Church. This has been manifested and confirmed in Canons 1013.1 and 1081.2, in *Casti connubii,* in the 1944 decree of the Holy Office, in Pius XII's discourses, and in the jurisprudence of the Rota antedating Vatican II.
>
> (2) The *communitas vitae* and the various goods of marital love belong not to the juridical essence of marriage but to its integrity, its completeness.
>
> (3) Those who think the foregoing should be revised in view of *Gaudium et spes* and *Humanae vitae* err on two counts. First, *Gaudium et spes* did not intend to do away with the traditional teaching (Pinto cites the responses of the conciliar commission in its *Expensio modorum* on the pastoral intent of the constitution

in support of this interpretation). Secondly, it would be impossibly difficult to draw the line of distinction between the allegedly essential *communitas vitae* and the elements of marriage which all admit are merely complementary and completing. He singled out Germain Lesage's inventory of necessary qualities of character as an example of the disagreement that would follow acceptance of heterosexual interpersonal love into the juridical essence of marriage.

How peripheral to the juridical essence of marriage Pinto regarded the heterosexual love relationship he made clear in his decision of April 14, 1975, in which his *turnus* denied a petition for nullity of a marriage in which the husband was transsexual and a transvestite. He had fathered three children, although in order to have intercourse he had admittedly to imagine himself a woman. The judges of the *turnus* admitted that his condition was a serious sexual aberration. But they denied that it prevented the husband from exchanging his right to those sexual acts capable of conceiving. Therefore he was capable of the consent creating a marriage. That his aberration seriously damaged and even destroyed the affectivity of his heterosexual relationship was irrelevant to this capacity to form a marriage, lamentable though it was.

Pinto anticipated a rejoinder in making the following claim for the juridical nonessentiality of the community of life and love:

> From what has been said it is clear that the marriage of transsexuals, even though they be on occasion capable of complete sexual relations, would be invalid if it were proved that at the time of entering marriage they were unable to give and receive the right to the body *in perpetuum*.
>
> The fulfillment of this [duty] is not impeded by the fact that the man must imagine himself to be a woman in order to have sexual intercourse, or vice versa, just as the use of aphrodisiacs does not impede the consummation of a marriage (Holy Office, February 2, 1949).
>
> There is no objection [to our argument] from the fact that the expert Côté admits that it was impossible for the Defendant "to fulfill the duties of marriage in a healthy way and to establish a community of life and love." For first of all [the same expert] states: "It is not juridical freedom which is at issue here, but the aptitude to effect a happy marriage"; but this does not belong to the essence of marriage, however desirable it may be.[42]

This thinking Pinto confirmed in a decision of October 28, 1976, using the argument that a community of life and love offering the mutual help appropriate to marriage cannot belong to its essence because such a community could be formed between a brother and a sister. Nothing in this community or this mutual help names exactly enough the specific, differentiating element that makes such a relationship a marriage. This element can be nothing other than the exchange of the right to the parties' sexual acts.

In a decision of March 12, 1975 Sebastiano Masala developed the argument for his conclusion in part by tracing the history of its entry into Christian thought of the Roman concept of marriage as the *consuetudo* or *communitas vitae.* He did what so many of his predecessors had done: he reduced the meaning of the intimate community, insofar as it refers to the essence of marriage, to the spouses' exchange of the right to their sexual acts. He admitted another sense of the *communitas,* and this too was reductionist: it is cohabitation. And it does not belong to the juridical essence of marriage; it is not substantial to the object of marital consent.[43]

A decision written by Pinto on July 15, 1977 denying on appeal a petition for nullity on the ground of the woman's emotional incapacity for marriage deserves consideration at length because it defends so clearly the thesis that *Gaudium et spes* changed nothing of substance in the Catholic jurisprudence of marriage that had developed by 1962.[44]

Pinto began the decision with a succinct definition of marriage drawn without change from the Code of Canon Law. Having set this as a criterion for defining, he then cited and criticized paragraphs from the first-instance decision rendered in the tribunal of Toulouse.

> The appealed decision claims that the traditional teaching about the juridical structure of marriage has been changed through the years, for it observes that "one must take into account the recent evolution of the juridical concept of marriage, which emphasizes the quite central role that must be given the couple's harmonious relationship, to their marital love, and to all those elements that support and consecrate and continue them in the married state. . . . Especial note must be taken in this area of the directives and teaching coming from the Second Vatican Council, "The intimate community of marital life and love. . . ." These passages and the commentaries they have inspired mark a clear and welcome liberation from a concept of marriage too exclusively juridical, preserved until now under the aspect of marriage the contract. But we mean to speak now of "a profound community of life and love" wherein "the spouses offer an eminent witness of harmony and fidelity. . . ." If love does not "create the marriage," happily one can acknowledge that it contributes a great portion of it.
>
> From this it appears that the evolution of the juridical concept of marriage, about which the appealed sentence writes, consists in this: that we must now consider as the intimate community of life and love not only the *matrimonium in fieri,* i.e., the contract, but also the *matrimonium in facto esse.* From

this it follows that along with the consent's creating the marriage, so too does love create it in great part. And a deficiency in this love results in the nullity of the marriage.

Pinto began his refutation of the Toulouse sentence in first instance with a quite inclusive and generic interpretation of *Gaudium et spes.*

The appealed sentence's claim that the Second Vatican Council changed the juridical structure of marriage is without merit. For the council dealt with marriage not under the juridical aspect of validity, but under the pastoral aspect of its orientation to eternal salvation.

The Central Commission did in fact criticize the Theological Commission's *schema* on chastity, virginity, marriage and family as "frequently too biological and juridical, and taking too little account of love and charity. . . ."

But on the other hand *Adnexum* II to the first draft of *The Church in the Modern World* written in 1964 said: "However the validity of consent and thence of the marriage does not depend on a particular degree of perfection in this love, as long as the consent is free and unity, indissolubility and fecundity are not positively excluded." No one doubts how richly love ought to be present in the act of consent and how it ought to grow throughout all of the married life. . . . Therefore, granted the serious need for marital love in the existential order, yet the juridical question about the validity does not depend on this, that the spouses have made their consent out of love; but on this, that they have made it in the way that the law requires.

In no way can it be admitted that Vatican II rejected the contractualist concept of marriage just because it accepted the personalist, with the consequence that one can no longer speak of a marriage's validity or nullity, because the conjugal rights depend not on the contract but on the personal union of the spouses; and with the consequence that indissolubility is not a juridical but a real entity.

The Patronus [the Rotal advocate who presented the appealed decision to the *turnus*] insists that the essential right to the communion of life consists, according to the Second Vatican Council, in the *integral* self-giving of the spouses.

But this is inadmissible. The constitution *Gaudium et spes* does indeed speak of the mutual self-giving of the spouses either as the object of marital consent (n. 48) or in relation to marriage *in facto esse* (nn. 48 and 49). But in saying this it in no sense intended to change the formal essential object of consent as this is formulated in Canons 1081.2 and 1086.2. For many of the bishops were displeased with the clause, "In such a human act by

which the spouses mutually give over and accept one another."
They asked that it be changed and suggested two formulas as alternatives: ". . . by which the spouses mutually . . . and legitimately grant to and accept from one another the specific rights
and duties" (thirty-four proposed this); and ". . . by which each
party gives and accepts the perpetual and exclusive right to their
bodies in their orientation to acts which are *per se* apt for generation."

The reasons these bishops offered for their reformulation of
the clause were these: the object of marital consent is not the persons (*sese*) but rather the actions of persons. The expression "the
giving over of their own persons" is to be avoided (cf. AAS 36
[1944] p. 103) [this is the Holy Office's warning against the theory proposed by Doms *et al.*].

But this requested change the Commission did not accept,
and for the following reasons: "A right does not exist without its
object (which was not specified in the first formulation); and in
marriage this looks to the persons of the spouses. The expression,
'the giving over of the person' is not at all rejected in AAS 36
(1944) p. 103.[45] In fact the encyclical *Casti connubii* uses this
term explicitly. . . . And in a document which is *pastoral,* which
seeks to start up a dialogue with the world, the juridical elements
listed in the second of the proposed formulations are not needed"
(*Schema Constitutionis Pastoralis de Ecclesia in mundo huius
temporis,* Expositio modorum Partis Secundae, 1965, pp. 12 et
13). Hence the second formulation was rejected [only] because it
did not agree with the style used in the Pastoral Constitution,
and not because the council in any way rejected Canon 1081.2.

Before taking up a major appellate decision written by the Sacred Roman Signatura in 1975 I would take notice of one handed down by the Rotal judge J. M. Serrano on November 18, 1977, on a petition for nullity on
the ground of inability to fulfill the duties of marriage.[46] A brief passage
from it is especially valuable in part because its radical disagreement at a
certain point with the decisions of Pinto and the other conservative judges
re-emphasizes how divided the officers of the Rota are, and in part because
it uses a magisterial source for the most part neglected—and strangely neglected—in this Rotal jurisprudence. I refer to Paul VI's encyclical *Humanae vitae.*

Serrano leads up to his citation from *Humanae vitae* by asserting the
juridical significance of *relative* capacity and incapacity for marriage.

For surely if it is beyond doubt that in order to be capable of
marriage a person must have the capacity for interpersonal relationship, it follows that we must take seriously the *relative* capacity for this element of marriage.

Therefore it is entirely in order to speak of a unique or singular capacity which would keep a certain two persons from being able to marry validly, while at the same time admitting that either could have the capacity for marriage with hypothetical other persons.

The qualities of such a relationship, qualities which belong to it as its substance, these are the essential properties and ends of marriage. Therefore it is worthwhile that one name the characteristics of the marital union so that persons' capacity for marrying may be more clearly established.

The marital community [*consortium*] demands that a person be capable of forming an intimate and personal union—an intimacy that is oriented to bearing and nurturing children in a decent, human way. This person must be capable of forming an exclusive personal relationship—exclusive in the positive sense that he or she finds the relationship fulfilling and satisfying, so that the exclusivity does not become an intolerable burden. He or she must be capable of a perpetual relationship, one possessing the strength that can create and sustain a certain unfailingness. . . .

From here Serrano moves on to *Humanae vitae* and quotes from its paragraph 9 Paul's detailed descriptive definition of marital love. Finally he makes this evaluation of Paul's statement:

This serious teaching of Paul VI has juridical valence. This is so both because of the supreme authority that it has by nature, and because of its express naming of marital consent. Therefore it must be taken into careful account by the Church's tribunals.[47]

A Decision of the Roman Signatura

Quite possibly no decision on a petition for nullity has had a greater weight of authority behind it since Vatican II than one handed down not by the Rota but by the Sacred Signatura, on November 29, 1975.[48] And none has gone to greater pains to argue that the jurisprudence putting the intimate community of life and love in the juridical essence of marriage cannot claim *Gaudium et spes* for its source and its warrant. At some points the decision is virtually an interpretation of *Gaudium et spes'* chapter on marriage and family. For these reasons, after detailing the original, first-instance decision and its sources, I will quote the Signatura decision at considerable length.

But first some theoretical background that may help explain the innovative juridical logic and conclusion produced by the court of first instance in this case.

There is no doubt, from all that we have seen of them thus far, that

Gaudium et spes and *Humanae vitae* say that a characteristic love is substantial to a marriage. But they leave room for disagreement about the weight of this substantiality. Is this love so substantial as to be essential to a marriage, so that if this love is absent from a relationship, or deficient in it, the relationship fails to be a marriage?

These documents leave another uncertainty in their wake. They describe marriage in terms that suggest a process. *Humanae vitae* especially says that it is a communion, a sharing, a coming to personal completion, a growing toward union in being. If these do not imply that the marriage itself comes only gradually into existence in a process, they leave an opening to say that it comes into existence at some hard-to-identify moment in a continuum of psychological growth. And this may or may not be the moment of public and mutual consent.

If, as these documents say, a marriage is a community of love—if what a marriage is, is an intimate sharing of life and love—it would seem to follow that a relationship is a marriage *as long as* it is such a community, such an intimate sharing. If these endure for a lifetime, the marriage endures for a lifetime. But what if a relationship that was these things for a while deteriorates and ceases to be such? Is it still a marriage? If so, what keeps it such when the elements said by the council and by the encyclical to make up its nature have vanished? Or do they only *seem* to say that the community and the sharing belong to marriage's nature essentially—so that even though they disappear, what is truly essential in marriage goes on?

An attempt to answer these questions by implication was made in a decision at first instance in the tribunal of Utrecht in the Netherlands.[49] The case was that of a native-born Italian couple who had come to that country and had exchanged marriage vows in Arnhem on February 12, 1963. A child was born to the union three months after the wedding; a month later the supposed husband deserted the wife and went to Switzerland. In May 1970 the tribunal of Utrecht accepted the woman's petition for a decree of nullity on the ground of defect of consent. On August 12, 1971 it rendered a favorable decision: "It is evident that this marriage was null on the ground of defect of consent, that is, of moral impotence."

The tribunal of Haarlem took this decision on regular appeal, and on September 28 of the same year sustained it, agreeing that the attempt at marriage had been invalid because of relative moral impotence and on the subsidiary ground of defect of consent.

On September 5, 1972 the tribunal of Utrecht communicated the favorable decision to the Signatura in Rome to be transmitted to Italian authorities for the implementing of its civil effects. On reading the decision some officials of the Signatura took alarm and asked for the *acta* of the case in both first and second instances. And having read these, Cardinal Staffa asked the Apostolic See to appoint a commission of Signatura cardinals to study, in third instance, the merits of the lower-court decisions.

Paul VI authorized the forming of this ad hoc commission on July 9, 1973.[50]

It seems evident that what drew the attention of the Signatura was the *in iure* argument of the first instance decision in Utrecht. The main elements of it were the following.

Since, according to *Gaudium et spes*, a marriage is to be understood as an intimate community of life and marital love, it can dissolve and disintegrate. Because a marriage is a communion, the ancient axiom "It is the consent of the parties that creates the marriage" takes on exceptional meaning. For if the marriage is a union, the "consent" is no longer to be seen as an instantaneous juridical act granting a juridical right, given once for always. It has the more existential nature of a commitment to a union of lives.

That a true marital union be brought into existence, the parties must really will it in all its fullness. Thus to verify defect of consent in a particular case it is enough to verify that it has not been seriously willed in all its fullness. If a couple has really willed a life-union, this will show itself subsequently, with the passing of time, as the marriage evolves. But if the relationship is flawed from the beginning and clearly degenerates with the passing of time—with its qualitative curve going downward rather than upward—there arises a strong presumption for defect of consent.

The phrasing of the key clause in its favorable appellate decision by the Haarlem tribunal tells much about the theory of marriage and of marital consent underlying it: "Reading this case one comes to the spontaneous conclusion that this short-lived union (of hardly four months) could not have been a true marriage. *It did not have the chance to develop to the point of becoming a normal community of life and love*" (italics added).

The Signatura's quasi-appellate judgment on these two decisions of the lower courts in the Netherlands is a long and severely negative critical analysis. Rather than examine it in its own sequence I shall do so topically.

It assayed the juridical relevance of *Gaudium et spes* in a way that we have already seen done by Pinto and others among the Rotal judges, interpreting it in a way that would dilute its value as a source or premise for knowledge about marriage. It said of the conciliar document's chapter on marriage and family, "We must first recall that its intent was only to make some statements about marriage and family, and to do this by throwing light on their importance and their existential value, rather than on their properly juridical aspects." It quoted the comments in *modi* 15a, 15e and 15f from the *Expensio modorum* of the December 3, 1965 general assembly of the council: "In a pastoral text, which is intended to establish a dialogue with the world, these juridical elements are not needed. . . . Moreover, in a text which speaks to the world in a direct and pastoral style, it seems that one should avoid terms which are too technical."

About the essential nature of marriage this commission insisted that it is a juridical relationship, a bond, by which a man and a woman are constituted husband and wife. With the Dutch courts' judgments in mind, that a marriage can disintegrate and go out of existence, it added that this bond continues to subsist independently of any subsequent will of the contracting parties, so that not even a positive revocation of their consent, once given, can affect its validity.

It acknowledged that *Gaudium et spes* has defined marriage *in facto esse* as an intimate partnership of life and marital love. But it insisted that this innovates nothing in Catholic thought, because such terms as the following are common in canonical tradition: "communion of conjugal life," "sharing in the whole of life," "a union retaining a common life."

It was clearly about the nature of the act that creates a marriage that the commission was concerned, because of the new and startling interpretation of this creating coming from the Dutch courts—that it is a gradual, processual forming of a union that is never complete, a forming that can halt and even come to an end. In criticizing this the commission searched into not only the kind of act that creates a marriage, but the object that this act bears upon.

It is a bilateral and free act of the will, in the nature of a contract, albeit unique, of its own kind. It is also (in the words of *Gaudium et spes*) "a marital covenant of irrevocable personal consent." The object of this consent is the spouses themselves: "The human act by which the partners mutually surrender themselves to one another." To say this another way, the persons of the spouses, under the specific marital aspect, constitute the object of consent. It is the nature of this consent that once it has been legitimately posited it produces its effect once for all, the juridical effect of giving and surrendering. This effect continues throughout the entire life together of the spouses, independently of and impervious to any subsequent revocation on the part of the spouses. This effect, understandable also as a bond, does not cease to exist if later love between the spouses ceases, or if the intimate communion of life and marital love, with its so-called existential nature, ceases.

Since the commission drew all this from its interpretation of *Gaudium et spes,* it suggested this preliminary summation: "It is clear from the above that it is false to say that the Council changed the doctrine about matrimonial consent, as if it had substituted for the traditional notion a certain so-called existential consent, so that when this ceases the matrimonial bond automically ceases to exist."

How little this commission thought the council's teaching on marriage to differ from the juridical interpretation of it in the Code of Canon Law and in the jurisprudence derived from it emerges in its closer exegesis of the key passages in *Gaudium et spes*. Take such terms designating marriage as "communion of life" or "a communion of love," and the statement that a marriage is a man's and woman's mutual gift of their persons by which they establish an intimate partnership of life and love. About them the analysis asks if the formal object of marital consent includes the communion of life, or if it includes only the parties' right to sexual acts for the conceiving of new life.

The reply of Cardinal Staffa and the others to these, their own questions, took the form of a logic of derivation and thence a familiar subordination. First the logic of derivation: *from* the marital relationship's essential orientation to procreation and nurture there naturally derives the need for a communion of life, for a permanent society of the man and the woman. Or to read this logic in reverse and bring the subordination to light, the spouses' mutual gift of their persons to form the communion of life and love has as its goal, its specific object, this gift's orientation to sexual acts apt for procreation and nurture.

Thus what distinguishes this communion, this community from all others—from that between a sister and brother or between friends—is the specific goal that is offspring. Here by way of confirmation and illustration the analysis quotes Chapter 1 of Augustine's *The Good of Marriage:* "For there could be in both sexes, even without copulation . . . a certain friendly and familiar union"; and Aquinas' singular exegesis of Genesis 2: "It is said that the woman was created as a helper to the man, but not in any work except that of generation, for in other works a man could be helped more by another man than by a woman" (*S. Theol.* I, 98, 2).

The necessary place in marriage of the communion of life is that without it the right to sexual intercourse, which is the juridically essential object of marital consent, cannot be exercised in its essential perpetuity and exclusivity. That is to say, this right could not, without the communion of life, be exercised maritally.

> From the perpetuity and exclusiveness of the right to conjugal acts there necessarily arises communion of life, without which the right itself cannot be exercised. Hence "communion of life," or "undivided common life," or "sharing of the whole of life," pertains to the essence of marriage insofar as it is understood as a perpetual right, that is, not an interrupted one, to conjugal acts, or as a condition sine qua non, without which the right itself cannot be exercised.
>
> Therefore by matrimonial consent is brought about that individual type of life for the spouses which, for the very fact that its purpose is the generation and education of offspring, necessarily implies an intimate and, as it were, morally continuous communion, which rightly can be called a communion of love. . . .[51]

This reconciling of the new with the old by identifying the two and reducing the former to the latter is most explicit in the commission's interpretation of the communion of life and love by reducing it to the Augustinian good of marriage that is *fides,* or *bonum fidei.* And the whole

communion of married life is thus reduced to the union of maritally sexual
acts.

> Indivisible union of sexual life, or communion of love, can be re-
> duced to the *bonum fidei.* And so far there is no evidence of any
> other right pertaining to the essence of the communion of conju-
> gal life, except this right to an undivided union of sexual life: that
> is, the communion of matrimonial life, properly so called, con-
> sists in the communion of life as to matrimonial acts properly so
> called.[52]

The Signatura on the Nature and Object of Marital Love

The Signatura concluded this critical judgment with a detailed interpretation of marital love. The interpretation is in fact two things. First, it is
a prescription for the kind of love that can be admitted into the essence of
marriage when the latter is defined according to the hierarchically subordinated ends and according to an object of consent that is the parties' right
to their sexual acts. Second, it is a distinction drawn between this essentially admissible love and a love admissible because it helps for the well-being
of a marriage, for the happiness of the spouses.

First of all, this admissible love cannot be either erotic inclination or
an affection rooted in the will. That is, it cannot be an habitual state of
soul. The reason for this is that as an habitual state it cannot enter into the
marital consent. For love has relevance in law only as an act of the free
will legitimately manifested, by which a marriage is created. (The obvious
assumption here is that only those elements of marriage are essential
which can have relevance in law.)

Marital love must be understood as an act. This act is related to marriage as its necessary and essential efficient cause (but apparently not as
marriage's formal cause, giving it its nature, or its final cause, giving it its
goal).

> But then love, or the mutual act of love by which the spouses
> give and accept one another, is the same thing as matrimonial
> consent. *It is therefore an act of the will,* not to be confused with
> inclination, passion, impulse or motive which brings the subject
> to make and express the act of the will. Love, understood as this
> impulse or motive, has no relevance in law: it can be changed, or
> cease, or fall short, while on the contrary matrimonial consent is
> irrevocable. . . .[53]

A second premise excluding from the essence of marriage (which is to
say, from canonical-juridical relevance) any love that is an habitual state of
soul is that to admit such a love would be to undermine the indissolubility
and the unity of the marriage bond. Here the criticism turns particularly to

the tribunals which have acknowledged love the habitual state of soul. It says that these have violated the indissolubility of marriage by finding nullity on the ground of such love's failure.

Again the only love belonging to the essence of marriage is the act of will which is the marital consent. And here an ambiguity appears. First the criticism said that by this act the parties give and accept one another's persons, and this for the sake of acts which of their nature are most expressive of conjugal love. But now it says that this act of will has as its object and effect the exchange of the right to sexual acts.

> If, on the contrary, love is taken as an act of the will by which the spouses mutually give and accept each other and are constituted as husband and wife, then love is the same thing as matrimonial consent. By this act each spouse makes a gift of his own person to the other, and accepts the person of the other, and this for life and exclusively, for the sake of acts which by their nature are most expressive of conjugal love. Unless there is such an act of the will which is essentially an act of giving oneself—and therefore an act of love—marriage is not contracted. In this sense and only in this sense love pertains to the efficient cause, intrinsic and essential to the matrimonial contract, and in this sense consent could also be called an act of love, by which the will of both parties gives and receives the *ius in corpus,* perpetual and exclusive, for acts which of themselves are apt for the generation of offspring, that is, for acts which are proper to conjugal love.[54]

In the end, concludes the criticism, confusion would be avoided if the act creating a marriage were understood to do so not specifically as an act of love, but as a covenanting act.

> Nevertheless, to avoid confusion, it must be affirmed that matrimonial consent produces its proper effect, namely the *matrimonium in facto esse,* not inasmuch as it is an act of love, but inasmuch as it is an act of the will of a pactual nature, namely one by which each of the parties intends to set up a conjugal society with the rights and duties which are proper to marriage. . . . Therefore marriage is not constituted by just any kind of love, or any kind of mutual giving, as we have already said above, but by a mutual giving which is truly conjugal, that is, a mutual, perpetual and exclusive giving of one's body for the sake of the matrimonial act, through which the spouses become one flesh (cf. Pius XII, Discourse of Oct. 29, 1951 . . .).[55]

In short, the love that belongs to the essence of marriage is the act of will by which the parties exchange the right to their sexual acts. Indeed for

Cardinal Staffa and the other four prelates nothing in the Church's teaching on the essential nature of marriage had changed.

Paul VI's Discourse to the Rota

By the end of 1975 and early in 1976 Pope Paul himself was sufficiently alarmed by interpretations made in turn of Vatican II's interpretation of marriage that he thought it necessary to say some things that are themselves interpretations of the council's mind. What he said can be seen in no other way than as a chapter in the unfolding of the Catholic Church's definitive understanding of marriage. This is contained in his annual address, on February 9, 1976, to the judges, the advocates and the *officiales* of the Roman Rota at the beginning of this court's judicial year.[56] It is to this discourse that I have referred a number of times already; I offer here a précis of it, with an ample quotation from it at an essential point.

Paul observed that certain thinkers and writers at times exaggerate those goods of marriage that are marital love and the personal perfection of the spouses, even to the point of subordinating to them that fundamental good that is offspring—some even to the point of ignoring the latter. They make of marital love such an important element even in the law that the validity itself of marriage depends on it. And they thereby open the way to divorce, for they say that once marital love fails—or rather once the initial amorous longing fails—the validity of the irrevocable marital covenant also fails, a covenant created by the full and free consent of love.

Surely, he continues, the Second Vatican Council attributed great importance to marital love. The bishops called it the fulfilled condition and the desired goal of marriage. But what he, Paul, wished to make emphatically clear in this address is that no Christian teaching on marriage can acknowledge a concept of marital love which leads to abandoning or even diminishing the force and meaning of the principle, *matrimonium facit partium consensus* ("It is the consent of the parties that creates the marriage").

In virtue of this principle a marriage exists from the moment the spouses make a juridically valid consent. This consent is an act of the will having the character of a pact—or of a covenant, to use the expression preferred nowadays to the term "contract."

His next words I quote in full because they touch the essence of marriage, or touch at least close by it, as Paul understood it in his address.

> At the instant it is made this act of consent produces a juridical effect, the marriage *in facto esse,* a living state. The act of consent has no subsequent effect on the "juridical reality" which it has created. A consequence of this is that once the consent has created its juridical effect, which is the marital bond, this consent becomes irrevocable and loses any power to destroy what it has created.

Even though it is a pastoral document, *Gaudium et spes* taught this doctrine clearly, as is evident in its words: "The intimate partnership of married life and love has been established by the Creator and qualified by his laws. It is created by the conjugal covenant of irrevocable personal consent. Hence by that human act whereby spouses mutually bestow and accept each other, a relationship arises which by divine will and in the eyes of society too is a lasting one. For the good of the spouses and their offspring as well as of society, the existence of this sacred bond no longer depends on human decisions alone" (n. 48).

Hence we firmly deny that with the failure of some subjective element such as marital love the marriage itself no longer exists as a "juridical reality." For this reality has its origin in a consent once for all juridically efficacious. So far as the law is concerned this "reality" continues to exist, since it in no way depends on love for its existence. For when they give their free consent the spouses do nothing other than to enter and be fixed in [*inseruntur*] an objective order or institution, which is something greater than themselves and in no way depends on them for either its nature or the laws proper to it. Marriage did not take its origin in the free will of men, but was instituted by God, who willed it to be reinforced and enlightened by his laws.[57]

If not at the Dutch tribunals as exclusively as Cardinal Staffa and his ad hoc commission had, Paul nevertheless aimed his remarks at those Catholics, the Dutch judges principal among them, who were seeing in Vatican II's insertion of marital love into the Church's understanding of marriage an effect on marriages in real life akin to the effect of *affectio maritalis* in pre-classical and classical Roman law.

According to that law the cause internal to the parties enabling their mutual consent to create and maintain a marriage was this *affectio,* their *will* to create and maintain it. As long as by their *affectio* they willed the marriage, it continued to exist. If and when they withdrew it, the marriage went out of existence. What Paul saw and heard some saying was that *Gaudium et spes* had made active marital loving an ingredient of the essence of marriage, with this consequence: that when the loving ceases, an element essential to marriage departs the relationship and it necessarily ceases to be a marriage. (If this is what he perceived, he was not quite accurate in saying that this interpretation opens the way to divorce. A divorce puts an existing marriage out of existence. But this interpretation would see marriages passing out of existence this side of divorce. He is also not accurate in applying the epithet "initial amorous longing" [*primigenia cupiditas amoris*] to the marital love whose death some say can end a marriage. To no explanation of marital love I have ever read can that predicate be referred accurately.)

Some Implications of Paul's Discourse to the Rota

A credible case can be made that *Gaudium et spes* did not state exactly the place of love in a marriage. Certainly the bishops thought this love grievously important to the happiness and survival of a marriage. They acknowledged that it is in fact the most common source of modern marriages, and that the realizing of this love's possibilities is marriage's goal. But did they say that it belongs to marriage's nature in such an essential way that its absence keeps the relationship from being a marriage?

To this question Paul's answer in his discourse is an emphatic "no." But he just as emphatically did not leave the matter there. He went on to explain how it is that a marriage is brought into existence apart from this love, and how it is that apart from this love, even despite its failure and disappearance, a marriage stays in existence.

He explained that what creates a marriage as its immediate cause, a cause both necessary and sufficient, is the parties' consent provided that it is made freely. Their love has no essentially necessary place in this creating.

Again, what this consent has as its immediate and proportioned effect is not the spouse's love, not a process of growth in them of love and perfection—which are not elements essential to a marriage in any case. What this effect is, is the marriage in actual existence (*in facto esse*). It is decidedly not marriage in the process of coming into existence (*in fieri*).

And, most significantly, Paul said of marriage *in facto esse* that it is a *juridical* effect, a *juridical* reality. Continuing his exact predicating he named this effect, this reality, the marital bond. It is, he said, a thing of the objective order. The partners create it by their consent. But once they create it, it takes on a kind of existence of its own, apart from their minds and wills, and has an unassailable immunity from the latter. Nothing they can do subsequently can affect it. Even their will to end the bond, the withdrawal of their consent, leaves it untouched. By their consent they enter an institution which exists in its own right, and they cannot exit from it in any way short of death. (Here, without Paul's naming it, we have the return of the contract invented by the medieval canonists—a unique invention in legal history, because the contract is non-voidable. In reintroducing the non-voidable contract in order to reassert a marriage's invulnerability to subsequent withdrawal of wills by the spouses, Paul accompanied Cardinal Staffa and his commission in their departure from the teaching of *Gaudium et spes,* which placed the unfailingness of marriage not in the indissoluble juridical bond, alias the non-voidable contract, but in the spouses' irrevocable personal consent.)

Questions and Doubts That Remain

Despite their character as attempts at exact answers to questions made inevitable by *Gaudium et spes* and *Humanae vitae,* these precisions did not bring clarity to the Church's work of defining marriage. What follow are my reasons for thinking this.

It is worth rehearsing yet again the specific things that the bishops of Vatican II said about the nature of marriage. They said that it is a community of love (*communitas amoris*); an institution (*institutio* or *institutum*); an intimate partnership, or sharing, of marital life and love (*intima communitas vitae et amoris coniugalis*); a sacred bond (*vinculum sacrum*); a marital covenant (*foedus coniugale*), although this may refer more to the covenanting act that creates a marriage; an intimate union of their persons and actions (*intima personarum atque operum coniunctio*).

Pope Paul said that a marriage is in essence a juridical reality, that what marital consent as a cause produces is an effect that is a juridical reality. If he had the predicates above in mind when he said this, did he mean that all of them signify juridical realities only? That not all of them but some of them do this, and that the essence of marriage is found in those that are juridical but not in the others? If he meant the latter, he left uncertainty and confusion by failing to point out which of the predicates designate the juridical reality and which do not.

One may guess that those Paul meant to belong to the imperishable juridical reality are "institution," "sacred bond" and perhaps "marital covenant." But to say this is to guess, since *Gaudium et spes* makes no distribution of these predicates among juridical essentiality and non-essentiality. Nor does Paul himself make the distinction and distribution.

Or is it possible that Paul, as well as Cardinal Staffa and commission, imply that in a marriage there are two essences, two substantial realities? The use of the adjective *juridical* essence, *juridical* reality hints at this—another but unspecified and anonymous essence and reality in a marriage. If this other is, as it seems to be, the sum of all the qualities of a marriage named by *Gaudium et spes,* even in elaborating richly on them the bishops failed to speak of the essence of marriage because in speaking *only* of them they failed to deal with *real* essence of marriage, the juridical essence. (Such at least, by reduction, is Paul's and the Signatura commission's interpretation of what the bishops did and did not do. And one must wonder if the bishops were aware that they were speaking of what is non-essential and contingent in marriage.)

To get at a particular point, one may wonder if the Signatura commission would remain consistent in its claim that *Gaudium et spes* stayed away from the juridically essential even when the bishops said that a marriage is formed by the spouses' irrevocable personal consent. For the commission used this statement from *Gaudium et spes* when refuting the Dutch tribunals' judgment about the nature of the act that creates a marriage. If the Signatura kept this clause from *Gaudium et spes* because juridically relevant, but set aside all its others because juridically irrelevant, one may wonder also at the commission's criterion for inclusion and exclusion.

Let us come back again to the insistence by Paul and the Signatura commission that what marital consent produces as its effect is a juridical reality. By definition this effect must be the object of marital consent. There will be some difficulty, I think, in reconciling this insistence with the revised canons on marriage at certain points. New Canon 242.1 calls the act creating a marriage a covenant. Joining this with Paul's and the commission's insistence, one would have it that the act of covenanting, an act certainly to be understood according to its biblical model, has as its principal effect a juridical entity.

What is more, this same canon says that the act of covenanting has for its effect the spouses' intimate sharing in all of life. Can this be the juridical effect that Paul and the Signatura meant? It would seem not, since the intimate sharing in all of life is precisely one of the predicates of marriage from *Gaudium et spes* that they appraised as non-juridical.

The conflict is compounded by the inclusion of this same juridically irrelevant "intimate sharing (or joining) in all of life" in the new Canon 243, which is the canon in the revised Code that most nearly defines marriage formally. And as we know from the vote at the meeting of the *plenarium* of cardinals in Rome in May 1977, this phrase defining the nature of marriage was kept in the new canon with full awareness that it would in the future be used in the Church's judicial decisions. For the *caveat* that accompanied the vote to keep the phrase urged that words and phrases susceptible to misinterpretation in favor of easy divorce and annulment be kept out of the canons on marriage.

Finally the ambiguity and even conflict become complete when one notes that in the revision of the canon stating the object of marital consent (this is now new Canon 244) this object is named as the man's and woman's mutual *donatio,* their giving of themselves to one another in an irrevocable covenant.

To resolve the conflict one would somehow have to turn this biblically grounded self-donating into a juridical reality. Or if one were to reject this as an impossible wrenching of reality, then only two courses seem open: either to rewrite these recently rewritten canons so as to state in them an object of marital consent that is unambiguously juridical—in order to not disagree with Pope Paul and the Signatura commission—or at the other extreme to admit that while there may be *a* juridical dimension in a marriage and in the object of marital consent, there is another dimension in both of these that transcends the juridical.

If the latter course were to be the one taken generally in the Church, there would remain the painful decision needed to answer the question, "By which dimension shall marriages in the Church be ruled—by the juridical, or by that which transcends the juridical?"

NOTES

1. As this is being written no part of the revised Code has yet been promulgated. And it appears that the incumbent Pope, John Paul II, has decided to pro-

mulgate all the parts of the Code simultaneously. Therefore the revised formulation of the few canons I examine here is tentative.

2. He published this as the final chapter in a book of essays titled *Alternatief Kerkelik Huweliksrecht* (An Alternative Church Law on Marriage), published by the Dutch society, Thijmgenootschap in 1974, and republished in German translation a year later as *Für Eine Neue Kirchliche Eheordnung.*

3. In "Report of the Special Committee of the Task Force of the Canon Law Society of America on the Marriage Canons of the Proposed *Schema Documenti Pontificii Qua Disciplina Canonica de Sacramentis Recognoscitur* (an unpublished document), p. 5.

4. In *Communicationes,* Vol. 9.1 (1977), pp. 118–119. In a word, the subcommission decided to evaluate the general criticisms not according to their intrinsic merit but according to the majority or minority size of the judgment they represented. But it is not apparent that this principle of writing the law to please the constituency holds throughout the rest of the revision.

5. *Doc. cit.,* p. 21.

6. "1. Matrimoniale foedus, quo vir et mulier intimam inter se constituunt totius vitae communionem, indole sua naturali ad bonum coniugum atque ad prolis procreationem et educationem ordinatam, a Christo Domino ad sacramenti dignitatem inter baptizatos evectum est."

7. This explanation is in the record of the subcommission's pre-1975 deliberations, published in *Communicationes,* Vol. 9.1 (1977), pp. 117–146.

8. This canon was number 295 only in the subcommission's first proposal in 1971. It was later relocated among these introductory canons of the marriage law as no. 244. The compelling reason for its relocation was that in prescribing the consent needed to create a marriage it completes the law's quasi-definition of marriage begun in Canons 242 and 243.

9. "1. Matrimonium . . . est (intima) totius vitae coniunctio inter virum et mulierem quae, indole sua naturali, ad prolis procreationem et educationem ordinatur."

10. In *Communicationes,* Vol. 3 (1971), p. 70.

11. I have this from a conversation with one of the consultors in the subcommission in the spring of 1977.

12. This I have from one of the members of the *plenarium,* one of those to whom the warning was addressed.

Cardinal Palazzini was mainly correct in his apprehensive judgment. The inclusion of the terms about which he warned would have severe consequences in the Church's juridical and judicial control of marriages. A contemporary German canonist explains why this would be so: "If we attribute to marital love a constitutive function for the valid creating of a marriage, then in many petitions for nullity courts would have to deal with the question of sufficient presence of marital love at the time the marriage was contracted—an almost impossible task, since love is far from amenable to juridical evaluation. The consequences in civil law would be beyond imagining. Ecclesiastical judges would have to keep a huge open-mindedness for the needs of civilly married couples in order to declare their marriages null. Given clever use of evidence it would be no great task to verify deficient or even absent love between the parties on the evidence of trouble in the relationship before the marriage. With this the Church's judicial decisions would lose all serious grounding and degenerate into a kind of caricature, since for any and every failed marriage there could be found a ground of nullity that could not be determined on objective criteria" (Paul Wirth, "Das Neue Kirchliche Eherecht: Kurzer Überblick und Kritische Würdigung," in *Seitschrift für Katholisches Kirchenrecht,* 1975, pp. 331–332).

13. In *Communicationes,* Vol. 9.1 (1977), pp. 79–80.

"*Ia Quaestio,* De notione matrimonii

    (a) Utrum in Codice praebenda sit notio matrimonii. Quatenus positive:

    (b) Utrum in definitione includere oporteat elementum 'coniunctionis vitae' ('communio', 'consortium') tamquam expressionis aspectus personalis matrimonii (*Gaudium et spes,* n. 48). Quatenus positive:

    (c) Quaenam sit vis huius elementi in ordine ad validitatem matrimonii?"

14. In *Communicationes,* Vol. 9.2 (1977), pp. 211–212. The vote was two in favor, two in favor with amendments (*iuxta modum*) and two opposed.

15. In *Communicationes,* Vol. 3 (1971), p. 75.

16. ". . . consensus proponitur ut actus quo vir et mulier foedere inter se constituunt consortium vitae coniugalis, perpetuum et exclusivum, indole sua naturali ad prolem generandam et educandam ordinatum" (*ibid.*).

17. "Consensus matrimonialis est actus voluntatis quo vir et mulier foedere irrevocabili sese mutuo tradunt et accipiunt ad constituendum matrimonium."

18. "Ut matrimonialis consensus haberi possit, necesse est ut contrahentes saltem non ignorent matrimonium esse societatem permanentem inter virum et mulierem ad filios procreandos."

19. "Ut consensus matrimonialis haberi possit, necesse est ut contrahentes saltem non ignorent matrimonium esse consortium permanens inter virum et mulierem ordinatum ad prolem, cooperatione aliqua physica, procreandam."

20. "At si alterutra vel utraque pars positivo voluntatis actu excludat matrimonium ipsum, aut omne ius ad actum coniugalem, vel essentialem aliquam matrimonii proprietatem, invalide contrahit."

21. "At si alterutra vel utraque pars positivo voluntatis actu excludat matrimonium ipsum aut ius ad ea quae vitae communionem essentialiter constituunt. . . ."

22. Fellhauer, *op. cit.,* pp. 122–123.

23. In this I shall follow the division made by Fr. Fellhauer in his essay, and shall borrow heavily from his data. He reports on the first of these periods on pp. 126–127.

24. The term *coram* ("before") plus the name of the Rotal judge designates that the decision was handed down by a *turnus* of three judges chaired by that one among them whose name follows the *coram.*

25. In Fellhauer, *op. cit.,* p. 126.

26. *Ibid.* The same evaluation of the *intima communitas* was made in a decision of May 18, 1968 *coram* Vincenzo Fagiolo. He acknowledged that the bishops of Vatican II called marriage the intimate community of married life and love. But like the decisions *coram* Bejan and *coram* Fiore, he equates this *communitas*—translated into the terms *vitae consortium, communis vitae consuetudo* and *vitae communio*—with no more than cohabitation, which is non-essential to marriage (*ibid.,* p. 127).

27. The decision is available in full in *Ephemerides Iuris Canonici,* Vol. 26 (1970), pp. 419–442. Fellhauer examines it in *op cit.,* pp. 128–131.

28. The translation of this passage is taken from Fellhauer, *op. cit.,* p. 128.

29. *Ibid.,* p. 129.

30. *Ibid.,* p. 131.

31. *Ibid.,* p. 133.

32. *Ibid.*

33. Taken from an unpublished transcript of the decision.

34. In Fellhauer, *op. cit.,* p. 136.

35. *Ibid.*

36. *The Documents of Vatican II,* p. 253.

37. Fellhauer, *op. cit.,* p. 137.

38. *Op. cit.,* pp. 139–140.

39. This is in Lesage's essay, "The *Consortium vitae conjugalis:* Nature and Applications," in *Studia Canonica,* Vol. 6 (1972), pp. 99–113.

40. "Evolution récente de la jurisprudence matrimoniale," in *Sociétè Canadienne de Théologie, Le Divorce* (quoted in Fellhauer, *op. cit.,* p. 131).

41. In Fellhauer, *op cit.,* pp. 143–144.

42. *Op. cit.,* pp. 145–146.

43. *Ibid.,* p. 146.

44. This decision is reported in *Ephemerides Iuris Canonici,* Vol. 34 (1979, 1–2), pp. 165–176.

45. "AAS" are the initials of *Acta Apostolicae Sedis.*

46. Reported in *Ephemerides Iuris Canonici,* Vol. 33 (1978, 3–4), pp. 346–353.

47. *Loc. cit.,* p. 350.

48. While the ordinary court of appeal in marriage cases is the Rota, these cases can come to the Signatura via an expediting or a reviewing of procedure. The principal function of the Signatura is to rule in procedural questions in diocesan tribunals as well as in the Rota itself.

49. A report of the case, both in its first instance proceedings and in its review and reversal by the Signatura was distributed in 1976 by the regional tribunal of Vancouver, Canada, after its translation by Rev. Bernard Rossi of that tribunal.

50. It consisted of Cardinal Staffa himself, prefect of the Signatura, and of Cardinals Egidio Vagnozzi, Francesco Carpino, Pietro Palazzini and Giacomo Violardo.

51. *Doc. cit.,* pp. 13–14.

52. *Ibid.,* p. 14.

53. *Ibid.,* p. 15.

54. *Doc. cit.,* pp. 16–17.

55. *Ibid.*

56. The discourse is in *Acta Apostolicae Sedis,* Vol. 68 (1976). pp. 204–208.

57. *Loc. cit.,* pp. 206–207.

12. CRITICAL REFLECTIONS

Even though canonists have at intervals denied that a formal definition of marriage has ever been written in Catholic law, there is no denying that at intervals exact though informal definitions have been proposed. When saying marriage is a contract canonists from the twelfth to the twentieth centuries implied that it is a species of the genus "human relationship." When naming marriage's ends and its contractual good-to-be-exchanged they identified a subdifference of this species.

Without doubt the Church needs to understand marriage in its nature. This is so for three principal reasons. For one thing the Church as a society needs to understand herself, her own life. This is made up of kinds of conduct that congeal into relationships and then into sub-societies of the inclusive society. Marriage is the most substantial of these sub-societies. If the Church does not understand marriage in its nature she does not understand her own. For the Church's nature is to be a society in which the belief, the trust and the caring love absolutely necessary for happiness are learned and carried on. But these are learned and carried on in families first and more than in any other relationship.

Secondly marriage the natural relationship is the matrix of marriage as sacrament. Lacking an understanding of the natural relationship the Church could not understand her most commonly and frequently used sacrament. What is more, the Church is in a sense the sum-total of her sacramental actions. They are the primary experiences in which the belief, trust and caring love mentioned above are learned.

Finally for now, the Church, like any society, must keep internal order. To do this in the domain of sexual conduct and of the consequent procreation and nurture of children within herself, she must know who is committed and accountable to whom in sexual conduct so that they may be held accountable for the good they ought to do and the harm they ought to avoid, as well as helped to do this good and avoid this harm.

But whether they think their attempts at defining marriage formal or informal, the bishops of the *magisterium* and the canonists have always owed obedience to the rules of defining. Now there are two kinds of definitions, the descriptive and the prescriptive. About them it is a student's le-

328

gitimate curiosity to ask to which of these kinds the canonical definitions of marriage have belonged (and even to ask to which the canonical definers have intended them to belong).

In descriptive defining the definer and his definition come after the thing to be defined. The definer comes upon this thing; it is already there constituted in its nature and existing in that nature. In defining it he seeks to say what its nature is both inclusively and exclusively. His definition is accurate if he describes this nature accurately.

It seems impossible that the canonical defining of marriage can have been descriptive. By their own intent the definers have sought to define marriage with universal reference. I have never read their disclaimer of intent to define marriage as it has always been and everywhere, and as it will always be everywhere. But any attempt to write a single accurate descriptive definition of marriage breaks up on the shoals of cultural diversity and historical change. Consider only the 1917 Code of Canon Law's definition of marriage. It does not describe accurately all marriages that have existed everywhere and for all time. According to this definition unity and indissolubility are essential properties of marriage. But unity means, among other things, monogamy. And many societies of the past, and some in the present, accepted and accept polygamous marriage. So the definition does not describe them. (If one says this is due to a fault in the polygamous relationships that keeps them from fitting the definition and thus from being marriages, one has passed from descriptive defining to prescriptive.)

Therefore the most we can say of the Code's definition as a description is that it tells accurately of marriage in a certain number of societies but not in all of them across the span of history or even within one epoch.

A prescriptive definition, on the other hand, is a priori. It involves the kind of defining a design engineer does, to borrow an example. The designer comes first. He designs in his mind the reality he plans to produce as an effect of his design. Men and women have designed societies, both large and small ones. Benedict, Francis, Dominic and Ignatius all designed small ones. Adams, Jefferson, Franklin and their colleagues designed a large one.

The designers of a society, if they have the power and authority to do so, can make it what they wish within broad limits. This they do in stating its goals. These will be some conception of the well-being at some level of the persons who are to be members making up the society.

Even if it were not inescapable by process of elimination that the bishops and canonists through the centuries (including the bishops of Vatican II) have defined marriage prescriptively because it is impossible that they have done so descriptively, their prescriptiveness would be evident in the sequential variations in their definitions that we have noted all through this volume. In short, Catholic churchmen have for centuries been writing prescriptions for marriage. Since they have varied the prescription, we can say that they have redesigned it. To say it another way, like any designers of marriage they have said which kind of sexually expressed relationship is acceptable in their society, and within which conditions. Their judgment appears in every case to have been at least in part pragmatic in the best sense. That is, they have specified the kind of sexual relationship acceptable in order to protect persons—sometimes the spouses, sometimes persons in the Church and in civil society generally, sometimes the Church itself hypostasized as a person, or even civil society conceived of in the same way.

It is worth pointing out in this regard that marriage conceived of as it is in the Code of Canon Law—a non-voidable contract in which a man and a woman exchange their right to sexual acts—is a contract invented by the Church's canonists. The non-voidability was part of the invention, since no contract before that time had ever been thought non-voidable by the parties who had entered it. And we ought to acknowledge too that the divine command for the lifelong fidelity of spouses was on the record long before this invention and hardly depends on it for its holding force.

Questions About Method

All this inspires some questions about the methods that churchmen have used in defining marriage, about the motives (conscious and acknowledged as well as unconscious) for their choosing this or that prescriptive definition over others, and about the consequences of these methods and choices.

The first although not the most important question asks in what degree the prescriptions of marriage have been motivated by the magisterial desire to preserve those goods of the Church that are continuity and invariability of teaching. This is not merely to glance at the crippling habit among some Scholastics of doing theology mainly by repeating their predecessors and adding not much more than new syntheses, finer distinctions and current applications, while neglecting inductive exploration and the riches that could come from carefully examined human experience. But it is to point out the reluctance to change Catholic teaching even in less than doctrinal territory just because that would relinquish what was said in the past. This conservatism is most transparent in the insistence by Vatican II's Theological Commission, and by the conservative Rotal judges since the council, that the understanding of marriage in *Gaudium et spes cannot* be definitive because it disagrees with traditional teaching—teaching contained, be it noted, not in the constitutions and decrees of any general council of the Church, but in two papal encyclicals, the Code of Canon Law, some papal discourses and some decisions of Vatican congregations. Is it too obvious to suggest that the latter documents' understanding of marriage may not be definitive because it disagrees with that of a general council of the Church?

In looking to both societal and personal goods when writing their prescriptions for marriage have some of the designers begun by doing to the Church what they have done to marriage—reified it, turned it for purposes of jurisdiction and judicial control into a juridical collective entity? And if they have, have they done this on the assumption that this juridical entity must be protected in its juridical character and, acting on this assumption, have they designed marriage in such a way as to gain this protection?

In reality the Church is the people of God, a society of persons on pilgrimage toward the happiness that God offers all men in Christ. The good of the Church is nothing other than the good of the persons, of the men and the women who make her up—this good distributed in the needs of persons as a community as well as in their private needs taken singly. Have the writers of the prescriptions for marriage been principally concerned for the goods of the persons, of the men and women who because of what they prescribe are in great measure going to be either happy or unhappy in marriage? After all it is not the Church taken in abstraction as a juridical entity but these men and women who will go to either salvation or damnation, possibly to either because of what they experience in marriage.

A case in point here: since the designers of marriage, whether conservative or progressive, write prescriptions, they really do have the choice of either writing love and the intimate community into their definitions of marriage or of keeping them out. One gets the impression that the conservative canonists have appealed to the good of the Church taken in abstraction as a reason for barring love and the community from their definition. (To be fair one must also acknowledge that they at times appeal also to the concrete good of persons, as is evident in their concern lest marriages be abandoned easily by easy annulment, to the serious harm of vicitimized spouses.) But just as compelling a case could be made for defending, at the beginning of marriages, potential victims of unions too easily entered precisely because no love has to be verified, and no capacity for forming the intimate community—because, in turn, love and the community have been written out of marriage's essence and therefore out of the object of the consent that creates a marriage.

To continue this question of including love and the intimate community in the definition of marriage or excluding them from it, I urge again that when the definers write a prescription for marriage, they really do have the option of including them or excluding them. But again, marriage is a constituent society of one or two larger, inclusive societies—of civil society and of the religious society, the Church. The designers of marriage therefore exercise their option to include or exclude love and the intimate community reasonably according as they judge one or the other will better help secure the goals of the larger communities.

To state the goal of the Christian community, the Church, most simply, it *is to be* a quasi-family whose members meet the invisible Creator through the audible word of the Gospel and the visible-tangible-audible sacraments, and thereby grow in the faith, the trust, the caring love that begin eternal life on earth and continue it beyond death. It is central to this understanding of the Church that caring love, *agape*, is not a mere helpful accessory to this life. It is of the essence of it. In still helpful old-time religious language, the work of the Church is to communicate Christ's saving grace.

In view of this, since the Catholic definers of marriage cannot write a *descriptive* definition of marriage for the entire human race in all of its history and are therefore left only the possibility of writing a prescriptive definition of it, and since in writing the latter they cannot escape setting some one set of societal goals as the principal norm of inclusion and exclusion in writing the definition, it is surprising that some of the Catholic definers have for their prescriptive norm set aside the goals of the Church and chosen instead goals appropriate to a secular and civil society. (To the instant objection that not everyone wants to be a Christian, but even a Christian definition ought to allow everyone to marry, I suggest that this concern is valid only if one presumes that there can be at all a single, universal definition of marriage. In other words, taking the Church and its goals as the norm and model for the Catholic prescriptive definition of marriage would not involve an offensive forcing of the sacred on the secular, because this kind of defining tries neither to describe the secular nor to either protect or attack its secularity. It is an effort by the appointed Christian teachers to design a form of sexual community that will best help men and women to reach the happiness God holds out to them in the larger community, the Church.)

A Definition of Marriage the Matrix of the Sacrament

Saying all this is to recommend that in writing their prescriptive definition of marriage the Church's teachers write one that makes of the marriage they design a matrix for the Christian sacrament of marriage. Let me offer a resumé what I said of the notion of matrix in this volume's first chapter. Every one of the sacraments consists of a fundamentally human kind of conduct, one capable of signifying a reality other than itself and even transempirical. This is a kind of conduct which, used in a ritual way by the Christian community, brings the participants within reach of God's gracing action, and does this by imaging in its specific way Christ's rescuing sacrifice of his life. In baptism such human conduct is the washing with water. In confirmation it is the laying on of hands in blessing and the anointing with chrism. In the Eucharist it is the blessing and sharing of bread and wine. In every case the human conduct *is* the essential sensate substance of the sacrament. Its creaturely status itself is incorporated in the gracing activity. Therefore as a matrix it must be in itself suitable for what the particular sacrament images. Water could not serve as the matrix of baptism by functioning as a reflecting-pool; bread and wine could not serve as the matrix of the Eucharist by reposing at a food fair.

To get from its further side at the prescriptive defining of marriage that may supply the Church with a matrix for the sacrament, it seems to me that those churchmen and canonists who insist that love and the intimate community do not belong to the essence of marriage must as a consequence rethink the theology of marriage the sacrament quite thoroughly. For centuries Popes, bishops and theologians have explained that the marriage of two baptized persons is a sacrament in this: that their union is an earthly image, a sacrament, of the love union of Christ and the Church. But obviously a marriage cannot be such an image unless love is in it.

For at least a century and a half Popes and bishops have also insisted that in the case of two baptized persons the marriage itself becomes the sacrament, that the sacrament is simply the marriage as natural human relationship—as the bond, the contract—elevated to become a grace-bringing image of the love of Christ and his Church. Since therefore love cannot not be in a marriage if it is to be a sacrament, where, according to the conservative canonists, does love make its entry and take its place? Though not in the *juridical* essence of marriage the natural relationship-contract-bond, could it be in some other essence that is in it? And is it this other essence that is elevated to become a grace-giving sign while the juridical essence is left in its natural, non-gracing state?

Or do they say that although a marriage's juridical essence need not have love in it for the contract to be just that, a contract, however it must have love in it if it is to be elevated to a sacrament? But if they hold to the juridical rule that the marriage of two Christians cannot be a contract unless it is also a sacrament, do they allow that if a relationship fails to be a sacrament because it lacks the love needed for the sacrament, then neither is the relationship a contract—and thus fails to be even a marriage because the love is missing?

Or do they say that the sacramentally needed love comes to and informs the contract according to the hylemorphic model, wherein the contract would be the *materia* and the imaging of the love relationship of Christ and the Church the *forma*? No magisterial or juridical document explains the relationship of contract and sacrament in this way. But supposing this explanation were accepted, would it entail destroying the contract? Its nature has been explained for centuries as an equal exchange of rights, an exchange whose effect is mutual obligations in commutative justice to grant the exercise of these rights—so that this exercise is called "the rendering of the debt." But it is impossible to interpret the relationship of Christ and the Church as an exchange of rights producing mutual obligations in commutative justice. Christ can render no debt to the Church. His love is gracious, covenantal, self-giving; so too ought the love of the Church to be. To avoid this absurdity do the traditional canonists say that the sacramentality elevates the natural contract of two Christians above its contractuality? But if the marriage of two Christians is a sacrament the moment it is contracted, as the same canonists insist, then no such marriage has ever in fact been a contract. And contractuality must therefore be left to the marriages of the unbaptized.

Why a Juridical Essence in Marriage?

We have seen in three kinds of ecclesiastical statements—in the Signatura commission's critique of the Dutch courts, in Paul VI's discourse to the Rota, and in the decisions of the conservative Rotal judges—a number of almost synonymous claims that any marriage is in essence a juridical entity. These claims show small variations. The Signatura commission said that the assertion in *Gaudium et spes* that a marriage is a community or sharing of life has no juridical relevance. Paul said that when love and the sharing of life vanish from a marriage, its essence remains nonetheless, because this is the marital bond, which is a juridical entity, imperishable by nature. The judges have said in various ways that though the sharing of life and marital love are most desirable and are necessary for happiness in marriage, they are not needed for the existence itself of a marriage. This is because the nature of this existence is the juridical bond, and neither love nor sharing is needed for this bond's existence. What is more, this bond can be created by the parties' mutual consent alone, which is a contractual act of the will.

In every case here the defining is prescriptive. None of these kinds of statements describes marriage as it has been understood in all and different societies in history. For example none has room in it for the ancient Roman tradition that marriage is a *consuetudo*, a sharing, produced by the parties' *affectio maritalis*, their will to be married—a sharing that can also be ended by the withdrawal of their *affectio*. Thus, since their definitions of marriage as a juridical bond are prescriptive, they are statements of what Paul, the Signatura commission and the Rotal judges *want* marriage to be. And this prompts two compelling questions. First, what do they signify by the adjective in their predicate: "Marriage is a *juridical* entity"? Second, why do they prefer to define marriage in this way?

The attempt to answer the first of these questions is difficult because it is an attempt to interpret other persons' thought without benefit of their explanation. But from my reading of the magisterial and juridical documents I discern the following elements of meaning for "juridical bond" where this predicate is affirmed of marriage.

1. It is a relationship of person with person.

2. It is a relationship they are obligated to sustain, obligated in such a way that their refusal to sustain it is moral fault in them.

3. It is a relationship whose creating can be examined and verified empirically, therefore whose existence too can be thus examined and verified.

4. Since it is thus empirically amenable, it can be evaluated and judged forensically—by judges in a court of law.

5. Because the parties to the relationship are persons living by nature in society, persons whose well-being is a participation in the well-being of society both civil and ecclesiastical, they are in this bond obligated to seek the well-being of these societies and accountable to them for this seeking.

6. Because the relationship has in it morally holding obligations of person to person and of the persons to the societies that can be verified forensically, authorities in the societies have a legitimate interest in the relationship's well-being. And this interest is authoritative; it can both legislate for the relationship generally and command it judicially in particular cases.

Let us grant for the moment that it is good to define marriage as a juridical bond in this multiple sense, good for the parties and good for the societies of which they are members. What seems so dubious in this prescriptive defining, and indeed arbitrary, is the insistence that only those elements of a marriage that are juridical in this sense belong to its essence, and that any others, precisely because they are not juridical, do not belong to it. In the minds of the conservative definers, as we have seen, the sharing of life and marital love are not juridical.

This leads to the attempt to answer the second of the questions: Why the insistence on defining marriage prescriptively in such a way that only elements definable as juridical are to be allowed in the definition?

I think the answer here can be gleaned from many places in the discourses and writings of the Popes, bishops and canonists. In one inclusive word, the reason is anxiety. Said more fully, it is pastoral concern for what would happen if authorities in the Church could not control Catholic marriages in that way and degree that legislation and judicial procedures can control them. They are concerned that great harm will come to the Church, to civil society and to persons. But this control is possible *au fond* only if authorities in the Church can verify who is married, and who is married to whom. And to verify these the authorities must have a criterion for verification that can yield empirically verifiable judgments. Thus their defining of marriage is in fact the designing of a pastorally motivated instrument for social control.

They are correct. The kind of control they deem necessary is possible even in minimal degree only if they have as a criterion for verifying marriage and non-marriage a definition of marriage that excludes all but juridical elements. Granted this as a premise, it is reasonable that marital love be excluded. There are so many conceptions of love from culture to culture and even within a single culture. Love is a creature of the emotions as well as of the will. It goes on in the recesses of the psyche, and when it manifests itself it does so in notoriously ambiguous signs. Who can say for sure if it is present in a person? And even if it is, who can verify its kind and its degree? Justice, if it is to be justice really and functionally in a society, ought to be reasonably uniform in principles, procedures and effects from judge to judge. But it is obvious from the reports of the Rotal decisions that not even the judges of a single court can agree on the nature of marital love nor on the degree of it needed for creating and sustaining a marriage.

The *communitas vitae*, the community or sharing of life, offers hardly less difficulty. The sharing of what in the conjoined life of the spouses?

And what degree of sharing in which ways? For example, few features of a man's or woman's life are more substantial and precious than love of parents. But suppose that a husband cannot abide the presence of his wife's parents, dislikes them intensely, avoids them, ignores them. He is otherwise a stable person, while they are in fact immature, interfering, quarrelsome, prying, disruptive. Can he not marry this woman because he cannot share an attachment and love that are precious to her?

Certainly it is this difficulty in verifying love and the sharing of life—difficulty that passes over into impossibility—that has inspired pastors and canonists in the Church to write love and the sharing of life out of their prescriptive definition of marriage.

What then do they think the bishops of Vatican II in *Gaudium et spes* and Pope Paul VI in *Humanae vitae* defined descriptively in marriage?

Their answer in its briefest form is that the council and the encyclical stated those characteristics and conditions of marriage that are necessary for its *bene esse* rather than for its *esse*—for its well-being rather than for its being at all. And when we examine their reasons for so interpreting the council, we circle back and come upon a logic by now familiar to us. It proceeds in the following syllogistic way.

> For the good of the Church as a whole, and for the good of individual persons in the Church as well as outside it, ecclesiastical authorities must be able to make judicial decisions about marriages.
>
> But to make these decisions they must be able to examine and judge marriages forensically and within the limits of forensic method.
>
> But this method can examine and verify only within the empirical domain, only on the strength of evidence verifiable in time and place.
>
> Therefore any transempirical, forensically non-verifiable elements of marriage must be excluded from the definition of its essense, or at least from the definition of its "juridical essence."

It was on the strength of this logic that the Signatura commission, the Rotal judges and Pope Paul insisted that *Gaudium et spes* does not touch the juridical essence of marriage, because it does not speak of the contract nor of the exchange of the right to an empirically verifiable act, but of empirically non-verifiable realities such as intimate sharing, a communion of life, a giving of the person, an intimate joining of persons and actions.

Let us say for a moment that they were and are correct in this interpretation of *Gaudium et spes*. But it is a begging of the question on their part to move on to the preliminary conclusion of their logic that because the bishops of the council did not speak of the juridical essence of marriage as they (the commission *et al.*) define it, they did not speak of its essential nature at all.

In his decision of July 15, 1977 reversing a judgment of nullity by the tribunal of Toulouse, the Rotal judge José Pinto criticized this judgment's *in iure* reasoning that *Gaudium et spes* has changed the juridical structure of marriage. Pinto denied this, saying: ". . . the council dealt with marriage not under the juridical aspect of validity, but under the pastoral aspect of its orientation to salvation." The disjunction Pinto states here is a surprising one. Does he mean that marriage in its juridical essence lacks the most serious of religious elements, the personal orientation to salvation, and that this orientation, because it does not belong to the essence of marriage that Pinto acknowledges, is secondary and dispensable in the marriages even of Christians?

Or does he imply something about the ontology of marriage that has been hinted at earlier in these pages? This is suggested by the consistent and traditional use of the modifier "juridical" when naming the essence of marriage. What does this use imply? That in a marriage are to be found plural essences, the juridical, the anthropological (which is philosophical-psychological-cultural), and also the religious? Though seemingly a speculative bandying of words the questions are serious ones whose answers have serious consequences. I doubt that Monsignor Pinto, educated Scholastic that he is, would indulge the crude nominalism of saying that in a marriage there are plural *substantial* essences, the juridical, the anthropological and the religious. This, if it were conceivable, would make of one marriage plural realities. But if not plural substantial essences, then are there one substantial essence and plural modifying, accidental essences? But if this is marriage's structure, then which of the essences is substantial?

A reasonable reply at this point is the same as that made earlier. When one is on the brink of defining marriage prescriptively, one ought to choose, as his criterion for the prescribing, the most valuable good that can come to both the Church collectively and to men and women singly from their marrying. This good is the final goal, the most thorough happiness they acknowledge. Since the men and women in question here are Christians as well as human beings, this goal is just the salvation that Pinto said has no relevance to the juridical essence of marriage.

Marriage Verifiable Under Any Definition?

One of the principal arguments for excluding love and the intimate community from the juridical essence of marriage travels on a boomerang trajectory. This argument is not only that it is impossible to decide the nature of the love and the community, or sharing, that are allegedly essential to marriage, but that the presence of either in a marriage is beyond the reach of forensic verification. But isn't it also true that the fact of marital consent as this is defined in the current Code of Canon Law—the consent of the will to exchange the right to sexual acts—is itself beyond the reach of such verification? This is so because a person's decision escapes forensic verification. Such verification can get at only exterior manifestation—but supposed manifestations of interior acts can always be deceptions.

The Catholic marriage law recognizes this in acknowledging simulated consent as a cause of the nullity of a supposed marriage. The judgment that a court can make about the fact of consent can never be better than probable. And traditionally the Catholic marriage courts, like all courts, have been satisfied with such probability as a warrant for their decisions provided that it is well grounded in evidence. Thus for the purposes of judicial control the difference between defining marriage as an intimate sharing caused and formed by a loving self-donation, and marriage as a juridical bond formed by consent of the will, is a difference in the quality of forensic verifiability. It appears then that the conservative determination of the nature of marriage has been ruled in some degree by a presumably better accessibility of forensic verification.

I suggest that this pragmatism, though well-intentioned because motivated by pastoral concern, should not rule the Catholic understanding of marriage. Humility is called for in defining marriage. Even where this is admittedly prescriptive defining it cannot ignore the reality for which it is prescribing; it must be reasonably descriptive. In this case it must reckon with the evidence that men's and women's act of creating their marriages, and their conduct in living their marriages, may simply go beyond the reach of judicial method.

In this regard I asked one of the judges of the Rota, in the spring of 1977, if he were confident that he and his colleagues could, at a distance of thousands of miles, and with evidence available to them only in written transcripts of lower court proceedings, judge the existence and non-existence of real-life marital relationships. His reply was that he and his colleagues could make such judgments "with sufficient accuracy." I did not press him to explain what he meant by the adjective "sufficient." But he did admit at least implicitly that his court, like all courts, makes probable judgments—such being the nature and natural limitation of judicial decisions.

But the merely probable judgments of secular courts and those of ecclesiastical courts have very different effects in the lives of the adjudicated. Secular courts can do no more to persons' conduct than to compel it in the public domain. While they have only minimally effective means for such compelling, ecclesiastical courts can seek to compel conduct by binding consciences. Their judgments carry the implication that refusal to abide by them is the moral fault, the sin of disobedience.

In some matters ecclesiastical courts can easily show good reason why their merely probable judgments should bind consciences. If serious harm would be done to the common good of the Church—for example, if a bishop has evidence amounting to strong probability that a pastor is leading a dissolute life—authority in the Church can compel persons on the strength of this probability. The good, the happiness of the individual, in this case of the man as a pastor, cannot override the good of his own and neighboring parishes, even where the evidence of his immoral life comes only to high probability.

But man-woman relationships are frequently so different. Suppose a woman has become privately certain, after ten years of married life, that her husband has never willed her well-being and has therefore never really loved her, but she cannot bring to the marriage court available to her the quantity and quality of evidence needed to gain from it a judgment of nullity. What reason can ecclesiastical authorities give her justifying their judgment that she is bound in conscience to regard herself as the man's wife, bound to him by an imperishable bond as long as they both live, when *she* judges honestly that her happiness is possible only in a marriage with a man who truly loves her, and when she judges that happiness will be within her reach even in eternity only if she lives this life in such a marriage?

To tell her that she must be held to the presumed marriage despite only the probability, at best, of its existence lest the structure of marriage in the Church and in secular society crumble more disastrously than it has is to adduce a reason quite different from that given to the pastor when he is removed. The Church as a society of persons—not as a reified institution—exists for the happiness of those persons. The life of the Church is a collective effort at bringing the experiences of trust, belief and caring love for them. The pastor does not need a parish pastorate in order to experience these, nor certainly to gain eternal happiness. But the woman may have an unqualified need of a lasting heterosexual experience of trust, faith and caring love in order to experience happiness at all. To hold her to a marital relationship in which these are denied her because the nullity of her marriage is only probably evident according to the method of empirical adjudication, and to do this for the well-being of the Church, is to invert the nature itself of the Church.

The Sacrament as Source and Model

Surely the Catholic Church can provide from her own resources an understanding of marriage that is at one and the same time objectively descriptive and prescriptive in a way that is Christian. For the descriptive element the Church's teachers could follow the example of the Roman jurists, Ulpianus and Modestinus, who wisely included only the most generic elements in their informal definitions of marriage: the joining of men and women in a single, or undivided, sharing in all of life. Or if even this description fails at universal descriptiveness because it excludes polygamous marriage, the adjective—whether "single" or "undivided"—could be omitted.

It is the prescriptive element of the definition that then must specify the kind of sharing by men and women that forms a marriage. Here the

Church's teachers must choose a criterion for this sharing, even a model. This they must do by naming the final goal they intend for it, which is the highest good that men and women may seek in it.

Here is the juncture in the Church's defining of marriage at which a substantive change has been needed since the thirteenth century, the juncture at which the bishops of the Second Vatican Council have in fact made such a change. Since that century the goal of the Church's prescriptive defining of marriage has been to simultaneously accomplish two tasks, one of them virtually forced on the medieval canonists by a tradition as old as the Synoptic narratives of Christ's conception. This was to account for the possibility of Mary's preserving her virginity while yet being truly married. This the canonists and theologians of the twelfth and thirteenth centuries did by making the object of marital consent the exchange of only the right to sexual intercourse (a right which need not be used), but at the same time by keeping sexual intercourse within the object of marital consent and thus keeping in it the element of the man-woman relationship that makes it marital and nothing else.

The other task was to design a definition that would be an effective instrument for judicial regulation of marriages for the good of both civil and ecclesiastical societies. By happily adroit design the definition that served the first task served also this second one. The definition of marriage seemed sufficiently amenable to judicial verification when the act creating it was defined as a consent of the will by both parties creating a juridical bond which is a contract, which is in turn an exchange of the parties' right to sexual intercourse. With this named as the object of marital consent, the primary good of marriage as Augustine had named it—procreation and nurture (understood subsequently as the primary end of the contract)—could easily be written into the definition.

What of the understanding of marriage the sacrament that was fixing itself in Catholic thinking at the same time—of the marriages of Christians as images of the love of Christ and the Church? When the reconciling of this biblical vision of the sacrament with the juridical definition of marriage was not simply ignored, it was forced quite simply. The love of Christ and the Church was said to be imaged in Christian marriages by the partners' exchange of the right to their sexual acts, by their use of this right, and by their confining their sexual activity faithfully to the exchanged right, but most especially by their confining it there permanently, until the death of one of them.

What I proposed a few pages earlier to hold in abeyance is now due for full statement. I urge that the criterion and model for the prescriptive, specifying element of the Catholic Church's definition of marriage be found in the sacrament. Note again that such a criterion ought to contain the highest good, the ultimate goal that marriage as a societal relationship can bring to those who enter it, who create it by their marital consent. Where men and women form this relationship as Christians, presumably they do so with the goal in mind that is the vision of God and his intimate love—do so with the intent to begin this vision and love this side of death in order to continue them endlessly beyond death.

Presumably too they intend to make their way to the unending condition of this vision and love in the next life by experiencing in their marriages in this life a love that images the love of Christ and the Church. But this love was and is, before all else, a self-giving and even sacrificial love— a self-donation made for the sake of the beloved's happiness.

This love has always been fertile, creative, constructive on the part of Christ in that it has bred in men and women in the Church belief, trust, selfless caring and the willingness to forgive and to heal damaged relationships. It has been fertile and creative on the Church's part in her striving, in the persons of Christian men and women, to make up in their own lives what is still incomplete in the sufferings of Christ.

It is not unreasonable that the Church's teachers define marriage the human relationship so that it may serve as the matrix of the sacrament understood in this way. If I understand what the bishops of Vatican II said in *Gaudium et spes*, they have indeed defined it in this way. The specifying element in their definition, the element which most proximately readies the relationship to become the sacrament, is the self-giving love that they examine and set forth in their paragraph 49 (which is titled "Marital Love"). Only if they define marriage in this way, with love as the cause creating it and as the abiding *forma* making it to be what it is, can they account reasonably for the marital unions themselves of Christians being sacraments.

The severe reluctance of the Signatura commission and of the conservative Rotal judges to admit love into the definition of marriage is in one sense understandable, but in another baffling. It is understandable because there are so many kinds of love, and because they are aware that couples have tried marriage because of romantic fascination and have abandoned marriages because of it. At close range, in Rome and nearby, they saw Roberto Rossellini, the exemplary Catholic and splendid Marian sodalist, abandon his wife and children for Ingrid Bergman in the 1950's when both were making a film on location on the island of Stromboli—with Rossellini pleading a shared love that Miss Bergman described at the time as "eternal."

The bafflement comes from two sources. The first is the failure of the prelates and the judges to understand that since, as prescriptive definers of marriage, they could keep out of its definition whichever kinds of love they thought ought to be kept out, then a fortiori they could keep out of it the silly infatuation that survived between Rossellini and Bergman for a filmland eternity of about six years. The second source is their failure to see that there has been ready at hand since the beginning of Christianity a love that they can write into the heart of the definition of marriage, and by doing so make of the latter a prescription for a responsible, morally rich, fruitful and holiness-producing man-woman relationship. The model for this love is there in the beginnings of Christian tradition—the self-giving love of Christ for his people.

To honor again for a moment the prelates' and the judges' concern for the accessibility of marital love to judicial verification, their concern would be justified if into the understanding of the love were allowed infatuation, emotional attachment, or auto-erotic projection. But I know of no Catholic thinker or writer who wants these in the understanding of marital love. The love that *Gaudium et spes* puts into marriage "leads the spouses to a free and mutual gift of themselves, a gift proving itself by gentle affection and by deed. Such love pervades the whole of their lives. Indeed by its generous activity it grows better and grows greater." It is hard to see that there is less judicial verifiability in a man's and a woman's mutual commitment to this generous activity than there is in their mutual exchange of the exclusive and permanent right to their sexual acts. (To say that sexual intercourse after the presumed exchange proves the exchange would, as Catholic marriage law itself implies, beg the question.)

A Dubious Philosophy of Defining

When Pope Paul VI and the conservative canonists predicate the terms "juridical reality" and "juridical essence" of marriage they raise a question about the philosophy—the epistemology— that rules their mode of defining. The use of the adjective "juridical" either modifies the nouns to a signification that is confused or implies a meaning in the minds of its users that is dubious. The confusion in signification is that the use of the adjective suggests that there are plural essences in a marriage, of which the juridical is only one. The dubiety of meaning, which really amounts to error, is the suggestion that the only essence in marriage is juridical.

The accurate use of the adjective would take the formulation "the juridical dimension or quality of marriage," which would imply accurately that this is one dimension or quality among others, and would leave open the question whether this is the substantial, fundamental dimension. Judged by the criteria of juridical identity that I listed earlier in this chapter, marriage surely has this dimension.

This confusion becomes a misfortune for the Church because of something current in the minds of the Catholic people that the judges and other canonists who agree with them surely know of and apparently take for granted. This is that the Catholic married do not experience their marriages as juridical realities and do not understand them as such. That the people are not thought by these canonists to experience and think of their marriages in this way emerged in the *expensio modorum*, the explanation and disposing of amendments, of the final text of *Gaudium et spes* in the general assembly of the Vatican II bishops on December 3 and 4, 1965. The reader may recall that a number of traditional-minded bishops asked earnestly at the eleventh hour of the council that the established predicates defining marriage—hierarchy of primary and secondary ends, exchange of the contractual right, marriage as a sacred bond—be kept in the text of *Gaudium et spes*. The reply from the Mixed Commission presenting and explaining the document was that the canonical precision this *modus* asked for is not needed in a pastoral statement, that juridical and excessively technical terms are to be avoided in a document addressed to the world. Since it is most unlikely that the people of the world would understand marriage as a juridical entity *apart* from these terms that the Commission said are not appropriate, it is accurate to conclude that the people do not and would not understand that juridical description of the nature of marriage. In other words, marriage as it is understood in the world by the Catholic people is not marriage as it is understood by the canonists who wanted these technical terms kept in *Gaudium et spes*.

But what kind of law would legislate for a relationship—marriage—conceived of in a mode of existence unfamiliar to, indiscernible by, and even alien to the persons who live the relationship? Putting it epistemologically, where does the "marriage" exist for which such a law would legislate? If not in the consciousness of the married, in their minds, wills and emotions, then where else? In asking this question we are only repeating what Doms *et al.* asked in the early 1930's about the phenomenological emptiness of the Church's traditional concept of marriage in the 1917 Code of Canon Law, its lack of reference to anything that goes on in lived reality.

The answer to the question about the kind of law that would legislate in this way is that a law grounded consciously or unconsciously in a Platonic vision of reality would do so. In this vision reality is found in truth and is synonymous with truth, and truth is by nature immutable. Therefore reality is not to be found in lived daily life, which is contingent and changing. It is found in the ideal models of persons, things and relationships. The models are indeed models, for they are the criteria according to which the concrete, this-life approximations are measured. Thus the definition of marriage coming from this epistemology is a design of the ideal model of marriage. Man-woman relationships are to be shaped according to this ideal and their correspondence to truth is to be measured by it. So, to the question "Where does the 'marriage' exist for which such a law would legislate?" the answer is: "In the mind of the legislator."

Intelligent layfolk to whom I have detailed some of this history of the defining of marriage by churchmen have at times asked: "How can *they* say what a marriage is in reality? A person can't say what a marriage is unless he has some experience of it. What experience have they had of marriage in real life?" It has seemed to me accurate to explain that with the traditional-minded churchmen saying what marriage is in real life has not been their concern in defining marriage. What these lay friends see as reality in marriage is not what the churchmen see and is not what they are concerned about. Their concern is to define what they think ought to be the ideal model of marriage— an ideal for their working out effectively a pastoral regulation of marriage.

Shortly before this was written the Synod of Catholic Bishops met in Rome with Pope John Paul II. The American bishops, represented by Archbishop John Quinn of San Francisco and Archbishop Joseph Bernardin of Cincinnati, asked that the Church's proscription of contraception be re-examined, and cited as a reason for this that there is an injurious discordance between the minds of the Church's teachers and those of the Catholic married at least in the United States. In support of this statement of fact Archbishops Quinn and Bernardin cited the statistical finding of the Gallup poll showing that about seventy-five percent of the Catholic married women in the U.S. disagree with the magisterial judgment, with approximately as high a proportion of priests sharing this disagreement. The reflection of Cardinal Pericle Felici on this (if the press reported his statement accurately) was: "Statistics don't mean anything."

What Cardinal Felici said may sometimes be true. Statistics may in certain cases not touch reality. But this depends on what the statistics are about, and even more on how close to the examined facet of reality the persons polled may be. If statistics reported the percentage of middle Europeans in 500 A.D. who replied when asked if they thought the earth is a sphere or a disk, the statistical finding would not mean anything. But, contraception aside, if the statistics report on the understanding of marriage in the minds of the Catholic married, and the overwhelming majority of them do not experience marriage as it is defined by a few churchmen, then the persons on one or other side of the disagreement are out of touch with reality. And this is not without meaning.

Paul VI's mind was working in a transparently Platonic way when, in his discourse to the Rota in February 1976, he explained why a marriage does not and cannot disintegrate and pass out of existence even though the spouses' love and intimate sharing vanish. He said that a particular, real-life marriage exists in an objective order—that "when they give their free consent the spouses do nothing other than to enter and be fixed in an objective order or institution which is something greater than themselves." Two paragraphs earlier he had said that the spouses' marital consent produces a juridical effect which is the marriage *in facto esse*, a living state.

It is the ontology of marriage, as Paul suggests it here, that is interesting. He seems to have meant quite deliberately that what exists in marriage's irreducibly essential existence in the objective order is not the relationship of spouse with spouse, not their sharing, not the intimate community that *Gaudium et spes* identified, not the habitual attitude, or set, of the spouses' wills toward one another. It is not something *of them* that exists, not a condition modifying their existence interiorly, not something existing *in them* or *linking them*. Rather he meant that their marriage is something "objectively" there, apparently distinct from them, created by them—but once created, existing of itself, a juridical category *in which* they exist. The verb he used to designate how they enter their marriage was *inseruntur;* they are "inserted" into this juridical category. In brief, as Paul saw it, the heart of the existence of a marriage (underneath the person-to-person relationship, the shared life, the union of wills, the communion of their being that he had named in his encyclical *Humanae vitae*) is not different from the existence, say, of a person's citizenship. It is a prepared juridical category, objectively there, into which one may choose or not to be "inserted." And, for Paul, this is the heart of the reality of a marriage, because this is what survives even if all else in it vanishes.

Intent in Defining in *Gaudium et spes*

If one were to agree with Pope Paul, the Signatura commission and the conservative Rotal judges, one would accept implicity that the Catholic Church has two definitions of marriage, one according to its juridical essence, the other according to its anthropological essence. If the history of the Church's defining of marriage is not at an end, the next move in this history ought obviously to be either a reconciling of these two definitions, if possible, or a selecting of one or the other.

Did the bishops of Vatican II intend that the Church have these two definitions? Only an explicit statement from them that as a group they rejected one or the other would remove the last doubt about their intent. But the accumulation of evidence, and the preponderance of it, is against their consciously wanting two definitions or their unwittingly allowing two. What follows here is this evidence.

If they accepted the two definitions that were proposed, they accepted one which the people understand, which more clearly describes marriage as the latter experience it, and another which only churchmen, the magisterial authorities and the canonists, are expected to understand, and by which these regulate and adjudicate marriages. A priori it is not believable that the bishops would either install or permit this damaging discordance between two sides of the Catholic consciousness.

Folded into this question of installing or permitting two definitions of marriage is the subsidiary question asking if the bishops intended that in *Gaudium et spes* they state to Catholics what is the essential nature of marriage. Certainly Cardinal Ottaviani and the Theological Commission intended that the council state this, although they meant the statement to reiterate *Casti connubii*, the Code of Canon Law, the 1944 condemnation of Doms *et al.* by the Holy Office and Pius XII's fuller version of this condemnation in 1951. As Cardinal Ottaviani said, the statement was to be "... pastoral, but pastoral and *doctrinal*, not pastoral-disciplinary." Nowhere did the Preparatory Commission void this doctrinal intent for the council's statement on marriage.

The progressive members of the Preparatory Commission—Cardinals Döpfner, Alfrink, Suenens, Léger, König—who argued successfully against accepting the Theological Commission's *De castitate, virginitate, matrimonio, familia* for consideration by the council, argued not because they wanted no more than a description of the non-essentials of marriage. They did so expressly because that document limited its understanding of marriage to its juridical traits and failed to describe it as the Catholic married experience it. That is, as an attempt at describing the nature of marriage to the married of the world it was inadequate.

The conservative prelates in the general assembly of the council clearly thought that the statement on marriage they were to promulgate was to set forth the essential nature of marriage and its single essential nature. That they thought this was evident in their struggle to write the traditional definition into the statement—the definition according to the hierarchy of subordinated ends and the right to the parties' sexual acts as the object of marital consent. They tried to do this because they thought that the text of *Gaudium et spes* as it came to the general assembly in October 1965, and as it survived substantially unchanged until the council adjourned on December 8 of that year, did not set forth marriage's essential nature at all, or because they thought it did so erroneously.

The intervention by the authority "higher than the papal Secretary of State" on November 24, 1965, a week after the deadline for proposing amendments to the text of *Gaudium et spes*, shows that this "higher authority" himself understood that the constitution's statement on marriage was to set forth the essential nature of marriage. This intervention ordered that where *Gaudium et spes* spoke of the ends of marriage in its paragraph 50, a word be deleted. The deletion was intended to so revise the formulation as to make clear that the document reasserted the hierarchy of subordinated ends in marriage. The way in which the council's Mixed Commission, which supervised the drafting of *Gaudium et spes*, dealt with this *modus* shows that it too understood that the defining of marriage's essential nature was at issue. It deleted the word as requested. But it added to the paragraph the clause that marks so clearly the crossroad in the Church's magisterial teaching on this subject: "Hence, while not making the other ends of marriage of less account. . . ." I say that the evidence is clear because for centuries the crucial terms exposing the essential nature of marriage had been *fines matrimonii*. That *Gaudium et spes* uses these terms at this juncture evidences the intent to speak of this nature.

That the bishops in general assembly understood *Gaudium et spes* was intended to state the essential nature of marriage is just as evident in the severest of the *modi* put before them on December 3. These criticized the constitution's chapter on marriage as theologically immature, as either equivocal or silent on some essential points, and as speaking of marriage in a way discordant with the Church's constant teaching, especially as this was expressed anew in *Casti connubii* and by Popes Pius XII, John XXIII, and the incumbent Paul VI. These *modi* demanded, among other things, that the chapter state clearly the hierarchy of subordinated ends in marriage, the validity of a marriage even where love is absent, and the object of marriage as the exchange of rights and duties proper to marriage.

The first of these *modi* came from only two bishops. It was followed by another coming from thirty-four bishops urging that the same object of marital consent be written into the statement. It in turn was followed immediately by a *modus* coming from one hundred and ninety bishops demanding the reinstatement of the doctrine of traditional ends of marriage in hierarchical order and of the traditional object of marital consent. And this, finally, was followed by a *modus* from ten bishops urging, as a counter-demand, that the object of consent be stated as a mutual giving and receiving of the spouses' persons.

Again this is evidence that the bishops on both sides of the disagreement, the conservative and the progressive, understood what was at issue, the Church's understanding of the essential nature of marriage.

The Mixed Commission's reply to these *modi* has played a serious role in the history of the Church's defining of marriage that was hardly foreseeable at the time it was made. Understanding the reply in one way a student could say that the Commission, a *de facto* author of the council's statement on marriage, undercut the general assembly's assumption that the statement was meant to define the essential nature of marriage, and that the reply in effect quieted the conservative prelates' anxiety over the abandoning of the conceptual system of hierarchically ordered ends of marriage and the exchange of rights as the object of marital consent. The question is crucial for this history of defining: Did the following reply to the *modi* say that *Gaudium et spes* was not intended to be a defining document and that the bishops were mistaken in thinking it such? The reply said that ". . . the canonical precision requested in the *modi* is not called for in a pastoral statement"; ". . . in a statement that is pastoral, that seeks to start up a conversation with the world, these juridical details [hierarchy of ends, object of marital consent] are not called for"; ". . . in such a document excessively technical terms [such as "hierarchically"] are not called for".

Yet even as the Mixed Commission's reply made these distinctions it sought to show that the statement on marriage did not contradict the traditional teaching. It explained that the inclusion of the persons of the spouses in the object of marital consent along with their right to sexual acts is necessary because rights inhere in persons. It explained that the hierarchy of the ends of marriage can be considered under diverse aspects, and it pointed out that even in *Casti connubii* Pius XI had said that if marriage is considered in its fuller sense, the fulfillment and sanctification of the spouses can be taken as its primary end. And finally, in order to banish all doubt that *Gaudium et spes* sustains the centuries-old tradition of the essentiality to marriage of procreation and nurture, the Commission pointed out the following paragraph in its text: "By their very nature the institution of marriage itself and marital love are ordered to the procreation and nurture of children, and find in them their ultimate crown." It was *Gaudium et spes* containing this assertion that the general assembly of the bishops accepted by an overwhelming majority vote.

Students of the subject must decide from their own examination of the evidence which of two things the council did. Because it produced only an admittedly pastoral statement had it no intention of resolving the disagreement about the primacy of procreation and nurture among the ends of marriage; therefore its clear aligning of these ends in parity cannot be taken as changing their traditional hierarchical alignment? (Clearly the Rotal judges José Pinto, Giuseppe Palazzini and Sebastiano Masala have chosen this interpretation. So too did Cardinal Staffa and the Signatura commission, and along with them Pope Paul VI in his 1976 discourse to the Rota. A more recent affirmation of this interpretation was made by Cardinal Pietro Palazzini during the Catholic synod of bishops at Rome in October of 1980. It is reported that he ". . . made the astounding statement that although Vatican Council II had not used the term 'principal and secondary ends of marriage,' that term had been implicitly retained in its teaching. As a consequence, traditional Church doctrine that procreation is the primary end of marriage has to be upheld in keeping with the constant mind of the magisterium."[1])

Or did the council intend to state once for always the essential nature of marriage, even though *Gaudium et spes* is admittedly a pastoral rather than a dogmatic constitution, and in replacing the hierarchical ordering of the ends of marriage with a statement of their parity, it resolved definitively the disagreement about this ordering in favor of parity? (Just as clearly the other Rotal judges, Lucien Anné, Vincenzo Fagiolo, J. M. Serrano, Ignace Raad—to name the most active among them—have opted for this interpretation.)

A most authoritative group of prelates seems also to have taken this interpretation. In its meeting in Rome during the last week of May 1977, the *plenarium* of cardinals supervising the revision of the Code of Canon Law voted to keep a defining concept of marriage in the revision (in new Canons 242 and 244) and voted that in this definition be included the element of "conjoining, or sharing, of life" as an expression of the personal aspect of marriage. And the *plenarium* took this phrase expressly from paragraph 48 of *Gaudium et spes*. As a consequence these two defining canons now read in their formulations awaiting promulgation (in those of their paragraphs pertinent to the definition of marriage) as follows:

242.1 The marital covenant, by which a man and a woman create between themselves an intimate sharing in all life, a sharing of its nature oriented to the good of the spouses and to the procreation and nurture of children, has been raised, when it is of baptized persons, to the dignity of a sacrament.

244.2 Marital consent is an act of the will by which a man and a woman give themselves and accept one another in an irrevocable covenant in order to create a marriage.

The cardinals' insistence that a defining conception of marriage be written into the revision of the law (insistence, we recall, over the worried objection of their conservative colleagues, with Cardinal Palazzini the most explicitly worried) and their taking the defining conception *verbatim* from *Gaudium et spes* seem clear evidence that they thought the council had meant in this document to state the essential nature of marriage. After all, they had themselves been members of the council and presumably remembered after an interval of eleven and a half years from the adjourning of the council in December 1965 what they had voted to say in *Gaudium et spes*. And they surely meant new Canons 242 and 244 to state this nature, since they were aware that their promulgation in the revised law would establish them as the criteria by which marriages would be adjudicated in the long future.

This is the latest point of arrival in the long history of the Catholic Church's defining of marriage. Whether it is the ultimate point, whether this history has come to its end and the Church has a final and fixed definition, remains to be seen. That the bishops' descriptive (or prescriptive?) definition, in *Gaudium et spes*, of marriage's nature did not resolve all doubts and end disagreements is evident in the disparate interpretations of their statements that have filled the years since the council. Therefore the continuation of this history will most probably be the effort to resolve these doubts and the disagreements they breed.

The process making up this continuing history, the work of resolving the doubts, is concentrated currently in the jurisprudential activity of the Church's marriage courts. It is to be expected that the two sides of the dialectic would work most clearly in these courts. We see this in the disagreeing judgments on nullity of marriages coming from different *turnus* of judges in the Rota, disagreeing because the several judges comprising the *turnus* bring disagreeing definitions of marriage to their work.

Let me close with a point made earlier and at greater length. It seems obvious that the Catholic Church's definition of marriage cannot be a single *descriptive* definition, one that looks on marriage in all of history in all its cultures and finds univocity in them. Marriage has been understandable univocally from culture to culture only in its most generic trait, in that it has been in all of them a more or less stable heterosexual relationship.

As the only alternative then, this definition must be prescriptive. And this is no misfortune. It is better that the inclusive Christian family, the Church, design her own most precious intra-familial relationship. But who shall do this designing? To be sure, the promulgating of the design is the acknowledged function of the Church's appointed teachers, her bishops with the bishop of Rome at their head. But the design cannot be drawn out of thin air; even a prescription must prescribe a relationship possible and productive in real life, and must therefore be to some degree descriptive. For the design must be the design of a form of life that helps men and women to the happiness that is available in intimate, persevering and sexually expressed love. Only those men and women who have searched for happiness in this kind of relationship can say which forms and sub-forms of it work. The bishops must ask the married about this. In another of their statements promulgated in the council, their Constitution on Divine Revelation, they suggested to themselves, in a roundabout way, the necessity of their going to those in the Church experienced in specific ways of life, if they are to teach well. In naming the persons in the Church who work to gradually clarify the meaning of tradition coming down from the apostles, they spoke of ". . . the meditation, the pondering carried on by the faithful who hold these things [this tradition] precious . . . through their personal, intimate understanding of the spiritual realities they experience."[2] Since they are the Christian married who experience marriage in the Church, they are its proper definers.

NOTES

1. This statement by Cardinal Palazzini was reported by Francis X. Murphy in his essay "Of Sex and the Catholic Church" in *The Atlantic Monthly,* January 1981, p. 55.

2. Par. 8 (in *The Documents of Vatican II,* p. 116).

INDEX OF PROPER NAMES

Abbott, Walter, editor: *The Documents of Vatican II,* 34, note 3

Abelard, Peter; *Epitome of Christian Theology,* 153

Albert the Great: *Commentarium in IV Libros Sententiarum: Petri Lombardi,* 188; *De Matrimonio,* 178

Alfrink, Cardinal Bernard Jan, 252, 253–255, 262

Albigensians, 177

Alexander II, Pope, 153

Alexander III, Pope, 168, 169, 193, 194

Ambrose: *Exposition of the Gospel According to Luke,* 119, 145

Anné, Lucien, 300–302, 306, 307

Anselm of Laon: *Sententiae: Tractatus de Matrimonio,* 152–153

Antinoous, 84

Commission for the Apostolate of the Laity of Vatican II, 258

Aquinas, Thomas: *Commentarium in IV Libros Sententiarum Petri Lombardi,* 179, 180, 181, 182; *Summa Theologica,* 303, 317; *In Decem Libros Ethicorum Aristotelis ad Nicomachum Expositio* 182–183

Aristotle: *The History of Animals,* 112; Nicomachean Ethics, 107, 109, 112–114, 115–116; *Politics,* 105, 107, 108; *Rhetoric,* 112; *In Stobaeus' Eclogues,* 109

Arndt, W.F. and Gingrich, F.W.: *A Greek-English Lexicon of the New Testament and Other Early Christian Literature, Second Edition,* 67, note 2

Anthanagoras: *Supplication for the Christians,* 117

Augustine, Aurelius, 10–11, 13, 20, 74, 91, 93, 145, 177; *De Adulterinis Coniugiis (On Adulterous Marriages),* 35–36, note 11, Chapter 5 *passim; De Bono Coniugali (On The Good of Marriage)* Chapter 5 *passim;* 35, note 8; 177, 317; *De Bono Viduitatis (On The Good of Widowhood),* 162; *De Genesi ad Litteram (Commentary on the Literal Meaning of Genesis),* 129; 132; *De Civitate Dei (The City of God),* 143; *Contra Faustum Manichaeum (Against Faustum the Manichee),* 138, note 26; *De Moribus Ecclesiae Catholicae (On the Morals of the Catholic Church),* 141; *De Nuptiis et Concupiscentiae (On Marriage and Concupiscence),* Chapter 5, *passim; De Peccato Originali (On Original Sin)* 129, 132, 133, 134

Bandinelli, Rolando (Alexander III), 168–169

Barth, Markus: *Commentary on Ephesians (In the Anchor Bible,* Vol. 34A), 68, note 13

Basil of Caesarea, 145

Basilides, 87

Bea, Cardinal Augustin, 257
Bejan, Ovidiu (Judge of the Roman Rota), 299, 301
Benedict XIV: *Constitution Dei Miseratione,* 212
Bernardin, Archbishop Joseph, 344
Bonaventure: *Commentarium in IV Libros Sententiae Petri Lombardi,* 183–185
Boniface VIII, Pope, 194
Bouscaren, T. Lincoln and Ellis, Adam C.: *Canon Law: A Text and Commentary, Third Revised Edition,* 10; 34, note 4
Browne, Cardinal Michael, 255–256, 262
Brueggemann, Walter: "Of the Same Flesh and Blood", in *The Catholic Biblical Quarterly,* Vol. 32,4 (1970), 66, note 2

Callistus I, Pope, 77
Camara, Bishop Helder, 258
Canon Law Society of America, 285–286
Carpino, Cardinal Francesco, 327, note 50
Carpocrates and the Carpocratian Gnostics, 84, 87
Cassianus, Julius, 83
Cathars, 177
Central Preparatory Commission of Vatican II, 248, 252
Chapuis, John, 193
Chrysostom, John: *On Virginity,* 92–93
Cicero: *De Finibus,* 106
Clement of Alexandria: Stromata, 83, 84, 85, 87, 88, 89, 97
Clement I, Pope, 192
Mixed Commission of Vatican II, 262–264, 271
Congregation of the Holy Office, 225, 249, 272, 273, 289, 309
Congregation of the Sacraments, 241, 248
Corbett, P.E.C.: *The Roman Law of Marriage,* 79, note 1

Daube, David: *The New Testament and Rabbinic Judaism: Part II, Legislative and Narrative Forms,* 123, note 8
Dearden, Archbishop Charles, 263, 264
Deferrari, Roy J., editor: *Hugh of St. Victor: On the Sacraments of the Christian Faith,* 174, note 5
Denzinger-Schönmetzer: *Enchiridion Symbolorum* 175, note 37; 222, notes, 1, 4; 269
DeVaux, Roland: *Ancient Israel,* 47, 98
Diogenes Laërtius: *Lives and Opinions,* Book 7, 105
Doms, Heribert: *The Meaning of Marriage,* 218, 225, 231–235, 245, 246, 279
Donovan, Rev. J., editor: *Catechism of the Council of Trent,* 222, note 6
Döpfner, Cardinal Julius, 252–253, 262

Ebertz, Otfried: *Vom Aufgang und Niedergang Des Männschlichen Weltalters,* 226
Encratite Gnostics, 83
Epictetus: *Discourses,* 105

Fagiolo, Vincenzo (Judge of the Roman Rota), 301, 303, 348
Felici, Cardinal Pericle, 264, 284, 290, 344, 348
Fellhauer, David E.: "The *Consortium Omnis Vitae* as a Juridical Element", in *Studia Canonica,* Vol. 13,1 (1979), 79, notes 1, 2, 4; 211–213
Fiore, Ernesto (Judge of the Roman Rota), 299, 300, 301

von Gagern, Friedrich: *L'Amour des Epoux,* 246, note 19
Gasparri, Cardinal Pietro: *Tractatus Canonicus de Matrimonio,*

204–205; 223, note 21; 246, note
11; 293
Gaudemet, J.: *La Definitio Romano-
Canonique du Mariage*, 75
van Gaytenbeek, A.C.: *Musonius
Rufus and the Greek Diatribe*, 27,
note 4
Goodall, Jane, 144, note 35
Gratian: *Decretum*, 158–164
Gregory VII, Pope, 154
Gregory IX, Pope: *Liber Decretalium*,
170, 172–173, 193
Gregory of Nazianz, 145
Gregory of Nyssa: *De Opificio Mundi*,
91–92, 145

Haarlem, regional tribunal, 314
Hadrian, Emperor, 84
Häring, Bernard: *Ehe in Dieser Zeit*,
246, note 246; 239
Hierocles, 109
von Hildebrand, Dietrich, 225,
227–229; 245, note 1
Hillel, Rabbi, 42
Hincmar of Rheims, 150
Hugh of St. Victor: *De Sacramento
Coniugii*, 155–158; *De Beatae
Mariae Virginis Virginitate*, 155;
*Hugh of St. Victor: On the
Sacraments of the Christian Faith*,
174, note 5
Huizing, Peter, 285
Hypollitus, 77

Ignatius of Antioch, 77
Innocent III, Pope, 170, 194
Irenaeus of Lyons: 105; *Adversus
Haereses*, 84, 85, 87, 89

Janssens, Louis, 239
Jeremias, Joachim: *Jerusalem in the
Time of Jesus*, 47–50
John XXIII, Pope, 193, 248, 271, 283
Justin Martyr, 105; *First Apology* 117
Justinian: *Digesta*, 73, 146; *Instituta*,
73, 146

Jerome: *Commentary on the Epistle to
the Galatians*, 119; On Ephesians
5 in the Vulgate New Testament,
67, note 12; *Epistola 100*, 91;
Against Jovinian, 111

Keating, John R.: *The Bearing of
Mental Impairment on the
Validity of Marriage: An Analysis
of Rotal Jurisprudence*, 35, note 7
Kerns, Joseph: *The Theology of
Marriage*, 119
Koch, Anton: *Lehrbuch der
Moraltheologie*, 226
Krempel, Bernardin, 245, note 1

Lactantius: *Divine Institutes*, 118
Larraona, Cardinal Arcadio, 257;
279–280, note 18
Fourth Lateran Council and
clandestine marriages, 194, 197
Leclercq, Jacques: *Le Mariage
Chretien*, 246, note 19
Léger, Cardinal Paul Emile, 252, 262,
264
Leo I, Pope: *Epistola 167, Ad
Rusticum*, 151
Leo XIII, Pope: *Encyclical Letter:
Arcanum Divinae Sapientiae*, 213
Lercaro, Cardinal Giacomo, 258
Lesage, Germain: "The *Consortium
Vitae Coniugalis:* Nature and
Applications", in *Studia
Canonica*, Vol. 6 (1972), 307–308,
309
Linsermann, F.X.: *Lehrbuch der
Moraltheologie*, 226
Lombard, Peter: *Libri Sententiarum*,
164–167
Luther, Martin: *On Marriage Matters*,
196

Mary, Mother of Jesus, 340
Mackin, Theodore: "Consummation:
Of Contract or of Covenant?" in
The Jurist, Vol. 32,1 and 32,2, 246

Marcion, 83

Martin, J.-P.: *De Matrimonio et Potestate Ipsum Dirimendi . . .*, 202

Masala, Sebastiano (Judge of the Roman Rota), 310–33, 348

McKenzie, John L.: *Dictionary of the Bible*, 124, note 14

Melancthon, Philip, 196

Merleau-Ponty, Maurice, 225

Michel, Ernst, 226; 245, note 1; 279, note 12

Minucius Felix: *Octavius*, 105

Modestinus (Definition of Marriage), 73–74, 146, 339

Moeller, Charles, 239; 280, note 21

Montini, Cardinal Giovanni Battista, 258

Musonius Rufus 109–110

Navarette, Urbano, 212–213, 246, 296, 307

Nicholas I, Pope: *Responsum ad Bulgaros*, 148, 150

Nicolaitian Gnostics, 85

Noonan, John T., Jr.: *Contraception*, 122, note 1

Ocellas Lucanus: *Universal Nature*, 111

Onan and onanism, 101

Oraison, Marc, 239; 246, note 19

Palazzini, Giuseppe (Judge of the Roman Rota), 304, 348

Palazzini, Cardinal Pietro, 290; 327, note 50; 349

Paucapalia, 164

Paul VI, Pope: On marital love in *Humanae vitae*, 19, 20; On the meaning of marriage in *Humanae vitae*, 28–29; 36, note 14; Argument against contraception in *Humanae vitae*, 246–247, note 21; Discourse to the Roman Rota of February 9, 1976, 25, 30, 214, 320–322, 344; Debate on *Gaudium et spes*, 264–265, 271, 289

Philo: *On Abraham*, 103; *On Joseph*, 103, 109; *De Opificio Mundi*, 102; *Special Laws*, 102, 104

Phyntis, 109

Pinto, José (Judge of the Roman Rota), 304, 308, 309, 310–311, 337

Plenarium of Cardinals (meeting of May 22–28, 1977), 286–287, 298, 324, 348

Pius V, Pope and the Catechism of Trent, 198

Pius XI, Pope: Encyclical Letter, *Casti Connubii*, 215–218, 251, 259, 277, 289, 346–347

Pius XII, Pope, 225, 271, 289; Discourse of October 29, 1951 to the Union of Italian Catholic Obstetricians, 219, 237, 238, 263, 319; Discourse to the Roman Rota of October 3, 1941, 246, note 18; Discourse to newlyweds of March 18, 1942, 246, note 18; Discourse to the Second World Congress on Fertility and Sterility, 246, note 18

Plato: *The Republic*, 105, 106

Pliny: *Epistles*, 84

Pompedda, Mario (Judge of the Roman Rota), 302

Pontifical Study Commission on Population Control, 271, 275

Prodicus, Roman Gnostic, 85

Quinn, Archbishop John, 344

Raad, Ignace (Judge of the Roman Rota), 307–308, 348

Rabbi Bibbi, 101

Rabbi Eleazar, 101

Rabbi Hillel, 42

Rabbi Shammai, 42

Raymond of Peñafort, 193

Regimund, 150

Reidlich, Gertrude: *Die Hierarkische Struktur der Ehe*, 246

Reinhardt, Marion Justin and Arella, Gerard J.: "Essential Incompatibility as Grounds for Nullity of Marriage", in *The Catholic Lawyer*, Vol. 16 (1970), 33, note 1; 33–34, note 2

Reuss, Bishop Josef of Mainz, 262

Rondet, Henri: *Introduction a L'Etude de la Theologie du Mariage*, 246, note 19

Rosset, M.: *De Sacramento Matrimonii*, 203

Rossi, Bernard (regional tribunal of Vancouver, Canada), 327, note 49

Rufinus: *Summa* of the Decretum of Gratian, 172

Rynne, Xavier: *The Fourth Session: The Debates and Decrees of Vatican Council II*, 280, note 32

Sacred Congregation of the Sacraments: ruling of August 2, 1958 on consummation, 36, note 15

Commission for the Discipline of the Sacraments in Vatican II: *Decretum de Sacramento Matrimonii*, 259

Sanchez, Tomás, 199–201

Scheler, Max, 225

Schillebeeckx, Edward, 239

Schwendinger, Fidelis, 227

Scotus, Duns: *Commentarium in IV Libros Sententiarum Petri Lombardi*, 185–186

Papal Secretary of State in the conflict over *Gaudium et spes* in Vatican II, 263–264

Seneca, 111

Serrano, J.M. (Judge of the Roman Rota), 305–306, 312

Shammi, Rabbi, 42

Socrates, 106

Signatura (Special Commission), 334; Decision of November 29, 1975, 313–320, 322–324

Stephen of Aquitaine, 150

Tacitus: *Annals*, 84

Tatian, 83

Tertullian, 105

Theodosius I, Emperor, 69

Theodosius II, Emperor, 72

Theological Commission of Vatican II, 249, 258, 269, 330, 345

Trent, Council of: 24th Session, 196–198

Tromp, Sebastian, 263

Touzy, Synod of, 150

Ulpianus, 73, 75, 146, 167, 171–172

Urban II, Pope, 169

Urban III, Pope, 194

Vagnozzi, Cardinal Egidio, 327, note 50

Valentinus, 86

Regional Tribunal of Vancouver, Canada, 327, note 49

Violardo, Cardinal Giacomo, 327, note 50

Vorgrimmler, Heribert: *On The Documents of Vatican II*, 280, note 21

Wernz, F.X.: *Ius Decretalium*, 189–190

William of Auvergne: *De Sacramento Matrimonii*, 189–190

William of Auxerre: *Summa Aurea*, 189

William of Champeaux: *De Coniugiis*, 153

Wynan, Arthur (Judge of the Roman Rota), 219–221, 299

Xenophon: *Oeconomicus*, 109; 126, note 55; *Memorabilia*, 109

Yves of Chartres: *Decretum*, 151; *Panormia*, 151

SUBJECT INDEX

Adversary procedure in Catholic
nullity cases, 242–243
Affectio maritalis as a cause of
marriage, 321
Affinitas superveniens as an
impediment to marriage, 150
Androgynous God of the Gnostics,
87–88
Aristotle and the reasons for marriage,
107–111

Capacity to form a marriage, 244
Casti connubii on the nature of
marriage, 215–218
Celibacy as the more perfect state of
life, 93–97
The Church, a definition, 331, 339
Code of Canon Law, Title VII: *De
matrimonio*, 34, note 1; its
production under Cardinal Pietro
Gasparri, 204–209; Canon 1012,
110, 207–209, 285–287; Canon
1013.1, 10, 11, 56, 209, 213, 218;
Canon 1013.2, 11, 13, 209; Canon
1015, 37, note 15; Canon 1081.1,
12, 210; Canon 1081.2, 12, 13,
210, 213, 219, 248, 300, 311;
Canon 1082, 211, 214, 219;
Canon 1111, 214; Canon 1129,
214; Canon 1130, 214; Canon
1131, 214
Canons defining marriage in the
revised Code: Canon 242 (1012),
287–288, 294, 324, 348; Canon
243 (1013), 288–291, 295, 324;
Canon 244 (1081.2), 292–294,
324, 348; Canon 298 (1082), 37,
note 15
Collections of Catholic law, 192
Communitas vitae in the jurisprudence
of the Roman Rota, 300–313
Concept of marriage in *Gaudium et
spes*, 15–17, 259–262
Clandestine marriage, problem and
resolution, 194–198
Concept of marriage in *Humanae
vitae*, 274–276
Concupiscence: its nature according to
Augustine, 134–136
Connubium (the right to marry in
Roman law), 70
Marital consent: dispute over the act
that creates a marriage, 146ff; the
dispute between Bolognese and
Roman-Parisian scholars,
158–168; resolution of the
dispute, 168–172
Consummation of marriage, 29–30
Contraception: moral evaluation,
243–244; Paul VI's moral logic in
Humanae vitae, 246, note 21; 276–278
Contractuality of marriage: in St. Paul,
57; in Roman law, 72, 78; in
Thomas Aquinas, 180–181; in
Duns Scotus, 185–186; at the end
of the medieval period, 186–189

Marriage as a covenant, 50–52; the Deuteronomic notion of covenant, 24; 35, note 9

Decretal development of marriage law, 193ff
Rotal decisions denying the juridical relevance of the *communitas vitae*, 308–313
Defender of the Bond in nullity cases, 242
The defining of marriage: the need for a definition of marriage in the Church, 328; method in defining marriage, 330–332; descriptive and prescriptive defining, 328–330; the philosophy involved in defining marriage, 342–345; the definition of marriage in the Code of Canon Law, 213–214; the definition of marriage in the revised Code, 283–291

Early Christian communities and marriage, 76–79
Ends of marriage, 11; 26–29; 35, note 11
Ends of marriage: hierarchy and subordination, 218–222; essays in debate about the ends of marriage, 1937–1943, 245, note 1
Essential incompatibility as a ground of nullity, 33, note 1
Expensio modorum of *Gaudium et spes*, Part II, Chapter 1, 271–274

Council of Florence on the goods of marriage, 212
Forensic verifiability of marital consent, 337–339
Frankish marriage tradition, 148
Friendship in marriage according to Plato, 111–112
Friendship in marriage according to Aristotle, 112–114
Friendship in marriage according to Augustine, 139–141

Friendship in marriage according to Aquinas, 181–182

Gallup poll on Catholic use of contraception in the U.S., 344
Gasparri and the writing of the Code of Canon Law, 204–209; Gasparri's use of the traditional sources in writing the canons on marriage, 212–215
Gaudium et spes' understanding of marriage, 15–17, 259–262
Doctrinal valence of the definition of marriage in *Gaudium et spes*, 345–349
Genesis account of the first couple, 43–47
German marriage tradition, 148
Gnostic condemnation of marriage, 80–88
Gnostic antinomianism, 84–87
Orthodox refutation of the Gnostics, 89–93, 116–120

Homosexuality as a reason for nullity in marriage, 300–303

The image of Christ and the Church in Christian marriage, 340
The indissolubility of marriage, 11, 22–26, 210

Jewish marriage, 38–43
Marriage as a juridical entity, 334–337, 342–345
Episcopal exercise of civil jurisdiction, 146–147
The jurisprudence of marriage since Vatican II, 297ff

Lombard marriage tradition, 147

Marital love in the defining of marriage, 335
Roman Signatura on the place of love in marriage, 318–320

Manichee teaching on marriage,
127–128

Marital love 19–20

Marital love in Pius XI's *Casti
connubii*, 217–218

Marital love in the definition of
marriage, 331

Marital love in *Gaudium et spes*, 341

Matrimonium initiatum (inchoate
marriage), 151

Marriage of Mary and Joseph, 151

Matrix of the sacrament of marriage,
332–333

The meaning of marriage according to
Dietrich von Hildebrand,
227–229

The meaning of marriage according to
Heribert Doms, 230–235

Method in defining marriage, 17,
330–332

Mixed Commission and the *modi* in
Vatican II, 347–348

Object of consent in the defining of
marriage, 189–190, 201–204

Original sin and sexuality, 90–93

Original sin according to Augustine,
131–134

Patristic use of the pagan teaching on
marriage, 104ff

Paul's interpretation of Christian
marriage in I Corinthians 7,
54–61

Paul's interpretation of Christian
marriage in Ephesians 5, 61–66

Paul VI's discourse to the Roman
Rota of February 9, 1976,
320–322

Personalist challenge to the canonical
understanding of marriage,
225–235

Condemnation of the personalist
understanding by the
Congregation of the Holy Office,
April 1, 1944, 235

Philo's influence on the Christian
teaching on marriage, 102–104

Philosophy of the defining of
marriage, 342–345

The *Pléroma* in Valentinian
Gnosticism, 86–87

Primary end of marriage, 79

Primary end of marriage in *Casti
connubii*, 217–218

Primary end of marriage in the Code
of Canon Law, 209–212

Marriage as a process, 314

Procreation as a goal of marriage,
26–29

Procreation as a goal of marriage in
the Scriptures, 97–100

Rabbinic Judaism: the Christian
inheritance, 100–102

Reification of marriage in nullity
cases, 242–243

Revision of the Code of Canon Law
on marriage, 283–284

Ancient Roman understanding of
marriage, 69–73

Classic Roman law on marriage,
73–76

Roman-Parisian interpretation of
marital consent, 173–174

Medieval Roman interpretation of
marriage, 147

Judges of the Roman Rota, 298, 299,
330

Paul VI's discourse to the Rota of
February 9, 1976, 320–322

Decisions of the Roman Rota: Coram
Anné, February 25, 1969,
300–302; Coram Anné, July 22,
1969, 302; Coram Anné, February
6, 1973, 306; Coram Anné,
March 11, 1975, 306–307; Coram
Anné, December 4, 1975, 307;
Coram Bejan, March 1, 1967,
299–300; Coram Fagiolo, May
18, 1968, 326, note 26; Coram
Fagiolo, October 30, 1970, 303;

Coram Fagiolo, November 27, 1970, 303; Coram Masala, March 12, 1975, 310; Coram Palazzini, June 2, 1971, 304; Coram Pinto, July 20, 1969, 304; Coram Pinto, November 12, 1973, 308; Coram Pinto, April 14, 1975, 307; Coram Pinto, October 28, 1976, 309–310; Coram Pinto, July 15, 1977, 310–311; Coram Pompedda, December 22, 1969, 302; Coram Raad, April 14, 1975, 307; Coram Serrano, April 5, 1973, 305; Coram Serrano, April 30, 1974, 305; Coram Serrano, July 9, 1976, 305; Coram Serrano, November 18, 1977, 312–313; Coram Wynan, January 22, 1944, 219–221, 299

Sacrament of marriage, 20–22
Sacrament as marriage as source and model of the definition, 339–342
Marriage the matrix of the sacrament, 31–33, 332–333

Roman Signatura on marital love, 318–320
The Signatura's review in 1975 of the Utrecht-Haarlem decision 313–318
Synod of Bishops, October 1980, 348
Synoptic Gospels and marriage, 52–54

The Theological Commission and preparation for a document on marriage in Vatican II, 248–257
Marriage Tribunal of Toulouse, 332

Utilitarian understanding of marriage in Plato and Aristotle, 230
Utrecht-Haarlem decision on nullity, August 12, 1971, 313–315

Catholic teaching on marriage on the eve of Vatican II, 239–245
Second Vatican Council's preparation of a document on marriage, 248–257
Debate and vote on *Gaudium et spes* in the fourth session of Vatican II, 262–265

INDEX OF PUBLISHED WORKS

On Abraham of Philo, 103

Acta Apostolicae Sedis: Vol. 36(1944), 219, 312; Vol. 68(1976) 204–208; 327, note 56

Acta Synodalia, 278–281, notes *passim*

Acta Synodalia, etc., *Prooemium*, 267

De Adulterinis Coniugiis of Augustine, 35–36, note 11; Chapter 5, *passim*

Adversus Haereses of Irenaeus of Lyons, 84, 85, 87, 89; Chapter 4, *passim*, 122, note 2

Alternatif Kerkelik Huweliksrecht, by Peter Huizing, 325, note 2

Ancient Israel, by Roland DeVaux, 47, 98

First Apology of Justin Martyr, 1:29, 117

Teaching of the Twelve Apostles (*Didascalia*), 6:78, 119

The Apostolic Constitutions, 192

Arcanum Divinae Sapientiae, encyclical letter of Leo XIII, 213

De Bono Coniugali (On The Good of Marriage) of Augustine, 35, note 8; 177, 317

Canon Law: A Text and Commentary, by T. Lincoln Bouscaren and Adam C. Ellis, Third Revised Edition, 10; 34, note 4

"Report of the Special Committee of the Task Force of the Canon Law Society of America on the Marriage Canons of the Proposed *Schema Documenti Pontificii Qua Disciplina Canonica de Sacramentis Recognoscitur* (unpublished document), 325, note 3

Casti Connubii, encyclical letter of Pius XI, 215–218, 236, 251, 255, 263, 264, 271, 273, 277, 346–347

De castitate, virginitate, matrimonio, familia, document of the Theological Commission of Vatican II, 249–252; 278–279, note 9

Catechism of the Council of Trent 198, 217

Christian Marriage, Second Edition, by George H. Joyce, 174, notes 1 and 3

Clementinae of John XXII, 193

Codex Theodosianus, 73

Communicationes: Vol. 3 (1971), 325–326, note 10; Vol. 5 (1973), 37, note 15; Vol. 9.1 (1977), 325, note 4; 325, note 7; Vol. 9.2 (1977), 326, note 14

"*The Consortium Vitae Coniugalis*: Nature and Applications", by Germain Lesage, in *Studia Canonica*, Vol. 6(1972) 307–308

Constitution on Divine Revelation (*Dei verbum*) of Vatican II, Par. 8., 350

Constitutio Iustiniani, 72
Constitutio Theodosii, 72
Corpus Iuris Canonici, 193
Contraception, by John T. Noonan, Jr., 122, note 1; 124, notes 15 and 16

Decretals of Gregory IX, 170
Decretum of Gratian, 159; 160, note 19; 163, 164
Decretum of Yves of Chartres, 151
In Defense of Purity, by Dietrich von Hildebrand, 226
Dei Miseratione, Constitution of Benedict XIV, 212
Dictionary of the Bible, by John L. McKenzie, 124, note 14
Digesta Iustiniani, 73, 146, 164
Discourse to the Roman Rota of Paul VI, February 9, 1976, 214
Discourses of Epictetus, 105
The Documents of Vatican II, Part Two, Chapter 1, "Fostering the Nobility of Marriage and the Family", 34, note 3; 36, note 12; 327, note 36
Dogmatic Constitution on the Church (Lumen Gentium) of Vatican II, 266

Eclogues of Stobaeus, II, 7, 26, 109
Die Ehe, by Dietrich von Hildebrand, 226
Ehe, Eine Anthropologie Der Geschlechtsgemeinschaft, by Ernst Michel, 279, note 12
Enchiridion Symbolorum, Editio 32, n.766, 222, note 8; n.827, 269; 175, note 37
Ephemerides Iuris Canonici: Vol. 26 (1970), 326, note 27; Vol. 33 (1978), 327, note 46; Vol. 34 (1979), 327, note 44
"Essential Incompatibility as Grounds for Nullity of Marriage", in *The Catholic Lawyer*, Vol. 16(1970), 33, note 1; 33–34, note 2

"Evolution récente de la jurisprudence matrimoniale", by Germain Lesage in *Société Canadienne de Théologie: Le Divorce*, 327, note 40

De Finibus of Cicero, III,20, 106

Commentary on the Epistle to the Galatians of St. Jerome, 119
Gaudium et Spes (Pastoral Constitution on the Church in the Modern World), 17, 18, 24, 26, 27; 34, note 3; 35, note 10; 243; 246, note 14; 314, 336, 345–346; Part II, Chapter 1, "On the Nobility of Marriage and the Family", history of its composition, 246, note 14; 259–265, 268–271, 273, 289, 293, 298, 303–305, 311, 321
Gospel of Thomas, 122, note 2
Greek-English Lexicon of the New Testament and Other Early Christian Literature, by W.F. Arndt and F.W. Gingrich, Second Edition, 67, note 8

Third Homily on Genesis of Origen, Chapter 6, 118
Fifth Homily on Genesis of Origen, Chapter 4, 118
Humanae Vitae, Encyclical Letter of Paul VI, 15, 20, 28, 29, 243, 246–247; 246, note 11; 274–278; 281, note 46; 312–314, 336, 345

Institutes of Justinian, 146, 164, 171–172
Isidorian Decretals, 195

Jerusalem in the Time of Jesus by Joachim Jeremias, 47–49
On Joseph of Philo, 103, 109
Against Jovinian of Jerome, 111

The Laws of Plato, 110

Liber Sextus Decretalium of Boniface VIII, 186

Lives and *Opinions* of Diogenes Laërtius, 105

Luther's Works, Jaroslav Pelikan and H.T. Lehmann, general editors, Vol. 46, 222, note 3

De Matrimonio of Albert the Great, 178

De Matrimonio et Potestate Ipsum Dirimendi Ecclesiae Soli Exclusive Propria, by J.-P. Martin, 202–203

The Meaning of Marriage by Heribert Doms, 225–226; 279, note 12

Memorabilia of Xenophon, 109

The Bearing of Mental Impairment on the Validity of Marriage: An Analysis of Rotal Jurisprudence, by John R. Keating, 35, note 7

Musonius Rufus and the Greek Diatribe, by A.C. van Gaytenbeek, 125, note 27

The Nicomachean Ethics of Aristotle, 109

Novellae of Justinian, 73

De Nuptiis et Concupiscentia of Augustine, 35, note 8; 162, note 13

Octavius of Minucius Felix, 117

Oeconomicus of Xenophon, 109; 126, note 55

De Opificio Mundi of Gregory of Nyssa, 90–91

De Opificio Mundi of Philo, 124, note 17

Panormia of Yves of Chartres, 151, 158

Papal Teachings: Matrimony, edited by Michael J. Byrnes, 224, note 40; 246, note 15; 281, note 48

Pseudo-Isidorian Decretals (The False Decretals), 192

The Politics of Aristotle, 105, 108

The Republic of Plato, 105, 106

Responsum ad Bulgaros of Nicholas I, 78

The Roman Law of Marriage by P.E.C. Corbett, 79, note 3

De Sacramento Coniugii of Hugh of St. Victor, 155

De Sacramento Matrimonii of William of Auxerre, 189–190

De Sacramento Matrimonii, by M. Rosset, 203

Sacrosanctum Oecumenicum Concilium Vaticanum II: Constitutiones, Decreta, Declarationes, 281, note 34

Schema 17: The Dignity of Marriage and the Family, in Vatican II, 259–261

Schema de Concilio Oecumenico of the Congregation of the Holy Office, 249

Libri Sententiarum of Peter Lombard, 164–167

Commentarium in IV Libros Sententiarum Petri Lombardi of Albert the Great, 188

Summa Aurea (Commentary on Book IV of Lombard's *Libri Sententiarum*) of William of Auxerre, 189

Commentarium in IV Libros Sententiarum Petri Lombardi of Thomas Aquinas, 179–182

Commentarium in IV Libros Sententiarum Petri Lombardi of Bonaventure, 184, 185

Commentarium in IV Libros Sententiarum Petri Lombardi of Duns Scotus, 186

Sententiae of Alexander III, 168

The Special Laws of Philo, 102, 104

De Nuptiis Stephani et Filiae Regimundi Comitis of Hincmar of Rheims, 150

Stromata of Clement of Alexandria, 83, 84, 85, 87, 88, 89, 97

Summa Rolandi of Alexander III, 168

Summa Theologica of Thomas Aquinas, 303, 317

Supplication for the Christians of Athanagoras 117

Synod of Elvira, Canon 54 78

The Talmud, 100

Talmudic Commentaries, 101

Tametsi, Decree of the Council of Trent, 196–197

The Theology of Marriage by Joseph Kerns 119

Tractatus Canonicus de Matrimonio of Cardinal Pietro Gasparri, 204–205

Universae Naturae of Ocellas Lucanus, 111

De Bono Viduitatis of Augustine, 162

De Beatae Mariae Virginis Virginitate of Hugh of St. Victor, 155

On Virginity of Clement of Alexandria, 117–118

On Virginity of John Chrysostom, 92–93

Vulgate New Testament, 64

SCRIPTURE INDEX

Old Testament

Genesis

1	43, 53, 88, 187
1:27b	43, 45
1:28	98
2	43, 52, 53, 88, 187, 228
2:18	44
2:21–22	44
2:24	45, 187
3	40, 64, 88, 90
3:6	46
3:13	47
3:16	47, 50
3:17	47
15:4	98
16:1–4	98, 99
16:10	98
18:15	49
20:18	98
22:17	98
24:60	98
26:4	98
30:2	98
30:3	99
30:9	99
38	101

Exodus

19:5	35, note 9

Leviticus

15:16–24	101

Deuteronomy

21:15–17	124, note 13
24:1	42, 43, 48
28:1–2	35, note 9
28:15–20	35, note 9
30:15–18	35, note 9
31:12	49

Hosea

———	50–52
1:1–3:35	40; 67, note 6

Isaiah

54:5–10	67, note 6
62:1–5	67, note 6

Ezekiel

———	50–52
16	40; 67, note 6

Psalms

128:3	98
127:3–5	98

Proverbs

17:6	98
31:10–28	67, note 5

Ruth

4:11–12	98

Tobit

6:16–22	119–121

Judith

—————   66

New Testament

Matthew
Infancy narrative   95
5:28   77
5:48   82
10:37b   96
18:20   97
19   43
19:3   48, 57
19:4   43
19:5   44
19:6   53
19:29   96
22:29–30   91, 96
24:19   82, 95

Mark
3:33–35   96
7:22   89
7:27   55
9:43   55
10   43, 99
10:2   57
10:7   43, 44
10:8   44
10:9   53
12:18–27   96
13:17   95

Luke
Infancy narrative   95
1:43–45   119
2   151
5:11   96
8:19–21   96
12:59   85
14:20   82, 96
14:26   96
18:28–30   96
20:27–38   96

20:35–36   82
21:23   82

Romans
—————   105
1:18–32   99
3:14   95
5   131

I Corinthians
6:13–20   55, 89
7   54–61, 94–95, 136
7:1   82
7:2   100
7:5   95, 100
7:7   83, 94
7:8   100
7:9   94, 95
7:24   94
7:25–38   77
7:28   94, 95
7:29   83, 94, 95
7:31   94
7:32–35   95
7:36–38   95
7:34   83
10:6–10   89

Galatians
—————   119
6:7–8   95

Colossians
1:15–20   86
2:8   123, note 7
2:15   123, note 7
3:18–21   97
3:18–4:1   67, note 11

Ephesians
—————   67, note 9
5   52, 53, 100
5:10   64
5:18–32   61–66
5:22   67, note 12
5:22–6:4   97

6:1–4	63	*I Peter*	
6:5–9	63; 64	3:1–2	100
		I Timothy	
		————	99
I Thessalonians	56	1:5–10	123, note 3
		2:10–11	97
		2:12–13	97
Titus		2:15	97
1:6	95	3:2	95